Medieval Narrative

Medieval Narrative:
An Introduction

Tony Davenport

OXFORD
UNIVERSITY PRESS

OXFORD
UNIVERSITY PRESS

Great Clarendon Street, Oxford OX2 6DP

Oxford University Press is a department of the University of Oxford.
It furthers the University's objective of excellence in research, scholarship,
and education by publishing worldwide in

Oxford New York

Auckland Bangkok Buenos Aires Cape Town Chennai
Dar es Salaam Delhi Hong Kong Istanbul Karachi Kolkata
Kuala Lumpur Madrid Melbourne Mexico City Mumbai Nairobi
São Paulo Shanghai Taipei Tokyo Toronto

Oxford is a registered trade mark of Oxford University Press
in the UK and in certain other countries

Published in the United States
by Oxford University Press Inc., New York

British Library Cataloguing in Publication Data

Data available

Library of Congress Cataloging in Publication Data

Data available

ISBN 0–19–925839–2

10 9 8 7 6 5 4 3 2

Typeset in Minion
by RefineCatch Limited, Bungay, Suffolk
Printed in Great Britain
on acid-free paper by
Ashford Colour Press Ltd, Gosport, Hampshire

Contents

Preface

This book was conceived as an introduction to the richest area of medieval English and European literature, the many narratives in verse and prose which survive from the eighth to the fifteenth century. It is intended for readers who already have some knowledge of major works of the Middle Ages, such as *Beowulf*, the *Decameron* and *The Canterbury Tales*, the *Chanson de Roland* and the *Morte Darthur*, and who wish to venture further. I have therefore assumed familiarity with some widely read texts, but have taken a more expository and frankly storytelling approach to less familiar and less readily available works. Some major poems such as Dante's *Divine Comedy* I have referred to without engaging in discussion, because of their scale and complexity: it is not difficult to find introductory accounts elsewhere. It seemed appropriate in a book about narrative to refer both to medieval definitions of its nature, and to modern theories of fiction and to attempt to establish some dialogue between them, but I had no wish to equip myself with any more than the bare necessities of the critical jargon of either medieval rhetoricians or modern narratologists and have used technical language sparingly, though I hope with an indication of the aspects of medieval tale-telling to which modern theorists have paid attention. I have not aimed to write a history of medieval narrative but rather to indicate its main types: *exemplum* and fable; chronicle, epic, and romance; fabliau and novella; voyage and dream; tragedy; the tale collection. Though this is a fairly long list, inevitably some things have had to be left out.

I have enjoyed the support of the English Department of Royal Holloway, University of London in my work on the book and owe thanks to the Heads of Department during the period of writing, Kiernan Ryan and Robert Hampson, for their affording me the role of retainer. Some of the topics included here are subjects I have taught as part of the course in Medieval Narrative for the Royal Holloway degree of M.A. in Medieval Studies; I am grateful to the students on the course whose interest has helped to develop my own awareness. I am grateful also to my medievalist colleagues in the English Department, Rosalind Field, Ruth Kennedy, and Jennifer Neville, who have shared the formulation of the syllabus and, together with Marion Gibbs in German, Ruth Harvey in French, and Jane Everson in Italian, different stages and versions of the teaching; I hope they are not too dissatisfied with my versions of topics which they know a good deal more about. To the secretarial staff of the English Department and to the staff of the libraries of Royal Holloway and the University of London I extend thanks for various kinds of help which contributed to my research. My thanks go also to Robert Eaglestone for his hospitality in cheerfully accepting me as a part-time squatter in his college space. My greatest debt is as always to my wife, Hester, who has put up, day in, day out, with the stresses of composition and who has provided encouragement, corrections, and advice.

Abbreviations

AMA	Alliterative *Morte Arthure*
CT	*The Canterbury Tales*
EETS ES	Early English Text Society, Extra Series
EETS OS	Early English Text Society, Original Series
EETS SS	Early English Text Society, Supplementary Series
MS	*Mediaeval Studies*
OUP	Oxford University Press
PMLA	*Publications of the Modern Languages Association*
TC	*Troilus and Criseyde*
U.P.	University Press

The idea of
Medieval Narrative

Look on a shelf labelled 'Medieval Narrative' nowadays and you are as likely to find the adventures of Brother Cadfael or Sister Fidelma, or a trilogy called *Merlin* or *Guenevere*, as a copy of the *Nibelungenlied* or *The Canterbury Tales*. The Middle Ages has, from the sixteenth century on, repeatedly been reinvented : *King Lear*, *The Eve of St Agnes*, *News from Nowhere*, and many other plays, poems, novels are indicators of writers' interest in using their historical imagination on actual stories from the medieval past, or invented situations placed in medieval settings or idealizations of medieval political systems and living conditions. To use the remote past as the setting for modern fiction gives some sorts of freedom to the writer: Victorian poets could write of sex and adultery through the figures of Lancelot and Guenevere, Tristan and Isolde; today's detective-story writers can create a welter of murder and violence without the trappings of modern police investigation. For some the difference between past and present is the point of invoking medieval society and literature, so that a mirror may be held up to modern life, as with the time-travelling heroes in Twain's *A Connecticut Yankee at the Court of King Arthur* or Ford Madox Ford's *Ladies whose Bright Eyes*. Others have expressed a mythical or mystical interest in the past through recreations of lost realms or the pursuit of Grail quests, or surrounding figures such as Merlin and Morgan la Fay with alchemical mumbo-jumbo. Much modern 'medieval' narrative is obviously superficial, as in the contrived exercises where known historical figures such as Chaucer appear as detectives in medieval whodunits. More often a perhaps naive story is combined with esoteric historical detail, what Umberto Eco called 'Salgarism' (after Emilio Salgari, late-nineteenth-century author of exotic adventures); his example is of characters escaping through a forest pursued by enemies who stumble over a baobab root and 'the narrator suspends the action in order to give us a botany lesson on the baobab—it should not be done'.[1] Pseudo-medieval fictions find it difficult to avoid scattering arcane details around the text. Here is Sister Fidelma investigating a monastic mystery:

The key fitted into the lock, and she turned it slowly. Then she turned it back and took it out, slipping it into her marsupium. Finally she reverted her attention to the piece of parchment. It was a note in Ogham.[2]

However, there are a few writers, Tolkien and Eco in particular, who have done more than create modern stories dressed in tabards; both academic writers, professors at Oxford and Bologna respectively, they published analytical essays on medieval literature and art as well as creating their own modern versions of the medieval in their fiction; their ideas of medieval narrative do provide signposts which may be followed by anyone interested in looking at the actual narratives of the past. The continuing interest in using medieval material for modern fiction, which is indicated by Eco's *The Name of the Rose* and *Baudolino*,[3] the seemingly ceaseless stream of Arthurian sagas, the many children's fantasy adventures in the tradition of C. S. Lewis's Narnia chronicles, and a spate of adult novels such as Barry Unsworth's *Morality Play* or Peter Ackroyd's *The Clerkenwell Tales*, is evidence of something of a cultural shift over the last twenty-five years, since the time, that is, when there was a flurry of insistence on the 'alterity' of medieval literature, the sense of its being on the other side of a chasm. This idea was expressed particularly forcefully by Hans Robert Jauss who went as far as to say: 'for us medieval literature is even more alien than that of the antiquity which is further away in time'.[4] It is striking that in reviewing Eco's *Baudolino* Tom Shippey says exactly the opposite: 'The Middle Ages retain their

---

[1] Umberto Eco, *Postscript to The Name of the Rose*, tr. William Weaver (New York, Harcourt Brace Jovanovitch, 1983), p.36.
[2] Peter Tremayne, 'Death of an icon', in Mike Ashley (ed.), *The Mammoth Book of Historical Whodunnits* (London: Robinson, 2001), p.124.
[3] Umberto Eco, *Il Nome della Rosa* (1980), trans. William Weaver as *The Name of the Rose* (London, Secker & Warburg, 1983); *Baudolino* (2000), trans. William Weaver (London, Secker & Warburg, 2002).
[4] Hans Robert Jauss, 'The alterity and modernity of medieval literature', in *New Literary History* 10 (1978–9), 181–228 (quotation from p.187).

attraction for the present-day because they are in vital respects still present, changed and reshuffled, but active in everyday life in a way which is not true of Classical tradition'.[5] How does one explain the apparent contradiction? Is the medieval past a foreign country or a place where the modern reader has a strong sense of recognition of things that still operate in present-day life?

Jauss was arguing, as the title of his essay indicates, that neglect of medieval literature, particularly in university syllabuses, had created an opportunity for new approaches to the subject to be developed: scholarly concentration on literary theory had left medieval literature untended and, Jauss suggested, therefore waiting for the aesthetic pleasure of 'the otherness of a distant text-world' to be rediscovered. This difference, or strangeness, of the medieval text had been disguised by the 'illusion of historical continuity', the nineteenth-century model of history which interpreted modern forms of writing as evolving from old, and therefore classed medieval literature as a sort of seedbed for later growth. Jauss saw medieval texts on the other side of the great divide between oral and written composition, between manuscript and book culture, and distinguished between the modern sensibility which thinks of tradition as written, authorship as single, the text as an autonomous work, and medieval reception of texts as intertextual, communal, and unfixed. Jauss takes as his example the medieval French *chanson de geste*, in particular the *Chanson de Roland*, and the often-discussed question of whether it is a unified work: if the poem was the product of improvised performance in a formulaic style, then there was never a final form of the text, but rather a repeated cyclical creation; medieval narrative normally admits a succession of repetitions, sequels, and alternatives within itself. Having exposed the 'alterity' of medieval texts, Jauss proposes ways in which modern theory can establish communication with their otherness, emphasizing in particular the *exemplum* and the fable which I intend to examine in a later chapter.

There is much that one might want to debate in Jauss's argument. Even such an obvious contrast as that between oral and written literary composition is more complex than he suggests. The only medieval literary texts that survive are written documents so that the

[5] Tom Shippey, 'Texts, relics and clever forgeries', review of *Baudolino* by Umberto Eco, trans. William Weaver, *The Times Literary Supplement*, 11 October 2002, 21–2.

modern reader has to experience the past as a written culture, whatever the form of the original communication between artist and
audience. The distinction between orality and literacy, particularly
associated with the work of Walter J. Ong,[6] is a concept based on the
difference between primitive cultures, where tribal memory exists in
the form of oral narrative, and more advanced cultures where written forms of record are available. This does not apply to the medieval period in Europe, a highly literate age even if education was
available only to part of society: the literary texts that achieved written form are *ipso facto* a record of literacy. What one encounters is
not an oral but a 'performance' culture, where texts show awareness
of the dual form. *The Canterbury Tales* is full of references to speaking and hearing as each pilgrim 'seyde as ye may heere', but Chaucer
can still tell his audience to 'turne over the leef and chese another
tale', clearly envisaging a reader holding a book. John Burrow
pointed out at the time of Jauss's essay that his intellectual position
was based on the situation in continental Europe, particularly in
France, and that 'the repression of medieval literature by the aesthetic canons of the Renaissance' and the cutting of the study
of medieval literature from the university curriculum had not
occurred, at least not to the same extent, in some other countries,
including Britain.[7] Nevertheless, Burrow accepted that modern theory, particularly in its rejection of the idea of texts as 'works' by
individual authors, brings attractive benefits to consideration of
codified, impersonal poems of the medieval period such as courtly
love lyrics, and that intertextuality is a concept that makes a good
deal of sense in medieval literary analysis. However, insistence on the
alterity of medieval texts does not convince when modern analysts
use medieval texts simply to reflect their own concern with, for
example, the self-referentiality of literature. What this debate about
alterity suggests is that, in the 1970s and 1980s, the British or American
reader was less likely than a continental European one to approach
medieval literature as something alien and requiring a new set
of scientific tools for its dissection. This partly explains an English

---

[6] Walter J. Ong, *Orality and Literacy: The Technologizing of the Word* (1982) (London, Routledge, 1995).

[7] John Burrow, 'The alterity of medieval literature', *New Literary History* 10 (1978–9), 385–90.

eclectic approach to medieval literature, which I am happy to follow, with a combination of medieval and modern critical terms. There was plenty of medieval literary theory and the modern reader needs to engage in dialogue with it; the simple imposition of modern critical terms on the medieval text does no more than replicate the critic's polemical position. Dialogue between past and present is helped, in my view, by the indicators in the writings of some modern creators of medieval narrative.

Tolkien's fiction amounts to a statement that medieval narrative provides the forms through which the modern imagination can visualize the conflict between good and evil. The journey and return motif, or 'there and back again' as the subtitle of *The Hobbit* expresses it, is the basic form also of *The Lord of the Rings*, and this, together with the quest to be fulfilled, themes of alliance and betrayal, concern with the continuity of dynasties and the honour of the tribe, all mark the origins of Tolkien's stories in the material of medieval epic and romance. His appeal in these two main fictions is to the childlike reader, ready to be absorbed in the unfolding of multiple, interlaced events that are held together by the central idea of the rings of power and their fate; the intellectual background provided by the myths of races, civilizations, and wars, the invented languages, the maps and mythical geography, the references to folklore, ballads, and lyrics telling of the past, are all scaffolding, and work less well by themselves, though they are the fruit of Tolkien's lifelong obsession, stretching from the First World War to his death, with proliferating layer upon layer of invented history. Tolkien was, of course, a linguist and philologist and a teacher of Old and Middle English and Norse texts, a literary explicator and translator more than a historian of culture and ideas. His best-known essays, on *Beowulf* and *Sir Gawain and the Green Knight*, are both defences of the combination of magic and morality, while his discussion of fairy stories offers several insights into his own creative intentions and his concepts of narrative. 'There is no better medium for moral teaching than the good fairy-story', he claims in his essay on *Sir Gawain*. What fairy stories offer he defines as 'Fantasy, Recovery, Escape, Consolation', attributing the power of the fairy story to the inner consistency of its unreality. Dismissing the idea of 'the willing suspension of disbelief', he describes the working of the fairy story in the following terms: 'What really happens is that the story-maker proves a successful "sub-creator". He makes a

Secondary World which your mind can enter. Inside it, what he relates is "true": it accords with the laws of that world. You therefore believe it, while you are, as it were, inside'.[8] In the making of his Secondary World Tolkien may be thought to have drawn on many literary sources: Charles Moseley suggests that there are elements (among others) from the Gothic novel, from Victorian and Edwardian fantasy literature—George Macdonald, *Peter Pan*, Rider Haggard, Kenneth Grahame—but concludes that: 'the nearest parallels to Tolkien's work lie in medieval romance, in the Irish *imram* or journey narrative, in saga, in epic: these genres formed his critical criteria and inform his own fiction'.[9] These parallels are most obvious when he re-creates literary images of societies as he does with the kingdom of Rohan, based on *Beowulf* and other Teutonic narratives, with scenes reminiscent of the mead-hall at Heorot and funeral rites for Theoden which echo those for Beowulf. In such scenes there is no doubt that one can apply to his fiction words such as Tolkien himself used of *Sir Gawain*: 'For it belongs to that literary kind which has deep roots in the past . . . It is made of tales often told before and elsewhere, and of elements that derive from remote times, beyond the vision or awareness of the poet'.[10] From old tales, Tolkien argues, the poem 'receives part of its life, its vividness, its tension'.

In the writing of Eco there is a much more intellectual concern with the idea of medieval narrative as text: he faces the scholarly investigator with an enigma, taking a postmodern, semiotic pleasure in the complexity of the problem. Like Tolkien, Eco had, by the time of publishing his medieval fictions, been thinking about aspects of the Middle Ages for a number of years. One of his earliest critical works, written in 1958 when he was twenty-six years old, was a chapter in a multi-authored work on the history of aesthetics which he later turned into a self-contained short book;[11] in this essay he is

---

[8] J.R.R. Tolkien, 'On fairy-stories', in *The Monsters and the Critics and Other Essays*, ed. Christopher Tolkien (London, Allen & Unwin, 1983), pp.109–61; the essay was originally a lecture (St Andrews, 1939) and later appeared in a revised form in *Tree and Leaf* (1964). This collection also reprints the essays on *Beowulf* and *Sir Gawain*.

[9] Charles Moseley, *J.R.R. Tolkien*, Writers and Their World Series (London, Northcote House in association with the British Council, 1997), p.33.

[10] J.R.R. Tolkien, '*Sir Gawain and the Green Knight*', in *The Monsters and the Critics and Other Essays*, pp.72–108 (quotation from p.72).

[11] Umberto Eco, *Art and Beauty in the Middle Ages*, trans. Hugh Bredin (New Haven, Yale U.P., 1986).

largely concerned with artistic form, with proportion, decorum, and symmetry in medieval art (as in the diptych or triptych), with the interweaving of several themes in medieval narrative, and with symbolism, such as that of the five-petalled rose. He displays an awareness of a wide range of medieval ideas about art and aesthetics, including medieval treatises on rhetoric, Jean de Meun's introduction into *Le Roman de la Rose* of the difference between Art and Nature, and the signs of change from the twelfth-century scholastic conception of art and poetry as didactic, 'in which clear, pre-existing knowledge provided the exemplary idea and was expressed in accordance with rules', into later conceptions (in Dante, for example) of 'creativity unambiguously tied to a world of passions and emotions'.[12] Though there are in this discussion the seeds of themes and ideas later used in *The Name of the Rose*—the rose itself as a symbol, Aristotle as the starting point for debate about art—by the time he wrote his novel it was the modern reader's uncertainties about the medieval text that he took as a keynote. So he provided the book with a 'modern' preface which gave details of a book of 1842 purporting to be a translation into French by one Abbé Vallet of a fourteenth-century manuscript written in old age by the monk Adso of Melk about events that had happened in his youth; the author translates this work while escaping from Prague in wartime and travelling to Melk, where there is no trace of Adso's manuscript; when the Abbé's book disappears the author is left only with his translation and notes which fail to correspond to bibliographical records in Paris or to the knowledge of other medieval scholars (and here Eco introduces the names of some actual medievalists, such as Etienne Gilson). Was the book a forgery? Then he finds in Buenos Aires the Italian translation of a Georgian book *On the Use of Mirrors in the Game of Chess* which quotes lengthily from Adso's manuscript . . . and so Eco goes on multiplying the layers of textual complexity and uncertainty. It is not surprising that the story of the novel is about a labyrinth, uses mirrors, and is itself a conundrum full of disguise, intricacy, and mystery. The image that Eco presents of medieval narrative is thus of an absorbing but unstable text like the one which is the subject of his tale, the supposed manuscript of Aristotle's Comedy. In the commentary that Eco subsequently wrote about the composition of his novel,

---

[12] Eco, *Art and Beauty*, p.111.

he shows how closely he based his writing on the actual words of medieval texts:

I set about reading or rereading medieval chronicles, to acquire their rhythm and their innocence. They would speak for me, and I would be freed from suspicion. Freed from suspicion, but not from the echoes of intertextuality. Thus I rediscovered what writers have always known . . . books always speak of other books, and every story tells a story that has already been told.[13]

Eco carries his games of books speaking of other books even further in *Baudolino*, the story of a liar who speaks all languages making his way through a kaleidoscope of medieval history and myth as he tells his life history and seeks to resolve the locked-room mystery of the murder of his master, Frederick Barbarossa. For the postmodern reader for whom virtually everything is to be read within ironic inverted commas Eco's novels may suggest that any modern fiction set in the medieval period must be some sort of pastiche, but that the actual narratives of the Middle Ages represent the original language of storytelling. This is not, of course, quite the case but it does provide one motive for learning to read medieval narrative in its own rather than in modern terms.

Medieval narrative is not just one thing and perhaps a more honest title for this book would have been 'Some varieties of medieval narrative'; part of my intention is to discuss the main narrative genres of the period and to identify the characteristics of some of the best-known examples of different forms. I am not attempting a history of narrative nor a survey but rather an introduction to the span of kinds and of narrative sophistication within those kinds; each type of narrative exists in simple and more complex versions, with authorial attitudes stretching all the way from unquestioning acceptance to ironic subversion. The perspective will be mainly English, with *The Canterbury Tales* as a central point of reference, but, without claiming any form of comprehensiveness, I have made reference to a range of well-known European narrative texts. The chapter that follows is more general and explores some aspects of medieval theories of narrative and of the debates that arise from placing medieval definitions in the light of modern narratology, at least in some of its forms.

---

[13] Eco, *Postscript to The Name of the Rose*, pp.19–20.

2

Narrative

Theory, medieval and modern

Narrative theory is not a twentieth-century Russo-French invention but existed in classical Greek and Roman times and was familiar to educated writers and readers of the Middle Ages. Plato, Aristotle, Cicero, Horace were cited as authorities even when the actual texts (particularly of the Greek philosophers) were not available to be read and when their teaching was known only because it was quoted by translators and transmitters such as Boethius. However, while Plato's criticism of poets as tellers of untruth, his and Aristotle's concern with the imitation of nature in poetry (*mimesis*) and Aristotle's definitions in the *Poetics* of the structure and the scope of plot, the relationship of epic and tragedy, and the differences between history and poetry had all become touchstones of thought in medieval scholarly tradition, it was the name of Cicero that dominated medieval rhetorical thinking and it is to him that one must go to find narrative defined. For Cicero its exemplifying function was the starting point for thinking how narrative worked. In his *De inventione* he explains the ways in which narrative can be used in stating a case in the law courts. His basic definition of *narratio* is 'an exposition of events that have occurred or are supposed to have occurred': the assumption is that this is an account of actual events, a statement of the facts of the case, or, if not, a hypothetical account which is like a sequence of actual events. The ideal form of narration for forensic purposes should be brief, focussed exclusively on the business in hand, chronological, and lifelike, though digressive material might be included for comparison or in order to entertain the audience. However, completely imaginary sequences of events could be used for training purposes or simply for amusement. Cicero distinguishes several different types of narrative: firstly, narrative mainly concerned with events, which might be an account of actual past occurrences (*historia*), or a fictitious, hypothesized but plausible set of events (*argumentum*), or an account of fantastic, unlifelike incidents (*fabula*); secondly, narrative centred on persons, in which not only events but also conversation and mental attitudes might be shown. Cicero interestingly envisages the possible effects in the latter type of narration:

This form of narrative should possess great vivacity, resulting from changes in fortune, contrast of characters, severity, gentleness, hope, fear, suspicion, desire, dissimulation, delusion, pity, sudden change in fortune, disaster, sudden pleasure, happy ending to the story.

(*De inventione*, Bk I, xix)[1]

So, though he is initially concerned with basic definitions of the types of narrative which may legitimately be included in legal speeches and whose purpose is to strengthen legal argument by providing a clear account of events or by illustrating legal principle, Cicero develops, almost as an afterthought to his professional categorization, a theory of narrative, accounting both for factual history and the fictional tale. In these ideas about the functional and the merely theoretical and playful uses of narrative material one can see the germ of medieval debates between those who accept stories as an effective way of proving a point in sermons and those who reject stories as a distraction from devout thought; this is an extension of the recurrent question of truth as opposed to fiction.

Most medieval rhetorical treatises on the subject of writing and speaking convert Cicero's recommendation of 'great vivacity' into recipes for shaping the narrative material (good ways of beginning and ending, how to abbreviate or to amplify the matter, good devices for adding stylistic interest, and so on), rather than with the nature of narrative itself. A stronger sense of asking questions about the general function and nature of narrative is found in medieval manuals about preaching, where Cicero's insistence on brief, cogent accounts of events is echoed, and where the fables of poets are seen as providing model structures for the preacher. So Thomas of Salisbury in his thirteenth-century *Summa de arte praedicandi* takes Virgil's *Aeneid* as an example, and uses the composition of poems as a model for a three-part structure for the sermon, consisting of theme, prayer,

---

[1] M. Tullius Cicero, *De inventione*, ed. and trans. H.M. Hubbell, Loeb Classical Library (Cambridge, Mass., Harvard U.P., 1949).

and narration. The exposition of a theme by means of a tale is the medieval idea of narrative associated particularly with the tradition of *exemplum,* an illustrative example in the form of a short story used to confirm the moral point. It is this idea of narrative which accounts for a large proportion of medieval tales.

The distinctions Cicero makes lie behind later rhetoricians' division of narrative into several kinds, as one can see in a rhetorical textbook such as John of Garland's *Parisiana Poetria* (written about 1220). John clearly thinks of himself as writing a gloss on what Cicero had said, as is obvious in his enlarged definitions of the three terms for types of narrative that Cicero used, *fabula, historia,* and *argumentum.* John emphasizes, as do virtually all medieval writers on the subject, the untruth associated with *fabula:* 'A fable contains events that are untrue, and do not pretend to be true: it follows that avoiding vice in fabulous narratives means lying with probability.'[2] The second term, *historia,* is seen as simply reporting an event that has taken place in the past, but it is here that literary formality and decorum are thought to belong: in order to write *historia* well the poet should include 'in order, proposition, invocation and narration'; also desirable is an epilogue, 'whereby the mind of the listener . . . understands what is to come'. There is a firm sense here that a particular sort of subject matter, that is the serious material of actual history, needs an orderly, conventional literary structure in order to express its truth. On the other hand the *argumentum,* that is the hypothetical case, the 'fictitious event which nevertheless could have happened, as is the case in comedies', is seen as an inappropriate place for invocation, with its implication that a divine ordering may shape the narrative. A three-grade hierarchy of narrative value and style shadowily emerges, with *historia,* a narrative of real events, told in a formal style with the appropriate structural machinery of introduction and conclusion, at the top of the ladder, the *argumentum,* realistic but invented, occupying the middle ground and by association with comedy introducing the concept of a less orderly narrative universe, while *fabula,* frankly full of lies, has to work by craft to make its untruths as convincing as it can.

This threefold division of narrative overlaps with other categories.

---

[2] *The Parisiana Poetria of John of Garland,* ed. and trans. Traugott Lawler (New Haven, Yale U.P., 1974), p.101.

There is the question of genre, which I will deal with more fully in the next section of this chapter: John of Garland includes within historical narrative many different literary forms, including epitaph, bucolic and georgic, invective and satire, tragedy and elegy. Elsewhere John turns to what modern critics would see as part of the question of 'point of view', when he fuses distinction of type with the question of the voice adopted by the writer: he defines discourse (*sermo*) as either dramatic, by which he means that all the words are spoken by voices other than the poet's, or narrative which is entirely in the poet's voice, which John calls expository, hermeneutic, or interpretative (he includes both Cicero's plot-centred and his people-centred narratives under this heading), or, thirdly, mixed, where both poet and *personae* speak, which John calls didactic or instructive. This distinguishing of three voices in poetry is a recurrent idea, traceable as early as Plato's *Republic* and Aristotle's *Poetics*, and passed on through Latin encyclopaedists such as Isidore of Seville in the seventh century to late medieval writers. The terms are still found in post-medieval times, though redefined, as one finds, for example, in T.S. Eliot's *The Three Voices of Poetry* (1953) where the three voices distinguished are:

(i)   the voice of the poet talking to himself—or to nobody;
(ii) the voice of the poet addressing an audience;
(iii) the voice of the poet when he attempts to create a dramatic character speaking in verse.[3]

The three voices are often labelled 'lyric', 'epic', and 'dramatic' and Eliot says later in his lecture that 'the voice of the poet addressing other people is the dominant voice of epic, though . . . there is heard also, from time to time, the dramatic voice'; this is close to what John of Garland means by his 'mixed' voice. Isidore of Seville defines the three 'characters' of poetry partly by examples, citing Virgil's *Georgics* as his instance of the lyric voice and the *Aeneid* as his example of the mixed/epic voice, both distinct from the dramatic voice used in tragedy and comedy. A slightly different tradition is represented by the great Anglo-Saxon scholar Bede in his *De arte metrica* where he gives Biblical instances to demonstrate the three 'kinds': the lyric voice is found in the Book of Proverbs, in Ecclesiastes and in the Psalms; the

---

[3]   T.S. Eliot, *The Three Voices of Poetry*, (Cambridge U.P., 1953).

mixed voice is exemplified not only by classical epic but also the Book of Job (because it is partly poetic and partly homiletic); the dramatic voice is represented in the Song of Solomon (because it is in direct speech).[4] These interpretations of the voices are as interesting as the definitions since they indicate the applicability of the idea to narrative. Though, strictly speaking, only the mixed/epic voice is apt to narrative, it becomes clear from such examples as Bede's that the distinction is being made between first-person narration, such as one finds in medieval dream poems and in lyric narratives such as Dante's *La Vita Nuova*; third-person narration, as in chronicles, fables, *exempla*, and other teaching narratives in the voice of the preacher; works in direct speech (not only drama but literary dialogues and debates); and the various mixtures of the poet's voice and the voices of fictional characters that one finds in epic and romance.

Medieval teachers of rhetoric adapted the body of knowledge which they inherited from classical writers to the formation of rules for composition; their immediate concern was teaching schoolboys and university students how to write Latin poetry and how to handle well-known story material in ways that would make it intelligible and interesting to a new audience. Many medieval writers were influenced by the 'Arts of Poetry', such as were written in the twelfth and thirteenth centuries by Geoffrey de Vinsauf, Matthew de Vendome, and John of Garland, either directly from the study and application of their texts as part of their own education, or indirectly from the absorption of the rules into the textbooks of later generations: from training in composition writers acquired a sense of basic ideas about narrative, about where to begin a story, how to shape it so that it worked effectively, and how to give it colour and interest by appropriate uses of description, dialogue, and a range of stylistic flourishes which would add force to the expression. Because they were written in the form of textbooks, medieval rhetorical manuals are more concerned with specific matters of technique (grammar, versification, ornament) than with expressing general ideas about creative literature and it is not easy for the modern reader trained to understand narrative largely by reading eighteenth- and nineteenth-century prose fiction to find points of contact with medieval concern with, say, the art of amplification. Under this heading medieval theorists

[4] See P.B. Salmon, 'The "Three Voices" of poetry in medieval literary theory', *Medium Aevum* 30 (1961), 1–18.

list methods by which a writer may deliberately set out to expand a
basic story (which, it is assumed, will have been taken from known
historical source material); once one has understood the devices of
enlargement it is easy to recognize that eighteenth- and nineteenth-
century novelists were using them, or others like them, all the
time. One of the most useful general concepts, famously expressed by
Geoffrey de Vinsauf, is the idea that the creative writer has a mental
plan of his work, a sort of blueprint:

If a man has to build a house, his hand does not rush to the task impetuously:
the heart's intrinsic measure first compasses the work, the inner man pre-
scribes the design, ordering the unfolding with sureness, the hand of the
heart forms the whole, before the physical hand does so. The work first exists
as an archetype, then as a physical reality. Let poetry see in this image what
rule must be given to poets.[5]

This is not only a revealing confirmation that medieval literary works
were expected to have an overall design but, because it is quoted by
Chaucer, it provides an indicator of the relationship between theory
and practice. Chaucer adapts this idea of literary premeditation to the
character of Pandarus in *Troilus and Criseyde*, as he promises to help
his friend Troilus to win the love of Criseyde and goes on his way
'thenkyng on this matere' and plotting the best time, place, and
method for persuading his niece to accept the royal prince as lover:

> For eueri wight that hath an hous to founde
> Ne renneth naught the werk for to bygynne
> With rakel hond, but he wol bide a stounde,
> And sende his hertes line out fro withinne
> Aldirfirst his purpos forto wynne.
> Al this Pandare in his herte thoughte,
> And caste his werk ful wisely or he wroughte.
> (*Troilus and Criseyde*, I, 1065–71)

By taking over Geoffrey de Vinsauf's image Chaucer recognizes the
relationship between plotting a narrative poem and plotting a love
intrigue and creates in Pandarus an artist within the world of the
poem; the imagined narrative spaces become measurable by the
love-architect's plumb line. The narrative perspective is thus enriched

---

[5] Geoffrey de Vinsauf, *Poetria Nova*, 126–31, trans. Ernest Gallo in *The 'Poetria Nova'
and its Sources in Early Rhetorical Doctrine* (The Hague, Mouton, 1971). The passage is
discussed in Ernest Gallo, 'The *Poetria Nova* of Geoffrey of Vinsauf', in *Medieval
Eloquence*, ed. J.J. Murphy (Berkeley, University of California Press, 1978), pp.68–84.

by a kind of doubleness: Chaucer the poet manoeuvres the story material but Pandarus manoeuvres the action and may be watched as he does it. *Troilus and Criseyde*, like *The Canterbury Tales*, provides a commentary on the narrative process in the course of its unfolding.

The idea of narrative process in medieval works has, however, often seemed to modern readers puzzling in itself, though difficulty in understanding may sometimes have its source in the conditions of survival of medieval texts: some narratives exist only in incomplete or garbled forms; some major works (*Le Roman de la Rose* is the obvious instance) are the work of more than one writer; some works (again there is an obvious case in *Piers Plowman*) exist in more than one form. Putting aside such peculiar problems, one may still easily compile a list of medieval narrative works which have seemed to modern eyes dislocated or strangely constructed. Theories of Gothic structure, based on analogies between writing and the visual arts, have produced ideas such as the literary diptych to account for poems which seem to consist of two loosely linked parts: if they are seen as a diptych, then the two parts may be read as complementary phases— *Beowulf* and Chrétien de Troyes's *Perceval* are famous examples. The *Chanson de Roland* too, which significantly often leaves the reader groping for explanations of the conduct of the characters and reasons for the action, has sometimes been interpreted (starting with Auerbach in his influential book *Mimesis*[6]) in terms of parataxis— scenes, like sentences, standing side by side without continuity or subordination. Perhaps, though, instead of thinking in terms of strange medieval forms for which special terms and conditions have to be defined one does better to recognize that in every period narrative uses a range of genres, and that alongside the plain versions of narrative there exist works which question or subvert the standard features of current narrative forms. Over a period of time there are cycles of fashion in literary awareness, in what writers think they should focus on: there is a continuity in the idea of narrative which persists through the vagaries of local change. As Frank Kermode notes, though the repetitions and lack of coherent transitions in the *Chanson de Roland* may create difficulty for the reader, the narrative processes are not uniquely medieval: 'Roland dies three times, always

---

[6] Erich Auerbach, *Mimesis: The Representation of Reality in Western Literature* (1946), trans. Willard R. Trask (Princeton U.P., 1953).

with a difference, almost as in a novel by M.Robbe-Grillet.' Similarly, modern judgement that a work such as Chrétien's Grail romance lacks coherence and the qualities expected of well-formed narrative, such as closure, may be caused less by a peculiarly medieval narrative idea and more by narrow modern expectations.[7] Pre-modern narratives are, in fact, very varied: some types, such as *fabliaux*, are relatively realistic and plot-dominated; their actions are presented so that events are specifically motivated and occur within a logical sense of space and time. But in less realistic types of fiction, such as romances, actions may be related to each other because of a numerical pattern, or a symbolic correspondence as much as a causal sequence. In some works, such as *Sir Gawain and the Green Knight*, plot and pattern may combine, though this sort of distinction has been overtaken by modern narratological discussion of plot and story, which it is appropriate to touch on before going further.

We owe to Aristotle the sense of the centrality of plot in the study of narrative literature: 'the ordered arrangement of the incidents is what I mean by plot' (*mythos*), he says in the *Poetics*, though it is of tragedy that he is speaking, and elaborates by distinguishing between simple plots, which have a single, continuous action not dependent on reversal or discovery, and complex actions, where discovery and/ or reversal will occur, both needing to be probable consequences of what went before.[8] On the basis of the primary importance of plot Aristotle develops statements of its basic characteristics: it should deal with an action complete in itself, have a beginning, middle, and end, and be of appropriate length to be grasped as a unity. An influential strand in modern discussion of narrative, beginning with the Russian Formalists in the twentieth century, has taken Aristotle's sense of plot as its base in classifying narratives in terms of the plot elements they contain and in developing distinctions between plot and story.

The first of these took as its focal point the construction of narratives from recurrent motifs and incidents which appeared in regular sequences: the ideas are especially associated with the formalizing and

---

[7] Frank Kermode, 'Novel and narrative', in *The Theory of the Novel: New Essays*, ed. John Halperin (New York Oxford, U.P., 1974), pp.155–74.

[8] Aristotle, *On the Art of Poetry*, in *Classical Literary Criticism*, trans. with an Introduction by T.S. Dorsch (Harmondsworth, Penguin Books, 1965), ch. 6.

codifying by Vladimir Propp[9] of the similar actions and underlying patterns of incident in Russian fairy tales. So, although the heroes of such tales are asked to perform many different tasks and tests, from ordeals by fire or sewing shirts to drinking lakes or decapitating dragons, all such trials occur in the same sequence of action: the hero has to perform a difficult task and does so; he is recognized as hero, the false hero is exposed, and the hero wins the princess and ascends to the throne. Plot is seen as primary and characters secondary, though analysis leads to the abstraction from the tales of seven basic roles or agents: villain, donor, helper, princess and father (in terms of agency a single element), dispatcher, hero, and false hero. Propp was aiming at a formal syntax of narrative, a scientific, formulaic representation of the fixed patterns, or 'functions' as he called them, which are the constants and the basic units of the narrative language in the sort of stories he was dealing with. This structuralist model which treats narratives as bodies of material to be tabulated is obviously best adapted as a critical method to the large-scale examination of stories of like kind—Mills and Boon romances, Hollywood westerns, sci-fi stories of new planets—with the intention of identifying the basic narrative recipe and the range of variations on it. The aspect of medieval narrative that makes most sense in structuralist terms is the recognition that medieval societies, certainly western European ones, shared a storehouse of folk tales and oral material and that in large groups of medieval stories such as chivalrous romances one finds the same patterns recurring in the stories of the deeds of different knights. *Sir Gawain and the Green Knight* is recognizable as a type of Arthurian episode in which Arthur and his court at Camelot provide the setting and point of reference for the arrival of a suppliant/ challenger at the court who will cause one of Arthur's knights to embark on a quest to find an unknown foe, to meet temptation and contest before returning to the court; in this particular case the poet plays subtle games with the formulaic elements but the sense of the narrative relies on the reader's recognition of them. Propp's identification of a regular narrative grammar working on a linguistic model and the later elaborations of structuralist narratology in the writings of Greimas and Todorov are readily adaptable to the analysis of

[9] Vladimir Propp, *Morphology of the Folktale* (1928; first translated into English 1958), trans. Laurence Scott, 2nd edn (Austin: University of Texas Press, 1968).

medieval narrative genres and the common features of a mixed bag of anonymous stories, but critics of structuralism have tended to fault the approach as unresponsive to the individual qualities of particular texts.

The same may be said of other large-scale studies of folk-tale material. Stith Thompson, in stating the fundamental principle of the study of folk tales as 'the adequate collecting of the stories', points out that this now generally accepted axiom is part of the nineteenth-century development of 'serious investigation of stories as an important part of human culture'. Actual medieval versions of folk tale are of interest only because they may be the earliest recorded form of a story: for the folklorist's purposes its excrescences have to be discounted.

Thus, many of our well-known tales appear in the most diverse literary treatments . . . The Prince as Bird is retold by Marie de France in her octosyllabic couplets and brought into the general circle of chivalric romance [i.e. in Marie's lay *Yonec*]. Many oral jests were worked over into poetic form and made into fabliaux and traditional animal tales were given a satirical twist in the *Roman de Renart*.[10]

The study of folk tales, therefore, is not the study of medieval narrative except incidentally: whereas the literary student is most interested in what the medieval text has made of its source material, the folklorist looks through the variations of genre, of form and style, of point of view, and so on, to the narrative motifs which link medieval tales to later occurrences of the same material. The study of stories en masse, by grouping, classifying, tabulating, according to shared subject matter and recurrent actions, continues to leave its mark on discussion because medieval writers borrow their basic story-material, and it is a customary stage in the study of a medieval narrative to trace its source and to identify what body of story-material it belongs to—in the case of romances very familiarly in terms of the three great 'matters',[11] the Matter of Britain (the stories of Arthur and his knights), the Matter of France (Charlemagne and his douzepers),

---

[10] Stith Thompson, *The Folktale* (1946), (Berkeley, University of California Press, 1977), pp.406–7.

[11] The distinction goes back to Jean Bodel in the twelfth century defining the subject matter for the poet as the three *matières* 'de France, et de Bretagne, et de Rome la grant'.

and the Matter of Rome (Troy, Thebes, Alexander, and so on), together with supplementary categories invented to mop up other romances such as the Matter of England (romances loosely based on English history such as *Havelok the Dane*). The limitations of these mass approaches have often been pointed out, as Dieter Mehl, for example, does in his standard work on the English romances: 'It is easy enough to demonstrate that there is in most cases no logical and unambiguous correspondence between material and form, between a certain story and a poem based on it. Even the connection between some stories and the *matières* is occasionally open to doubt.'[12] The preoccupation with the history of motifs and with the study of sources goes along with the structuralist approach that stems from the work of Propp and others on folk-tale material.

The second line of plot-based theory which has made a major contribution to modern discussion of narrative is the distinction between plot and story made by the Russian Formalists in the terms *fabula* and *sjuzet*, defined as a distinction between the logical ordering of events which could be abstracted from a narrative and the actual sequence of events as they are narrated. The original idea may be thought of as a recognition that, for example, a mystery story may be summarized for someone who has not read it, either by an analytical, demystified, 'what-really-happened' version of the action (the thing reviewers of detective fiction are supposed not to reveal) or by a 'what-happens-next' outline of events. The terms *fabula* and *sjuzet* were taken up by theorists of narrative but have proved rather slippery in translation: translated into French as *histoire* and *discours* or *récit*, they have usually become 'story' and 'plot' in English, though both of these terms are ambiguous, or 'story' and 'discourse'. Most writers on narrative feel obliged to define the terms. So Paul Cobley says: '*fabula* refers to the chronological sequence of events which make up the raw materials of the story: *sjuzet* is the way the story is organized'.[13] The refinement of the Russian Formalist distinction between story and plot by Genette into a division of narrative into three levels—*histoire* (story), *récit* (plot/discourse), and *narration* (narration, narrating)— has proved an adaptable tool and the terms, despite their ambiguities,

[12] Dieter Mehl, *The Middle English Romances of the Thirteenth and Fourteenth Centuries* (London, Routledge & Kegan Paul, 1968), pp.31–2.

[13] Paul Cobley, *Narrative* (London, Routledge, 2001), p.15.

are ones that correspond to most people's sense of how narrative works.[14] For a theorist like Peter Brooks[15] who sets out to reinstate 'plot' as a significant critical term, 'the design and intention of narrative, what shapes a story, and gives it a certain direction or intent of meaning', the terms *fabula* and *sjuzet* are to be argued with as not quite tallying with our sense of story, plot, and narration. Without trying to get back to the original Russian definitions, one may find in the pragmatic development of these terms and distinctions a language that one can adapt to the reading of medieval narrative. *Sir Gawain and the Green Knight* may serve as a test case.

The story-material of *Sir Gawain* is basically widespread Arthurian matter which includes the figure of Morgan la Fay, who had first appeared in Geoffrey of Monmouth as one of a group of nine healing sisters in the Isle of Avalon and then in Chrétien as Arthur's (half-)sister, but who had in the French prose romances developed into an enemy of Guenevere and of Camelot and Arthur; in this role in the poem she uses her supernatural power temporarily to transform a knight (identified at the end of the poem as Sir Bertilak de Hautdesert) into a green giant, who first appears at Camelot on New Year's Day to offer a challenge, allegedly a Christmas game but actually a mutual beheading contest. The gruesome beheading and the green knight's uncanny survival had been intended to cause Queen Guenevere to suffer mortal shock, but the challenge, which is successfully taken on by Arthur's nephew, Gawain, leads instead to an extension of the original idea into a testing of Gawain (as Camelot's representative), who has had to pledge his honour to seek out the green knight by the time of the next new year in order to receive his own neck blow. To the Arthurian story-material and characters, and the familiar idea of a quest for an individual knight who must leave Camelot for the adventure and then return, the poet has added the motif of the beheading game and subsequently uses other recognizable romance elements in the knight's arming and journey, his arrival at a strange castle, temptation of the hero by the lady of the castle, and another testing game of exchanged winnings, before reverting to

[14] Gérard Genette, *Narrative Discourse* (1972), trans. Jane E. Lewin (Ithaca, N.Y., Cornell U.P., 1980; Oxford, Basil Blackwell, 1982).

[15] Peter Brooks, *Reading for the Plot: Design and Intention in Narrative* (Cambridge, Mass., Harvard U.P., 1984).

the second appearance of the green knight and the completion of the adventure in explanation and Gawain's crestfallen return. The story-material is familiar and yet defamiliarized, partly by the interweaving of the known figures of Arthur and Gawain and unknown quantities (the green knight, his wife and court, all of whom remain anonymous until the naming of Bertilak and Morgan in the closing stages), but largely by playing off typical romance scenes and actions against unexpected plot management. Among the prior events that belong to the concept of *fabula* is the knowledge that, whatever happens in this adventure, Camelot, Arthur, and Gawain will survive it: the poet tells us that 'al watz þis fayre folk in her first age'(l.54), which is to say that the events occur in the early years of Arthurian confidence and pros-perity and that there is, therefore, still a substantial, known future for this court to be narrated elsewhere.

The plot, that is 'the ordered arrangement of the incidents', or *sjuzet*, does not carry such reassurances because it is the unique chronological course that has been cut through the story-material. Circumstances force Gawain to take on a dangerous adventure, which he might have done better to avoid, and to make a blind promise to seek out an unknown opponent who has been given the right to chop off his head, without Gawain's being allowed to defend himself or fight back. He has to leave the court where he is at home to ride through unknown winter territory and, when he finds shelter at Christmas in an unknown castle, he must learn new social rules, make more promises, and steer a tricky course around social traps, while all the time keeping up the courage he will need when he faces the green knight's axe. One may feel confident that Gawain will sur-vive the crucial encounter but one does not know exactly what will happen at the end of the poem; Gawain's return to Camelot, 'knyȝt al in sounde'(l.2489), is yet not a hero's triumph but a sort of compen-sated humiliation outside the normal range of romance closure. The plot moves the protagonist from known to unknown, and a major part of the plot strategy is concealment: the reader does not know who the people at Hautdesert are, what their motives are or where Gawain's experiences are leading, until the careful build-up of sus-pense is exploded into anticlimax and explanation. Varied story-material has been selectively and allusively dovetailed to create a single plot-line following the hero (except for the hunting scenes in which Gawain is not present). The relationship between *fabula* and *sjuzet* is full of irony as the unknown of the plot resonates against the known of the story, as, for example, in the temptation scenes where the knowing reader of French romances about Gawain could well expect an erotic seduction but where this particular Gawain devotes himself wittily and ingeniously to avoiding the sexual boldness of his hostess's bedroom visits.

The narrating of these events is by means of an apparent directness and simplicity of voice in combination with sophisticated devices of structuring and perspective. Initially the tale-teller's stance is that of an oral narrator conveying directly to his audience in traditional minstrel style a story of Arthurian adventure which he has heard: we are asked to 'lysten þis laye bot on littel quile' and promised a 'stori stif and stronge' in poetic style which has 'lel lettres loken', that is, in regular alliterative metre. There are, however, few signs of such a process of oral narrating in what follows, especially if one compares *Sir Gawain* to a romance composed throughout in an oral style such as *Gamelyn*. There is a reminder to the hero not to forget what he has promised at the end of Fitt I, a direct assertion to us in Fitt II that our storyteller is deliberately going to delay matters while he explains the symbolic appositeness of the pentangle to Gawain (and one notes that this explanation is in fact a rather bookish thing to include), and a reassurance at the end of Fitt III that our hero has nearly achieved his quest and that if we sit still a little longer all will be revealed. By the time he gets to the end the poet has left off this flimsy cloak of social storytelling and refers twice to the book-reading which lies behind the poem (and to which occasional reference has been made, as at l.690—' þe boke as I herde say') and with which it belongs. For the most part the narrating is in the voice of an omniscient narrator, apparently present as a witness to all the scenes in the story, able to enter, when he chooses, the thoughts of his hero (and even, briefly, the thoughts of the anonymous lady of Hautdesert). There is frequent shifting from past to present tense so that the reporting of an adventure that happened long ago is constantly being expressed in terms of the vivid moment, as, for example, when Gawain leaves Camelot and 'gef hem alle goud day/He wende for euermore' and then 'Mony wylsum way he rode': with a new stanza the very same verb jumps into the present tense—'Now ridez þis renk þurʒ þe ryalme of Logres'. The same effect occurs with the many passages of direct speech when the fact of utterance is reported as past—'quoþ Gawan' and so on—but the speeches themselves (and more than a quarter of the poem is in direct speech) are in the present tense and the first person. This flexible confident voice, which at times seems to identify closely with the hero, 'oure luflych lede', can also step outside the adventure and include the comments of anonymous bystanders and find space to put the story within the perspectives of history (at the beginning and end), of seasonal time and mutability (at the beginning of Fitt II), of moral allegory (in the pentangle passage), and of fourteenth-century aristocratic life (in the hunting scenes particularly). The narration is conspicuously structured by the echo of the opening at the close, by the division into fitts and particularly by the elaborate three-part scheme of Fitt III with its three days each divided into scenes of simultaneous action, and by the choice of a unique metrical scheme of 101 stanzas of no fixed length combining unrhymed alliterative long lines with the short rhymed lines of the bob and wheel: this is about the nearest any medieval English poet came to the effect of French *laisses* (as used in the *Chanson de Roland*), again combining regularity with flexibility.

The development of narratology in the 1970s and 1980s from earlier structuralist approaches to narrative thus provided a language that fits comfortably with medieval narrative and which enables the reader to bring out the rich and complex effects of a sophisticated poem. But one could argue that the richness and complexity were there in the text and that the terms which were known in the poet's own time can probably be made to work with a similar result. In the Ciceronian terms from which I began in this section *Sir Gawain* is *fabula* (in the sense of an unlifelike and untrue narrative—with a green giant, a non-fatal beheading, an aunt with magic powers, it is clear that this is fantasy land) pretending to be *historia*, and doing so with remarkable panache and persuasion; the terms may be different but both medieval and modern theories recognize the text which plays off one effect against another.

Genres

For medievalists the concept of genre is enmeshed in the problem of dealing with a large body of anonymous works. For pragmatic, bibliographical reasons these have to be classified and subdivided and the headings under which they are grouped, once the known authors (Chrétien, Boccaccio, Chaucer, or whoever) have been separated off, are usually genre labels: chronicles, romances, debates, dream poems, tales, fables, allegories, dramatic pieces, lyrics, and so on. Critical exposition of individual works may take issue with the labels they have been given and many essays have been written which consist essentially of the author arguing that though *x* is usually called a romance, it demonstrably fulfils the criteria for some other category, whether it be saint's life, parable, folk tale, saga, family myth, or something else.[16] But in order to appreciate an individual medieval work one must read it, and to read it one must find it, and finding it usually means looking it up under a generic heading in order to locate an edition: before one can argue about its genre one must know what genre it belongs to. Genre-labelling is thus associated with approximation: it is a tool of convenience, with a provisional quality about it, rather than part of a precise system. It is therefore not surprising that modern discussion of medieval genres has consisted often of expressions of irritation at the lack of a regulated scheme and attempts to negotiate more precise terms.

It is not that there is any lack of genre words in medieval usage. Paul Strohm lists, with reference to medieval English narrative genres, *comedie/tragedie, cronicle, ensample, fable, geste, legende, lyf, myracle, passioun, pley, proces, romaunce, spelle, storie, tale, tretys,* and *visioun.*[17] One could add to this list from Chaucer's usage alone *dreme, epistel, lay, parable, sweven,* together with words referring to short poems, now usually called lyrics, which may sometimes include narrative elements. Strohm claims to be providing 'A taxonomy of Middle English narrative terms' but the word for scientific classification promises more than can be substantiated: no system emerges from the alphabetical list of words, many with senses overlapping with others, though Strohm argues that there was enough coordination, at least before the fifteenth century, for writers to 'choose among these terms with some confidence in the significations and expectations

---

[16] For example, Francis Lee Utley, 'Five genres in the *Clerk's Tale*', *Chaucer Review* 6 (1971–2), 198–228, in which he considers Chaucer's version of the story of Griselda as drama, *exemplum*, fairy-tale, *novella*, and religious allegory.

[17] Paul Strohm, 'Middle English narrative genres', *Genre* 13 (1980), 379–88.

they would evoke'. So, on the basis of the history of the origins of the words and of their adaptation into English, he suggests that, among other terms, *geste* ('a narrative replete with vigorous deeds or actions'), *romaunce* (from its original identification of the vernacular, usually French, language in which a work was written developing in English mainly to refer to 'accounts of the deeds of a single hero, with emphasis not only on martial but also on amatory and fanciful episodes'), *spelle* (an oral tale with popular appeal), *storie* (factual, historical tales or at least realistic ones), and *tale* (a spoken narration, including both true and fictitious material), were sufficiently distinct to communicate the right expectations to a medieval audience. He cites several examples, such as reference to *Havelok the Dane* as a *spelle* (raising expectation of 'a compact and immediate narrative') or *Kyng Alisaunder* as a *geste* (leading to expectation of 'predominance of diverse actions over fantasy or amorous by-play'), but these are debatable, particularly since in these two cases one might object that *Havelok* is not especially compact and the fantastic element in *Kyng Alisaunder* is quite strong; one suspects that *spelle* refers to the manner of the telling and *geste* to the content (the acts of a great leader) and that the two words could be exchanged with no great loss in the expectation aroused. There is plenty of evidence for the interchangeability of many medieval terms for narrative kinds. Strohm himself notes that some of the so-called English Breton lays are particularly varied in the way they refer to themselves: allegedly based on *storie* and *romaunce*, in the course of its telling *The Erl of Tolous* refers to itself as *tale*, *geste*, and *lay* and *Emaré* similarly claims to be based on *storie* and *romaunce* and calls itself *songe*, *story*, and *lay*. Caroline D. Eckhardt points out that in different manuscripts of *The Canterbury Tales* the same tale may receive different descriptions: so *The Manciple's Tale* and Chaucer's *Tale of Melibee* are both in different places labelled *narratio*, *fabula*, *tale* with a few other designations such as *tretis* and *proverb*.[18] Maldwyn Mills examines two manuscripts in which romances occur and finds that none of them is identified as a romance: they are named variously *hystorye*, *treatyse*, *jeaste*, *lyfe*. This contrasts with the well-known Thornton collections which include a large number of romances and use the word *romance* in many of their

---

[18] Caroline D. Eckhardt, 'Genre' in *A Companion to Chaucer*, ed. Peter Brown (Oxford, Blackwell, 2000), pp.180–94.

titles.[19] Perhaps 'romance' was by the fifteenth century already seen
by some as too broad and general to be a useful indicator of content
and, just as modern surveys of romance create subclasses relating to
content, theme, metre, and so on, so fifteenth-century compilers used
genre words such as *geste, story, lay* as subheadings within the larger
category. It is clear that some terms (*legende, lyf, myracle, passioun,
visioun*) usually refer to religious material, though the promise of
Chaucer's Miller to tell 'a legende and a lyf' reminds us to be cautious
even here; some apply to teaching uses of narrative (*ensample* and
fable, though the latter has the wider sense of an invented plot, distinct from true events); others are applied mainly to secular material,
as in the case of those already listed, together with *comedie, tragedie,
cronicle*, but none of these terms seems to have very sharp edges.

Strohm's discussion of the expectations which genre words raise in
the audience's mind was stimulated by the influential analysis of
genre by Hans Robert Jauss, whose views on medieval alterity were
referred to earlier; he is one of the theorists associated with the
'aesthetics of reception', an aspect of reader-response theory.[20] Jauss's
argument is that 'every work belongs to a genre', which is to say that
'for each work a preconstituted horizon of expectations must be
ready at hand': to establish what this horizon of expectation is for any
given genre requires historical study of genre as a kind of language
which changes over a period of time. In pursuit of this Jauss examines
the relationship of medieval classifications to the classical distinctions
of voice, identified in the preceding section of this chapter, and of
style (humble/low, medium, grand/high) and to the formulations of
the rhetoricians, as in John of Garland's groupings according to form,
delivery, closeness to reality, and feeling or mood (invective, satirical,
tragic, elegiac). He argues that 'the new literary genres of the Romance
vernaculars' did not proceed in a linear development from this tradition. To insist on continuity with classical categorizations is to ignore

---

[19] Maldwyn Mills, 'Generic titles in MS Douce 261 and MS Egerton 3132A', in *The
Matter of Identity in Medieval Romance*, ed. Phillipa Hardman (Cambridge, D.S.
Brewer, 2002), pp.125–38. The Thornton collections are Lincoln Cathedral Library MS
91 and British Library MS Additional 31042.

[20] Hans Robert Jauss, 'Theory of genres and medieval literature', first published in
French in *Poétique* (1970), 79–101, and incorporated into *Towards an Aesthetic of
Reception*, trans. Timothy Bahti (Brighton, Harvester, 1982); extracts from the essay
are included in *Modern Genre Theory*, ed. David Duff (Harlow, Longman, 2000),
pp.128–47.

the development of a Christian aesthetic in which a humble style may be used for lofty ideas: the Bible itself was a compendium of literary forms in prose and verse, containing chronicle, legend, saga, biography, parable, allegory, lyric, sermon, epistle, dialogue, and so on. In a period that did not yet feel any 'separation between religious life and literary culture' (a statement obviously easier to accept for some European countries and for some parts of the huge period covered by the word 'medieval' than for others), the forms of literature are to be defined in terms of religious and social functions, becoming literary and autonomous only by gradual process. This process is not one of organic development or evolution but rather of periodic alternation of dominant and subordinate roles. So, for example, Jauss cites (and he is thinking mainly of medieval French literature) the new appearance of the courtly romance which, in mid twelfth century, struggles for dominant position with the older *chanson de geste*, to be followed early in the thirteenth century by the prose romance and in mid thirteenth century by allegory. What Jauss thinks desirable is a sense of genre as part of a given period's system, but, of course, the problem of dating many medieval works often blurs any perception of what the hierarchy of genres might have been at any one time.

Although Jauss's phrase 'horizon of expectation' has often been repeated in modern discussion of medieval genres, the difficulty of establishing what that horizon was for specific medieval works and kinds remains. The works that most clearly display the identifying features of a genre tend to be parodies, because, as Ardis Butterfield pointed out, 'the humour of parody is . . . that it draws attention precisely to those features of style, content and form which the source of the parody presents as unexceptional'.[21] A case in point is Chaucer's treatment of romance in *The Canterbury Tales*, where a definition of the genre would be quite difficult to work out from, say, *The Knight's Tale* and *The Man of Law's Tale*, but the absurdly exaggerated parody in *Sir Thopas* provides a very recognizable outline of its typifying features: a knight riding out on a quest, the love of a fairy bride, a fight with a giant, the arming of the hero whose handsomeness and virtue are praised in superlatives, the spirit of adventure and chance, and so on. Jauss's idea that to understand medieval generic concepts

[21] Ardis Butterfield, 'Medieval genres and modern genre theory', *Paragraph* 13 (1990), 184–201 (quotation from p.186).

one must limit oneself to identifiable sets of expectation within the medieval period really requires that medieval writers provide unambiguous labels for their works; only a few do so. Chaucer is one who does and he does it conspicuously and often enough to mark genre-labelling as a feature of his work.

So in *Sir Thopas* the hero, as he prepares to arm in order to fight a three-headed giant, calls for his:

> . . . mynstrales
> And geestours for to tellen tales,
> Anon in myn armynge,
> Of romaunces that ben roiales,
> Of popes and of cardinales,
> And eek of love-likynge.
>
> (*CT*, VII, 845–50)

Chaucer conveys here not only the genre name that his imitation belongs with but also the grand social level that is expected in such tales, and again later in the parody he places *Sir Thopas* in terms of genre name and of some comparable examples:

> Men speken of romaunces of prys,
> Of Horn child and of Ypotys,
> Of Beves and sir Gy,
> Of sir Lybeux and Pleyndamour—
> But sir Thopas, he bereth the flour
> Of roial chivalry!
>
> (*CT*, VII, 897–902)

These are the only places in *The Canterbury Tales* where Chaucer uses the word 'romance' (except for the reference to *The Romance of the Rose* in *The Merchant's Tale*). Of the names referred to here, Horn, Bevis, and Guy are well-known young romance heroes, 'sir Lybeux' is the young hero, son of Gawain, in the romance *Lybaeus Desconus* ('The Fair Unknown') and Ypotys is the eponymous hero of a pious legend written in a popular romance style, included perhaps because he is a boy hero; 'Pleyndamour' is the only mystery, possibly a tongue-in-cheek invention by Chaucer of a particularly foppish name for a hero. *Sir Thopas* is a genre joke carried into imitation of elements of form (the tail-rhyme stanza and the use of bob lines as in *Sir Gawain and the Green Knight*) as well as subject matter and style, and the names and genre words act as signals to the reader. But, of course, this tale is interrupted and condemned by the Host for its poor quality, accused of 'verray lewednesse', 'drasty speech', 'drasty ryming', and of being 'rym dogerel'—all identifying the supposed ignorance of the teller, the well-known poet Chaucer, who elsewhere in *The Canterbury Tales* is credited with having written so much that virtually all tales have come from his pen:

> And if he have noght seyd hem, leve brother,
> In o book, he hath seyd hem in another.
>
> (*CT*, II, 51–2)

The Man of Law, though, has prefaced this with the undercutting proviso that 'he kan but lewedly/On metres and on rymyng craftily' (*CT*, II, 47–8). Thus an in-joke about the author's own abilities gives an extra spice to the bluff dismissal by the unliterary Host of this story teller who proves capable only of amateurish romance hackwork. In this instance the genre-labelling is the signal for catcalls of disapproval.

Something similar occurs in Chaucer's composition of the other ostentatiously interrupted tale in the Canterbury series, *The Monk's Tale*. In this case the tale-teller, resisting the implications of the Host's teasing that he might entertain the pilgrims with a story about sex, announces that it is his intention to tell tragedies and then provides an explicit definition in case we may be in doubt of what that means:

> Tragedie is to seyn a certeyn storie,
> As olde bookes maken us memorie,
> Of hym that stood in great prosperitee,
> And is yfallen out of heigh degree
> Into myserie and endeth wrecchedly.
>
> (*CT*, VII, 1973–7)

The seventeen stories that follow, varying in length from a single eight-lined stanza to sixteen, are all tales of the great and powerful whose time of prosperity is brought to a sudden end by the turn of Fortune's wheel; stretching from Lucifer and Adam to Bernabò Visconti, who had died as recently as 1385 (and whom Chaucer had met in 1378), they cover the whole of history and illustrate both the definition of tragedy found in Boethius (as glossed by Nicholas Trevet and translated by Chaucer in his *Boece* [Bk II, prose 2] as 'a dite of a prosperitee for a tyme that endith in wrecchidnesse') and the idea of the falls of great ones narrated in Boccaccio's Latin prose work *De casibus illustrium virorum* ('Concerning the falls of famous men'). This is close enough in theme to Chaucer's work to look like the model for it, though it is not certain that Chaucer knew Boccaccio's text; Boccaccio does not in any case call his narratives 'tragedies', emphasizing the protagonist's own rash and sinful acts rather than the blind arbitrariness of Fortune. This is an instance of Chaucer's defining a genre in a manner which makes it sound a more clearly established literary type than was probably the case. John of Garland contrasts comedy ('a humorous poem beginning in sadness and ending in joy') with tragedy, which is defined as 'a poem composed in high style, beginning in joy and ending in grief'.[22] Dante associated tragedy with lyric forms, though he applies the word in the *Inferno* to the story of Dido and Aeneas; Boccaccio uses the word only in association with classical instances.[23] However, whether or not Boccaccio thought his stories of the falls of the great were moralistic demonstrations of punishment for overweening pride (and hence *exempla* rather than tragedies), Chaucer (in *The Monk's Tale* at least) interpreted such tales as what has become known as '*de casibus* tragedy' and he was imitated by Lydgate and others in the fifteenth and sixteenth centuries: so if he did not find an existing genre, he invented a new one. In *Sir Thopas* Chaucer confirmed the type by alluding to other known romances, but here the series confirms the opening definition again and again, so that if the reader did not know what a tragedy was at the beginning, by the time the Knight breaks in and stops the Monk going through the whole set of a hundred tragedies which he says he has in his cell, we have been given seventeen illustrations of the type. Rejection in this case is not because of the slipshod quality of the narration but because of the depressing nature of the content and the monotony of the repetition: as the Knight says, 'litel hevynesse/Is right ynough to muche folke'.

These two cases interestingly show Chaucer being specific about genre but with the intention of displaying the tales as examples of unsuccessful narration which fails to hold the audience's attention.

---

[22] John of Garland, *Parisiana Poetria*, ch.4.
[23] See H. Ansgar Kelly, 'Interpretation of and by genres in the Middle Ages', in *Interpretation: Medieval and Modern*, eds. Piero Boitani and Anna Torti, 8th Series of J.A.W. Bennett Memorial Lectures (Cambridge, D.S. Brewer, 1993), pp.107–22.

Such genre names imply a literate awareness in his intended readership and his sense that one possibility opened up by using a
wide variety of narrators is to create conflicts of style among them.
His collection of tales is not, as most medieval tale collections
were, a compilation of tales of the same kind but an anthology of
varied tale types selected with a sense of appropriateness to the
supposed storytellers. So the Prioress is given a Marian miracle
(referred to as 'this *miracle*') and the Second Nun a saint's life
(referred to as 'the *lyf* of Seinte Cecile'), while less pious characters
such as the Reeve and Shipman are given comic tales of sex and
trickery (referred to as '*tales*'), and so on. However, beyond this
Chaucer uses his pilgrims not only as narrators but also as audience and includes their reception of the stories (though not,
unfortunately in all cases, since *The Canterbury Tales* was left
unfinished at Chaucer's death): the reception varies from delighted
approval to bored condemnation. The implication for thinking
about genre is that Chaucer found genre-labelling a useful focussing device in this creation of cross-currents between the narrator
and the narratee.

This was not always for the purpose of exposure of the limitations
of narrative types. A more complex instance is the identification of
The Franklin's Tale as a Breton lay. This subclass of romance has a
slightly better defined history than some types of courtly narrative.
Marie de France, writing in the late twelfth century in England but in
Anglo-Norman, possibly for the court of Henry II, provided a definition for her collection of *Lais* (twelve poems surviving in its fullest
form as a collection in British Library MS Harley 978) which presup-
poses an earlier type of lay, which Marie refers to in terms that make
it sound like a sung ballad, from which she claims to have reconsti-
tuted the story: there is little evidence to support Marie's statements
that the noble Bretons composed lays to preserve for posterity adventures they had heard (in the prologue to *Equitan*) or that the 'lay . . .
which is performed on harp and rote, was composed from the tale
you have heard' (epilogue to *Guigemar*). In effect, whatever the real
antecedents for Marie's poems, she created the genre and set herself
to justify her texts and her chosen poetic mode in her prologue,
where she presents herself as not wishing merely to do as others have
done by translating a Latin work into French, but looking for a more
original path:

So I thought of lays which I had heard . . . composed, by those who first
began them and put them into circulation, to perpetuate the memory of
adventures they had heard. I myself have heard a number of them and . . . I
have put them into verse, made poems from them and worked on them late
into the night. (Marie's *Prologue* to the *Lais*)[24]

The Anglo-Norman writer Denis Piramus provides, in the prologue
to his life of St Edmund (written about 1180), a contemporary tribute
to the popularity of 'les vers de lais' composed by 'Dame Marie'
among both the male and female members of the court and it seems
reasonable to think that other surviving anonymous French lays were
written in imitation of her. Some English poems were either translated or adapted from her lays (*Lai le Freine, Sir Landevale, Sir Launfal*),
while other short romances in English, notably *Sir Orfeo*, ally themselves to the Breton lay tradition. There is some evidence for knowledge of the lays in late-thirteenth-century England.[25] Chaucer
prefaced *The Franklin's Tale* by his version of what Marie had said in
her prologue and in the introductions to several of her lays:

> Thise olde gentil Britouns in hir dayes
> Of diverse aventures maden layes,
> Rymeyed in her firste Briton tonge,
> Whiche layes with hir instrumentz they songe.
> Or elles redden hem for hir plesaunce;
> And oon of hem have I in remembraunce,
> Which I shal seyn with good wyl as I kan.
>
> (*CT*, V, 709–15)

Here then is another of Chaucer's conspicuous genre labels, slightly
puzzling in that one can not suppose that Chaucer knew Marie's
work directly and the two-hundred-year gap between her lays and
late-fourteenth-century recall of the tradition is not all that easy to
span. What 'horizon of expectation' would the idea have evoked in
Chaucer's time? Breton lays are usually defined as short romances
(though Marie's vary from 118 lines in octosyllabic couplets to 1184
lines), concerning idealized, even if sometimes adulterous, love, with

---

[24] *The Lais of Marie de France*, trans. with an Introduction by Glyn S. Burgess and
Keith Busby (Harmondsworth, Penguin Books, 1986), p.41.
[25] See Elizabeth Archibald, 'The Breton lay in Middle English: genre, transmission
and the Franklin's Tale', in *Medieval Insular Romance: Translation and Innovation*, eds.
Judith Weiss, Jennifer Fellows, and Morgan Dickson (Cambridge, D.S. Brewer, 2000),
pp.55–70.

supernatural elements: such a definition would fit Chaucer's tale, though he is clever enough to make the adultery a threat avoided and the supernatural a transformation readable as ingenious illusion. Explanations for Chaucer's invocation of the Breton lay tradition have varied from Laura Hibbard Loomis's idea that Chaucer knew the Auchinleck MS, in which *Lai le Freine* and *Sir Orfeo* with their shared prologue listing the topics favoured by the Bretons in their lays both occur,[26] and that this manuscript represented a fourteenth-century revival in England of interest in a form that had ceased to be fashionable in France, to the idea that Chaucer was characterizing the Franklin by deliberately using an old-fashioned type of narrative, or the notion that, since the Breton lay was a more emotional, even lyrical, kind of romance narrative, Chaucer's interest in combining narrative with complaint may have led him to seek out a story with opportunities for emotional monologues.[27] His use of the label does not seem here, any more than with *Sir Thopas* and *The Monk's Tale*, to be simply a matter of offering a helpful pigeon-hole to the reader. His drawing attention to the genre is again to point to the variety of literary forms within *The Canterbury Tales* and can be linked to his other literary signposts, such as the specific identification of Petrarch as the source for *The Clerk's Tale*, the review of his own writings which he included in *The Man of Law's Prologue*, and the repeated renewal in the prologues and link passages of a running debate about the truth and the qualities of fiction.

Mixture of genres is a major feature of *The Canterbury Tales*, so much so that it can be read as a virtuoso display of the narrative kinds that Chaucer knew: even with what might seem the most limited part of the medieval writer's repertoire, preaching discourses, Chaucer is able to ring the changes from historical *exemplum* (*Physician's Tale*), saint's life (*Second Nun's Tale*), miracle (*Prioress's Tale*), sermon with *exemplum* (*Pardoner's Tale*), animal fable (*Nun's Priest's Tale*), to the two prose treatises (allegorical dialogue in *Melibee* and discourse on repentance and the sins in *The Parson's Tale*). The variety of narrators' voices is matched by the range of kinds. Even at the moment

[26] Laura Hibbard Loomis, 'Chaucer and the Breton lays of the Auchinleck Manuscript', *Studies in Philology* 38 (1941), 14–33.

[27] See Archibald's essay and the chapter on *The Franklin's Tale* in my earlier book, W.A. Davenport, *Chaucer: Complaint and Narrative* (Cambridge, D.S. Brewer, 1988), pp.178–97.

when all fiction is apparently rejected as untruth, when in *The Parson's Prologue* Chaucer has his poor parson express the extreme of rhetoricians' disapproval of the falsity of *fabula*—'Thou getest fable noon ytold for me'—even here the alternatives are indicated as the Parson declares:

> But trusteth wel, I am a Southren man;
> I kan nat geeste 'rum, ram, ruf,' by lettre,
> Ne, God woot, rym holde I but litel bettre;
> And therfore, if yow list—I wol nat glose –
> I wol yow telle a myrie tale in prose
> To knytte up al this feeste and make an ende.
>
> (*CT*, X, 42–7)

It may be a moral choice that the Parson is making but it is expressed in terms of stylistic competence and preference: no alliterative poetry, with its associations of 'geeste' (presumably referring to the celebration of heroic deeds in alliterative poems like the *Morte Arthure*), and no rhyming stuff either (again perhaps alluding to popular romance writing), but a pleasing discourse in prose. Here the horizon of expectation is created by discarding some ideas that are seen as inappropriate. Sometimes the variety is marked by placing tales together in generic opposition as is most strikingly the case with the two opening tales of the series, the stately *Knight's Tale* and the slapstick *Miller's Tale*. And it is at the changeover between these two that Chaucer puts his statement of generic intent. In *The Miller's Prologue* he speaks as the compiler of a tale collection, aware that tales are of different literary kinds and that each kind may please an audience differently. He has chosen, obviously in order to create variety within the series, to include comic and vulgar material and so, like Boccaccio in the *Decameron*, he has to divert the possible disapproval of his audience by distancing himself from supposedly irrepressible story tellers. In Chaucer's case these are condemned as 'cherles' whose 'harlotrie' can not be avoided, but of course the reader can ignore it:

> And therfore, whoso list it nat yheere,
> Turne over the leef and chese another tale;
> For he shal fynde ynowe, grete and smale,
> Of storial thyng that toucheth gentillesse,
> And eek moralitee and hoolynesse.
> Blameth nat me if that ye chese amys.
>
> (*CT*, I, 3176–81)

Three categories are identified: 'cherles tales/harlotrie'; tales that are 'storial' and concern 'gentillesse'; and tales that express 'moralitee' and/or 'hoolynesse', and I am happy to accept this broad classification as an indicator of a suitable genre division for discussion in the rest of this book.

The didactic kinds, the 'moralitee and hoolynesse', are the simplest to define, though, as I indicated above, their range is quite wide: exemplary modes are the nearest to rhetorical theories of narrative and to that basic idea of *narratio* which Cicero saw as the essential statement of the facts. I shall deal with *exemplum* and *fable* as representative didactic genres. Chaucer's 'storial thyng that toucheth gentillesse' brings first to mind the medieval romance but it can also be seen as representing the Ciceronian idea of *historia* as a major category of narrative, including chronicle, epic, and biography together with their extended forms in romance, legend, and saint's life. The 'cherles tales' are usually in modern times called *fabliaux*; in Ciceronian terms they belong to the category of *argumentum*, the 'fictitious event that nevertheless could have happened, as is the case in comedies' (as John of Garland put it). The one area that Chaucer's categorization leaves unspecified, though there is plenty in *The Canterbury Tales* that connects with it, is the fantastic or dream narrative, that sense of *fabula* which Cicero connected with unlifelike incidents. These four groups will form the material of Chapters 3–6 which follow. Before that, however, a look at prologues is needed.

Prologues and narrators

The main place where medieval authors set themselves to control the expectations of the audience is in prologues, which is where much of the application of medieval critical theory is to be identified; it is here that writers define their attitude to what is to follow and give the reader necessary clues to understanding.[28] It is probably more appropriate to think of thresholds of expectation than of horizons.

---

[28] See the collection of vernacular prologues assembled in *The Idea of the Vernacular: An Anthology of Middle English Literary Theory 1280–1520*, eds. Jocelyn Wogan-Browne, Nicholas Watson, Andrew Taylor, and Ruth Evans (Exeter, University of Exeter Press, 1999).

There are basically two types of prologue: firstly writers' prologues to their own poems or prose narratives, in which they establish a relationship between their audience and their subject and identify, or at least cast some light on, orientations concerning genre, point of view, the role expected of the reader, and the voice of the narrator; secondly the prologues that scholars/editors wrote as introductions to their commentaries on works by others, which were designed to direct readers to an accurate evaluation of the text.[29] Both of these were capable of being developed and shaped to a variety of roles and functions as in introductions by adaptors, translators, and compilers.

As with narrative itself, so with prologues: there was an established, classically based tradition of text-division which indicated what was expected of prologues. In the sections on Invention in *De inventione* and *Rhetorica ad Herennium*[30] Cicero defined the basic outline and division of the text as an introduction, the narration/statement of the facts, the pros and cons of argument and the conclusion. Isidore of Seville in the seventh century shows a simplified version of this classical tradition in four sections: *exordium, narratio, argumentatio,* and *conclusio*; i.e. introduction, statement of facts, proof, and summing up. In the *exordium* the speaker prepared the hearer's mind for attention, which he might do, if the material to follow is straightforward, by a direct approach to the subject—a brief summary, open exhortation to listen, an appeal to the audience's interests—all these could be accommodated in the direct opening or *prohemium*. If, on the other hand, the material was controversial or difficult, an indirect, subtle approach, or *insinuatio*, might be required; Cicero has various recommended devices for this, including the use of jokes, puns, innuendo and ambiguity, banter with the audience, and so on. The prologue is designed to create receptivity in the audience, whether by direct involvement in the material and the occasion, or by dissimulation and suggestion.

John of Garland is one of the rhetoricians who defines prologues explicitly. In the *Parisiana Poetria*, which draws on material traceable

---

[29] See *Medieval Literary Theory and Criticism* c. 1100–c. 1375: *The Commentary Tradition*, eds. A.J. Minnis and A.B. Scott with the assistance of David Wallace, revd edn (Oxford Clarendon Press, 1991) especially ch. 1, 'An anthology of literary prefaces: introductions to the authors', pp.12–36.

[30] M. Tullius Cicero, *Rhetorica ad Herennium*, ed. and trans. Harry Caplan, Loeb Classical Library, (Cambridge, Mass., Harvard U.P., 1954).

to the *Rhetorica ad Herennium*, Horace's *Ars poetica*, and Geoffrey de Vinsauf, John makes distinctions between the *exordium* (a rhetorical beginning whose purpose is persuasion) and the *proemium* (an advance outline of the book's contents, whose purpose is instruction); thus we meet a clear separation between the emotional and the explanatory functions of openings, and the basis of what elsewhere is seen as a difference between the extrinsic and intrinsic prologues. John further defines the *prologus* (an introductory discussion to the work) and several techniques for opening. These distinctions were already being used at an earlier date in the writings of a commentator such as Conrad of Hirsau (*c*.1070–1150) in his *Dialogue on the Authors*, a master/pupil dialogue in which the master defines terms:

> The proem is the preface to the work. The prologue is a preliminary statement before a discourse . . . the prologue makes the reader or listener readily taught, attentive, and well-disposed. Every prologue is either apologetic or commendatory.[31]

In his commentary on Sallust, Conrad later develops a distinction between two types of prologue: the *prologus ante rem* (a pre-text prologue), which is introductory to the subject matter and which presents the main contents of the work to follow; and the *prologus praeter rem* (a beyond-text prologue), which goes beyond the subject matter and which does not deal directly with the content of the work, but which presents a context of themes and ideas for what is to follow. Thus the exact terms used change to some extent, but both in classical and medieval times theoreticians find it necessary to recognize that prologues are not all the same and that they often fuse together at least two purposes, one concerned with influencing the audience's attitude and the other concerned with the actual contents of the work.

From the twelfth century onwards writers aware of rhetorical precepts demonstrate a variety of ways in which prologues could create perspective. What one might call the traditional medieval poet's prologue offers a justification and explanation of the text in terms of the writer's own experience and qualifications for the task, the reason for writing, which might include dedication to a patron who has commissioned the work, some reference to the writer's own life and

---

[31] See Minnis and Scott, *Medieval Literary Theory and Criticism*, p.43.

circumstances, the stimulus to the writing, the intention of the work, and the source material. Later in the period it is common for the writer to offer protestations of modest talent, inadequacy for the task, and so on. The Prologue which Marie de France wrote to her collection of *Lais*, mentioned in the previous section, provides one late-twelfth-century version, particularly interesting because of the scarcity of known women authors in the medieval period. Marie is not afraid to declare her faith in her own talents, 'the gift of knowledge and true eloquence' which it is her duty to use, and for which she has sought a literary task that will not merely repeat what others have done, translations from Latin into French: and so she explains her intention of turning the lays she has heard into poems and dedicates them to the 'worthy and courtly' king, possibly Henry II of England. Marie knows that a prologue has to make a case for her work and to do so she formulates an interesting general characterization of the type of poem she is embarking on together with oblique implications that her works will be courtly, virtuous, carefully composed, worth reading, and subtle in their meaning. Marie is clearly educated in rhetorical patterns of thought and knows how to gain her readers' confidence.

The careful shaping of prologues is as much the concern of Chrétien de Troyes, whose works show the marks of school training and who left at least five instances of ambitious narrative, written in the 1160s and 1170s, each with a carefully structured rhetorical opening, as Tony Hunt has demonstrated.[32] Chrétien's prologues display a chronological development in confidence and ambition from the coherent, conventional justification of the text in the prologue to *Erec*, where, after an opening *sententia* or proverb, he names himself, identifies his source-material and enhances his subject-matter by characterizing the role of the poet as that of drawing wisdom and delight for the audience from a story that others have neglected or misunderstood. By the time he wrote *Cligés* Chrétien was sure enough to offer evidence of his experience and skill by giving a list of his works in the prologue before impressing the worth of the story upon his reader through its occurrence in an ancient volume in a nobleman's library: the implication is that the tale will communicate

---

[32] Tony Hunt, 'Tradition and originality in the Prologues of Chrestien de Troyes', *Forum for Modern Language Studies* 8 (1972), 320–44.

the value of the chivalry and learning of the past. The best-known but most debated of the prologues is the one Chrétien wrote for *Lancelot*, where his references to his patron, Marie, countess of Champagne, daughter of Eleanor of Aquitaine, express such devotion and obedience to her commands that some have read it as ironic: does his famous statement that Marie provided the *matière* and the *sens* for the poem mean that she told him to write about the love of Lancelot and Guenevere and to treat it as illustrating the concept of ideal or 'courtly' love, or is Chrétien simply paying tribute to Marie's providing the occasion and the stimulus for his work? The prologue shows a greater degree of modesty in the poet's references to his own talents and makes a more subtle appeal to the reader's good will by a less direct approach. With *Yvain* Chrétien appears to dispense with a prologue by moving directly into the opening scene of the Arthurian court at Pentecost, but this leads him to a commendation of love and to praise of the courtliness of Arthurian society: a concealed prologue (Hunt reads it as an *insinuatio*) subordinates the poet's voice to the theme; Chrétien does not name himself and delays some of the effects of prologue (direct address to the audience to capture interest in the material and so on) until the speech of Calogrenant to the court at l.149ff.—'Lend me your hearts and your ears!' With his last, unfinished work, *Li contes del graal* ('Perceval'), Chrétien devotes his prologue to a forthright tribute to his greatest patron, Philip, count of Flanders, and relates the worth of his subject, 'the finest story ever told', to Philip's charity and piety, thus cleverly enhancing both patron and topic by mutual reflection; the poet's own role is simply that of the sower of the seed of romance in fertile soil. This is a mature and self-assured piece of writing. These prologues, individually and collectively, display Chrétien's high degree of consciousness of himself as artist (as well as his rhetorical training and classical education) and define the medieval poet's role of using his imaginative skills to interpret materials from earlier sources: from his source in a story, 'un conte d'aventure', the poet makes a well-structured composition, 'une molt bele conjointure' as he says in the prologue to *Erec*, and he might be providing the vernacular restatement of that rhetorical precept quoted earlier from Geoffrey de Vinsauf, that the poet must have a mental image or blueprint of the work before it is begun.

An even more high-flown example of the literary prologue is that of the *Tristan* of Gottfried von Strassburg (*fl.* 1210). Gottfried was

writing in the period of the production of the main examples of the
medieval 'Arts of Poetry', and is thought to have learned directly from
them. His prologue is usually seen as a great example of medieval
rhetoric in practice. It consists of 240 lines in two different metres.
The first forty lines are in gnomic quatrains, using wordplay and an
acrostic of the patron or dedicatee's name, Dieterich, and dealing with
the relationship between criticism and art, the poet's need of a
discriminating audience, and the difficulty of high achievement:

> Hei tugent, wie smal sint dine stege,
> wie kumberlich sint dine wege!
> die dine stege, die dine wege,
> wol ime, der si wege unde stege!

(O Excellence! how narrow are thy paths, how arduous thy ways! Happy
the man who can climb thy paths and tread thy ways!)[33]

This strophic prologue is an intellectual fulfilment of the rhetorical
idea of creating benevolence in the audience: Gottfried ingratiates
himself by flattering his hearers as the discriminating listeners his fine
talent needs. The prologue then switches into couplets (the metre for
the rest of the work) to establish the worth of his subject by declaring
that the poet will create pleasure for a select circle of 'noble hearts'
who accept the contraries of love. The sources of the poem are
acknowledged and, in an incantatory passage, the poet praises love,
which ennobles the spirit, enforces constancy, is a blessed state necessary to worth and honour, and whose sorrows must be borne. Tristan
and Isolde endured sorrow and so their story comforts others; their
names live on and their life and death are 'our bread . . . the bread of
the living'. Gottfried's prologue combines the artist's professional
concerns with reference to the poem's theme, its source and purpose,
and the emotion and mystical fervour it contains. Critics have argued
a good deal over the years about how the different parts of the prologue relate to one another. Since the story of Tristan and Isolde was a
tale of adultery and betrayal, which might have challenged the moral
code of the audience, could the prologue be read as another example
of *insinuatio*, in which Gottfried enlists the reader's sympathy
indirectly by establishing in the mind the power of love, the mystical
sustenance which the story offers, and so on? Or is it a composite

---

[33] Gottfried von Strassburg, *Tristan*, trans. A.T. Hatto (Harmondsworth, Penguin
Books, 1960), p.40.

prologue fusing together aspects of the two types of prologue mentioned above (*ante rem* and *praeter rem*), and so combining a claim for the significance and value of the work with the opening of a dialogue with the reader? Few medieval authors—only perhaps Dante —go further in claiming for their subject such intense meaningfulness and in employing such stylistic sophistication and sublimity.

These high-style, courtly prologues designed to win the good will of the hearers also define the audiences that the texts require: the sophisticated, educated language tells us what kind of readers we are expected to be, discriminating, interested in moral choices, capable of responding to fine feeling. Obviously not all medieval narratives have the same expectations. Contrast Gottfried's prologue to *Tristan* to the earlier version of the story in the *Tristrant* of Eilhart von Oberge (written between 1170 and 1190) which Gottfried probably knew. Eilhart's manner is lively, personal, and informal and his prologue, like his telling of the story, is blunter and more prosaic: he first tells those who do not want to listen to the story to leave, or at least to keep quiet, before promising the true tale of Tristrant and Isalde 'just as I found it in the book':

Hear a story, just as I tell it, of both joy and grief. No one ever knew a better tale of worldly feats, of manhood, and of love, and therefore you should listen all the more carefully.[34]

This is an example of what is sometimes called the 'pre-courtly' style but one could make the same point by looking at later texts. Contrast the clever, embedded prologue of Chrétien's *Yvain* with the opening of the English version of the poem, the fourteenth-century romance *Ywain and Gawain*, which takes no trouble to be subtle but assaults the audience straight on:

> Almyghty God that made mankyn,
> He schilde his servantes out of syn
> And mayntene tham with might and mayne
> That herkens *Ywayne and Gawayne*;
> Thai war knightes of the Tabyl Rownde,
> Tharfore listens a lytel stownde.[35]

---

[34] Eilhart von Oberge, *Tristrant*, trans. J.W. Thomas (Lincoln, Nebr., University of Nebraska Press, 1978).

[35] *Ywain and Gawain*, ed. Maldwyn Mills, Everyman's Library (London, J.M. Dent, 1992), p.1.

Such a popular entertainer's call for attention is a secular version of the preacher's direct, controlling manner. Marie de France, for example, in her *Fables* takes a much more robust line with her readership than in her *Lais*:

> Those persons all, who are well-read,
> Should study and pay careful heed
> To fine accounts in witty tomes,
> To models and to axioms:
> That which philosophers did find
> And wrote about and kept in mind.
> The sayings that they heard, they wrote,
> So that the morals we would note;
> Thus those who wish to mend their ways
> Can think about what wisdom says.
>
> (Prologue, 1–10)[36]

A prologue may thus be the poet's identification of him or herself as artist and a call for the audience to become sensitive intelligent appreciators of the fine points of a tale or it may be more simply the reciter's call for attention where the voice adopts 'minstrel' mannerisms and expects no more of the audience than the courtesy of keeping quiet, or the instructor's bringing the audience to heel. It is a definition of the assumed narrator as well as the assumed hearer and should answer a number of questions: are we listening to the artist sharing the hard-won fruits of mental labour and tuning our response to the text's stylistic finesse or just sitting down for a comfortable, undemanding hour or two to hear a journeyman retelling some tale he has picked up second-hand and aspiring to be no more than a temporary entertainer, or sitting up straight to learn a lesson while hoping that it is convincing and humane?

For the modern reader there is also the problem of how medieval narratives were originally 'published': we have only such written records as survive and therefore all medieval texts are now a matter of book-reading, words printed on the page, but at the time of composition some were oral (and the version of the performance which was written down may be incomplete, inaccurate, or distorted), while others were composed to be read in or from manuscript texts. This difference is reflected in the stance that narrators take up: prologues

---

[36] Marie de France, *Fables*, ed. and trans. Harriet Spiegel (Toronto, University of Toronto Press, 1994), hereafter referred to as Spiegel.

function to locate that role somewhere in a spectrum ranging from the scholarly book-compiler to the popular entertainer. Narrative designed to be read aloud encourages the composer to think in terms of speaking directly to the audience, but even so the degree of personal involvement in the story varies a good deal. Chrétien speaks as the teller of the tale but detaches himself from it by partly referring to himself in the third person: 'Chrétien begins his tale, following his source' (*Cligés*) and again 'Chrétien begins his book about the knight of the cart . . . Now he begins his story' (*Lancelot*) or at the close 'Thus Chrétien brings to a close his romance of the knight with the Lion, I've not heard any more about it.' (*Yvain*). It is no surprise that these narratives are presented in the voice of an omniscient narrator (even if he confesses that there are things he does not know). Orality is much more consciously exploited by narratives that are either supposed first-person accounts of experience, as in dream poems, or storytelling in an assumed, 'dramatic' voice.

First-person narrators are, as I said earlier, an aspect of the 'lyric' voice and lyrics, both secular and religious, may form a part of 'autobiographical' narratives. One model for medieval writers was Boethius' *De Consolatione Philosophiae*: written in alternating passages of Latin verse and prose, the work combines a first-person account of Boethius' own imprisonment and despair at the loss of worldly position with an unfolding process of consolation expressed as a dialogue between the afflicted sufferer and the teaching figure of Philosophy. This dialogue is, as the reader gradually comes to understand, a mental debate by means of which Boethius brings to bear on his loss of position, his banishment and exile the resources of his own mind and education so that he is slowly reconciled to his fate, but it is presented as a dramatic confrontation in which self and other are envisaged as the human Boethius and the superhuman Philosophy who takes him patiently through a learning sequence. There is no explanatory prologue here: the work begins with a lyric lamenting old age and the fickleness of fortune, but these supposed quiet thoughts of the narrator are soon challenged by the magisterial figure who appears before him and scorns the Muses of Poetry at his bedside as 'hysterical sluts'[37] who are making matters worse by

---

[37] As translated by V.E. Watts: Boethius, *The Consolation of Philosophy* (Harmondsworth, Penguin Books, 1969); Chaucer in his *Boece* calls them 'thise comune strompettis' (Bk I, prose 1).

indulging his sickness of mind and preventing the working of Reason. Dramatic allegory is thus combined with the creation of two levels of discourse: rational discourse in prose is interspersed with intense poetic expressions of passion at this early stage; later the lyrics are more often quiet meditations, interpreting the arguments of the prose passages through images and instances, such as the retelling of the story of Orpheus and Eurydice in the lyric that ends Book III. The echoes of Boethius may be heard in many medieval first-person narratives. Though *De Consolatione Philosophiae* is not itself a dream yet it provided a blueprint for the consolatory dream poem in which troubled or confused narrators encounter divine or learned figures who teach and enlighten (the basic pattern of *Piers Plowman* and *Pearl*) as well as other non-dream spiritual journeys and dialogues of which *The Divine Comedy* is the major instance; the double level of discourse provided the pattern for works which combine narrative with inset lyrics (as in Dante's *La Vita Nuova* or Guillaume de Machaut's *Le Voir Dit*). In poems of both types the figure of the narrator is a combination of poet/ observer who controls the experience, has perhaps been through it and is now supposedly recalling and recording it, and the protagonist whose confusions are the subject of the dream or quest.

Several commentators on medieval dream poetry have linked the doubleness in this use of the narrator to Genette's ideas about the different levels of narrative or diegesis:[38] a narrator who is above the story (the voice remembering and interpreting the experience, the waking narrator in dream poems) is the figure who in Genette's terms is extradiegetic (outside the story), but he is also in the story (intradiegetic) and not able to understand the moment-by-moment phases of the adventure. Medieval poets often highlight this doubleness by attributing to their extradiegetic narrators 'autobiographical' details (as when Langland's narrator calls himself Long Will or Chaucer in *The House of Fame* has his dreamer addressed as Geoffrey) so that we are encouraged to identify them with the author, while at the same time characterizing their intradiegetic selves as of limited understanding—even making them downright stupid at times—so that the dreamer is some 'other' self.

---

[38] As, for example, in Piero Boitani, *English Medieval Narrative in the 13th and 14th Centuries*, trans. Joan Krakover Hall (Cambridge U.P., 1982), pp.188–9 and Helen Phillips in the 'General introduction', in *Chaucer's Dream Poetry*, ed. Helen Phillips and Nick Havely (Harlow, Longman, 1997), pp.11ff.

A different combination of narrator's voices and stances is found in another widely influential work, *Le Roman de la Rose*, largely because of the peculiar history of the poem, which was begun by one poet, Guillaume de Lorris, between 1225 and 1230, and completed, in a continuation about four times longer, by Jean de Meun (who was, like Chaucer, a translator of Boethius) between 1269 and 1278. Guillaume's prologue provides the pattern later adopted by many writers of dream poems, notably Chaucer and his imitators: outside the dream is an opening discussion of whether dreams are true or not, with reference to Macrobius and the dream of Scipio as dream authority, and the poet's explanation that what is to follow is his own dream now recalled in the service of love and expressed as a romance, called 'The Romance of the Rose'; within the dream the poet describes a May morning and the pleasure of the woods in spring, full of singing birds, into which the dreamer happily sets off on his adventure. This classic opening represents a development from the earlier type of rhetorical prologue; the poet's voice still provides authority for the material by referring to a classical instance of dream (others use the biblical authority of dreams interpreted by Joseph and Daniel), opens a dialogue with the reader on the themes of dreams and love, explains the origin of the work, and identifies its genre and name. However, the passage into dream involves a sliding from one self-characterization to another and 'romance' proves not to be an account of adventures of a named chivalrous hero but a first-person account of a fantasy adventure into the world of personifications. The representation of love and courtship against a background of springtime energy and scenic pleasure is psychological, an exploration of the self within a courtly world. Critics have allied the narrator-figure envisaged by Guillaume with the tradition of the French courtly love-lyric, by means of which the poet/lover expresses his ardour. As Leslie Topsfield describes it, the process of falling in love in *Le Roman de la Rose*: 'is expressed in terms which a thirteenth-century audience would immediately associate with the courtly love lyric and the situation in which the troubadour or trouvère pleads for mercy with his lady.'[39] Comparison of the first 4000 lines of the poem with the rest exposes a change of personality and of literary effect when Jean

---

[39] Leslie Topsfield, 'The *Roman de la Rose* of Guillaume de Lorris and the love lyric of the early troubadours', *Reading Medieval Studies* 1 (1975), 30–54 (quotation from p.45).

de Meun took over. In place of the delicately expressed, abstract but recognizable, allegory of Guillaume, the later poet substituted a series of scholarly, encyclopaedic, and digressive discourses which often ignore the allegorical fiction and use the personifications as mouth-pieces for satirical, at times cynical, exploration of varied themes. Jean de Meun's narrator is no longer a lovelorn troubadour but a more picaresque first-person voice, closer to the tradition of the French courtly *dit* or love-adventure, not now pursuing an idealistic courtship but willing to listen to advice on seduction.[40] Because he is eclectic Jean de Meun does not maintain a single, consistent voice or point of view, which adds to the work's complexity. Jean de Meun's broadening and shifting of the stance of the narratorial voice explains why the poem was so widely known (it survives in over 200 manu-scripts) and the at times contradictory voices of the two poets of *Le Roman de la Rose* account for something of the variety in later medi-eval narration, particularly to be observed in the writings of Chaucer.

In *The Book of the Duchess* Chaucer combines two types of first-person narrator. First comes the poet/dreamer who identifies himself in the prologue and rounds off the work, expressing the poet's mental anxieties and preoccupations and explaining the impulse of the poem as the creator's troubled mind seeking to complete a task; the poem is usually identified as an occasional poem marking the death of Blanche, duchess of Lancaster, first wife of John of Gaunt, and the task, therefore, is that of composing a suitable poetic tribute to a highly regarded noblewoman, but Chaucer also expresses it as an artistic search for a suitable subject for poetry. At the end of the poem, it is 'done', the topic found and treated and the artistic design fulfilled. The prologue here is in an informal, anecdotal style about the poet's sleeplessness and his 'sorwful ymagynacioun', both of which are massaged away by his reading of the story of Ceyx and Alcyone (from Ovid's *Metamorphoses*) from which the transition is made into the dream and, with a flourish of authoritative dream names (Joseph and Pharaoh, Macrobius and Scipio), we pass to a May morning scene adorned with birdsong and literary images, which provides the setting for the beginning of the 'consolatory' dream experience and makes clear the poem's debt to Guillaume de Lorris. Early in his career as a writer Chaucer had translated at least

---

[40] See Sarah Kay, *The Romance of the Rose* (London: Grant & Cutler, 1995), pp.33–44.

the beginning of *Le Roman de la Rose* and his early dream poems are the place where the effect is most visible. In the main body of *The Book of the Duchess* the narrator becomes a scene-painter and then a questioner before the rather brisk summing up of the experience at the end which, given the very leisurely opening, takes one by surprise.

> Thoghte I, 'Thys ys so queynt a sweven
> That I wol, be processe of tyme,
> Fonde to put this sweven in ryme
> As I kan best, and that anoon.'
> This was my sweven; now hit ys doon.
> (*The Book of the Duchess*, 1330–4)

The effect is of an opening which implies that the poet/narrator is the focal point of the narrative but which is gradually counteracted as this narrator steps back, becomes an observer, a deferential confidant, merely the channel through which the subject is flowing.

The first-person role is virtually ceded to the figure encountered in the dream, the Black Knight whose bereavement becomes the poem's central theme and whose account of his own falling in love, courtship, and loss becomes the poem's main narrative. This narrator is the lyric lover from Guillaume de Lorris's poem recalling, describing, celebrating his feeling for the beautiful woman he admired and loved. Chaucer includes two lyrics: the Black Knight's first words, overheard, are those of a sorrowful complaint (ll.475–86) and later he gives a sample of the sort of love song he composed to woo the beloved (ll.1175–80); both have a rhyme scheme that distinguishes them from the octosyllabic couplets of the rest. The dialogue between the two speakers becomes very one-sided as the dreamer's role dwindles into that of facilitating the knight's confession. While one can read the strategies Chaucer employs here as an ingenious way of dramatizing and fictionalizing an actual event and of disguising the figures so that they achieve a semi-allegorical status, the Black Knight as a personification of sorrow and the dead Blanche as 'fair White', an ideal of pure beauty, at the same time one can recognize them as enabling Chaucer to write courtly love poetry without himself taking up the stance of lover. The double narration means a shift in the poet/dreamer's role from teller to listener, which is a shift Chaucer may also be seen to make in *The Canterbury Tales*. In Chaucer's other early dream poems, *The House of Fame* and *The Parliament of Fowls*, something comparable occurs in the narrative strategy. Love is again the theme of both and the role in which the poet casts himself is that of a seeker for knowledge of love as the necessary material for a writer. The resources he explores are those of books and dreams, beginning both poems in a voice of anxiety or uncertainty, in the case of *The House of Fame* by echoing Guillaume de Lorris in an opening debate with the reader as to whether there is truth in dreams, and in *The Parliament of Fowls* by linking the difficulty of defining love with the philosophical questions raised by the classic dream text, Macrobius' commentary on Cicero's *Dream of Scipio*. Having clothed himself in the narrator's garb of seeker after truth (with a few touches to elevate the poet's role taken from Dante) he is nevertheless happy to slip out of the prominence of being the central first-person consciousness in both poems, again using the dream to introduce other dominant voices and to reduce the narrator's function to that of bemused observer.

In *The Canterbury Tales* Chaucer gives to most of the storytellers a prologue so that they can act not only as dramatic voices narrating their own tales, but have an opportunity to define their narrative stance. These prologues, though often assumed simply to be dramatic monologues or sections of dialogue between pilgrims in which character is extended from the description in the *General Prologue*, themselves spread out along the extradiegetic/intradiegetic line. Some of them are literary, 'artist's' prologues, in the sense that they are used to define genre (as I have already indicated for the prologues of Monk and Franklin), or to locate the tale in relation to its source (as in *The Clerk's Prologue*), or to justify using prose in preference to verse and to privilege moral content (*sentence*) over verbal expressiveness (the prologue to *Melibee*) and truth over fiction (*The Parson's Prologue*). Some are formal prologues virtually independent of the context within the story of the pilgrimage: the most obvious of these is the prologue to *The Second Nun's Tale* which is concerned to justify saints' lives and to introduce this one by explaining the origin of the text, providing a suitable prayer to the Virgin and a lengthy explanation of the etymology of St Cecilia's name. Slightly more adapted to the Canterbury context is the comparable prologue to *The Prioress's Tale* where the opening prayer to Mary is gracefully turned to an expression of the narrator's modesty as she compares herself to 'a child of twelf month oold, or lesse,/That kan unnethes any word expresse'. In all these prologues Chaucer transfers to his narrators a degree of his own writerly concern and awareness of textual shaping and the need for justification. In one case, *The Man of Law's Prologue*, the transfer is only partly made and this is in any case a composite prologue, closer to the rhetorical definitions of the *exordium*, since it combines a thematic passage on poverty in rhyme royal stanzas (ll.99–133), with a longer passage relating to the text, though it does so obliquely with a review of Chaucer's writings. The comments on his own work are part of that separation of himself off into a third-person member of his own pilgrimage, which continues in his writing tales for himself, *Sir Thopas* and *Melibee*, which deliberately avoid fulfilling the role of great poet in his own person. Another indication of Chaucer's preference for withdrawing from the central first-person artist's role is the absence of a formal prologue to *The Canterbury Tales;* instead he used his opening (the so-called *General Prologue* though Chaucer did not call it that) to begin his frame story and to describe his gallery of narrators, with only a few passages of prefatory material towards the end (ll.715–46) where he tells his audience what is to follow and pretends to be merely the recorder of what the others say, for which he should not be blamed. Following this strategy of performing writer's functions only indirectly he hands over the responsibility for organizing the tale-telling on the way to Canterbury to his Host and lets his other comments seem to arise from the immediate situation (as in *The Miller's Prologue*, quoted earlier). Several of the pilgrims' prologues similarly are made part of the context and work mainly as a kind of continuity in the series (as in the prologues of the Cook, Merchant, and Nun's Priest): a number of prologues make more of this idea in the form of quarrelling among the storytellers (the prologues of Friar and Summoner particularly, but also that of the Manciple and, mixed with other elements, those of Miller and Reeve). There are a few tales without prologues at the beginning of the separate fragments in which the work survives (tales of Squire, Physician, and Shipman), but there are also a few tales in which there are disguised prologues at the beginning of the tale (the first thirty-four lines of *The Knight's Tale* and, arguably, the discourse on marriage at the beginning of *The Merchant's Tale*).

Totally undisguised are Chaucer's ostentatious 'oral-performance' prologues, the 'long preamble' that he wrote for the Wife of Bath, the confession prologue of the Pardoner, and the prologue of action and dialogue with which he prefaced *The Canon's Yeoman's Tale*. All three show interest in different aspects of speech mannerism and oral rhetoric, in using the prologue as a dramatic opportunity to establish character and attitude and to give to the audience in advance of the tales they tell a sense of what kind of narrators they are likely to be. They are all, in Wayne C. Booth's terms, 'unreliable', though to different extents, and these are the prologues which most clearly represent the degree of complexity in narrative layering that Chaucer achieved in *The Canterbury Tales*: the tales that follow these prologues have all been provided with an ironic subtext by what the prologues have shown.[41]

Not only in *The Canterbury Tales* but more widely in his work Chaucer shows an unusually large range of awareness of the choices available to him in the role of poet and in the function of narrators. The sources of the alternatives have been in part suggested above, what Chaucer learned from rhetorical precept in his early education, what he imitated or adapted from ancient authorities and from contemporary continental writers and so on, but the work of contemporary writers in English also provides evidence of the literary milieu in which Chaucer wrote. Academic and scholastic ideas about narrative and about how to present and to interpret it left their mark in Chaucer's work. His literary vocabulary shows an awareness of the terms of academic prologues written as introductions to classical authors and of the language of bible commentaries, as, for example, when he speaks of the author's 'entente' in the *Prologue to the Legend of Good Women* and refers in a number of places to the *mateere, maner,* and *effect* of writing; he even uses terms in *Melibee* ('the cause material', 'the cause formal', and 'the cause final', ll.1398ff.) which show knowledge of the Aristotelian causal scheme which was a major influence on the analysis of literary texts from the early thirteenth century onwards[42] Its effect was to focus interpretation of a text on the author and his reasons for writing in terms of the major causes of the work: the *causa efficiens* (the author), the *causa materialis* (the subject matter of the work), the *causa formalis* (the literary form in which it is expressed), and the *causa finalis* (the end or justification of the work). Chaucer approaches such

---

[41] Wayne C. Booth, *The Rhetoric of Fiction* (Chicago, U. of Chicago Press, 1961).

[42] See A.J. Minnis, *Medieval Theory of Authorship: Scholastic Literary Attitudes in the Later Middle Ages*, 2nd edn (Aldershot, Scolar Press, 1988), pp.28ff.

functional prologues most nearly in his educational texts. *A Treatise on the Astrolabe* has a preface which bears the signs of a teacher's prologue: the direct address to the intended reader, 'Lyte Lowys my sone', and a justification of the text, followed by an explanation of the purpose of the translation, a modest apology for the translator's inadequacies and finally an outline of the content. The presentation of a prose textbook needs to be clear and obvious in its strategies, but with fiction and with poetry the application to narrative of a body of theory devised originally for forensic oratory or for academic exegesis needs more room for manoeuvre. One can recognize in the *Prologue to the Legend of Good Women* a more literary version, wrapped up in the guise of a dream opening. Here Chaucer pays tribute to the literary masters of the past, whose old books are 'of remembrance the keye'. In his dream sequence Chaucer dramatizes himself in the role of author and offers a justification for the tales of martyred virtuous women which are to follow: the defence of the poet's intention, even the listing of his own compositions (which presumably predates the shorter version in *The Man of Law's Prologue*), added to the central images of the daisy, Queen Alceste and the God of Love, all mark this as a high-style, rhetorical, and intellectual prologue.

By the time Chaucer came to work on *The Canterbury Tales* his ideas had broadened and the prologues which he included are, as I hope to have indicated, flexible and varied: the *General Prologue* is a narrative opening more than a *prohemium* or an *exordium*, but one's sense of it becomes clearer in conjunction with contemporary writing. Reading the *General Prologue* alongside the prologues to *Piers Plowman* (particularly the A version) and *Confessio Amantis* suggests that there is a closer agreement about the possible subject matter of the prologue to a long poem among late-fourteenth-century English poets than about its form. All three can be read as 'three estates' prologues, surveys of English society as composed of nobility, church, and commons. It has often been suggested that Chaucer was influenced by Langland and there are many echoes of the figures seen in the field full of folk at the beginning of *Piers Plowman* in the descriptions of Chaucer's pilgrims, as Helen Cooper has pointed out.[43] Langland's A-text prologue works through twenty-seven

[43] Helen Cooper, 'Langland's and Chaucer's Prologues', *The Yearbook of Langland Studies* 1 (1987), 71–81.

estates, Chaucer thirty, and both include figures who are not standard members of Latin satirical surveys, notably cooks and pardoners, as well as the usual figures of knights, squires, lawyers, merchants, monks, friars, and so on. And, though Langland's version is the opening of an allegorical dream presenting in a tone of social complaint the scene which is to represent the world throughout the poem, whereas Chaucer is inventing a cast-list of potential storytellers for his narrative pilgrimage, beneath the differences are surprising conjunctions: Langland's allegorical figures are animated by vivid realistic touches and among Chaucer's individualized portraits are ideal representatives of their estates—Knight, Parson, and Plowman. Gower's treatment of the three estates in the prologue to *Confessio Amantis* is a less descriptive, more explicit piece of social generalizing, part of a *prologus praeter rem*, an extrinsic prologue, which bears more obvious signs of the academic, rhetorical tradition than the other two. All three illustrate the development of prologues from brief preliminaries to major introductory presentation of significant aspects of a work. Langland's 109-line A-text prologue (expanded to 230 lines or so in the B- and C-texts) is a substantial piece but a mere sketch compared to the 858 lines of Chaucer's *General Prologue* and the 1088 lines of Gower's prologue (plus several passages of Latin verse which point the stages of the text). Gower works hard to impress on the reader not only his purpose in writing (to combine *lust* and *lore* and to link examples from the ancient past with awareness of the modern world), but also the earnest seriousness of his enterprise:

> For this prologe is so assised [*composed*]
> That it to wisdom al bilongeth:
> What wysman that it underfongeth,
> He schal drawe into remembrance
> The fortune of this worldes chance . . .
> (*Confessio Amantis*, Prologue, 66–70)

Though the material of *Confessio Amantis* is to be a dialogue about love illustrated by a multitude of narratives, many of classical origin, the prologue stakes a claim as a philosophical, ethical work about divisions in society and within man's own nature and does this by a survey of the estates of society and their failings and a retelling of Nebuchadnezzar's dream of the great statue which Daniel interprets

as representing the history of the world and its decline; this leads back to the theme of corruption and instability in the modern world. None of this relates informatively to the actual content of the eight books that follow and Gower still needs to begin his first book with an intrinsic prologue leading into the theme of love and the narrative situation (the dialogue between lover and confessor) that controls the rest of the work. Gower's combination of the role of social philosopher, ready to embark on a review of the modern world equipped with scholarly Latin introductions and marginal glosses, with that of the confused suppliant within the fiction, hoping to enter Venus' court, is another version of that extradiegetic/intradiegetic fusion already observed as a characteristic of medieval dream poems. In the light of these contemporary examples Chaucer's choices look even more distinct. As Minnis points out,[44] the passages in the *General Prologue* and *The Miller's Prologue* which identify Chaucer in the role of compiler who aims no further than to record accurately the words of his pilgrim storytellers show as much awareness as Gower does of the academic prologue tradition, but Gower's choice of the wise authorized voice (in his prologue, that is) highlights Chaucer's preference for assuming a subordinate role, for hiding behind the mask of limited intent in order to have more room for manoeuvre.

Though it is not easy to sum up what prologues and narrators contribute to one's sense of medieval narrative, the evidence does suggest a number of significant points. There was a clear tradition of what prologues were expected to do and a set of topics that regularly appeared. However, over the span of the medieval period there is a good deal of variation and this might depend particularly on the degree and nature of the artist's own responsibility for the work and according to the level of sophistication of the writer and the expected audience. Paul Cobley states of the medieval period: 'The period witnessed narrative developments which extended the common understanding of what constituted "the poet's voice".'[45] There are signs of this in the development between the twelfth and fourteenth centuries of the prologue from a fairly strictly defined preliminary passage of negotiation with the reader to a discourse in its own right. Cobley identifies this extension particularly with

---

[44] Minnis, *Medieval Theory of Authorship*, pp.190–210.
[45] Cobley, *Narrative*, p.70.

Chaucer's multiplying the narrative voices in *The Canterbury Tales*: 'Whatever Chaucer meant, intended or thought is not, therefore, to be gleaned from an equation of the poet with the narrator of the prologue.'[46] Chaucer can place material in what look like prologues only for them to turn into narratives as one reads. The narrators who are, as it were, given a voice by medieval prologues prove to have an unexpectedly wide range of possibilities, among which one can distinguish: the authoritative controlling voice of the preacher who becomes an omniscient narrator; less obtrusive versions of the taleteller interpreting an acquired tale and sharing its interest with the audience, where the narrating voice may almost disappear but for the occasional 'as the book says' or 'as I in toun herde'; the autobiographical first-person narrator of dreams and supernatural experiences; the fictional storytellers who present narratives in a voice assumed by the poet in a kind of ventriloquism. The choice between authoritative and deferential roles is one way of expressing the span of the narrator's function in medieval narratives. Some writers manage to combine apparently contradictory roles and have more than one identity within a work. Such effects mean that some forms of medieval narrative may be said to approximate to the 'polyphonic' quality which Bakhtin has claimed to be the defining feature of the novel:[47] the idea that some texts are not 'monological' but achieve a multi-voiced effect both by juxtaposing several voices within the text and by a text's intertextuality has obvious relevance to medieval narrative. However, some forms of narrative in the period are at the other end of the spectrum, that is the didactic writer's use of narrative to preach or to teach and it is at that end that I intend to begin in the chapters that follow.

[46] *Cobley, Narrative*, p.71.
[47] Mikhail Bakhtin, *Problems of Dostoevsky's Poetics* (Ann Arbor, Mich., Ardis, 1973), originally published in Russian, 1929; cited and discussed by Shlomith Rimmon-Kenan, *Narrative Fiction*, 2nd edn (London. Routledge, 2002). pp.116–17.

3

Didactic narratives

Exempla—from lessons to lies

Chaucer's Pardoner, cynically exposing his own preaching techniques, tells us that the inclusion of stories in his sermons is a
sure-fire way of getting his gullible audience to hand over money:

> 'Thanne telle I hem ensamples many oon
> Of olde stories longe tyme agoon,
> For lewed peple loven tales olde;
> Swiche thynges kan they wel reporte and holde.'
> (*CT*, VI, 435–8)

What he refers to as 'ensamples' are usually called *exempla* in modern
critical parlance: the *exemplum* is an instance which illuminates
moral teaching, 'a short narrative used to illustrate or confirm a
general statement' as Mosher defined it,[1] or even more basically 'a
moralised anecdote'.[2] The illustrative function of brief examples is
clear in a teaching text like the *Ancrene Wisse*, as the author warns his
audience of devout women against the seven deadly sins, working
through exhortations and examples relevant to each in turn. Here
(with a modern English version) he is instructing the dear sisters to
maintain peaceful unity against the divisive force of anger:

Neomeð nu ʒeorne ʒeme bi moni forbisne hu god is anrednesse of luue ant
annesse of heorte; for nis þing under sunne þet me is leouere ne se leof þet
ʒe habben. Nute ʒe, þer men fehteð i þes stronge ferdes, þe ilke þc haldeð ham
feaste togederes ne muhe beo descumfit o neauer nane wise? Alswa hit is in
gastelich feht aʒeines þe deouel: al his entente is forte tweamen heorten, forte

---

[1] J.A. Mosher, *The Exemplum in the Early Religious and Didactic Literature of
England* (New York, Columbia U.P., 1911).
[2] G.R. Owst, *Literature and Pulpit in Medieval England* (1933), revd edn (Oxford,
Basil Blackwell, 1961).

bineomen luue þet halt men togederes. For hwen luue alið, þenne beoð ha
isundret, ant te deouel deð him bitweonen ananriht ant sleað on euche halue.
Dumbe beastes habbeð þis ilke warschipe, þet hwen ha beoð asailet of wulf
oðer of liun, ha þrungeð togederes—al þe floc—feste, ant makieð scheld of
hamseolf, euch of heom to oþer, ant beoð þe hwile sikere; ȝef eani unseli went
ut, hit is sone awuriet. Þe þridde: þer an geað him ane in a slubbri wei, he slit
ant falleð sone. Þer monie gað togederes ant euch halt oþres hond, ȝef eani
feð to sliden, þe oðer hine breid up ear he ful falle.

(Now take careful heed, by means of many examples how good are single-
mindedness in love and unity of heart, for there is no quality under the sun
that I would have you possess that is dearer or as dear. Do you not know that
when men fight in strong armies, those who hold fast together can not be
discomfited in any way? It is just the same in the spiritual fight against the
devil; his whole intention is to divide hearts, to take away the love that binds
people together. For when love dies down, then they are sundered and the
devil inserts himself between and kills in both directions. Dumb animals
have this same caution, that when they are attacked by a wolf or a lion, they
throng tightly together, the whole flock, and make themselves into a shield,
each for the other, and are safe while they do so; if any poor creature ventures
out, it is soon torn to death. A third example: if a single person goes alone
along a slippery path, he slides and soon falls; where many go together and
each holds another's hand, if anyone begins to slip, the next person holds him
up before he falls down.)[3]

The examples are short references to common knowledge and experience, though each of the three instances cited here could be enlarged
into a scene or narrated as a particular historical example of the type
of occurrence. Elsewhere in the *Ancrene Wisse* this happens, particularly in the well-known allegorical narrative of a lady besieged in a
castle and offered rescue by a chivalrous knight, interpreted as the
soul trapped in the body needing rescue by Christ. The use of full-
scale narrative to bring preaching against the sins to life in the minds
of the audience is the principal strategy in a confessional manual such
as Robert Mannyng of Bourne's *Handlyng Synne*, a free adaptation
of the French *Manuel des Pechiez*, into which Mannyng, writing in
1303 for the instruction of the novices and the lay brothers of the
Gilbertine order at Sempringham Priory in Lincolnshire, introduced
exemplary narratives of his own, some with local settings and references, to augment those already present in the text he was translating.

---

[3] *Ancrene Wisse*, Part IV, on Temptation, in *Early Middle English Verse and Prose*, eds.
J.A.W. Bennett and G.W. Smithers (Oxford, Clarendon Press, 1968), pp.229–30 (my
translation).

The *exemplum* can work quite simply, as in Mannyng's section warning against the dangers of sacrilege, and particularly of letting the mind be distracted from holy things by music, dancing, and the pernicious influence of minstrels:

> Daunces, karolles, somur games,
> Of many swyche come many shames.
> Whan þou stodyyst to make þyse,
> Þou art slogh yn Goddys seruyse.
> And þat synnen yn swych þurgh þe,
> For hem þou shalt acouped be.
> What seye ȝe be eury mynstral
> Þat yn swyche þynges delyte hem al?
> Here doyng ys ful perylous:
> Hyt loueþ noþer God ne Goddys hous.
> Hem were leuer here of a daunce,
> Of bost and of olypraunce,
> Þan any gode of God of heuene,
> Or ouþer wysdom þat were to neuene.
> Yn foly ys al þat þey gete,
> Here cloth, here drynke, and here mete.
> And for swych þyng telle y shal
> What befyl onys of mynstral.
> Seynt Gregory telþ yn hys spell,
> How hyt of a mynstral fell.
>   (*Handlyng Synne*, 4685–704)[4]

The function of the *exemplum* is signalled by the didactic introduction: the preacher's voice offers condemnation and warning, sketching the scenario of foolish action and its consequence, and then announcing his intention of turning to narrative to reinforce the point. With the backing of the authority of Gregory, the author adopts the stance of storyteller, the 'once-upon-a-time' formula and the required narration of a specific past event.

> A mynstral, a gulardous,
> Com onys to a bysshopes hous,
> And askede þere þe charyte.
> Þe porter lete hym haue entre.
> At tyme of mete þe bord was leyd
> And þe benesoun shulde be seyd.
> Þys mynstral made hys melody

---

[4] Robert Mannyng, *Handlyng Synne*, ed. Idelle Sullens (Binghampton NY, Binghampton U.P. 1983).

Wyþ gret noyse and loud and hy.
Of þe bysshop þe fame ran
Þat he was an holy man.
Þe bysshop sette hym at þe burd
And shulde haue blessed hyt wyþ wrd.
So was he sturbled wyþ þe mynstral,
Þat he hadde no grace to seye weyl al
Hys graces ryght deuoutely
For þe noyse of þe mynstralsy;
Þe bysshop pleynede hym ful sore,
And seyde to alle þat were þore
Þat he ne shulde make hys nycete,
Before þe graces of þe charyte.
He sagh hyt weyl þurgh þe spyryt
Þat þyr shulde come veniaunce alstyt.
'ʒeueþ hym þe charyte & lateþ hym go.
Hys deþ ys nygh þat shal hym slo.'
He toke charyte & toke hys gate
And als he passede out at þe ʒate
A stone fyl down of þe wal
And slogh þe mynstral.
Þat betokened þat God was noght
Payd of þat þe mynstral wroght,
Þat he dysturblede þe benesoun
And þe gode mannes deuocyoun.
Þys tolde y for þe glemennes sake
To loke whan þey here gle shul make,
And also for þo þat shulde hyt here
Þat þey loue hyt nat so dere,
Ne haue þer yn so gret lykyng,
Þe lesse to wrshepe heuene kyng.
(*Handlyng Synne*, 4705–42)

The punishment for interrupting a blessing is extreme but the exemplary purpose of the narrative clear-cut, announced at the beginning and restated at the end, allowing no demurring from its message, leaving the audience to store the instance in memory, and be warned.

Exempla in moral handbooks such as this, or the early-fifteenth-century *Jacob's Well*, a prose teaching book equally full of moral tales, are stories chosen for their representative quality: hence the characters are likely to be common types, 'average' figures in likely situations. Preachers appeal to their audience's experience and so represent men of a certain age, or of a certain condition in society, and women in their social roles as wives, daughters, mothers. There is a tendency towards various sorts of realism: *exempla* are often anecdotal and local. To be effective their picture of life needs to be recognizable and transferable. However, this commonplace aspect of the *exemplum* is to some extent in conflict with storytellers' tendency to pick up extraordinary and dramatic tales, and to adopt stories of famous figures of history and legend, whose experience is likely to be very peculiar.

Gesta Romanorum is the name given to a collection of tales first made probably in Latin in the late thirteenth century, either in England or in Germany; manuscripts survive in Latin and in vernacular languages and the contents vary considerably from one version to another. The work is representative of the impulse to assemble stories to provide convenient source-books, either for preachers or as some form of entertainment for the literate. The stories purport to be tales of the classical past, 'the deeds of the (Roman) emperors moralized', as the Innsbruck manuscript of 1342 calls it, but it draws on other medieval collections and the ultimate sources are widespread—the Old Testament, eastern tales from both written sources and oral tradition, writings of Fathers of the Church such as Augustine and Gregory, as well as a hotchpotch of tales set in the classical and early Christian eras. The declared purpose is instructive and the tales are marked by the often lengthy moralizations attached to them, though this is often the part that least convinces the modern reader and sometimes one suspects that the application of the story belongs to a separate layer of the writing. The collection was translated into English in the fifteenth century (three different English versions in fact survive in manuscript), and the text was printed by Wynkyn de Worde, Caxton's successor, in 1510. This great compendium of anecdotes, incidents, historical fragments, and retellings of ancient legends is a storehouse of narrative (all sorts of plots such as those of *Pericles* and *The Merchant of Venice* can be found here), and narrative seen primarily as *exemplum*. These tales work in the opposite direction from the *exempla* in instruction books such as Mannyng's. Many begin with the name of a ruler and move straight into the supposed historical circumstances:

Menelaus reigned in the Citee of Rome, that was right mercifull; therefore he made a law, that yf a mysdoer were take, and put into prison, yf he myght ascape, and flee to the paleys, he shuld have refute, without any contradiccion.[5]

After this ostensibly precise placing in historical time, the narrative proper shifts to anonymous figures:

It fille that there was a man-sleer taken, and put into prison, and put to his diete; wherefore he sorowed gretly, that he was put fro mannes sight, and fro the light of the sonne, save a litell wyndowe, by the whiche the lighte shone in; by the whiche light he toke his mete and his drynke of the kepers euery day, and ete at a certayn houre. And whan the keper of the prison was gone away, a Nightyngale was wonte to come in atte wyndow, and synge wondir swetly; of the whiche songe the knyght was gretly comforted. And after the songe, the brid fleigh into the knyghtes skirte, and the knyght euery day fedde the bridde with a porcion of his mete.

After this it felle vpon a day, that the knyght was wondir hevy, and said to the bridde sittynge in his skirte thise wordes:

'O! good bridde, what shalt thou yeve me, that have so many a day i-fedde the? bryng me into memorie, for thou art goddes creature, and I also.'

Whan the bridde had herd this, he flew forthe. And the third day he come ayene, and brought in his mouthe a precious stone, and lette it falle into the knyghtes skirte, and flew forthe. The knyght, whan he sawe the stone, he had grete mervaile. After it happed to falle on his feters, and anon all the iren that he was bound in was broken therwith. The knyght, whan he saw this, he was right glad, and arose, and touched the dore with the stone, the whiche opened; and anon he went out, and ranne to the paleys. The iayler sawe this, and whan he perseived it, he blew iii blastes with an horne, and brought all out of the Citee, and said, 'Se the theef! folow ye hym!' and all thei folowed, but the keper ranne before. The knyght sawe that, and shotte to hym with an arowe, and slough hym; and so the knyght ranne to the paleys, and there he found refute, aftir the lawe.

The story, which (after the historical prologue) begins in a realistic, circumstantial manner, gradually turns into fantasy, and the nature of the transition, when we are told of the bird that 'the third day he come ayene', prepares us for the lengthy allegorical interpretation that follows in the section headed in this version as *Declaracio*: the Emperor is God, the knight the sinner who may escape punishment by contrition and confession, the gaoler is the devil, the bird the voice of God, the precious stone Christ; and so the whole story is revealed as a code. The *exemplum* is often, as here, a form of parable in which

---

[5] *The Early English Versions of the Gesta Romanorum*, ed. Sidney J.H. Herrtage, EETS ES 33 (London, Oxford U.P., 1879), xix, p.334.

spiritual relations are expounded from an earthly fiction used as a similitude, though in the exegesis there are often awkwardnesses, inconsistencies, and forced parallels. Elsewhere the *Gesta Romanorum* offers fare as varied as the story of Aristotle's warning Alexander the Great against a beautiful princess who has been nurtured on poison, or the tale of Apollonius of Tyre told as an illustration of the tribulations of worldly life, simple historical instances told in a few sentences, long romantic sequences of adventure and vicissitude—all translated at their close into allegorical senses and moral maxims. So though the material is often far from the typical and everyday, the exemplary pattern is imposed upon the narrative and insists on the meaning which the reader must see in it. The reader is not, of course, always ready to do this.

Extreme instances, unusual events, and elements of fantasy, certainly supernatural and miraculous content, can compromise the force of *exemplum* and medieval writers can recognize this in the way they handle stories. Mannyng's famous story of the Dancers of Colbek is a case in point, as comparison with the simple story of the punishment of the noisy minstrel, quoted above, reveals. The theme is again that of sacrilege, here the desecration of churchyards by using them for dancing carols and disturbing the celebration of mass within the church. As usual Mannyng defines the didactic purpose of the story at the beginning and, though it is a continental tale set in Kölbigk in Saxony, localizes it in the England of Edward the Confessor and moves into the tale of twelve fools, including Robert the priest's daughter Ave, dancing a carol in the churchyard on Christmas Night led by Gerlew (OE Garlaf), and singing a three-line Latin jingle, making it likely that the leader of this coven of rioters is a relapsed priest, uncloistered monk, or at least a truant student. When they take no notice of the priest's forbidding them to continue interrupting the service, he curses them and brings on them God's vengeance, condemning the dancers to go on dancing and singing for a year: immediately their hands are stuck fast together. Up to this point the course of crime and punishment seems clear, but the narrative now takes an unexpected turn. Robert sends his son Azo to rescue Ave from the dance, but when he tries forcibly to drag her away, her arm comes off in his hand, while the rest of her body goes on dancing, and when the horrified father tries three times to bury the arm, it keeps leaping back out of the soil. And so the *exemplum* branches into two, as the son exposes the father's error:

> 'Þy cursyng now sene hyt ys
> Wyth veniaunce on þy owne flessh.
> Fellyche þou cursedest, and ouer sone;
> Þou askedest veniaunce—þou hast þy bone!'
> (*Handlyng Synne*, 9120–3)

For a whole year, come rain, come shine, the carollers go on dancing and singing their ironic refrain:

> 'Why stonde we? why go we noȝt?'

Three attempts to provide covering against the weather for them fail as did the burial of Ave's arm, but at last, as Yule returns, the hour of the curse is reached and the dancers separate, flying in the 'twynkelynge of an ye' into the church where they lie for three days, after which eleven of them rise, leaving Ave dead on the pavement. With startling effect their voice now takes on the role of judgement:

> Þey sett hem vpp and spak apert
> To þe parysshe prest, syre Robert:
> 'Þou art ensample and enchesun
> Of our long confusyun;
> Þou maker art of oure trauayle,
> Þat ys to many gret meruayle.
> And þy trauayle shalt þou sone ende,
> For to þy longe home sone shalt þou wende.'
> (*Handlyng Synne*, 9192–9)

And so Robert's death follows Ave's, leaving her arm as a holy relic and the rest of the dancers, though separated, suspended in time, still hopping, but with their nails and hair never growing. The preaching voice confirms the message at the end—both messages—but the effect of the *exemplum* has diversified: the basic story is fantastic, supernatural and grotesque, and Mannyng recognizes that some may dismiss it as 'but a trotevale', but it develops greater depth than might have been expected because the dancers identified as wrongdoers at the start strangely become sufferers and victims, leaving the priest, the one sinned against, apparently the voice of righteousness, to bear the greater punishment for his curse. This is not so much a practical lesson as a fearsome story from which no one emerges secure. The morality of such a tale is something other in its working than simply an illustrative instance from everyday life. Elements of realism in *exempla* can lead to their being interesting pieces of social history, and one learns much about social conditions and attitudes from Mannyng and from other instructive manuals that include illustrations from daily life, such as *Jacob's Well*. But realism is only one end of the stylistic scale which can extend to pseudo-history and tales of magic.

The aspect of *exempla* with which the modern reader has the greatest problem is the question of the authority of the narrator, a question at the heart of Larry Scanlon's attempt to redefine the *exemplum* in a way that bridges the gap between medieval function and modern theory: what he comes up with is 'an *exemplum* is a narrative enactment of cultural authority'.[6] Exemplary tales are used by teachers to enforce moral argument and therefore the characteristic tone in which they are expressed is authoritarian and demonstrative: the narrator lays down the law and presents the tale as 'proof' of the argument. The question often arises in the reader's mind of whether or how far one can accept the role of pupil that such writing assumes. How far does the narrative leave scope for the play of the reader's own intelligence? Is the assumption one of the audience's complete ignorance, foolishness, and weakness, requiring submission to the authoritative voice, or does the text engage in some form of exchange with the reader? The question is quite a complex one since the ideas of authority and proof come across to us with the seal of approval conferred by their use by medieval philosophers and theologians, or, as Scanlon puts it, 'the *exemplum*'s enactment of authority in fact assumes a process of identification on the part of its audience'.[7] Identification with the process of argument can deflect our own unease at being used as a blank notebook waiting to be filled with the teacher's opinions. Recognition of an audience for a piece of writing that is different from oneself can distance literary response and enable one to find a way of handling material at second hand and so redirecting one's critical faculties. Despite this, it remains true that *exempla* can be difficult to accept because narrators restrict narrative to mere

---

[6] Larry Scanlon, *Narrative, Authority and Power: The Medieval Exemplum and the Chaucerian Tradition* (Cambridge U.P., 1994), p.34.
[7] Scanlon, *Narative, Authority and Power*, p.35.

illustration, or, on the other hand, over-interpret their examples in order to hammer home the moral point.

It is precisely in this question of the authority of the preaching voice that the most sophisticated of medieval authors located the effects which they saw that the use of *exemplum* made available. We have seen that Mannyng could introduce a form of doubleness into an exemplary tale, whereby the moral direction announced at the beginning acquires a contrary flow: error is corrected but correction too is dangerous. Gower and Chaucer take the idea further by dramatizing the process of teaching, so that they do not cast themselves in the preaching role, but put it at sufficient distance for its ironies to emerge.

In *Confessio Amantis* Gower adapts the form of a confessional dialogue on the subject of the seven deadly sins to the secular process of preparing an aspiring lover to enter the court of Venus: so Venus' priest, Genius, takes on the role of teacher and lectures the lover, Amans (who is also 'John Gower' in some sense), illustrating the various aspects of his teaching with a multitude of *exempla*. Teacher and pupil are fictional characters: their dialogue is presented to the reader as a dramatic scene. The exemplification works in a variety of ways: the lover sometimes confesses his own weakness and allies himself with the proffered example, sometimes denies the error and distances himself from the behaviour in the story. Some of the *exempla* are brief and to the point, others, such as the tale of Constance (over 1000 lines), are long sequences of adventures displaying the twists and turns of fortune. Most interestingly, from the point of view of looking at the working of *exempla*, there are some stories which add another layer by including as part of the tale a process of teaching and learning. A character within the tale commits an act of folly or of sin and is given a lesson: one of the other characters takes on the role of demonstrator. An instance is the tale of the Trump of Death (*Confessio Amantis*, Book I, 2021–253) which Genius relates to warn Amans against pride. It tells of a king who, when reproved by his proud brother for demeaning his royal position by descending from his chariot to give succour to two frail and aged pilgrims, determines to teach the brother a lesson in humility, which he does by sending his trumpeter by night to announce the death penalty at his brother's gate; when the brother, his wife and children appear next morning at court, as weeping suppliants clad only in shirts and smocks, the king at first mocks them for their readiness to expose themselves merely in

fear of a human law, when his own action had been triggered by the
evidence provided by the two old men of:

> 'Min oghne deth thurgh here ymage,
> Which God hath set be lawe of kynde,
> Wherof I mai no bote finde.'
> (*Confessio Amantis*, I, 2230–2)[8]

More gently he advises his brother:

> 'Dred God with al thin herte more:
> For al schal deie and al schal passe,
> Als wel a leoun as an asse,
> Als wel a beggere as a lord.'
> (*Confessio Amantis*, I, 2246–9)

The lesson here is enacted within the story, as one character identifies
the error of another and offers the corrective, and the giving and
accepting of the lesson are both occurring at a distance not only from
the reader but even within Gower's overall fiction: this is unexpectedly made clear by the reaction of Amans which is to see that the tale,
however improving, is not relevant to his situation—it is an excess of
love, not an excess of pride from which he is suffering.

In *The Canterbury Tales* Chaucer shows such awareness of the
ironic narrative possibilities of *exemplum* in several different ways.
He uses the act of telling instructive stories as in itself a characterizing
feature for preaching figures. So in the *Summoner's Tale* the specious
friar, a figure as untrustworthy as the Pardoner, is given a substantial
speech on the theme of anger, vividly illustrated by a sequence of
stories, ultimately from Seneca but probably known to Chaucer from
some Franciscan collection of useful examples; the stories could
stand alone and are a good illustration of Chaucer's command of an
apt forensic style for narrative used in the service of argument, but
in the context acquire an ironic layer, since we read them as instances
of the oleaginous friar's art, and see his teaching on anger in the light
of the fact that the friar is himself incapable of controlling his own
rage when the worthy householder Thomas, to whom the friar's sermon is addressed, later plays a gross trick on him rather than handing
over some clinking coins. Similarly, the self-confident cockerel,

---

[8] *The English Works of John Gower*, ed. G.C. Macaulay (2 vols., Oxford, Clarendon
Press, 1900–01); *John Gower: Confessio Amantis*, ed. and abridged R.A. Peck (Toronto,
University of Toronto Press, 1980).

Chauntecleer, in *The Nun's Priest's Tale* conducts his argument with his wife as to whether dreams do really give advance warning of coming disaster largely through *exempla*, a succession of stories of truth revealed in foreboding dreams. Whether it is the satirical idea of a cockerel as preacher, or the idea that the Priest who is telling the tale is likely to argue in this way that dominates the reading, the stories themselves are again simultaneously cogent contributions to argument and yet comic in their use.

The Pardoner's Tale is a much more fully developed version of a similar idea. A brilliant *exemplum* showing how greed brings destruction upon itself (the story of the three blasphemous robbers who murder each other for a heap of gold) has a showy sermon attacking gluttony, drunkenness, gambling, and swearing attached to it, so that the combination of homily and tale is presented to the audience as a sample of the Pardoner's preaching art. The sermon is, strikingly, embedded in the tale rather than providing the didactic introduction for the example, so the order raises in the reader's mind questions of the relative priority of narrative and moral maxim. Here the story seems to generate the sermon, whose themes grow from the opening description of the tavern-haunters in Flanders, wasting their lives in eating, drinking, swearing, and ogling the girls who sell fruit and biscuits and entertain the company. From this, with a few stepping stones of short biblical *exempla*, the Pardoner finds his way into histrionic proclamation of a homiletic theme:

> O glotenye, ful of cursednesse!
> O cause first of oure confusion!
> O original of oure dampnacioun,
> Til Crist hadde boght us with his blod agayn!
> (*CT*, VI, 498–501)

So Chaucer gives a dramatic justification to the didactic part of his text, not merely providing a fictional preacher, but occasion and origin for the rhetorical display. The sermon combines short scriptural allusions and quotations with the local and anecdotal touches that *exemplum* often attracts: St Paul is cited to condemn gluttony, while drunkenness is illuminated by description of a drunken man, foul-smelling, addle-witted, and falling over like a stuck pig, and of the tricks of the wine-sellers of Fish Street and Cheapside. Examples crowd together to form a close texture of exhortation and allusion before the Pardoner returns to his main *exemplum* and unfolds the powerful sequence of vice and punishment. Since we know from the Pardoner's prologue (quoted at the beginning) that his own motives in preaching are entirely corrupt and his concern is simply to make as much money for himself by his rhetorical skill in manipulating his audience's feelings of guilt, the tale works cleverly to display both the process of exemplification and the questions about reader-response that the process involves.

Medieval uses of *exemplum* thus display an interesting range in degrees of distancing and self-awareness. The basic type of simple moral lesson presumes docile acceptance of the didactic point of view, though the nature of the story, commonplace or exotic, can set up ambivalences. The combination of several tales, or the placing of tales in a sequence or series, or the handling of tales so that complex cross-currents appear as in Mannyng's 'Dancers of Colbek', all demonstrate that *exemplum* is a narrative building block from which multiple structures can be constructed. The dramatization of the act of teaching puts the exemplary story at that useful distance from which one can observe its functioning and enjoy the author's manoeuvring as part of the narrative effect. Chaucer in particular plays with the authority of the teller, and produces challenging contradictions when his most cogent pieces of moral illustration are put into the mouths of his least reliable speakers.

Fables—from Aesop to Henryson

The longest continuous tradition of narrative from ancient times to the present is that of the fable, stretching from Aesop (at least as early as the sixth century BC) to Kipling's *Just So Stories*, Orwell's *Animal Farm*, and the adventures of Tom and Jerry. Associated with traditional wisdom, inherited maxims, and proverbs, and often using animals to make observations on human behaviour, fables present pictures of common experience. After the Bible, Aesop's fables, in some form or another, were the most widely read texts in the Middle Ages, usually encountered first in the schoolroom: the stories themselves were often criticized as mere fiction, 'fables' in the sense of something untrue, but they are always seen as valuable because of the moral truths they contain. The standard medieval view is stated many times by collectors of fables, translators and writers of textual commentary. Conrad of Hirsau puts a full version into his commentary on Aesop, of which the following is a part:

> because the role of poets is either to be useful or to give pleasure, this author, from his observation of human nature, wove together the false fictions of his fables, inventing nonsensical or at any rate illogical stories, intertwining the childish and the serious, and making it all serve as a comparison with human life. For fable is fiction, not fact ... fables were invented so that by introducing the fictitious conversation of dumb animals or insensible objects, certain similarities in human morals and behaviour might be criticized.[9]

Conrad goes on to distinguish between animal fables and fables in which human beings interact with animals, and to develop a discussion between teacher and pupil about the interpretation of the story of the wolf and the lamb, at the end of which the teacher again sums up the considered view of fables:

> *Teacher.* The author's intention is clearly seen from his choice of subject-matter. For through this work, assembled as it is from various invented stories, he wanted to delight and also to recall irrational human nature to its true self by a comparison with brute beasts. The final cause is the profit (*fructus*) to be derived from reading the book.[10]

The earliest examples of fable are often satisfied with a picture, working rather like a cartoon—hence the ancient definition of fable as 'a fictitious story picturing a truth'.[11] Later fabulists prefer to interpret the fable, to see the narrative as a disguised expression of truth which has to be uncovered and expounded, usually by reading allegorically, which might be in terms of simple equivalence (the fox is the devil and so on), or by more extended comment on the social and religious roles of the characters, or by introducing bestiary traditions and biblical parallels.[12]

---

[9] Conrad of Hirsau, *Dialogue on the Authors*: extracts translated in Minnis and Scott, *Medieval Literary Theory and Criticism*, p.47.

[10] Minnis and Scott, *Medieval Literary Theory and Criticism*, p.48.

[11] Introduction to *Babrius and Phaedrus*, ed. and trans. B.E. Perry Loeb Classical Library (Cambridge, Mass. Harvard, U.P., 1965), p.xx; see also *Aesopica* ed. B.E. Perry (Urbana, Ill., University of Illinois Press, 1952) and B.E. Perry, 'Fable', *Studium Generale* 12 (1959), 17–37.

[12] See Edward Wheatley, *Mastering Aesop: Medieval Education, Chaucer and His Followers* (Gainsville, Fl., University Press of Florida, 2000), pp.76ff.

Medieval tellers of fables regularly pay tribute to Aesop and claim him as their source and authorization, even though they had no direct contact with the ancient Greek tradition and only a blurred knowledge of what the early fables were like. The earliest texts of 'Aesop's Fables' are already a mixture, made up of several layers of tales, some of Greek origin, some from Egypt and other parts of North Africa, some from Asia Minor, as is obvious from the varied menagerie of animal characters from wolves and lions to camels and scarab beetles, and from the occasional appearance of exotic characters and places such as Ethiopian slaves and the River Maeander. It is thought that the oldest of Aesop's stories may be the mythological ones, such as 'Zeus and the Men':

Having made men Zeus entrusted Hermes with pouring over them some intelligence. Hermes, making equal quantities, poured for each man his portion. Thus it happened that the short men, covered by their portion, became sensible people, but the tall men, not being covered all over by the mixture, had less sense than the others.[13]

This is typical of the Aesopic fable in being brief and having the sting in the tail. By the time the collection was being written down some process of demythologizing may already be seen, as Perry[14] recognizes in such a tale as Fable 19, 'Aesop in a Dockyard', in which Aesop himself appears as a character, identified as 'a writer of fables', who is using the story of Zeus creating the earth to swallow the sea as a retort to the teasing of the dockers; so the myth element is distanced into fictional fabling. Although we find many familiar tales, such as 'The Fox and the Bunch of Grapes', 'The Lion and the Mouse', 'The Field Mouse and the Town Mouse', and 'The Tortoise and the Hare',[15] among the earliest collections, the overall nature of the content is unexpected. Most of these fables are very brief and animal stories are by no means the norm. Some are no more than observations of life, such as:

A fisherman drew in his net from the sea. He could catch big fish, which he spread out in the sun, but the small fish slipped through the mesh, escaping into the sea.

[13] Fable 120 in Aesop, *The Complete Fables*, trans. Olivia and Robert Temple (Harmondsworth, Penguin Books, 1998), p.92.: hereafter referred to as Temple.

[14] Quoted in Temple, p.xiii.

[15] Respectively nos. 32, 206, 243, and 352 in Temple.

The fable is on the verge of becoming a proverb but not quite the one that is attached to it as a moral:

People of a mediocre fortune escape danger easily, but one rarely sees a man of great note escape when there is a disaster.[16]

How far do such morals form an essential part of the fable? They are usually thought to indicate the taste of the collector more than the composer of fables; they indicate the use to which fables were put by preachers and rhetoricians. When apt, they work, but only too often they are inept, either by being clumsy and overstating the obvious, or, as here, by saying something different from the fable itself. In the best fables the meaning is embodied in the story, but in medieval usage it is an allegorical form and it may give rise to more than one interpretation. The characteristic form of the Aesop fable is that of a story with a twist, a final reversal, a turning of the tables or a witty answer, such as in one of the briefest, 'The Lioness and the Vixen':

A vixen criticized a lioness for only ever bearing one child.
'Only one,' she said, 'but a lion.'[17]

The best of the Aesop fables are jokes, often rather sharp ones, with many instances of brutality; early appreciation of them, such as Aristotle's, was for their pungency, their dramatization of proverbs and riddles. Later collectors tended to bowdlerize them and to emphasize the lesson element, which made fables suitable for adaptation into children's stories and textbook models.

There are two main branches of the European tradition of the fable. One developed from the first-century Latin collection of Phaedrus, in iambic verses, perhaps the first poet to treat the fables as a series; his stories were in turn further popularized by a fourth-century prose collection known by the name of Romulus (the collection purports to be translated from Greek by the Emperor Romulus for his son Tiberius); many derivatives, in both prose and verse, of the *Romulus* survive, including the French verse versions known as *Isopets*, and a twelfth-century Latin verse collection attributed to 'Walter the Englishman'.[18] The second branch developed from a col-

---

[16] Fable 25 in Temple, p.22.
[17] Fable 194 in Temple, p.143.
[18] Tentatively identified as the Walter who was chaplain to Henry II and tutor to William II of Sicily. His fable collection is in Léopold Hervieux, *Les Fabulistes Latins* (5 vols., Paris, 1893), ii, pp.316–51.

lection of the second century in Greek verse, attributed to Babrius; this was in turn put into Latin elegiacs in the fourth century by Avianus and derivatives of his version, known as the *Avionnet*, were the main sources of Christianized school texts of the fables, studied as part of the syllabus in rhetoric; over a hundred texts of such school manuals survive. Fable texts were copied out by pupils with spaces between the lines for insertion of glosses, translations, and explanations; texts were analysed as examples of Latin grammar and of rhetorical usage.[19]

When medieval writers began to turn these snippets of teaching material into substantial literary texts, different ways of reading and of applying fables developed. While individual fables recur and remain quite close to ancient versions, except for a little more detail or a more specific moral, the gathering of fables into a composite, continuous work accumulates these minor changes and acquires an overall character. The single fable is the narrative unit, but one's sense of the fable becomes a selection or an abstraction from a whole book of examples. The earliest vernacular European medievalization of these stories may be the Anglo-Norman collection of *Fables* by Marie de France, better known for her collection of Breton lays but composing her fables also for a late-twelfth-century court, identified by Marie as that of 'Count William'. Marie draws the first forty of her collection of 103 fables from some text of the *Romulus*, but the source of the rest is unclear, though most have analogues in other European and non-European versions. Marie made her own collection from a mixture of origins, and may have recorded some of the fables for the first time. Naturally Marie, like so many other medieval authors, cites authorities for her texts, referring in her prologue to Aesop as well as Romulus, and less expectedly in her epilogue also to King Alfred whose English version of Aesop she claims to be putting into French rhyme; no Old English fable collection exists and the text known as *The Proverbs of Alfred* is a piece of 'wisdom literature', rather conventional moralizing divided into sections, each one of which begins 'Thus queth Alfred'. Whether Marie's naming of Alfred and her supposed English source is a compliment to an audience in England, or whether there was an English version of Walter the Englishman's

---

[19] See Wheatley, *Mastering Aesop*, pp.59ff.; the first chapter is about different ways of defining fable.

collection (Marie's contemporary), is mere surmise, but Marie is typical of collectors of fables in giving her work a translator's frame, encouraging us to read the whole set of fables as a unified if composite work. From the prologue it is clear that she has a sense of the overall purpose of the collection, as offering morals and axioms of a practical nature, pieces of worldly wisdom which will teach the reader to avoid being tricked, as well as to recognize and judge pride, greed, and other kinds of sin and folly.

Fairly early in the series Marie's interest in the social and political themes in the fables is clear. Her second fable, the story of the wolf picking a quarrel with the lamb who is drinking from the same stream and, despite the lamb's innocence of any offence, using even protests of innocence as offence enough to justify slaughter, leads directly to a comment on oppression:

> Issi funt li riche seignur,
> Li vescunte e li jugeür,
> De ceus qu'il unt en lur justise:
> Faus acheisuns par coveitise
> Treovent asez pur eus confundre;
> Suvent les funt a pleit somundre.
> La char lur tolent e la pel,
> Si cum li fus fist a l'aignel.

> > (And this is what our great lords do,
> > The viscounts and the judges too,
> > With all the people whom they rule:
> > False charge they make from greed so cruel.
> > To cause confusion they consort
> > And often summon folk to court.
> > They strip them clean of flesh and skin,
> > As the wolf did to the lambkin.)[20]

Stories of greed and trickery that follow amass evidence of abuse of the law by the powerful, the collusion of the rich, the wickedness of lords, the lack of reward for the poor, who may find a rare opportunity for vengeance (as in Fable 10, 'The Fox and the Eagle') but are usually well advised to be content with their lot (Fable 9, 'The City Mouse and the Town Mouse'). Although most of Marie's fables are quite short, they are, in comparison with the epigrammatic quality of many of the early Aesopic fables, demonstrative narratives with some

---

[20] Spiegel, pp.34–5.

development of action and plot, as in Fable 18, 'The Frogs who Asked for a King', where the frogs' request for a king moves through several stages: the initial quest for stability and leadership, their acceptance of and then their dissatisfaction with a log as king, and then the consequence when fate sends them a hungry snake instead. Though some of the *Romulus* fables involve animals with human beings (such as the wry Fable 15, 'The Ass who Wanted to Play with his Master'), only a couple are stories entirely concerned with human relationships (the story of the widow who allows the corpse of her late lamented husband to be substituted for the missing body of a felon, and the Aesop allegory of man's stomach quarrelling with other parts of the body). The initial effects are of Marie's developing her several themes mainly through analogies with the animal world. Her longest tale, Fable 29, 'The Wolf King', is one of her most powerful.

This elaborate, developed instance of fable is a good illustration of Marie's neat narrative art: it has its own prologue which defines the original situation when the lion-king decides to resign and go into exile, which leads naturally into the beasts' controversial choice of the wolf as his successor, and to the lion's assessment of the pros and cons of their choice.

> He said to doubt not in the least
> That they had picked a clever beast,
> Extremely fast and versatile,
> Provided that his heart and will
> Were as they ought to be sincere.
> But one thing caused the lion fear—
> That wolf for counsellor would pick
> The fox who knew well how to trick;
> Both are insidious and base.
> If from the wolf they wanted peace,
> On holy relics he must swear
> That he'd touch no beast anywhere.
> And that forever he would not
> Eat any meat, no matter what.
> The wolf most willingly then swore
> To more than they had asked him for.
> (21–36)[21]

Then come three short episodes that test the worth of the wolf's

---

[21] Spiegel, p.103.

promises, as he faces three animals in turn with the test question, 'Does my breath smell?' The roe-deer who says that it stinks is legally sentenced to death for insulting the king; the second animal who says that it is the sweetest scent known is equally condemned for lying; the monkey, who has the wit to say he does not know, is caught by the wolf's feigning illness and getting his sycophantic doctors to prescribe as a cure that he satisfy his appetite, and, if monkey-flesh is the one thing that will cure him, monkey-flesh he had better have. 'Q.E.D.', as one might say, and Marie sums it up with her usual economy and aplomb:

> Thus by the wise man we are taught
> That we, no matter what, must not
> A wicked man e'er make seignior,
> Nor show to such a one honour.
> His loyalty's as much pretence
> With strangers as with his close friends.
> And toward his people he will act
> As did the wolf, with his sworn pact.
>
> (115–22)[22]

Marie's moral comments, the 'epimythium' as it is known, are of four, six, or eight lines and usually tied in aptly to the tale; pointed and often ironic, they show no inclination to heavy-handed generalization, nor to losing sight of the character and situation.

After the forty *Romulus* fables the collection becomes more eclectic, and alongside animal fables, many of which are familiar, Marie introduces a fair number of stories of human relationships, some of them closer to fabliau than to apologue, as in the case of Fable 42, 'The Doctor, the Rich Man and his Daughter', where the daughter's deception (substituting her own blood after she has accidentally spilt the sample of her father's blood which she was taking to the doctor) leads to a satisfying narrative climax (the doctor's discovering that the father is pregnant) which works as a good joke and does not need the further emphasis on the moral point that 'beguilers . . . / By their own deeds they will be caught'. One suspects that Marie's inclusion of such tales as this, or Fable 44, 'The Peasant who Saw Another with his Wife' or Fable 45, 'The Peasant who Saw his Wife with her Lover', both anecdotes that resemble the story used for the pear-tree episode in Chaucer's *Merchant's Tale*, are part of her aim of giving the

---

[22] Spiegel, p.107.

collection of fables variety in order to be entertaining for her audience. Recognition of women's shrewdness removes any antifeminist bite the stories may have had and keep morality at the level of everyday sense. Some of Marie's fables show her expressing the woman's point of view, in fables about pregnancy or female animals being tricked by a male.[23]

Marie's handling of fable is simple, easy, and clear. Her writing is at some distance, not only in terms of chronology but also in narrative fullness and structure, from the Aesopic epigram, but Marie does not play with the idea of allegorical exegesis: her tales show morality in action and need only a slight demonstrative nudge of 'thus this example shows . . .' to round them off. In common with other medieval redactors of fable material, Marie's versions are more socially specific, as Henderson has pointed out: 'They apply the ancient lessons of weak and strong to specific classes in a real society: rich and poor, *seigneur* and *vilain*.'[24]

Another of Marie's sources was the gathering of fox stories into the 'beast-epic', *Le Roman de Renart*. This work, like the fables of Aesop, is not the composition of a single author, but a collection of tales which grew over a period of time. It is made up of a series of short episodes linked together by the recurrence of key characters, particularly the clever, but deceitful fox, Reynard, and the fiercer, but stupider, wolf, Isengrim, with a supporting cast of character types. The earliest form seems to be the *Ysengrimus* (1149), a Latin poem composed by a Flemish cleric based on the conflict between fox and wolf, 'one of the finest masterpieces of all time' in the view of a modern expert on the topic.[25] Later versions—and nearly thirty branches of *Le Roman de Renart* seem to have been composed between 1174 and 1250—develop its strong strain of satire, so that the grouping of fables around the court of the lion, Noble, resolves into a mirror of the feudal, social hierarchy.[26] The comic interplay of

[23] See Spiegel, Introduction, pp.10–11. Fables 21 and 6 are about pregnancy; Marie's version of 'The Fox and the Bear' (Fable 70) emphasizes the deceit and oppression used against the female bear.

[24] Arnold Clayton Henderson, 'Medieval beasts and modern cages: the making of meaning in fables and bestiaries', *PMLA* 97 (1982), 40–49 (quotation from p.41).

[25] Kenneth Varty, Introduction to *Reynard the Fox: Social Engagement and Cultural Metamorphoses in the Beast Epic from the Middle Ages to the Present* (Oxford, Berghahn Books, 2000), p.xv.

[26] See H.J. Blackham, *The Fable as Literature* (London, Athlone Press, 1985), pp.40–51.

character, variations on recurrent situations, tricks, plenty of dialogue, elements of burlesque, all shift and reduce the moral force of
the tales in favour of the effects of situation comedy—a reduction of
point from proverb into catchphrase—though successful in terms of
lively enjoyability. The earliest vernacular English appearance of this
material is *The Fox and the Wolf* in MS Digby 86 (1250–75);[27] this
consists of nearly 300 lines in rhyming couplets, mostly telling
the story of the fox, the wolf, and the buckets in the well, though the
beginning sounds as if the story of the fox pretending to be dying in
order to wheedle his way into the hencoop was originally part of the
composite tale, which seems to be told for sheer enjoyment of the
comic effrontery of the fox, rather than as a cautionary story. Such
treatment of the fable as an individual work marks the distinction
between beast-epic and fable, in which the moral, even if it was added
by a later collector, has become an essential and identifying part of
the form. Reading fable as comic narrative rather than for its instructive point may release the story from enforced didacticism, but may
also take away its sense of direction. Nevertheless such use of the fable
runs alongside the serious uses of the form in the Reynard material.
The Reynard cycle did eventually get translated into English (from
Dutch in the fifteenth century by Caxton), but is mainly interesting
in England as a source for others, as it is for Marie and also for the
early-thirteenth-century Latin fabulist, Odo of Cheriton.

One is in no doubt in Odo's *Fables* that one is reading the work of
an instructor. He is identified as Magister Odo, meaning that he had a
master's degree, in 1210–11, later as Doctor Ecclesiae; he studied in
Paris and his land-owner father provided him with an administrative
office at the church at Cheriton (near Folkestone).[28] Odo's writings,
sermons and parables as well as fables, identify him as a priestly
teacher whose world is ecclesiastical, as he interprets fables in terms
of the satirical light they throw on members of the church.

Odo looses a menagerie of snail bishops, spider bishops, and rector flies, of
dog officials and crow officials picking the bones of the lesser clergy and,
ultimately, of the poor.[29]

His fables were based on some version of the *Romulus*, like those of

---

[27] Bennett and Smithers, *Early Middle English Prose and Verse*, pp.65–76.
[28] See Albert C. Friend, 'Master Odo of Cheriton', *Speculum*, 23 (1948), 641–58.
[29] Henderson, 'Medieval beasts', p.41.

Marie, but with additions from the Reynard cycle and elsewhere. They survive in a number of manuscripts, which are not consistent in their contents and order; if one adds together all the different fables that occur in the various manuscripts, they amount to over a hundred.[30] The fables vary in length and type: some are animal fables, some apologues—philosophical fables about human beings. Some are told square and plain, others elaborately treated as allegories; Odo's use of hypothetical cases identifies the theologian. He writes in Latin for fellow-priests primarily, but he is liberal with familiar quotations, often from the Vulgate, sometimes in English, as in Fable 10, 'The Buzzard and the Hawk's Nest', where the mother hawk pitches the nest-fouling buzzard chick out of the nest with the words 'Of an egge y the brouzgyt/bytt of thy kynde y maye nouzght' (i.e., 'I brought you out of an egg, but can't bring you out of your nature').[31] As with Marie and her reference to the supposed fables of Alfred, Odo is conscious of a vernacular folk tradition of fable sayings. In his treatment of narrative he can be forceful and terse, as Jacobs points out in his version of 'The Wolf and the Lamb who Were Drinking':

A wolf and a lamb were drinking from the same stream. And the wolf said: 'Why are you muddying my water?' 'I'm doing nothing of the sort,' the lamb replied, 'for you are drinking upstream; and the water flows down from you to me.' The wolf came back at him: 'Curse you! For you are contradicting me! Who are *you* to be so arrogant?' And he immediately devoured the lamb.

Thus rich men, for no cause at all—and regardless of how the poor respond—devour them.[32]

This is more economical than the versions in the *Romulus* and the moral application is so unequivocal as to make even Marie's modest comments, quoted above, seem diffuse. But in the majority of cases Odo is much keener to draw out the meaning of the fable, as he does with the story told, without any moral, in the Middle English *The Fox and the Wolf*; Odo's tale of 'The Fox, the Wolf and the Well-Bucket' (Fable 29 in Jacobs) is the same in its narrative outline, but interpreted as follows:

---

[30] The Latin texts of Odo's fables may be found in Hervieux, *Les Fabulistes Latins*, iv, pp. 173–250. They have been translated into English as *The Fables of Odo of Cheriton* by John C. Jacobs (New York, Syracuse U. P., 1985).

[31] Jacobs, *Fables of Odo*, p.93.

[32] See Jacobs, *Fables of Odo*, Introduction, pp.33–7.

The little fox signifies the Devil who says to man: 'Come down to me, down into the well of sin, and you will find delicacies and an abundance of other good things.' The fool acquiesces and goes on down into the well of sin and there finds no nourishment. In time enemies come and pull out the impious man, beat him, and kill him. The Devil promised Adam many good things; but in fact he delivers many evils.[33]

This sounds more like the daily teaching of the parish priest and has little of the edge that Odo can give to attacks on social ills, as, for example, his treatment in Fable 71, 'The Spider, the Fly and the Wasp'[34] where he announces his theme in the promythium: 'Against rich men who assault the poor, etc.', then presents the narrative succinctly:

When a fly comes into her web, the spider courageously strides forth and seizes the fly and kills it. When a droning wasp comes along, making an awful racket, the spider flees down her hole.

Then follows the epimythium, twice as long as the fable itself:

So it is with certain bishops and prelates. When a poor and modest man falls into the net of the bishops (on account of some wrongdoing or false charge) they eagerly seize him and have a great feast. But when a rich man comes along, shouting threats, then the bishop or prelate hides himself.

Even then he is not finished, but rounds it off with a quotation from Hosea. This shows Odo in full teaching mode and is the pattern of his more developed fables.

One of the most interesting of Odo's stories is one of the longest, where a more ambitious theme and a necessarily more elaborate way of reading are evident. This is Fable 40, 'Walter's Search for the Happy Place'. It begins as follows:

There once lived a man named Walter. He longed for a place and condition where he might rejoice for ever and suffer no affliction—either of flesh or spirit. So he set out on his quest. And he found a most beautiful lady whose husband had died.

Walter approached her. Then, when they had exchanged greetings, the lady wanted to know what he was seeking. Walter replied: 'I am in quest of two things, namely: a place where I may rejoice for ever, [and]a place where I may not suffer at all—in either the flesh or the spirit.' 'Be my husband and remain with me,' replied the lady; 'you will thus have all the things you need: homes, lands, vineyards, and the rest.'

---

[33] Jacobs, *Fables of Odo*, p.89.
[34] Jacobs, *Fables of Odo*, p.124.

She showed him an entrance and a chamber, both of which pleased Walter. And he asked where he would rest at night. So the lady showed him a bed. Surrounding it were, on one side, a bear—and a wolf on the second, worms on the third, and serpents on the fourth. Walter then asked: 'How long will I be dwelling with you? Will I indeed have delights like these for ever?' Said the lady: 'Not at all! For my husband died and, in time, you will have to also.' She continued: 'Do you see this bed?' 'I see it,' Walter responded. And the lady: 'The bear will slay you—but whether on the first night or after a year or during the tenth year or later on, I really don't know. Then afterwards the wolf, worms, and serpents will consume you.'

'All the other things,' said Walter, 'are good. But this bed terrifies me. I haven't the slightest desire to lie regularly in such a bed—whether to gain you or, even, the whole world.' And he made his exit.[35]

Walter continues his search and finds a country where the king has just died; he is offered the kingdom but on the same conditions as those offered by the lady. A third time he journeys and is offered lordship over splendour, but with the same drawbacks. The climax of the search, when it comes, is surprisingly swift.

At long last he came to a place where he found an old man sitting at the foot of a ladder; the three-rung ladder was leaning up against a wall. The old man asked Walter what he was seeking, and Walter told him. 'I am,' he said, 'looking for the place where I can for ever rejoice and suffer no affliction.' The old man said: 'If you use this ladder to ascend the wall, then there you'll find what you're seeking.' So Walter made the climb, and he found it.

The abruptness identifies a parable needing explanation, not a simple fable carrying its own complete meaning: the reversal at the end motivates the explanatory section which is headed, as a number of Odo's moralizations are, with the word *Mistice* (where 'mystically' implies revealing the hidden meaning). Odo's explanation is long and detailed, beginning with the overall sense:

Take any worldly man you like; he seeks these three things, or some part of them. He seeks (1) a beautiful woman, on account of his licentiousness, or (2) high position, on account of his vanity, or (3) gold and silver, on account of his greed. Yet if he looks carefully at the bed on which he must lie, he swiftly flees from all such things. For at the head of the bed stands the bear, that is death, who spares no one . . .

[35] Jacobs, *Fables of Odo*, pp.97–8.

The images are given their allegorical sense in turn: death, those who covet the worldly man's goods, the worms that devour the body, the devils that wait to carry off the soul. Once the picture is interpreted we are ready to see the meaning of the enigma as the last paragraph explains the ladder:

Climb up Jacob's golden ladder—the ladder whose first step is contrition of heart, whose second is true confession, whose third is full penance. If you will make the ascent up these rungs, you shall be transported unto the glory of eternal life—where without end you shall rejoice and not suffer affliction.[36]

In some respects this is Odo's most compelling story, but is such a mystical apologue outside the limits of fable? Cautionary tales, using human figures as representative, are part of the fable tradition from earliest times, and scattered through Odo's collection are a number of such tales, as for example, Fable 6, 'An Abbot, Food, and some Monks', or Fable 109, 'An Aged Father and his Son', or, in another vivid encapsulation of man's situation on earth, Fable 114, 'A Certain Man Flees the Unicorn',[37] in which the man, in fleeing the unicorn (which is later identified with death) half falls into a pit, grabbing a small tree on the way down—this position of suspense, with a threatening dragon below and the heads of snakes above, becomes an image of the human condition, carefully expounded in a final section, in this case headed 'Moralitas'. This sort of 'fabulous' Christian story is closest to the myths in the Aesopic tradition. At the other end of the spectrum are fables that emphasize naturalism, particularly in describing the world of animals, their natural habitats, and their patterns of behaviour.

With an individual fable, such as *The Fox and the Wolf*, or a fable put into a different context, such as Chaucer's *Nun's Priest's Tale*, the reader's sense of the tale is different. As part of *The Canterbury Tales* Chaucer's 626-line version of the story of the cock and fox (which Marie managed to tell in thirty-eight lines) has been placed within a medley of narratives, so that comparison is between fable and other kinds of storytelling: the idea of fable itself is offered for the reader's analysis and judgment. At the end of his inflated treatment, with all

[36] Jacobs, *Fables of Odo*, p.100.
[37] The three fables named are respectively Jacobs, *Fables of Odo*, pp.72–3, p.153, and pp.161–2.

its flourishes of description, rhetorical speech, debate, digression, and allusion, Chaucer, in the assumed voice of his priestly narrator, offers his audience a choice:

> But ye that holden this tale a folye,
> As of a fox, or of a cok and hen,
> Taketh the moralite, goode men . . .
> Taketh the fruyt, and lat the chaf be stille.
> (*CT*, VII, 3438–40, 3443)

One sense in which we might dismiss the tale as 'a folye' is the recognition that animals do not talk, let alone quote Cato and the Old Testament, and that the whole thing is obviously a pretence: for fable, or at least animal fable, to work we have to accept the metaphorical nature of the narrative, and the usual reason given in the Middle Ages for doing so is the worth of the moral message which is conveyed through the invented anecdote. At the same time to call such a tale foolish is a dismissive adult comment on the things of childhood and the schoolroom language of moral lessons is the tone in which cock and fox sum up their experience:

> 'For he that winketh when he sholde see,
> Al wilfully, god lat him never thee!'
> 'Nay,' quod the fox, 'but god yeve him meschaunce,
> That is so undiscreet of governaunce,
> That jangleth when he sholde holde his pees.'
> (*CT*, VII, 3431–5)

The moral force of the tale has, however, been diffused by the distractions that Chaucer has introduced. Chauntecleer's vulnerability to flattery no longer serves a practical warning against vanity; it has become a mirror reflecting the arrogance of masculine claims of superiority, the power of sexual desire to overcome prudence, the distance between academic reasoning and practical common sense, and so on—a range of ideas has given Chauntecleer a wider representativeness so that it is no surprise that the tale has been read as a comment on the fall of man. The ambivalence and adaptability of fable, which Chaucer exploits in his maverick telling, comes from the different applications that it had acquired by the fourteenth century: animal fables might bring echoes of infant lessons in self-discipline, but had also picked up associations from their use for older students of rhetoric, whereby fables became the framework for exercises in

the art of apostrophe, descriptio, and so on. What Chaucer does in
The Nun's Priest's Tale is to confuse the reader by playing a game
of shifting levels, not only levels of register, but also from the human
to the animal aspects of his characters, so that at one moment
Chauntecleer and Pertelote are engaged in academic debate, the next
pecking seeds, at one moment addressing each other as courtly lovers,
at the next coupling energetically and repeatedly. The morality of the
story becomes difficult to read because the world of the narrative is
unstable.

Within the black-and-white world of the poor widow, her two
daughters and the smallholding with pigs, cows, a sheep, and a yard,
gradually appears the technicolour world of Chauntecleer and his
harem; while the human beings in the story utter no more than 'Out!
harrow! and weylawey!/Ha, ha, the fox!' at the climax of the action,
the heraldically splendid birds are soon wordily exchanging opinions,
as, for example:

> 'Swevenes engendren of replecc:iouns,
> And ofte of fume, and of complecc:iouns,
> Whan humours been to habundant in a wight.'
> (*CT*, VII, 2923–5)

or, on the other side of the argument about dreams:

> 'That dremes been significac:iouns,
> As wel of joye as tribulaciouns,
> That folk enduren in this lif present.'
> (*CT*, VII, 2979–81)

The sheer length of Chauntecleer's speech defending the meaningfulness of dreams identifies him as not merely a caricature of human
preachers, but as an ironic example of the disparity between words
and action, since after his weighty argument he takes no actual heed
of his dream and still falls victim to the danger of which it warned.
Nevertheless, the key voice in the tale is that of the narrator. Here,
instead of a medieval ventriloquist adopting the voice of Aesop, or an
unobtrusive pointer of morals such as Marie, is a shape-shifting narrator, who for the first half of the tale seems content to be a behind-
the-scenes recorder of dramatic speech, handing over the argument
about dreams almost entirely to the voices of cock and hen, but who
then turns into an interfering commentator, whose intrusions and

digressions take over the comic role from the cockerel's preaching mannerisms. Is Chaucer parodying the working of fable in pushing to extremes its finding of morals?

> O Chauntecleer, acursed be that morwe
> That thou into that yerd flaugh fro the bemes!
> Thou were ful wel ywarned by thy dremes
> That thilke day was perilous to thee;
> But what that God forwoot mot nedes bee,
> After the opinioun of certein clerkis.
> Witnesse on hym that any parfit clerk is,
> That in scole is greet altercacioun
> In this mateere, and greet disputisoun,
> And hath been of an hundred thousand men.
> But I ne kan nat bulte it to the bren
> As kan the hooly doctour Augustyn,
> Or Boece, or the Bisshop Bradwardyn,
> Wheither that Goddes worthy forwityng
> Streyneth me nedely fo to doon a thyng— . . .
> I wol nat han to do of swich mateere;
> My tale is of a cok, as ye may heere . . .
>
>   (*CT*, VII, 3230–44, 3250–51)

Chaucer may be suggesting that, since fables are the vehicles for philosophy, the more philosophizing the fabulist puts in the better. What makes *The Nun's Priest's Tale* enjoyable is the comedy of inappropriateness that Chaucer develops and the bathetic shifts from high thought to low action, from the fall of Troy to the farmyard. It is the familiarity of the fable tradition and the cock and fox material which provides the strong foundation for this rhetorical game-playing. The link between a natural, homely tale of country life, with its *Roman de Renart* chase scene, the names of the dogs and the building up of hullabaloo, and the intellectual fantasy of courtly, book-reading animals playing out a drama of horrific threat, near tragedy, and providential escape, is, as it were, licensed by the trad-ition in fable of animal situations as metaphors of human behaviour. It is strong enough to survive even Chaucer's distortions and dis-proportions, though in commenting on its own literary form, it becomes a kind of meta-fable.

There are no such problems of understanding with Lydgate, who produced the first fable series in the English language in his collection of *Isopes Fabules*, some of which, if not all, were probably among his earliest works.[38] The idea of writing poetic fables could have been, in his case, an extension of studying rhetoric at Oxford (1405–10).[39] The seven fables vary in length, with the first four (which, with the prologue, follow the traditional opening order of the *Romulus* collections) given extensive treatment, while the other three are much shorter: perhaps Lydgate began with the idea of a substantial series but then broke off, adding the last three later. Written in rhyme royal stanzas and, initially at least, on a scale matching that of *The Nun's Priest's Tale*, Lydgate's fables show the first stages of his pedestrian treatment of Chaucerian forms, and at the same time a clear expression of late medieval fable theory. From the start Lydgate thinks in terms of 'Olde examples of prudent philosophers' who saw similitudes in nature from which 'Notable sentence of gret moralyte' might be drawn. Aesop expressed these in fables, which may be 'rude' but which enclose 'gret prudence':

> Perlys whyte, clere & orientall,
> Ben oft founde in muscle shellys blake,
> And out of fables gret wysdom men may take.
> (*Isopes Fabules*, 26–8)

Lydgate subscribes to the idea of the narrative in a fable as a covering over of morality, a rough curtain which the storyteller draws back to reveal the fineness of abstract truth, but, though he devotes the final stanzas of the fable (three stanzas in each of the first three) to this uncovering, he can not wait until then to find moral aspects to the story as he goes along. Possibly encouraged by Chaucer's Nun's Priest, Lydgate gives up the crispness of telling that suits fable best, in favour of a loose readiness to generalize. Even before the beginning of the actual story in Fable III, 'The Frog and the Mouse', several stanzas are given to moral reflection:

> Aftyr þeyr naturall disposicions
> In man & beste ys shewyd experyence:
> Som haue to vertew þeyr inclinacions,

---

[38] The collection is in *The Minor Poems of John Lydgate*, Part II, ed. H.N. MacCracken, EETS ES 107 (London, Oxford U.P., 1934), pp.566–99.

[39] See Derek Pearsall, *John Lydgate* (London, Routledge & Kegan Paul, 1970), pp.192ff.

> Oone to profyte, anoþer to do offence;
> Som man pesyble, som man doþ violence;
> Som man delyteþ in trouþe in hys entent,
> Anoþer rejoyseþ to be fraudulent.
>
> (*Isopes Fabules*, 372–8)

And so on. The mouse is as ready with literary references (to Croesus, Midas, Solomon, Alexander, Priam) as Chauntecleer and though such amplitude is acceptable in Chaucer, where it contributes to the comedy, in Lydgate it rather sounds as if amplification is being sought for its own sake and is being supplied according to standard recipes. By letting the moralization dominate the narrative Lydgate blurs the edges of fable: his own image of the story as the black shell with the gleaming pearl within is lost sight of because he can not keep story separate from meaning.

Lydgate's *Isopes Fabules* make an interesting comparison for, and may have been one of the sources of, the outstanding example of the late medieval fable collection, Robert Henryson's *Moral Fables*. It is, as with Lydgate, a matter of controversy whether Henryson had completed his collection and what order we should read them in: they survive only in texts nearly a hundred years later than their original composition; the thirteen fables which are printed in modern editions of Henryson's works[40] occur only in prints of about 1570, while the text, which is better in some respects, found in the slightly earlier Bannatyne MS (1568), has only ten of the fables in a different order. The most recent editor has argued for the unity and coherence of the collection,[41] but other critics have interpreted the variations in Henryson's treatment of the stories as evidence of several stages of composition, perhaps beginning with a series of six or seven fables based on a version of the *Romulus* (and since Henryson quotes from Walter the Englishman, it may be his version);[42] to these Henryson might then have added three fox stories (perhaps influenced by

---

[40] The authoritative text is *The Poems of Robert Henryson*, ed. Denton Fox (Oxford, Clarendon Press, 1981).

[41] *The Moral Fables of Aesop by Robert Henryson*, ed. George D. Gopen (Notre Dame, Ind., University of Notre Dame Press, 1987).

[42] These fables would be I, 'The Cock and the Jewel'; II, 'The Two Mice'; VI, 'The Sheep and the Dog'; VII, 'The Lion and the Mouse'; VIII, 'The Preaching of the Swallow' (though this could have been a separate poem); XII, 'The Wolf and the Lamb'; XIII, 'The Paddock and the Mouse'.

Caxton's translation of *Reynard the Fox* from the Dutch in 1481)[43] and finally appended three fables from Caxton's *Aesop* (1484).[44] The series of thirteen fables could have been compiled by sixteenth-century printers to make the fullest collection.[45] As they came to be put together these tales are examples of highly developed late medieval versions of fable: as Gopen points out, 'Henryson averages 230 lines per fable and 43 lines per *Moralitas*.' There is, however, variation of treatment within this overall pattern. The three 'Reynard the Fox' stories and the three 'Caxton's *Aesop*' stories concentrate on comic incident and intrigue: some of them have quite complex plots, especially Fable V, 'The Trial of the Fox', the longest story of the series, which has several different episodes in succession, and they interest the reader mainly by vigour of narrative and the twists and turns of the fox's wiles and of the rivalry between fox and wolf. Even the simplest of them, 'The Fox and the Wolf', Henryson's version of Chaucer's story of Chauntecleer and Pertelote, is distinguished by Henryson's introduction of a cheeky comic digression in the form of debate among Chauntecleer's three widows (as they think) about the nature and extent of their loss and the character of the departed rooster (first lamented in public language as 'our drowrie and our dayis darling,/Our nichtingall and als our orloge bell' but then scornfully dismissed as a poor lover and condemned as a proud and lustful adulterer). The morality drawn from these fabliau-like episodes is modest both in length and in content, which consists of comments on the sins of everyday worldliness, pride, sensuality, greed and so on.

Of the other fables 'The Two Mice' is the nearest to these essentially comic stories: Henryson gives space mainly to an imaginative, highly amusing retelling of the familiar tale, full of precise detail and sharp evocation of the animal world; he appends a short (four stanzas) moral section praising the simple life and being content with little, summing up, as he always seeks to do, in homely proverbial style:

---

[43] That is Fables III, IV, and V, 'The Cock and the Fox'; 'The Fox and the Wolf'; 'The Trial of the Fox'.

[44] That is Fables IX, X, and XI, 'The Fox, the Wolf and the Cadger'; 'The Fox, the Wolf and the Husbandman'; 'The Wolf and the Wether'. These three are the fables missing from the Bannatyne MS.

[45] This theory of the text is basically the view of John MacQueen, *Robert Henryson: A Study of the Major Narrative Poems* (Oxford, Clarendon Press, 1967), pp.187–93.

> Thy awin fyre, freind, thocht it be bot ane gleid,
> It warmis weill, and is worth gold to the.
>
> (Fable II, 389–90)

Even in these examples fable is not much of the time an affair of short, witty answers and turned tables, but rather a thoughtful balance between sharply imagined animal situations and sober reflections on human society. A more serious note is sounded in several of the others, particularly 'The Sheep and the Dog' and 'The Wolf and the Lamb', where the fairly simple action is placed in a medieval Scots law court and the tragic events provide occasions for lengthy meditations on injustice.

Henryson included two prologues in his series, one at the beginning and a more elaborate type of prologue in 'The Lion and the Mouse'. The initial prologue expresses some familiar ideas, as that the 'feinȝeit fabils of ald poetre' may not be literally true, though they may give pleasure by being well expressed, but that they perform a useful function as reproof of evil living: this they do because the invented story is the 'figure of ane vther thing'. Henryson's metaphor for this, in place of Lydgate's image of the mussel shell and the pearl, is of the tough shell of a nut enclosing the sweet kernel of doctrine. As Aesop is quoted as saying, though it is Walter the Englishman who actually provides Henryson with the words, '*Dulcius arrident seria picta iocis*' ('Serious things please more sweetly when adorned with jests'). Aesop, referred to twice in this first prologue, later appears to the author in the dream prologue as a venerable, white-haired Roman, bearing a roll of paper with pens in his ear; addressed as 'poet lawriate' he is at first reluctant 'to tell ane prettie fabill/ Concludand with ane gude moralitie' (ll.1386–7) but then yields to the request to compose 'Vnder the figure of ane brutall beist/Ane moral fabill' and is still the voice used after the story of lion and mouse is concluded, to provide the moral interpretation and to exhort Henryson to persuade his countrymen to fight for justice. There is thus a strong, literary and textual element to Henryson's presentation of his stories. Fables are rhetorically skilled and pleasing fictions inherited from the distant past to be used as figures of modern morality. Given this emphasis it is not surprising that Henryson, unlike Lydgate, usually observes a sharp division between storytelling and picture-making on the one hand and sententiousness on the other, so much so that in some cases the sweet moral kernel is quite different from what the outside of the nut seemed to promise.

This is most obviously the case in the first and shortest fable, 'The Cock and the Jasp', traditionally the opening story in *Romulus* collections and in this position in the fable collections of Walter and of Marie de France and Lydgate. Henryson's interpretation is the traditional one of seeing the cock's spurning of the jewel found in the rubbish heap as an example of ignorant failure to appreciate worth. As Marie expresses it:

> What for the cock and gem is true
> We've seen with men and women too:
> They neither good nor honour prize;
> The worst they seize; the best, despise.
> (Fable 1, 19–22)[46]

It is Lydgate who prefers a consistently moral view and in beginning by praising the cock as a dutiful timekeeper, a discourager of sloth, and a moral champion who teaches us to praise God with tuneful voice, he sets up a version of the story in which the cock's admiration of the jacynth shows a proper lapidary knowledge of the stone's virtue; assigning the gem as apt for jewellers and princes is part of a recognition of the propriety of nature in which each creature and object has its own function. The moral envoy praises diligence, being content with one's lot and knowing one's place:

> Suche as God sent, eche man take at gre,
> Nat prowde with ryches nor groge with pouerte.
> (*Isopes Fabules*, 216–17)

Though Lydgate's treatment of the tale is obvious common sense, in this he is rejecting the traditional way of reading the fable, which could have been an interesting departure if Lydgate had had rather more of Henryson's skill in imagining the events of the story. Henryson's reading, though following the inherited sense, is much more challenging because he concentrates on narrative first and gives it lively realization and then, like a magician, reveals the hidden figure. Fable (eight stanzas) and *moralitas* (six stanzas) come near to having equal weight, in contrast to Lydgate's laborious narrative

---

[46] Spiegel, p.33.

(thirteen stanzas) and three different points in the moral envoy (three stanzas). It is not any lively imitation of the natural world that Henryson embarks on here; what he imagines is a cock 'cant and crous, albeit he was bot pure' ('brisk and jaunty, though he was only poor'— which carries a clear hint of how we are to judge him later) scraping on the dunghill outside a house where the maids are careless enough to throw out with the sweepings a precious stone of jasper, and suddenly surprised into a confused soliloquy by the sight of the marvellous gem. Impressed by its beauty, the cock pays tribute to it as an object to be looked at but quite useless for filling 'my tume intraill' ('my empty guts'), rising to a crescendo of rhetorical address to the jasper:

> 'Quhar sulde thow mak thy habitation?
> Quhar suld thow duell, bot in ane royall tour?
> Quhar suld thow sit, bot on ane kingis croun
> Exalt in worship and in grit honour?
> Rise, gentill Jasp, of all stanis the flour,
> Out of this fen, and pas quhar thow suld be,
> Thow ganis not for me, nor I for the.'
> (Fable I, 106–12)

The cock leaves the jewel on the ground to seek more apt food while the poet seeks the 'inward sentence and intent/Of this fabill', which proves not to confirm any idea we might have that the cock is showing common sense—far from it: the cock is a fool who lacking knowledge, mocks it. The narrative is a neat instance of Henryson's playing with high and low diction, whereby the cock's appetite and the object of his scratching in the yard run as undercurrent to the flourish of poetic celebration; Chaucer's contrasts in *The Nun's Priest's Tale* echo in the background. There is no recognition of the cock's virtue but a conversion of the picture of bird and jewel into an emblem representing the folly of ignorance, as Douglas Gray points out:

'Emblem' and 'story' are simply two extremes of the same form. The fable looks towards emblem-books, and aspires to the condition of an image, a speaking picture, static, with simultaneous layers of significance, while at the same time it also looks towards the tale or the anecdote and demands a story with a consecutive and linear motion (even in 'The Cock and the Jasp' something happens).[47]

---

[47] Douglas Gray, *Robert Henryson* (Leiden, E.J. Brill, 1979), pp.83–4.

The *moralitas* works as an act of focussing as we move from story to meaning.

At the other extreme of challenging use of the *moralitas* there is no element of surprise but rather an intensification of meaning already clear in the narrative. The story of the wolf and the lamb, which as we have seen earlier in the versions by Marie and Odo can be told very succinctly, has in all versions the theme of tyranny against the poor. Lydgate in his Fable II discourses from the very beginning on this theme, bringing in other examples, such as 'Grete pykes þat swymme in large stewes,/Smaller fysshe most felly þey devour' (ll.239–40); he does not reach the story until his fourth stanza but tells it with some force mainly through dialogue between wolf and lamb, reaching the sudden killing of the lamb in his tenth stanza and then adding a further six stanzas of elaboration (concerning Old Testament parallels, allegorical shepherds, the usefulness of lambs, the inequalities of the law) before reaching his three-stanza *conclusio*, which can only cover the same ground since he has already used up his moral comments. This is one of the fables where one suspects that Henryson was aware of Lydgate's, since the pattern in the two versions is not unlike, with the dialogue forming the dramatic centre of both. But Henryson makes much more of the opportunities the story offers. He moves into the action with the very opening words: 'Ane cruell volff, richt rauenous and fell . . .'. His dialogue characterises the two speakers, the wolf abusive and combative, the lamb timorous and deferential but with a legalistic and priestly precision: the contest turns into a law-court debate with some tension and power. The focus is on the situation and the two voices: the moral comments are left to the long *moralitas*, where Henryson develops his argument into the opposition between the poor people and the various kinds and degrees of extortion practised by lawyers, powerful men, and hereditary landowners; to each Henryson gives two or three stanzas, combining description of the wrongdoing of the powerful with direct appeal to these men to relent, particularly forceful in the case of the landed men:

> Hes thow not reuth to gar thy tennentis sweit
> In to thy laubour, with faynt and hungrie wame,
> And syne hes lytill gude to drink or eit
> With his menȝe, at euin quhen he cummis hame?

Thow suld be rad for richteous Goddis blame,
For it cryis ane vengeance vnto the heuinnis hie
To gar ane pure man wirk but meit or fe.

O thow grit lord, that riches hes and rent,
Be nocht ane wolf, thus to deuoir the pure!
(Fable XII, 2756–64)

Henryson is the most ambitious of the medieval writers of fable and the most successful in using the form to explore the relationship between human and animal figures and to balance the pleasure of fantasy pictures of talking beasts with sober lessons about conduct in the society of which he was a member. The ample scale of the *Moral Fables* is a long way from the wry little jokes of Aesop, but the affinity between them is not in doubt: the recipe for fable and medieval understanding of its working do not change significantly. Each generation of poets will use the power of fancy to enliven the story, to make it graphic, typical, or highly unusual, but communicating from writer to audience through a shared pragmatic recognition of aspects of behaviour, animal and human; the covering of ingenuity can then be drawn back to analyse the fruit of identification and comparison. Given the long-lasting common sense of the logic and purpose of fable, it is remarkable that its medieval forms are so diverse.

4

Forms of history

Chronicle—fact and fiction

The Ciceronian rhetorical tradition which divides narrative into three kinds, *fabula, argumentum,* and *historia,* leaves the third of these terms to cover a huge variety of literary forms: if *fabula* is the label for works of fiction and imagination, *argumentum* the pigeon-hole for plausible hypotheses, then all writing about the actual events of real life and of factual matters in past and present has to be thought of as *historia.* Hence John of Garland includes a bewildering number of genres in this category. Poetry which refers to real events might include celebration of weddings and honourings at funerals and so *epithalamium* and *epitaph* are named; poetry about factual matters such as the conditions of rural life has to count as history and so *bucolic* and *georgic* appear; other celebrations of real experience might be the subject matter of *lyric* and *hymn,* while comments on actual events and current affairs are the material of *invective* and *satire;* narratives of unfortunate events and the sorrows of lovers make it necessary to include *tragedy* and *elegy.*[1] While this mixture (and John includes a few more genres than those I have listed) might seem to render the idea of 'history' so blurred as to be useless as a category, these terms are merely subdivisions of the larger idea that one main area of narrative writing is concerned with events of the past, and their variety recognizes that such narrative may be not only simple factual recording, but may interpret history and comment on it. The real ambiguities about the idea of 'history' as a literary term prove not to come from the variety of forms it includes but from the application of the word to material which is far from factual. Probably the best-known and most widely influential 'history' of the

---

[1] John of Garland, *Parisiana Poetria,* ch.v, ll.321ff.

medieval period, surviving in over two hundred manuscripts as well as translations into most of the European vernaculars, is Geoffrey of Monmouth's *Historia Regum Britanniae* ('The History of the Kings of Britain') and while this Latin work is written in the form of a history or chronicle, much of what Geoffrey has to say is not reliable history and includes a fair amount of the fictional and even of the fabulous.[2] Geoffrey's use of the word *historia* constitutes a claim that he is writing of real events of the past and of real men and women and their adventures, and he made use of existing chronicles (Gildas, Bede, Nennius) as well as Welsh material about which little is known but which may have been 'reliable' written sources. However, it is clear that he also invented many things in order to bolster his creation of a national myth of British history and the foundation of the English nation. This fact was recognized and criticized in his own time, most severely by the chronicler William of Newburgh, writing at the end of the twelfth century and so about fifty years after the composition of the work which William called 'a laughable web of fiction'. Among other criticisms of Geoffrey he says:

He has taken up the stories about Arthur from old fictitious accounts of the Britons, has added to them himself, and by embellishing them in the Latin tongue he has cloaked them with the honourable title of history . . . none except those ignorant of ancient histories can possibly doubt the extent of his wanton and shameless lying virtually throughout his book, which he calls *A History of the Britons*, when they come across it. He has not learnt the truth about events, and so without discrimination he gives space to fables without substance . . . The motive was either an uncontrolled passion for lying, or secondly a desire to please the Britons, most of whom are considered so barbaric that they are said to be still awaiting the future coming of Arthur, being unwilling to entertain the fact of his death.[3]

The distinction between accurate history and history compromised by the inclusion of fable and invention was thus being made by educated men of the period, but the student of medieval literature has to recognize that 'history' may be used as a generic description of works that are far from 'true'. Geoffrey was writing the history that ought to have been there and supplied it with the necessary

---

[2] Geoffrey of Monmouth, *The History of the Kings of Britain*, trans. with Introduction by Lewis Thorpe (Harmondsworth, Penguin Books, 1966).

[3] William of Newburgh, *The History of English Affairs*, Book I, trans. P.G. Walsh and M.J. Kennedy (Warminster, Aris & Phillips, 1988), Prologue.

authentification in the form of his supposed source in 'a very ancient book written in the British language'.

Even within the field of respectable historical writing distinctions have to be made among its different forms. Antonia Gransden has written authoritatively about medieval chronicles, that is 'serious historical writings' from which 'histories in the romance style' whose 'primary purpose was to entertain' are rigorously excluded, and in classifying them makes the distinction between 'annals' (chronicles with very short yearly entries), 'chronicles' (chronologically structured records), and 'histories' (selective accounts in literary form).[4] With reference to the latter pair she quotes the late-twelfth-century chronicler Gervase of Canterbury who said:

> It is characteristic of history to tell the truth, to persuade those who read or hear it with soft words and elegant phrases and to inform them about the deeds, ways and lives of anyone it truthfully describes; it is an essentially rational study. A chronicle, on the other hand, reckons the years ... and briefly tells of the deeds of kings and princes which happened at those times, besides recording any portents, miracles or other events.[5]

The distinction is intriguing, particularly in the acceptance of persuasive rhetoric in the writing of history and of superstitious material in the chronicler's record, and Gransden goes on to recognize that histories and chronicles in any case tend to overlap. Chroniclers may begin with a year-by-year record, like an annalist, but allow their account to spread when they reach an interesting or complicated topic, as happens in the well-known description of the reign of King Stephen in the Peterborough Chronicle. Also chroniclers may be compiling their text from earlier written records, whereas annalists are usually keeping a contemporary log. One could add other sorts of uncertainty about historical writing particularly emphasized by modern textual theory which encourages the reader to approach any record with scepticism: one historian's 'truth' and 'rational study' may be another's incompleteness and prejudice. A very large amount of medieval writing is, in one way or another, historical and the

---

[4] Antonia Gransden, 'The chronicles of medieval England and Scotland', *Journal of Medieval History* 16 (1990), 129–50 and 17 (1991), 217–43; reprinted in *Legends, Traditions and History in Medieval England* (London, Hambledon Press, 1992), pp.199–238.
[5] *The Historical Works of Gervase of Canterbury*, ed. William Stubbs (2 vols., Rolls Series, 1879–80), i, p.87, quoted by Gransden, p.200.

question of which historical categories one includes within one's sense of the literature of the medieval period is a complex one, particularly if one assumes that narrative includes any text which records an act, from 'the cat sat on the mat' upwards. Chronicles, even year-by-year annals are right up the street of narratology. At their simplest, annals are closest of all forms of narration to the basic definitions of what narrative is. In the Anglo-Saxon Chronicle the annal for 746 reads: 'Here they killed King Selred.'[6] This is a fair instance of a minimum linguistic act that everyone recognizes as a story, even if the nature of the reader's interest is an immediate set of questions. Sometimes in chronicles with the primary purpose of keeping an official record of births, deaths, reigns, succession, and so on, what results is a multitude of small narratives, unconnected and unexplained except by the sequence of time. At other stages the statements are full enough to form a more complex experience in themselves, and also to connect with the other annals that surround them, as, for example, in the following entry:

473. Here Hengest and Aesc fought against the Welsh and seized countless war-loot, and the Welsh fled from the English like fire.[7]

Here is a vivid snapshot of a phase in the Anglo-Saxon conquest, linking with other annals in the sequence dealing with the brothers Hengest and Horsa and the aftermath of Horsa's death when Hengest fights on with his son Aesc. It is all so long ago that one reads it like a verbal Bayeux tapestry, not so much a verifiable record as a strip cartoon of the past.

More developed are the few passages where events seemed more significant to the annalist than sticking to the strict chronology of year-by-year recording: the story of the death of the Wessex king Cynewulf is a case in point. This is recorded under the year 755 when Cynewulf and the Wessex council got rid of the reigning king Sigeberht, whose actions they judged unlawful, after only a year of rule; the aftermath, when Cynewulf tried to drive out Sigeberht's brother Cyneheard did not occur until 784 but the chronicler gets involved in the saga of blood feud and the testing of loyalties and so

[6] That is, as in *The Anglo-Saxon Chronicles*, trans. Michael Swanton (London, Phoenix Press, 2000).

[7] Winchester MS, *The Anglo-Saxon Chronicles*, trans. Swanton.

goes straight on to tell what happened. His account begins when Cyneheard

learned that the king, with only a small retinue, was enjoying the company of a woman at Merton, and he trapped him there and surrounded the chamber before the men who were with the king were aware of him. And when the king realised this and went to the door, he defended himself in exemplary fashion until he spotted the prince, and then he rushed out at him and wounded him severely; and the rest all went on attacking the king until they had killed him. And then by the woman's screams the king's thanes were alerted to the disturbance, and whichever of them was ready and quickest ran to the place. And to each of them the prince offered money and life, and not one of them would take it, but without pause they went on fighting until they all lay dead, except for one Welsh hostage and he was badly wounded.[8]

Matters do not stop there, of course, and next day when the king's thanes who had been left behind find out what happened, they attack Cyneheard who has barricaded himself in the stronghold and, despite Cyneheard's offers of money and land if they accept him as king, and despite the fact that among the men within are some of their kinsmen, they force their way in and take their revenge. The chronicler clearly is interested not just in the dramatic events but in the attitudes of the men on both sides, so much so that his account suddenly breaks into direct speech for a moment during the negotiations between kinsmen:

And they made an offer to their kinsmen, that they could leave the place unharmed; and they said that the same offer had been made to their comrades who had been with the king on the previous day, and that they did not care for the idea for themselves 'any more than your comrades who were slain with the king'.

With such an incident, where this is the only account that exists, the historical truth of the chronicle can not be the criterion by which the reader judges the effect of the passage: it is the story itself and the sense of immediacy, as with a piece of fiction, that makes its point.

As a literary work the Anglo-Saxon Chronicle proves to be no simple example of mere annual record. In the form in which its various texts survive it is a compilation begun probably in Alfred's time, based on existing chronologies and monastic annals, lists of

---

[8] The translation of this and the next quoted passage is mine.

kings and genealogies, and on various Latin histories for its earliest parts. It develops in style as it reaches more recent history, becoming more complex and more colloquial in expression and including some very expansive passages of historical writing, as with the lengthy obituary of William the Conqueror in 1086. It is remarkable as 'the first continuous national history of any western people in their own language'.[9] In striking contrast to the situation in England, where this vernacular chronicle writing is the basis of later romanticizations of history, it is only in the thirteenth century that vernacular prose chronicles develop in France from earlier literary forms such as epic and romance.[10] The Anglo-Saxon Chronicle forms a standard by which one can judge the rather different aims of the Latin chronicle writers of the twelfth century, the period usually thought of as the medieval golden age of history writing.

In contrast to the 'web of fiction' produced by Geoffrey of Monmouth in the 1130s, the histories written by William of Malmesbury (c.1090–1143) and Henry of Huntingdon (c.1088–c.1160) were serious attempts to give an account of English history from the time of Bede to the present; Bede's *History of the English Church and People* (which reached 731) was taken by both as their model. William is openly critical of the inadequacies of the Anglo-Saxon Chronicle in his *Gesta Regum Anglorum* which shows by his breadth of reading, discrimination in his handling of material, and his careful distinctions between what he knows from his own observation and what he knows only second-hand, a conscientious attempt to develop a proper historical method. His knowledge was wide enough for him to be aware of contemporary continental chroniclers and he was well educated and able to use classical historians, particularly Suetonius, as a stylistic exemplar. However, to the student of literature he is interesting not just as an example of good twelfth-century history writing but because he demonstrates that serious history could include lively depictions of character and a good deal of storytelling, often of tales of wonder and the supernatural. So, for example, his account of the necromancy of Gerbert, made archbishop of Ravenna

---

[9] *The Anglo-Saxon Chronicles*, trans. Swanton, p.xx.
[10] See Gabrielle M. Spiegel, *Romancing the Past: The Rise of Vernacular Prose Historiography in Thirteenth-Century France* (Berkeley, University of California Press, 1993).

by the Emperor Otho and rising eventually to be Pope Sylvester, includes the following tale:

There was a statue in the Campus Martius near Rome, I know not whether of bronze or iron, with the forefinger of the right hand extended, and on the head was written, 'Strike here'. The men of former times supposing this to mean that they might find treasure there, had battered the harmless statue with repeated axe-strokes. But Gerbert proved them wrong, solving the problem in a quite different way. Noting where the shadow of the finger fell at noon, when the sun was at its height, he placed a stake there; and went to the place at night, attended only by a servant carrying a lantern. The earth opening by means of his familiar arts, revealed to them a spacious entrance. Before them was a vast palace with golden walls, golden ceilings, everything of gold; golden soldiers amusing themselves with golden dice; a king of the same metal, at table with his queen, with servants waiting on and delicacies set before them; vessels of great weight and value, on which the sculpture surpassed nature herself. In the inmost part of the palace, a carbuncle, small in size but of the first quality, dispelled the darkness of night. In the opposite corner stood a boy, holding a bow bent, with the arrow drawn ready. While the exquisite art of everything ravished the eyes of the spectators, nothing could be touched though it could be seen, for as soon as anyone stretched forth his hand to touch anything all these figures appeared to rush forward to repel such presumption. Alarmed at this, Gerbert repressed his inclination: but not so the servant. He tried to snatch from a table a knife of admirable workmanship, supposing that in a booty of such magnitude, such a small theft would hardly be detected. Instantly, the figures all leapt up with loud clamour, the boy let fly his arrow at the carbuncle, and in a moment all was in darkness; and if the servant had not, at his master's warning, immediately thrown back the knife, they would both have suffered severely. In this manner, their boundless avarice unsatisfied, they left, the lantern directing their steps.[11]

Because he is simply presenting the evidence of tales told by others, William can include a good deal of what one would identify as fictional material: as he says a little further on, 'leaving these matters to my readers, I shall relate what I recollect having heard, when I was a boy' and so he moves into another tale of hidden treasure and a

---

[11] William of Malmesbury, *Chronicle of the Kings of England*, trans. J. Sharpe, revd J.A. Giles (London, Bell, 1911), pp.176–7. In the later edition, with the title *Gesta Regum Anglorum*, ed. and trans. R.A.B. Mynors, R.M. Thomson, and M. Winterbottom (2 vols., Oxford, Clarendon Press, 1998), I pp.285–7. Neither translation reads well at all points and I have, therefore, amalgamated the two. The story was adopted later into *Gesta Romanorum*.

magic bridge, such as one expects to find only in Mandeville's *Travels* or as a scene in *The Lord of the Rings*.

As a recent translator says of Henry of Huntingdon: 'In his world, history was a literary genre and the writing of history required imagination and rhetorical skills.'[12] So Henry composes speeches for historical figures in order to convey their character by appropriate words and style and, like William, following the example of classical historians, Sallust in particular, inserts the material that is needed to bring the history to life. Again like William, Henry liked stories and there are some well-known ones that seem first to have got on to the page of a book in Henry's version, such as the scene of King Canute staging his demonstration that the power of God was greater than that of a temporal ruler by his unsuccessful bid to control the waves of the sea, and the story that Henry I died of a surfeit of lampreys, but perhaps the most obvious indicator of Henry's mixed purposes in writing history is his inclusion of poetry, some attributed to tradition or unnamed poets but most of it probably composed by Henry himself, celebrating individual historical figures—Alexander, Alfred, Matilda—or marking significant events, such as the loss of the White Ship in 1120; his most ambitious poetic effort is a translation of the Old English poem on the Battle of Brunanburh in 937.[13]

I hope I have said enough to indicate that the 'serious' historians of the twelfth century include material that is of interest to the student of narrative: it would be possible to compile a substantial anthology of short stories from the writings of William of Malmesbury, Henry of Huntingdon, and a few other figures such as Walter Map and Gerald de Barri (Gerald of Wales), both of whom were educated at the University of Paris and learned to write polished Latin prose works which included many tales illustrative of moral lessons, the transitoriness of kingly power, the folklore of Britain, much of it about ghosts, devils, and fairies, and even the tales of love and chivalry that one thinks of as part of the history of romance. The twelfth century is a period when there was a vast increase in the amount of story material that was achieving written form and, despite the

---

[12] Henry of Huntingdon, *The History of the English People 1000–1154*, trans. Diana Greenway, World's Classics (Oxford U.P., 2002), p.xxiv.

[13] See A.G. Rigg, *A History of Anglo-Latin Literature 1066–1422* (Cambridge U.P., 1992), pp.36–40.

repetition of the condemnation of fable as untruthful, it seems clear that stories gradually became more and more acceptable as forms of entertainment, even in serious Latin works written by educated men for their peers. As Geoffrey Shepherd expresses it:

It can be assumed that stories of ancient things and modern instances existed in the oral repertoire of many peoples before literacy was established . . . But after a vast accession of story material in the eleventh and twelfth centuries stories quite commonly came to be written down; and the status of story-tellers who can now command manuscripts had obviously been greatly enhanced.[14]

It is in this company that Geoffrey of Monmouth's *Historia Regum Britanniae* has to be considered: it is not that Geoffrey is markedly different from other educated historians of the twelfth century in being interested in stories, in inventing material to fill out the gaps in the records or to give impressions of character, even in including myths, legends, and prophecies. What Geoffrey managed to do was deal with the early history of Britain so that it provided a foundation myth and read as a continuous sweep of the emergence of a nation, coming to a close before the more recent centuries of English history, which is what his more sober historical colleagues understandably concentrated on. It is Geoffrey who gives currency to the myth (which he took from Nennius) of the foundation of Britain on the isle of Albion by Brutus after the fall of Troy and the establishment of the city of New Troy (Troynovant), later to be called London after King Lud; and it is Geoffrey who joined up the discontinuous events in Nennius' ninth-century *History of the Britons* by inventing a long line of named British kings (which includes familiar names such as Lear and Cymbeline, but many unfamiliar ones such as Arviragus, Asclepiodot, and Gurguit Barbtruc) and by creating a pattern from the idea of the rise and fall of British power. The twelve-book structure may indicate that Geoffrey was thinking in Virgilian epic terms, but his narrative is largely composed in the style of chronicle, proceeding reign by reign with genealogies, interspersed with portraits of the outstanding rulers and frequent battle scenes. The only alien

---

[14] Geoffrey Shepherd, 'The emancipation of story in the twelfth century', in *Medieval Narrative: A Symposium*, ed. H. Bekker-Nielsen *et al.* (Odense U.P., 1979) pp.44–57, and reprinted in Geoffrey Shepherd, *Poets and Prophets: Essays on Medieval Studies*, eds. T. Shippey and John Pickles (Cambridge, D.S. Brewer, 1990), pp.84–97.

material is the life history and prophecies of Merlin in Book VII, betraying their origins as separate texts. The climax of Geoffrey's history, and the richest narrative seam in the work, is the story (in Books IX, X, and XI) of the rise and fall of Arthur, seen as king and conqueror, with victories over Scotland, Ireland, Norway, Denmark, and Gaul and ultimately over Lucius, emperor of Rome. The figure of this noble leader, rival to Alexander and Charlemagne, is essentially Geoffrey's invention. Here is the primary source of the vast amount of European narrative on the subject of Arthur and his court from that day to this, and the question of the degree of historical truth in Geoffrey's treatment ceases to matter; it takes on a life of its own and proves to be adaptable to many different interpretations and themes. Modern readings of Geoffrey have come to emphasize the idea that he was writing for Anglo-Norman patrons who were looking to substantiate their own independence from France, and that he was providing a legitimization of the Norman conquest of Britain by portraying its earlier history in terms of invasion and the play of imperial ambitions, with particular emphasis on glorifying the successes of Belinus and Arthur against the power of the Roman empire. It is difficult to see quite how Arthur, the Romano-British leader fighting against the Angles and Saxons, was accepted as an Anglo-Norman and eventually an English hero, but Geoffrey's history, though it ends with the fall of the Britons and recognition of the merits of Anglo-Saxon (i.e., 'English') rule, somehow manages the sleight of hand that makes readers feel on the winning side.

Of the various translations into vernacular languages of Geoffrey's work which soon followed its first appearance the most influential was the *Roman de Brut* by Wace, a Channel Islander by birth but taken to Normandy as a child where, after a period of education in Paris, he returned as a junior cleric (about 1130 when he was about 20) and began to write both historical and religious works. He probably conceived the idea of translating Geoffrey's history in the early 1150s, visited England to learn something of the topography, and produced the *Roman de Brut* by 1155, possibly under the patronage of Henry II; according to Laȝamon he presented a copy to Henry's queen, Eleanor of Aquitaine, and he was rewarded with gifts and the position of canon at Bayeux. In his translation Wace follows the substance of Geoffrey's Latin but elaborates in various ways. He is writing in verse (octosyllabic couplets) and so the writing is inevitably more rhythmic, more decorative, more style-conscious; he introduces new material, most significantly the Round Table, while discarding other parts, notably the whole book concerning the prophecies of Merlin; he casts a veneer of courtliness over the speeches and social relationships and moves towards that urbane, polished kind of romance narrative, where courtesy and knighthood are the dominant forms. Wace is clever enough to distance himself from the material to some extent, introducing passages of scepticism about some of the content, as in the following passage:

In this time of great peace . . . wondrous events appeared and the adventures were sought out which, whether for the love of his generosity, or for fear of his bravery, are so often told about Arthur that they have become the stuff of fiction: not all lies, not all truth, neither total folly nor total wisdom. The raconteurs have told so many yarns, the story-tellers so many stories, to embellish their tales that they have made it all appear fiction.

(*Roman de Brut*, 9785–98)[15]

This follows his introduction of the Round Table and so covers him against possible criticism, provides the appropriate rhetoric for the reader to accept him as a judicious translator but, of course, does not actually get in the way of the further circulation of whatever fictions he chooses to include. Wace tends to avoid controversy, which may explain his exclusion of Merlin's prophecies and which can be seen in his omission of some of the bolder political speeches. Wace's version is as much chronicle in nature as Geoffrey's and the essential features of the events and personalities remain the same, but the effect in Wace is blander and more generalized. One can see this in the presentation of Arthur's last battle. Geoffrey with his usual enthusiasm for battle tactics fills his account with details and numbers, as Mordred divides his 60 000 men into six divisions with 6666 men in each with those left in a single division under his own command; he deploys them carefully and goes round to encourage each. On the other side Arthur 'divided his men into nine divisions of infantry, each drawn up in a square, with a right and left wing. To each he appointed a commander.' Tactics then smoothly melt into leader's propaganda as part of a traditional build up to battle. Wace, on the other hand, reduces this to broad impressions, and does not 'know their number

---

[15] As translated by Judith Weiss, in Wace's *Roman de Brut, A History of the British* (Exeter, University of Exeter Press, 1999).

but there were many people. The king's army was large and he sought
Modret where he knew him to be, intent on killing him.' The difference is even sharper in the reporting of the result of the battle, where
Geoffrey records almost with the eyewitness annalist's zeal for the
specific:

On Mordred's side there fell Chelric, Elaf, Egbrict, and Bruning, all of them
Saxons . . . and the Scots and Picts, with nearly everyone in command of
them. On Arthur's side there died Odbrict, King of Norway; Aschil, King of
Denmark; Cador Limenich; and Cassivelanus, with many thousands of the
king's troops, some of them Britons, others from the various peoples he had
brought with him. Arthur himself, our renowned king, was mortally
wounded and was carried off to the isle of Avalon, so that his wounds
might be attended to. He handed the crown of Britain over to his cousin
Constantine, the son of Cador Duke of Cornwall; this in the year 542 after
our Lord's Incarnation.[16]

Wace is not dealing with the battle as much as with the text as he tries
to convey the picture:

great was the slaughter. I can not say who did best, nor who lost or won, nor
who fell or stood firm, nor who died and who lived. The losses were great on
both sides, the plain was strewn with dead and bloody with the blood of the
dying. Then perished the flower of youth, tended and gathered by Arthur
from many lands, and those of the Round Table, famous throughout the
world. Modret was slain in the fray, and the vast majority of his men, and the
flower of Arthur's people, both the strongest and the best.

Arthur, if the chronicle is true, received a mortal wound to his body. He
had himself carried to Avalon, for the treatment of his wounds. He is still
there, awaited by the Britons, as they say and believe, and will return and may
live again. Master Wace who made this book will say no more of his end than
the prophet Merlin did . . .[17]

Here the difference is encapsulated between the chronicler convincing his readership by apparent exactitude about what really happened (even if he is making it up at that moment) and the chronicler
who convinces his readership by an apparently honest attempt to
make sense of inadequate records. Wace can be detailed when he
chooses, as he is often in describing the places where battles occur

---

[16] Geoffrey of Monmouth, *History of the Kings of Britain*, trans. Thorpe, p.261.
[17] Wace, *Roman de Brut*, trans. Judith Weiss, in *The Life of King Arthur: Wace and
Lawman*, Everyman's Library (London, J.M. Dent, 1997), p.233.

and about naval equipment and storms at sea,[18] but his most important achievement is successfully to have converted a Latin prose narrative into a stylish French verse text which later writers perceived as
adaptable to other purposes. In particular Wace's *Roman de Brut* is
the main stepping stone between Arthurian chronicle and Arthurian
romance, notably the romances of Chrétien de Troyes. Alongside the
use of that material by the next generation and by subsequent writers
of French prose romance, the tradition of writing chronicles of
the whole of British history often took Wace as a base, as in the
verse *Chronicle* of Robert Mannyng in the early fourteenth century.
Continuations of and additions to Wace contributed to a composite
historical tradition, visible in the texts known corporately as the
French prose *Brut* or *The Chronicles of England* which probably ori-
ginated in the early fourteenth century but had been translated into
English versions by the fifteenth; Caxton printed a text in 1480 and it
was by then probably the most widely known national history.[19] The
most significant addition to Geoffrey and Wace that became part of
the traditional history was at the beginning, in a 'prequel' to the
Brutus foundation myth, telling of the establishment of Albion by
Albin/Albina, one of thirty daughters of a Greek king, all of whom
had been exiled for murdering their husbands and who, once settled
in this land, allowed the devil into their paradisal garden to engender
the race of giants eventually conquered by Brutus. This story, adapted
from the Anglo-Norman poem *Des Grantz Geantz* was circulating at
least as early as the beginning of the fourteenth century when it
appears in the Auchinleck manuscript in the verse chronicle known
as *An Anonymous Short English Metrical Chronicle*.[20] That this story
of civilization in Britain beginning with a feminist collective is added
to the 'factual' historical branch of the family tree of chronicle
texts that stem from Geoffrey and Wace provides another interesting
conjunction of fact and fiction in the medieval writing of history.

However, I am not attempting here to give an account of the development of medieval chronicles, which is a huge subject and would

[18] See Weiss, Wace's *Roman de Brut* (1999), pp.xviii–xxiv for a fuller account of
Wace's characteristics as a writer.
[19] See John Taylor, *English Historical Literature in the Fourteenth Century* (Oxford,
Clarendon Press, 1987), pp.110–72.
[20] *Anonymous Short English Metrical Chronicle*, ed. E. Zettl, EETS OS 196 (London,
Oxford U.P., 1935).

have to include reference to other important writers, such as Matthew Paris, writing in St Albans in the first half of the thirteenth century, and influential texts, such as Higden's *Polychronicon* written in the early fourteenth century and translated from Latin into English by the Cornishman John Trevisa in the 1380s, and works of particular literary interest, such as the *Chronicles* of Froissart whose descriptions of battles and pageantry are often quoted, but whose major contribution to chronicle-writing was the use of speech and dialogue in his accounts of events, including conversation with informants and eye-witnesses.[21] The aspect of chronicles that I have been hoping to draw attention to is the idea of the chronicle as a literary form and its relationship to other forms of historical narrative. The story of Arthur and the knights of the Round Table is one of the most widely treated subjects not only in medieval European writing but beyond. It first achieved currency as part of the material of chronicles of British history and the manner and form of chronicle left their marks upon the material, as one may observe in both the verse retelling by Laȝamon and in Malory's prose version over two hundred years later, but most medieval Arthurian texts have shifted from the world of chronicle towards some other literary form: epic and romance are the terms that most often come to mind.

Epic—from *Beowulf* to Boccaccio

There is no continuous tradition of epic writing in the medieval period and study of the medieval epic has partly to be a task of archaeological identification and reconstruction, sometimes hypothesizing from broken fragments what the shape of the whole work

---

[21] See Froissart, *Chronicles*, trans. Geoffrey Brereton (Harmondsworth, Penguin Books, 1968). The authoritative account of medieval chronicles is Antonia Gransden's two-volume work, *Historical Writing in England c.550 to c.1307* (Ithaca, NY Cornell U.P., 1973; London, Routledge & Kegan Paul, 1974) and *Historical Writing in England c.1307 to the Early Sixteenth Century* (Ithaca, NY, Cornell U.P.; London, Routledge & Kegan Paul, 1982). Some English verse chronicles are discussed by J.A.W. Bennett in *Middle English Literature* (Oxford, Clarendon Press, 1986), ch.4, 'History in verse', pp.90–120. A more general account is that by Andrew Galloway, 'Writing history in England', in *The Cambridge History of Medieval English Literature*, ed. David Wallace (Cambridge U.P., 1999), pp.255–83.

might have been. What does one look for?—poetic celebration of a nation's beginnings and heroes, with stirring accounts of crucial battles, conquests, and triumphs, or attempts to produce updated versions of Homer or Virgil, or simply long poems about the past which achieve epic quality by their size and scope? There are various definitions of epic, ranging from the flatfooted ('A long narrative poem, on a grand scale, about the deeds of warriors and heroes') to the flippant, as in Byron's labelling of *Don Juan*:

> My poem's epic, and is meant to be
> Divided in twelve books; each book containing,
> With love, and war, a heavy gale at sea,
> A list of ships, and captains, and kings reigning,
> New characters; the episodes are three:
> A panoramic view of hell's in training,
> After the style of Virgil and of Homer,
> So that my name of Epic's no misnomer.
>
> (*Don Juan*, Canto I)

Byron is describing the perception of the literary epic as it was at the beginning of the nineteenth century at which time Homer and Virgil are linked as the creators of a common ancient mode of treating heroic journeys, battles, and conflicts with the gods; at a later time they are often separated, Homer identified with the idea of oral or primary epic and Virgil with secondary or literary epic.[22] In primary epic the poet is most likely to speak as the channel through which narrative passes, the servant of the story. The subject matter has social and possibly religious significance and the meaning is communal. The poet speaks both to and for the audience:

> Hwaet! we Gar-Dena in gear-dagum
> þeod-cyninga þrym gefrunon,
> hu þa aeþelingas ellen fremedon.

(Listen! We have heard of the power of the kings of the Spear-Danes in days gone by, how the princes accomplished deeds of valour.)

(*Beowulf*, 1–3)

In secondary epic medieval and post-medieval poets usually accept a mould, often the twelve-book, hero-centred narrative of the *Aeneid* with either the poet's own hero substituted for Aeneas or some slice

---

[22] See C.S. Lewis, *A Preface to Paradise Lost* (London, Oxford U.P., 1942), chs. iii–vii.

of history shaped to the design. Primary and secondary ideas some-times meet when educated writers consider classical epic to be the form appropriate to historical subject matter but incorporate features of oral style such as repetition and formulaic phrases.

It is in the study of primary epic that the skills of the archaeologist are most called for. Even to make connections between the ancient Sumerian *Epic of Gilgamesh*, a series of episodes which describe 'a meeting of friends, a forest journey, the flouting of a fickle goddess, the death of the companion, and the search for ancestral wisdom and immortality,'[23], linked by the sense of transitoriness and lament, to the Homeric accounts of the Greeks and Trojans at war and the travellings of Odysseus requires a hypothetical bridge over a huge chasm, and the surviving fragments of later Germanic, Norse, and Slav heroic literature do not provide much more solid ground to stand on.[24] Nevertheless some idea of European epic poetry concern-ing origins and history can sketchily be seen in the few examples that there are.

The sixty-eight lines that are all that remain of the German text known as the *Hildebrandslied* were probably written down about 800 and take us to the heart of a heroic episode in which a warrior, Hildebrand, who had left the treacherous Odoacer with Theodoric the Goth and now returns to help his lord reconquer his kingdom in Italy, finds himself fighting in single combat against the bravest of Odoacer's warriors, Hadubrand, Hildebrand's own son. The father learns his opponent's identity from his opening taunts, which make the fight unavoidable. The fragment does not reach the outcome but Nordic versions of the story reveal that the father kills the son. This episode of Germanic duty outweighing personal feeling conveys something of the heroic view of life, and in its laconic style and terse dialogue suggests a poetic tradition of highly charged heroic lay. Simi-larly *The Fight at Finnsburg* (forty-eight lines) takes the reader into the exchanges between characters in a tense moment dealing with conflicting loyalties. Attitudes are more important to the poet than identities and plot details, and one can only understand the situation

---

[23] *The Epic of Gilgamesh*, trans. N.K. Sandars (Harmondsworth: Penguin Books, 1960), p.22.

[24] See *Heroic Epic and Saga: An Introduction to the World's Great Folk Epics*, ed. Felix J. Oinas (Bloomington, Ind., Indiana U.P., 1978), a collection of essays on epic traditions from ancient times up to some modern oral tales.

because the names can be linked to one of the historical 'digressions' in *Beowulf* and to material in the Old Norse *Atlakvitha* ('The Lay of Attila') and the Old High German *Nibelungenlied*. The background is the marriage between Finn, king of the Frisians, and Hildeburh, a Danish princess; this is the moment when Hnaef, Hildeburh's brother, lodged in his brother-in-law's guest-hall with his comitatus is attacked by followers of Finn who are unwilling to forget old enmities. The subject is the defence of the hall, expressed both by the voices of warriors on both sides, preparing for and urging to battle, and then in description of the fighting which lasts for five days and in which Hnaef is killed. The passage is vividly articulated and its significance is greater than its brevity might seem to warrant: the accumulation of heroic topics—the opening call to arms, the defence of the hall, the deadly feudal rivalry, moonlight gleaming on armour, the carrion birds and the wolf waiting for the battle-dead—offers a snapshot of the *idea* of heroic Germanic epic, as does *Deor*, a poem full of allusions to historic tales of endurance, or the list of heroic narratives in *Widsith*: the mnemonic function of historical poetry is clear in the travelling poet's examples, which include characters referred to both in *Beowulf* and in the *Nibelungenlied*.[25] The fragments of *Waldere* reinforce the idea of awareness of epic in the Germanic world, if only because the same narrative material formed the basis of *Waltharius*, one of the few texts where classical and Germanic epic traditions meet; this Latin epic of nearly 1500 hexameters written early in the tenth century, displaying the influence of Virgil and Statius, tells the story of the Burgundian princess Hildegund and her betrothed Walter of Aquitaine and their flight with stolen treasure from the court of Attila the Hun, only to be trapped by the Frankish king Gunther/Guthhere and Hagen, formerly their fellow hostage. In *Waldere* only two passages of dialogue survive in which Hildegyth urges Walter on and then Walter taunts Guthhere, but these tense speeches could have been part of a historic epic of about the same scale as *Beowulf* and they again presuppose a tradition of epic poems on historic subjects. However, the only Old English epic poem that

---

[25] Translations of *The Fight at Finnsburg, Deor, Widsith, Waldere* and *Beowulf* are in *Anglo-Saxon Poetry*, trans. and ed. S.A.J. Bradley, Everyman's Library (London, J.M. Dent, 1982). *Beowulf and the Fight at Finnsburg*, ed. F. Klaeber, 3rd edn (Boston, D.C. Heath & Co., 1950) is the standard edition. *Beowulf: A New Translation* by Seamus Heaney (London, Faber and Faber, 1999) is the outstanding modern version.

does survive complete, that is *Beowulf* itself, is rather a different proposition.

Although *Beowulf* is full of historical allusions and repeatedly locates its characters in terms of the remembered past of peoples whose origins were in northern Germany, Denmark, and Sweden, the poet uses as his main narrative material episodes of the hero's individual conflict with hostile supernatural forces, rather than large-scale battles or significant milestones in Anglo-Saxon history. Beowulf the Geat crosses the sea from Sweden with a small band of men to offer help to the Danish king, Hrothgar, in ridding his court of a terrible scourge, the cannibal monster Grendel who is attacking the hall, Heorot, night after night. Two-thirds of the poem deal with Beowulf's heroic struggle, first with Grendel and then, when the attack on the hall is renewed, with Grendel's mother. Beowulf's return in triumph to his own country leads to a passage of transition over a period of fifty years in which time Beowulf has become the Geat king and has, in his old age, to defend his people against a predatory dragon. This final battle occupies the last third of the poem. Considered simply in terms of effective narration the best part of *Beowulf* is the central one of the three episodes, Beowulf's fight with Grendel's mother. Here the hideous, bloodthirsty horror of the attack on Heorot and the death of Hrothgar's thane, Aeschere, is immediately followed by a summoning of Beowulf and his men to the hall and a speech by King Hrothgar which combines lament for the death of a noble warrior, appeal to Beowulf once again to save the Danes from destruction, and a vivid description of the desolate landscape where Grendel and his mother dwell. Beowulf's resolute response leads into the journey to the moor and a fuller scene-painting of the gloomy wood and turbulent lake, then to Beowulf's arming, his speech of intention, and his dive into the water, with the climax in the fight in the cave. Beowulf's victory over the fearsome opponent ends in his beheading her and then lopping off the dead Grendel's head. The narration cuts back to the watchers on the shore, where the sight of the blood in the water is enough to send Hrothgar and his retinue in pessimistic mood back to Heorot, leaving only the Geats to hope for their comrade's reappearance. Switching back to the scene in the cave the narrator envisages Beowulf watching the sword melt in the monster's blood, his survey of the treasures in the cavern and his return to the surface, to be received joyfully by his companions and accompanied back to the hall where he gives his account of the fight and is thanked by Hrothgar in a homily on kingship. This all demonstrates the poet's skills in unfolding an event with appropriate visualization, adjustment of pace, mixture of narrative, speech, and description. Though the fight is between a human hero and a fabulous monster, implausible in several respects—not least in the fully armed Beowulf's day-long dive into the depths of the lake—the handling of the sequence of scenes and actions is such that the reader can envisage a full (twelve books, if necessary) treatment of a story of national warfare being conducted in this style. But such epic narration is not in this case part of a sequence of military achievements or political actions, but is put into perspective by comparisons and generalizations about conduct (so that Beowulf is judged in relation to tribal expectations and comparative judgements related to the inherited culture of the peoples) and by the passing over of other parts of the story (especially the period of fifty years of Beowulf's time as king of the Geats). There is a sense that the immediate narrated events are out of step with, even on a different timescale from, the chronicled family, tribal, and inter-tribal history. The fight with Grendel's mother, like the preceding encounter with Grendel himself and Beowulf's later fight with the gold-guarding dragon, deals not with history, which is disconcertingly relegated to the margins of the narrative, but with fable, the symbolic and probably temporary triumph of good over evil.

This was the point of departure for what is still the best-known essay on the poem, Tolkien's 'Beowulf: The Monsters and the Critics',[26] in which he criticized scholars of an earlier generation for wanting the poem to be something it was not, particularly a heathen, heroic lay. Tolkien saw Beowulf not as a remnant of a heroic past but as a serious, sophisticated product from a literate poet at a meeting point between old and new (he places it in the age of Bede). Among the older aspects of the poem one would count the heroic ethos, which is expressed in many different ways, in Beowulf's offer of service to Hrothgar, loyalty to the group or comitatus, the ceremonies of the hall with the symbolic acts of gift-giving from the lord and the

---

[26] J.R.R. Tolkien, 'Beowulf: The Monsters and the Critics', Sir Israel Gollancz Lecture, British Academy, 1936, reprinted several times including in *The Monsters and the Critics and Other Essays*.

dispensing of mead by the women of the royal house, and other ceremonial acts, particularly the funeral of Beowulf which brings the poem to a close, Beowulf's acts of personal courage and physical prowess together with the major act of loyalty by Wiglaf in the last episode as he takes his stand by the aged and wounded Beowulf to help him overcome the dragon. The historical material too, whatever one makes of its relationship to mythic events, continually authenticates the poem. Some of the characters are real historical figures whose deeds can be dated and confirmed, as is the case with Hygelac, whose death in about 521 in a raid on Frisian territory is recorded by Gregory of Tours in his *History of the Franks*. From the background stories alluded to in the brief summaries, in the court minstrel's lays, in the outline of Beowulf's career between his feats at Heorot and his time as the Geat king and so on, it is possible to construct family trees of the Danish, Geatish, and Swedish royal houses and a chronology of the various wars, rivalries, and revenges that leave the Geats at the end of the poem staring war and the threat of annihilation in the face.

The verse form of *Beowulf* is also part of its representative force as an embodiment of an older poetic tradition: the alliterative line in its two halves, together with its use of formulaic diction and phrasing, reinforces the concept of a bardic style of recited or chanted verse referred to in the hall scenes at Heorot, even if the poem itself is a literate composition using these formulae to create an archaic effect; the contrast with the much simplified verse-form used in the later writing down of the *Nibelungenlied* is marked. Ranged against these various signals that might make one read *Beowulf* as a survival from the heroic Germanic past, conveying the cultural heritage which the Anglo-Saxons brought with them from the Continent, are characteristics which identify it as a later filtering of traditional culture through a modified historical sensibility. Most obvious among these are the Christian references which indicate that the heathen past is being reconstructed or at least adjusted. More significant is the poet's choice as hero of Beowulf, who in the absence of any external evidence has to be presumed fictional, and the way in which his career is treated. A third aspect of the poem which places it at some distance from the idea of national epic and the ancestral memory of the race is the elegiac mood of the whole: this is no celebration of the glories of the past but an ultimately melancholy meditation on the attempts of human society to stem the forces that threaten.

At a later stage of Anglo-Saxon poetic writing the contrast between chronicle and epic may be seen in the two battle poems *The Battle of Brunanburh* and *The Battle of Maldon*. The first is included in the Anglo-Saxon Chronicle under the year 937 and shows the application of the traditional poetic style to what the chronicler recognized as an incident of particular significance. In marking the importance of King Athelstan's victory over a mixed army of Scots, Welsh, and Dublin-based Norsemen the poet does not invent any stirring speeches but employs heightened poetic language to report how 'Athelstan, leader of warriors,/Ring-giver of men . . . struck life-long glory/In strife round Brunanburh.'[27] The chronicler describes the day-long fighting, the dead bodies left on the field, the flight of the Norsemen, and reaches a climax in the traditional images of the carrion beasts of the battle-field, 'the dusky-coated,/horny-beaked black raven,/and the grey-coated eagle, white-rumped,/greedy war-hawk, and the wolf'.[28] This is a celebration of victory but no recapturing of the heroic spirit of past times, whereas *The Battle of Maldon* was written in celebration of attitude more than occasion, which was a comparatively minor encounter when a band of Vikings in 991 attacked the Essex coast and sailed up the Blackwater estuary to be confronted by the ealdorman Byrhtnoth and a company of East Saxons. When Byrhtnoth unwisely in his *ofermod* ('pride'[29]) yielded his favourable position, where he could prevent his opponents' crossing from the island in the river, in order to fight on more equal terms, the Vikings killed him. It is not known how the poem came into being: among other suggestions is the idea that it was composed as a memorial to Byrhtnoth at the behest of his family, but whatever the reason the poet saw the encounter as the material for a heroic lay and filled out the events with idealistic expressions of fortitude, identifying the words and actions of Byrhtnoth as in the ancient mould of Germanic battle ethics. So in the early part of the incomplete text

---

[27] *The Anglo-Saxon Chronicles*, trans. Swanton, p.106. Swanton points out the contrast between the two poems in *English Literature before Chaucer* (Harlow, Longman, 1987), p.167.

[28] *The Anglo-Saxon Chronicles*, trans. Swanton, p.109.

[29] Or possibly 'excessive courage', as is argued by Katherine O'Brien O'Keeffe in 'Heroic values and Christian ethics', in *The Cambridge Companion to Old English Literature*, ed. Malcolm Godden and Michael Lapidge (Cambridge U.P., 1991), pp.107–25.

the Vikings' offer to call a truce in exchange for gold is met with a powerful display of defiance from Byrhtnoth:

> Byrhtnoth spoke, raised his shield,
> brandished the slender ash-spear, spoke these words,
> angry and resolute, gave him answer:
>   'Do you hear, seafarer, what this people say?
> They will give you spears as tribute,
> deadly point and ancient swords,
> war-gear that will profit you little in the fight.'
>   (*The Battle of Maldon*, 42–8)[30]

The word used in this last line for 'war-gear' is *herezeatu*, which has an ironic double edge, typical of the epic style, since it refers to the feudal right of the lord ('heriot' in later English) to claim weapons, horses, and other war-gear on the death of one of his tenants. However, Byrhtnoth's taunts turn in the end to the more bitter irony of his defeat and death, the desertion of the Essex company by some cowards, one of them on Byrhtnoth's own horse, and finally to the poem's expression of courage in defeat, another classic theme of epic verse. As he stands by the corpse of his leader and faces his own death, an old warrior rallies the last of his comrades:

> 'Thought shall be the harder, heart the bolder,
> courage the greater, as our strength grows less.
> Here lies our leader, all cut down,
> the valiant man in the dust. Ever may the man lament
> who now thinks to turn from this battle-play.
> I am old in years; I will not leave this place,
> but by the side of my lord,
> by so dear a man, expect to lie.
>   (*The Battle of Maldon*, 312–19)

That this style was still available to the poet and the expression of this theme thought valid at the end of the tenth century is remarkable: the poem is usually seen as a piece of antiquarian nostalgia, since the idea of Byrhtnoth as the leader of a comitatus seems to hark back to the seventh century. Some knowledge of such poetic tradition has to be

---

[30] *The Battle of Maldon*, ed. E.V. Gordon (London, Methuen, 1937); the translations are mine, but versions appear in *Anglo-Saxon Poetry*, trans. and ed. S.A.J. Bradley and several other anthologies of Old English poetry.

presumed still to be on hand to be called up as the suitable mode for epic themes when Laȝamon came to compose his English version of the material of Wace's chronicle in the early thirteenth century.

Similar histories seem to lie behind other major examples of medieval European epic, the *Chanson de Roland*, the *Nibelungenlied*, and the *Cantar de mio Cid*. The Middle High German *Nibelungenlied*, consisting of about 9000 lines in four-line stanzas, was written down about 1200, probably in Austria or Bavaria. Older hypotheses about its origins, fixated on the idea of folk poetry and oral tradition, explained the text as a linking of separate narrative episodes, perhaps originally individual lays, but the time of writing was far removed from any 'heroic age', or period of migration when heathen tribes were living in a state of perpetual strife.[31] The composition of the poem belongs to a period when Christian chivalry is the keynote of the court culture and the poet sounds like either a professional story-teller or an educated and sophisticated cleric. The poem is in two parts: the first tells of the coming of Siegfried to the Burgundian court, his marriage to Kriemhild, the rivalry between Kriemhild and Brunhild (the woman won with Siegfried's aid as a bride for Kriemhild's brother, Gunther), and the treacherous plotting which leads to the murder of Siegfried by Hagen, Gunther's vassal; the second half is the story of Kriemhild's second marriage to Etzel (Attila) and her eventual luring of her brothers and Hagen to the Hungarian court where she carries out her revenge for Siegfried's death. Though the different focus of the two halves suggests that this form of the work may be a composite created from an earlier hero-centred epic tale of the adventures of Siegfried and the material from Hunnish history which we have already encountered in *Waldere/Waltharius*, the poet has worked them together to make a convincing balance, linked by the figure of Kriemhild. A recurrent theme is that central heroic idea of the conflict of loyalties and all the main characters are defined in terms of the moral choices required of them. This too is a unifying idea since the motif recurs even with characters who do not

---

[31] *The Nibelungenlied*, trans. A.T. Hatto (Harmondsworth, Penguin Books, 1965), gives an account of the history of the text in various appendices and includes a long essay 'An Introduction to a Second Reading', pp.293–347, which explores the problems of interpretation. A survey of past ideas about the poem is included in the useful introduction to the work by Neil Thomas, *Reading the Nibelungenlied* (University of Durham, 1995).

appear until the second half of the story, as is the case with Rüdiger, the liege of Etzel who persuades Kriemhild to marry Etzel and becomes a friend of the Burgundians, only to be required later to be involved in Kriemhild's vengeful plan to kill them. The story concerns history, feud, and blood-revenge, but it is also a narrative of character, particularly well developed in the case of the central figure, Kriemhild, as she makes the transition from reticent young princess to the she-devil of the later episodes. It is as a result of such interest on the poet's part that the question arises as to whether epic concern with tribal need has been overcome by dramatization of private relationships: has the history of Huns, Burgundians, and Franks dwindled into family feud? The epic qualities might be thought to be essentially attached to the historical material and the *Nibelungenlied* can be read in conjunction with its numerous analogues, particularly those in Icelandic: lays about Sigurd/Siegfried among the *Poetic Edda*; the lay of Attila (*Atlakvitha*) mentioned earlier; and the prose sagas which tell a version of the story of Siegfried and Brunhild rather closer to that familiar from Wagner's *Ring* cycle (*Völsunga Saga*, probably composed in the late thirteenth century, and the thirteenth-century Norwegian compilation *Thidrek's Saga*).

Apart from the question of sources, the text has inconsistencies. The poet is interested in aspects of pomp and ceremony and includes many descriptions of clothing, with a particularly elaborate instance in the anxiety of Gunther, setting out for Iceland to woo Brunhild, to dress with style, when seven stanzas are devoted to details of his wardrobe. Such courtly interest in fashion sits uneasily with the stark savagery of some of the poem's actions and is one sign of a clash of cultures, which betrays itself as a conflict between *fabula* and *sjuzet*, between the story material and its treatment. The poetic form of the *Nibelungenlied* is another aspect of the work which it is difficult to pigeon-hole: the four-line rhyming stanza has replaced any sign of traditional alliterative metre, and the language of the poem is often rather flat, lacking epic formulae or other signs of traditional stylistic elevation. Hatto identifies a few features as echoes of 'the ancient epic manner'—shifting into direct speech at high points of the narrative, a liking for understatement and a scattering of poetic paraphrases,[32]—and suggests that great epic is particularly likely to result from 'an

---

[32] *Nibelungenlied*, trans. Hatto, p.344.

awareness on the part of a new and more literate age that an old order is passing'. Those who praise the *Nibelungenlied* highly take the view that the poet has made a successful fusion between historical subject matter and a 'modern' style, shifting from the idea of simply celebrating a heroic past to a tense and forceful narrative about the vulnerability of states to disunity and treachery.

At the time when this work was being put together, the main flush of epic writing in France, in the form known as the *chansons de geste*, was already fading. These songs of heroic deeds, of which about a hundred survive, grew up around a number of narrative centres: the figure of Charlemagne and his vassals, including the twelve peers who often play a more active role than Charlemagne himself; the adventures of William of Orange; the Crusades. They had a basis of historical fact but also admitted legend and invention and it seems likely that they were subject to continuous revision by the jongleurs whose repertoire they formed. They expressed the high ideals of feudal knighthood, motivated by the idea of honour in the service of France and of Christendom. They varied in length from fewer than 1000 lines to over 20 000, and were mostly composed in *laisses*, verse paragraphs of unrhymed (though often using assonance in the last word of the line) usually decasyllabic lines, though many were at a later date recast in rhyme and in the fourteenth and fifteenth centuries in prose. The masterpiece of the genre is the *Chanson de Roland*, probably also the earliest and possibly a model for many of the rest.

In some respects the poem is *The Battle of Maldon* writ large,[33] a story of heroism in defeat but here concerning a major war between Christians and Saracens at a level of national pride and security, rather than a local skirmish. It is based on an actual historical event in the year 778 which is recorded in the biography of Charlemagne written by Einhard (*d.*840), the *Vita Karoli Magnus*, which reports Gascon treachery during a crossing of the Pyrenees by the French army in the form of an attack on the baggage train as it passed through a narrow defile. In the attack the Basques killed the royal seneschal, a count of the palace, 'Roland, prefect of the Breton march and many others'. In the poem Roland becomes Frank rather than Breton, the Basque attackers are transformed into Saracens and the

---

[33] As was suggested long ago by W.P. Ker in his classic study *Epic and Romance* (London, Macmillan, 1908), pp.54ff.

situation aggrandized into part of the full-scale campaign of the Franks against the Muslims in Spain. It seems likely that the poem was composed near to the time of the First Crusade and that it reflects the zeal associated particularly with the Christian conquest of Jerusalem in 1099, although the claim made by Wace in the *Roman de Rou* (*c.*1160) that a song of Roland was sung to the Normans by the minstrel Taillefer before the Battle of Hastings in 1066 may indicate the prior existence of some version of the story. The fullest version of the poem, surviving in the early-twelfth-century Oxford MS Digby 23, has some Anglo-Norman features and so may have been copied in England. It falls into four parts: the rivalry among Charlemagne's peers, in particular the enmity of Ganelon towards his proud stepson Roland, which leads to Ganelon's treacherous plotting with Marsile, the Saracen king; the Saracen attack at Roncesvalles and the death of Roland; Charlemagne's victory over the Saracens (which includes the arrival of the Emir Beligant with his army to prolong the battle, an episode that some have seen as an interpolation); and, finally, the return to France and the punishment of Ganelon. At the very end of the poem, as Charlemagne expresses something of the bitterness that the whole episode has left, the poet puts his name to the text:

> 'Deus,' dist li reis, 'si penuse est ma vie!'
> Pluret des oilz, sa barbe blanche tiret.
> Ci fait la geste que Turoldus declinet.

> ('God,' said the king, 'how wearisome my life is!'
> He weeps and tugs at his white beard.
> Here ends the story which Turoldus relates.)[34]

Whoever this Turold(us) was, it would seem that he was conversant with rhetorical teaching and some Latin texts, since, for instance, the portrait of Charlemagne borrows from Einhard's biography. Thus the many oral features of the work, its use of formulaic diction and the dramatic style of jongleur recital, are probably the choices of a literate craftsman deliberately creating the effect of minstrel lay.

Within the major theme of Charlemagne's conflict with the Saracens and the feudal patriotic honour that goes with it, the poet develops a fascinating drama of character and relationships, particularly between Roland and his stepfather, Ganelon, and between

---

[34] *The Song of Roland*, trans. with an Introduction and Notes by Glyn Burgess (Harmondsworth, Penguin Books, 1990), pp.210 and 156.

Roland and his comrade, Oliver. Though the poet provides some kind of motive for Ganelon's hatred of Roland (that he had once tricked him out of gold and other goods), rather as Shakespeare does for Iago, the tense exchanges in the scenes where Roland nominates Ganelon to undertake the dangerous role of ambassador to Marsile and later Ganelon gives Roland no choice but to accept the even more perilous task of commanding the rearguard as the army crosses the mountains, make clear that the loathing is obsessive, that Roland's bravado is, to Ganelon, a kind of insult. The most frequently quoted line from the poem, 'Rollant est proz e Oliver est sage' ('Roland is brave and Oliver is wise') (l.1093) focusses the difference and the tension between the two friends, who quarrel in the battle because Roland will not blow his horn to call for Charlemagne's return; their reconciliation at the point of Oliver's death is one of the high points of the poem and one of the places where the poet's most striking effect, the use of repetition in 'parallel' *laisses*, may be seen in action. First we are told

> Oliver feels that his wound is mortal.
> He grips Halteclere with its burnished steel
> And strikes Marganice on his pointed helmet of gold,
> Sending its flowers and stones tumbling to the ground.
> He slices through his head right down to his front teeth;
> Raising his sword on high he flung him down dead.
> Then he said, 'Pagan, a curse on you! . . .
> Then he shouts for Roland's help.
>
> (Laisse 146)

So we are given one view of Oliver's dying moments, the resolute continuation in the task on hand, with the poet keeping the immediacy of the present tense until the enemy is killed. Then, it seems, he goes back to the point from which he started:

> Oliver feels that he has a mortal wound;
> Never will he have his fill of vengeance now.
> In the thick of the fray he strikes like a baron,
> Slicing through the lance shafts and the bucklers,
> Through feet and fists, saddles and sides . . .
> Then calls to Roland, his friend and his peer:
> 'Lord companion, come and fight at my side.
> In great sorrow we shall part this day.'
>
> (Laisse 147)

Even then the moment is not over: Roland comes, looks at the pale and bloodstained Oliver, faints upon his horse, and is struck by Oliver, his sight too blurred by blood for him to recognize Roland:

> At this blow Roland looked at him
> And asked him in gentle, tender tones:
> 'Lord companion, do you intend to do this?
> This is Roland who loves you so dearly;
> You had not challenged me in any way.'
> Oliver said, 'Now I can hear your voice,
> But I cannot see you: may God watch over you.
> Did I strike you? Pardon me for this.'
> Roland replies: 'I have not been hurt;
> I pardon you here and before God.'
> With these words they bowed to each other;
> See how they part with such great love!
>
> (Laisse 149)

The actual *laisse* (150) in which Oliver's death is reported is the culmination of these overlapping dramatized moments, each of them with the emotional punch in the final line of the laisse. The same technique is used in the treatment of the death of Roland himself, when, as Kermode pointed out in the passage I quoted earlier, Roland dies three times and each time differently (Laisses 174–6). By this effect the poet slows the narrative and gives due weight to crucial events, and by the repetition creates a heightening of significance in a form of ritualization. In a similar way the parallel between Roland and Oliver gives depth to the treatment of war in the poem. Oliver's prudence sets Roland's proud valour in perspective; Byrhtnoth's *ofermod* is translated into Roland's *démesure*, the heroic error of the lack of a sense of proportion. The poem presents a number of other striking characters on both the Frankish and the Saracen sides of the conflict, with the handsome, clever but flawed figure of Ganelon and the dominant icon of Charlemagne, who is disturbingly indecisive at times but in whose authority justice and the sense of honour and hierarchy reside, the names that are present almost from first to last.

The *chanson de geste* is the best-attested type of epic writing in the medieval period, producing this work of great literary power and a substantial body of other French poems on 'historical' subjects in a similar style. The influence of the *chansons de geste* can be seen outside France, in Italy, for example, and in the case of the medieval

Spanish epic, the *Cantar/Poema de mio Cid*.[35] As in Germany with the *Nibelungenlied*, the long-standing explanation for the Spanish poem was that it was the product of centuries of folk narrative and oral tradition, with its composition in laisses and its use of formulae seen as characteristics which had evolved from early orally transmitted ballads, lays, and lost epics.[36] However, the story of the Cid is not one of ancient history but of the adventures of Rodrigo Díaz de Vivar, standard-bearer to Sancho II of Castile, after the assassination of Sancho and the taking over of Castile by Sancho's brother Alfonso, king of Leon, who sent the hero into exile from 1081 to 1087 and again from 1089 to 1092. In the last twenty years the view that the poem was a 'modern' composition has gained ground. Colin Smith argues that 'the *Poema de mio Cid*, composed in or shortly before 1207, was the first epic to be composed in Castilian; that it was in consequence an innovatory and experimental work . . . and that it did not depend on [an] existing tradition of epic verse in Castilian.'[37] He sees the text as 'a kind of *chanson de geste*, an attempt to emulate and acclimatise the great French genre' and the work of a single author, Per Abad, a bilingual lawyer working in Burgos.[38] Smith locates the text, that is, very specifically in terms of early-thirteenth-century Spanish culture to produce another instance of the medieval idea of epic as a creation of a literate author imitating or inventing an apparently oral style. The subject matter is presented as history, with the Cid's capture of Valencia as the major military achievement at the heart, and to some extent the poet is precise about historical events. Many of the names mentioned refer to actual people and there is plenty of local detail in some parts of the narrative, but the facts of the second exile of the Cid, which forms the main material of the poem, are freely mixed with fiction. The poet turns two obscure figures from Alfonso's court into his main villains and invents as a major plot element the marriages of the Cid's daughters to the Infantes of Carrión and the insults done to

[35] *The Poem of the Cid*, trans. Rita Hamilton and Janet Perry, with Introduction and Notes by Ian Michael (1975) (Harmondsworth, Penguin Books, 1984).

[36] A summary of traditionalist views is provided by Merle E. Simmons in the chapter on 'The Spanish epic', in Oinas, *Heroic Epic and Saga*, pp. 216–35.

[37] Colin Smith, *The making of the* Poema de mio Cid, Cambridge U.P., 1983, p.1.

[38] Smith, *The making the* Poema de mio Cid, p.73. Like Turoldus, Per Abad/Abatt is named in the closing lines of the poem and, again as with the *Song of Roland*, he has been taken by some scholars to be merely the copyist.

them which the Cid must redress before they can be more honour-
ably wed and become queens of Navarre and Aragon. Enough detail
of names and incidents is included to give the appearance of histor-
icity but it is a clever construct. The *Poema de mio Cid* is centred on
the hero and the concept of honour. The hero is unusually not a
young bachelor but a middle-aged married man with daughters of
marriageable age and the honour he represents is linked to the virtues of a mature man fulfilling a role in society. He is defender of
justice and family obligation, capable of great leadership but also a
loyal vassal, courteous and generous but astute and practical. In
contrast to the *Song of Roland* this is no tragic celebration of valour
in defeat but a robust success story of a heroic fighter winning back
his fame and fortune. In this respect the poem is nearer to the spirit
of romance.

How far is the case of the early Middle English Laȝamon's *Brut*
parallel to the situation of these continental epic poems? The two
manuscripts in which the *Brut* survives, Cotton Caligula A ix and
Cotton Otho C xiii, seem neither to be much earlier than 1250, despite
the fact that the language of the Caligula version is a good deal more
archaic and in the past was thought to be at least fifty years earlier
than the 'modernised' Otho text, but the poet's adoption of a style
apparently modelled on Old English poetic traditions makes a date
much later than 1200 improbable. Perhaps this English variation on
the epic idea was written about a hundred years after the *Song of
Roland* and at roughly the same time as the *Nibelungenlied* and the
Poema de mio Cid. At 16 095 lines it rivals the longer *chansons de geste*,
but, since its length is the result of the poet's taking on the whole
chronicle history covered by Geoffrey of Monmouth and Wace, its
genre hovers between verse-chronicle and historical epic. Among the
epic qualities is a strong strain of patriotism in that Laȝamon sees
Arthur and other kings as the defenders of 'our island home' and
declares (in his prologue) that what he had in mind was 'That he
wolde of Engle þa aeþelen tellen' ('that he would tell of the noble
deeds of the English'); he shows particular interest in the antiquity of
the realm, to which end he emphasizes English sources (as with the
mention of Bede in his prologue). Whereas at the end of Arthur's life
Wace says that he remains in Avalon 'awaited by the Britons', Laȝamon,
having translated this, follows it up with Merlin's prophecy that 'an
Arþur sculde ȝete cum Anglen to fulste' ('an Arthur should come

again as a help to the English') and, while Tatlock[39] and others have taken this as a reference to Prince Arthur of Brittany (1187–1203), the grandson of Henry II, named as heir by Richard the Lion-heart, it seems consistent with other passages in the poem to read it also as an expression of Laȝamon's sense of himself as an English poet writing for English readers (whether these 'English' were Celt, Saxon, or Norman) about their national heritage.

He also sees his verse as traditional and adopts an archaic diction, showing knowledge of the specialized Old English poetic vocabulary and some use of stylized expressions such as kennings and poetic formulae, though these are merely traces in Laȝamon, not main features of style; enjambement, normal in Old English verse, is rare whereas similes, uncommon in Old English, are a distinctive feature of the style. There has been and remains controversy about the actual verse-form of the *Brut*, which resembles the rhythm and line pattern of Old English verse but does not have a regular four-stress structure with caesura and uses intermittent rhyme. The theory used to be that Laȝamon had inherited a 'popular' form of Old English verse, but that has been scotched and replaced by the (in some respects even more improbable) idea that Laȝamon's line develops from Old English metrical prose. Pearsall suggested that Laȝamon had learnt not only from Germanic verse but also from Anglo-Norman epic style in the *chansons de geste*, from which he might have acquired the use of simile, hyperbole, taunts, innuendo, and some other features of expression.[40] Wherever he got it from, Laȝamon writes with a consciousness of high style, creating his own formulae which by repetition give the effect of an accepted poetic code. He gives variety to the poetic language from time to time by the use of figures of speech, particularly simile. Arthur 'rushed like the fierce wolf when he comes from the wood hung with snow and thinks to bite any beast he pleases' (ll.10040–3). The mail-clad corpses of the Saxons defeated at Bath and left lying in the water are seen as 'steel fishes [that] lie in the stream, . . . their scales like gold-painted shields, their fins float as if they were spears!' (ll.10640–3). The tone can be aggressive, scornful,

<hr />

[39] J.S.P. Tatlock, *The Legendary History of Britain: Geoffrey of Monmouth's* Historia Regum Britanniae *and its Early Vernacular Versions* (Berkeley, University of California Press, 1950), pp.483–531.

[40] Derek Pearsall, *Old English and Middle English Poetry* (London, Routledge & Kegan Paul, 1977), p.112.

and triumphant, full of graphic detail, sometimes with a grim humour as when Uther kills Pascent by thrusting a sword into his mouth and we are told 'such food was strange to him'. Battle scenes and seascapes, heroic boasts and taunts, vivid passages of dialogue (a notable feature, for example, of the narration of the story of Lear and his daughters) continually illuminate the chronicle material but it is only in the Arthurian sections that the note of epic is continuously struck, and it is here that Laȝamon most consistently expands and develops the material he took from Wace and Geoffrey. He creates an archaic picture of a Saxon court with men on benches, wine-bearers, and ceremonial speech, removing Wace's moments of humour as lacking in dignity and paring away Wace's courtliness and chivalry. Laȝamon wants an Arthur who is a battle-leader, surrounded by fierce military men. The difference between the two is clear in the scene where Wace invents the Round Table so that Arthur could accommodate all praiseworthy knights from many lands.

Arthur had the Round Table made, about which the British tell many a tale. There sat the vassals, all equal, all leaders; they were placed equally round the table, and equally served. None of them could boast he sat higher than his peer; all were seated near the place of honour, none far away. No one—whether Scot, Briton, Frenchman, Norman, Angevin, Fleming, Burgundian or Lorrainer—whoever he held his fief from, from the West as far as Muntgieu, [i.e. the Alps] was accounted courtly if he did not go to Arthur's court and stay with him and wear the livery, device and armour in the fashion of those who served at that court. They came from many lands, those who sought honour and renown, partly to hear of his courtly deeds, partly to see his rich possessions, partly to know his barons, partly to receive his splendid gifts.[41]

Wace's urbane narrating manner is apparent even in translation: Arthur is portrayed as a generous, honoured, benevolent ruler, surrounded by fair fellowship, in an atmosphere of equality and courtesy, where the trappings of knighthood—'livery, device and armour'—are valued.

It takes Laȝamon a good deal longer to cover the same ground. Before the table is installed Laȝamon introduces a lengthy dramatic scene which conveys a court rather different from Wace's civilized picture:

---

[41] Wace, *Roman de Brut*, trans. Weiss (1997), pp.50–1.

Hit wes in ane ȝeol-daie þat Arþur in Lundene lai;
þa weoren him to icumen of alle his kinerichen,
of Brutlonde, of Scotlonde, of Irlonde, of Islonde,
and of al þan londe þe Arþur haefde an honde,
alle þa naexte þeines, mid horsen and mid sweines;
þer weoren seouen kingene sunes mid seouen hundred cnihten icumen
wiþuten þan hired þe herede Arþure.
Aelc hafede an heorte leches heȝe
and lette þat he weore betere þan his iuere.
Þat folc wes of feole londe; þer wes muchel onde
for þe an hine talde haeh, þe oþer muche herre.

(11346–56)

(It was on Christmas Day that Arthur lodged in London; then some had come from all his kingdoms, Britain, Scotland, Ireland, Iceland, and from all the lands he had in his possession, all the thanes of highest rank, with horses and servants; seven kings' sons had come with seven hundred knights in addition to the household that served Arthur. Each had proud feelings in his heart and thought he was better than his fellows. Those men were from many lands; there was fierce rivalry because if one thought himself great, the other considered himself greater.)[42]

The company here is much less continental than in Wace's court; Laȝamon later on translates the list of nations represented at Arthur's table and includes Wales, England, Scotland, Ireland, Normandy, France, Flanders, and Denmark, but at this point, when he is creating a dramatic scene, he makes it a northern assembly of proud rivals. Envy soon leads to conflict when food and drink are brought; blows are exchanged, loaves and bowls of wine thrown, and soon knives are picked up:

Þer wes faeht swiþe graet, aelc mon oþer smat,
þer wes muchel bold-gete, balu wes an hirede.

(There was fierce fighting, every man striking another; there was much bloodshed, there was chaos in the court.)

(11385–6)

The scene would look at home in *The Fight at Finnsburg*. With speeches from Arthur the riot is quelled and this leads to Arthur's

---

[42] *Laȝamon's Arthur: the Arthurian Sections of Laȝamon's Brut*, ed. and trans. by W.R.J. Barron and S.C. Weinberg (Harlow, Longman, 1989), pp.106–9. I have edited the translation in one or two places.

finding a skilled carpenter in Cornwall who makes the table at which all the knights can be seated and speak with each other 'as if they were brothers . . . all equal, both the great and the humble'. This is a particularly well developed instance of Laȝamon's moving the narrative towards the specific and dramatic, with vivid, physical detail, individuals named, action violent and emotional; even the creation of the table itself is dramatized through the figure of the carpenter. If one adds to the graphic qualities of the narration Laȝamon's interest in marvels and enchantment, seen in many references to the supernatural, the powers of fays and elves and prophetic dreams, and in his restoring some of the prophecies of Merlin which Wace had cut out, the *Brut* may be seen to be a complex amalgam of chronicle and epic. Its unique importance as an English interpretation of the Arthurian material inherited by later writers, particularly the author of the Alliterative *Morte Arthure* and Malory, is enhanced by its position as a bridge between Old English and later Middle English poetry. Weighing up the claims of the work to be considered a national epic, Barron and Weinberg point out the lack of 'the structural complexity, the variety of perspective, the thematic concentration of Virgilian or Homeric epic' but identify more generally some 'essential characteristics' of epic: '. . . great length, seriousness of treatment, concentration upon themes and values vital to a particular society, especially to its military survival, demonstrated in the careers of charismatic heroes of exceptional gifts and prowess.'[43] Laȝamon's narrative falls into three parts as Byron suggested all the best epics should, and the central Arthurian episode is the nearest to the career of the charismatic hero.

It is surprising that no full-length medieval Arthuriad was written (and that, despite Arthur's appearance in *The Faerie Queen*, the subject was still waiting for its epic poet when Milton was looking for a subject). The nearest to it in Middle English is the Alliterative *Morte Arthure* and it is in the contrast between this fourteenth-century poem and the contemporary English Stanzaic *Morte Arthur* that the difference between the epic and romance treatment of the Arthurian story may best be seen. For the alliterative poet Arthur is a military leader and conqueror whose story is one of battles, noble behaviour, and tragedy; Lancelot is merely one knight among many and love

[43] Barron and Weinberg *Laȝamon's Arthur*, p.li.

stories are ignored; the spirit is ironic and stoic. For the other poet, adapting the French *Mort Artu* into English, the story is about love, adventure, mystery, and magic; the court is the framework for diverse characters and episodes, Arthur a figurehead; here Lancelot, love, and adultery are in the foreground; the mood is melancholy and regretfully pious.

To find Homeric or Virgilian epic in the medieval period it is not to the story of Arthur but to older heroes that one must look. For much of the time Homer's words were unknown; his name was invoked as the chronicler of the siege of Troy, but it was the post-classical retellings of the tale by Dares and Dictys that were the source of medieval versions of the story. It was therefore Virgil's *Aeneid*, together with a few other classical Latin poems particularly the *Thebaid* of Statius, on which the medieval sense of epic as a poetic form was based. The existence of a text such as Walter of Chatillon's *Alexandreis*, written about 1180 and so roughly contemporary with the lays of Marie de France, the romances of Chrétien de Troyes, and the writings of Walter Map, is evidence of the awareness of classical epic among the educated of the twelfth century; the treatment of the heroic career of Alexander in ten books of Latin hexameters is modelled on Virgil and Statius, and its survival in over two hundred manuscripts with excerpts in florilegia and school textbooks[44] show that its contemporary reputation was as great as that of Geoffrey of Monmouth's *Historia*, though it had no long-lasting influence. Walter has been called 'perhaps the most accomplished Latin poet of his time';[45] some of that time he spent as a member of a circle at Canterbury where he became a friend of Thomas Becket, after whose death he returned to Reims where he wrote his epic while in the service of the archbishop. At about the same time Joseph of Exeter produced the first medieval verse epic on the Troy material in his *Frigii Daretis Ilias* ('The Iliad of Dares the Phrygian'), which tells the whole story from the voyage of the Argonauts to the fates of the returning Greek heroes in six books of unrhymed Latin hexameters. This survives in only five manuscripts though at least twice as many are known to have existed and the work was known to Chaucer, whose references to Dares in *Troilus and Criseyde* are probably to

---

[44] As Rigg points out in *A History of Anglo-Latin Literature*, p.156.
[45] By F.J.E. Raby in *The Oxford Book of Medieval Latin Verse* (Oxford, Clarendon Press, 1959), p.488.

Joseph's poem; he does make precise use of the text, particularly in the descriptions of Diomede, Criseyde, and Troilus in Book V. This 'high point in medieval Latin verse', praised by Rigg as 'a remarkable poem and quite untypical of its age',[46] was produced (*c*.1185) about thirty years after the French version of the Troy story written for Henry II's court by Benoît de Sainte-Maure in his *Roman de Troie.* This romance of antiquity developed the love story of Troilus for Briseida and his replacement by Diomedes, together with the love affairs of Jason and Medea and Achilles and Polyxena, and freely invented speeches and soliloquies; Joseph sticks much more closely to the events of war and portrays Troilus as a great warrior. In this instance one can see the academic prestige of the Virgilian epic almost answering back the more modern treatment of the classical material in terms of love adventure.

The involvement of epic in a medieval debate about the continuing validity of the liberal arts and the place of Latin poetry in culture is even more strikingly visible in the work of the great fourteenth-century Italian poets.[47] Petrarch's *Africa* is an incomplete bid for the high cultural prestige of epic achievement: based on the conflict between Rome and Carthage and the career of Scipio, this ambitious venture occupied Petrarch from the early 1330s for about twenty years. It was an attempt to rival Virgil and to provide a combination of the drama of battle scenes, the history and topography of ancient Rome, dreams and portents, a virtuous hero, a subordinate love story, and an allegory of truth. Serious, worthy, and ponderous, it contributed to Petrarch's reputation but has had nothing like the influence or the readership of his vernacular poetry. According to Boccaccio, Dante (twenty years before Petrarch embarked on his Latin epic) originally thought of writing his *Divine Comedy* in Latin but on reflection considered that the old traditions of the liberal arts were in decline and so decided to write in the vernacular. Dante took Virgil not as the model for his poetic form and style but as his guide within the poem, and so produced not an imitation of the classical epic but an intertextual debate with its themes and materials, turning himself into a modern Christian Aeneas and like him descending to the

---

[46] Rigg, *A History of Anglo-Latin Literature*, p.102.
[47] See Jane E. Everson, *The Italian Romance Epic in the Age of Humanism* (Oxford U.P., 2001).

underworld and then returning. And so, as with Benoît and Joseph, there is the sense that in Italy the older academic tradition of epic still had the prestige of poetic laurels to be won even though newer ideas were demonstrating its inadequacy. Dante is inventing the 'personal' epic, an autobiographical and spiritual journey in search of meaning and understanding, a class of poem to which later great works such as Wordsworth's *Prelude* belong, but the concept is closer to medieval dream than to that of the historical epic. Boccaccio stayed closer to the classical idea in his attempt to create a modern epic form in the *Teseida*.

In this last of his early works, written about 1340 while he was at the Angevin court of King Robert of Naples, Boccaccio was stimulated to fill the gap which had been identified by Dante in *De Vulgari Eloquentia*, that is the lack of any military poetry written in the Italian vernacular; he modelled the form of his work on Virgil, shaping his story into twelve substantial books with exactly the same number of lines as the *Aeneid*, but drew the material from episodes in Statius' *Thebaid*, elevating the figures of Arcita and Palemone into dual heroes whose rivalry for the hand of Emilia grows out of the story of Theseus' defeat of the Amazons and winning of Hippolyta and the aftermath of the war in Thebes. Though there are stirring battle scenes in Books I, II, and VIII and a muster of heroes in Book VI, Boccaccio's choice of *ottava rima* as his metrical medium and of a poetic diction that goes with it turns the expression of the poem towards the style of popular Italian romances, known as *cantari*, and the title he gave to the work, *Il Teseida delle Nozze d'Emilia* (i.e., 'The Epic of Theseus concerning the Marriage of Emilia') indicates his mixed purposes. This is not, as Petrarch's *Africa* is, an imitation of classical epic, but a modern hybrid form aimed at combining historical grandeur with adventure and lyricism, and balancing Virgilian heroics with echoes of Ovid and *Le Roman de la Rose*. The historical element is expressed by means of the classical machinery of invocations and elaborate similes, and through allusions to other ancient stories. A learned texture is created both by images drawn from nature, science, and myth and by the prose commentary in which Boccaccio added marginal notes on the poem's meaning and references (shades of *The Waste Land*). About sixty manuscripts of the fourteenth and fifteenth centuries survive, which indicates that the *Teseida* achieved a fair degree of popularity and circulation and it was one of the earliest printed books in Italy, published in Ferrara in 1475.

Modern judgments of Boccaccio's epic have tended to relegate it, in comparison to the *Decameron*, to the rank of minor work. W. P. Ker went as far as to call it 'the first example in modern history of the pernicious effect of classical studies', regarding the 'Olympian machinery, catalogues of armies, . . . elaborate battles, and epic similes, and funeral games' as fussy window dressing which disguised the fact that the story was too trivial to bear the weight of its classical pretensions.[48] He saw Chaucer's abbreviation of the story to a quarter of its Italian length in *The Knight's Tale*, therefore, as a more accurate weighing of the worth of the story—romance rather than epic. Piero Boitani expresses greater enthusiasm for Boccaccio's eclectic mix of themes (love and war), of classical and modern influences (Statius, Dante), of human drama and mythology, praising it, even if its contrasting elements are not always in harmony, as 'a wholly new piece of narrative poetry, poised between classical epic and medieval romance'.[49] Chaucer was obviously impressed by it, even if he was not quite sure what to do with it. He took the description of the temple of Venus from it for *The Parliament of Fowls* and experimented with its neo-classical high style and its mixing of love and war in *Anelida and Arcite*, apart from recasting it in *The Knight's Tale* as a tragicomic romance of chivalrous rivalry, love debate, and court ceremony. It seems likely too that it was from the *Teseida* that Chaucer took at least some of the epic machinery with which he embellishes *Troilus and Criseyde*, from his announcing the subject of his poem in the opening lines to the invocation of Calliope, muse of epic poetry, at the beginning of Book III, and the reference to Virgil, Homer, and Statius as he closes the poem. Boccaccio perhaps led Chaucer to explore some of the classical epic sources for himself and the Troy material had its own antecedents, but to some extent Boccaccio's hybrid epic represented for Chaucer a narrative idea from which he could profit, even if he did not himself choose to embark on a twelve-book English imitation. The several stances towards classical epic evident in the work of Dante, Petrarch, Boccaccio, and Chaucer, from rejection to acceptance, from modernization to selective borrowing, provide

---

[48] Ker, *Epic and Romance*, p.364.
[49] Piero Boitani, 'Style, iconography and narrative: the lesson of the *Teseida*', in *Chaucer and the Italian Trecento*, ed. P. Boitani, (Cambridge U.P., 1983), p.188.

informative indicators of cultural uncertainties and shifts in the fourteenth century. In earlier European epic writing one can identify
attempts in several languages to reclaim some idea of the heroic past,
perhaps in the service of contemporary dynastic quests for stability
and reassurance. The later ambivalences of epic are more probably
related to changes in the audience for courtly literature and in the
occasions for poetic recital. Firelit declamations of memorized or
improvised poetry celebrating ancient heroes may or may not be a
romanticized modern picture of the medieval past, but daylight readings from a book, such as Criseyde and her ladies are enjoying of the
story of Thebes in *Troilus and Criseyde*, are more likely settings for
fourteenth-century epic.

Romance—from Marie to Malory

Romance is notoriously difficult to define, largely because there is so
much of it that it spills over and needs subcategories and overflow
tanks.[50] The central medieval sense is of narratives of chivalry, in
which knights fight for honour and love, but it also has to serve as a
term for historical adventures in a courtly setting, tales of recovery of
lost fortune and of virtues tested but in the end triumphant over evil.
In English the word 'romance' first conveyed the origin of stories in
French and so could apply to any translated narrative, but it eventually became identified with the content rather than the language.
Because the word has continued to have literary currency until the
present day it is hard to avoid attributing to medieval romances the
qualities that it acquired in later phases of its history, sentimentality,
escapism, lack of realism, acceptance of the supernatural, idealized
characters and settings, and so on, but medieval romance is not

---

[50] Whereas in the past scholars set out to define romance (notably Nathaniel A.
Griffin, 'The definition of romance', *PMLA* 38 (1923), 50–70 and Dorothy Everett, 'A
characterization of the English Medieval romances', *Essays and Studies* 15 (1929),
98–121, reprinted in D. Everett, *Essays on Middle English Literature*, ed. P.M. Kean
(Oxford, Clarenden Press, 1955), pp.1–22), recent writers are more apt to say, for
example, 'the category of "romance" is loose and fuzzy at the edges': Ad Putter, 'A
historical introduction', in *The Spirit of Medieval English Popular Romance*, eds. Ad
Putter and Jane Gilbert (Harlow, Longman, 2000), p.1.

necessarily romantic and can be surprisingly prosaic and literal, especially in some of its local details. It was also a serious form of writing, turning away from the emphasis on national sovereignty or tribal loyalty that animated the epic and the *chanson de geste* towards exploration of individual ambition and satisfaction. In locating the beginnings of romance writing Eugene Vinaver looks at the prologue which Marie de France wrote to her *Lais*, as I did earlier in the section on prologues and narrators, and suggests in her justification of her own work a general principle: Marie sees herself in relation to ancient writers as one of those who came later, whose task it is to 'gloser la lettre' (construe the text) and 'de lor sen le sorplus mettre' (add their own thoughts). Vinaver concludes that: 'What a good romance writer is expected to do, then, . . . is to reveal the *meaning* of the story . . . adding to it such embellishing thoughts as he considers appropriate.[51] With that thought in mind Marie's romance narratives, and the kinds of meaning she reveals, may serve as a possible starting point for reading romance.

Marie de France has the distinction of having virtually invented a medieval narrative genre. Though she claims to be translating a lyric source (the *lai*) into a narrative (the *conte*), since our knowledge of the supposed Breton originals is only what Marie tells us, it is her works that are called *lais* and the phrase 'Breton lay' translates into English the idea of 'a love-related adventure of long ago, often containing elements from Breton, or more generally Celtic, tradition, particularly magic or supernatural motifs'.[52] Her twelve lays are all short narratives, though the really brief ones (*Chevrefoil* [118 lines] and *Laüstic* [160 lines]) communicate more clearly what one might mean by a lay, as a subclass of romance, than the poems with more complex plots (*Guigemar* [886 lines] and *Eliduc* [1184 lines]), in which action moves through several phases over a period of time. *Chevrefoil* takes an episode from the story of Tristram (and though roughly contemporary with the work of Eilhart, Thomas, and Béroul, shows that the story is already well known) when he is living alone in the

[51] Eugene Vinaver, *The Rise of Romance* (Oxford, Clarendon Press, 1971), p.17.

[52] Paula Clifford, *Marie de France*, Lais, Critical Guides to French Texts (London, Grant & Cutler, 1982), p.13. The standard edition of Marie's poems is Jean Rychner (ed.), *Les Lais de Marie de France*, 2nd edn (Paris, Champion, 1981). A convenient translation is *The Lais of Marie de France*, trans. with an Introduction by Glyn S. Burgess and Keith Busby (Harmondsworth, Penguin Books, 1986).

forest after being exiled by King Mark. When he learns that the king will be spending Pentecost at Tintagel he knows that Yseult will pass that way, and so he shapes a hazel branch and cuts his name into it; the queen looks for a sign, sees it and stops, supposedly to rest on her journey but really to go into the wood and find Tristram. She tells him to go back to Wales whence Mark will summon him and they part in tears. This poignant, allusive poem does not tell more of a story than an incident in a wood, but the encounter is given meaning by the image Marie applies to the two lovers who resemble the honey-suckle clinging to the hazel. The image is focussed in the lay's title, which in the closing lines Marie gives both in French (*Chevrefoil*) and in English (*Gotelef*)—the naming of the lay becomes a significant expression of meaning. Similarly in *Laüstic*, a story of unfulfilled adulterous love, the sympathies of poet and reader are concentrated in the poetic symbol of the nightingale, whose song is the wife's excuse for rising from her bed in the night secretly to converse at the window with the neighbouring knight who loves her, and which becomes the pitiful victim of the husband's obsessive instinct to capture and destroy. The wife uses the dead bird as a message to the lover who enshrines the body in a precious casket. This too becomes fused with the lay's title, *Laüstic*, though again Marie gives the name not only in Breton but also in French and English:

> Ceo est russignol en franceis
> E nihtegale en droit angleis.
> (*Laüstic*, 5–6)

The association between name, image, and tragic love is Marie's most powerful and penetrating literary effect, showing not only how to create intense feeling in narrative but also a sophisticated literary self-awareness in the framing of the effect within the idea.

In the longer lays Marie is more explicit about the ethics of the love relationships which she explores. Like Yseult and the wife in *Laüstic*, the wives in *Guigemar* and *Yonec* are trapped by marriage, in their cases to jealous older husbands who literally imprison them; they are released into the arms of younger lovers by magic. Guigemar arrives in a magic ship and the romance is more his story than that of the unnamed wife, a symbolic tale of a hero's reluctance to love overcome after he shoots a deer and is wounded but spirited away in the waiting ship, which sails to find the imprisoned wife in a seaside castle behind a marble wall, in a beautiful chamber with a chapel of Venus at its entrance. Guigemar soon turns from a wounded hunter being secretly cared for by the lady and her faithful companion into a wounded suitor, emboldened by love to reveal his feelings and to be accepted as the lady's lover. It takes a year and a half for the husband's steward to notice that Guigemar is being kept in the lady's quarters, but with discovery comes rupture as the hero is forced to return to the ship; the lady is imprisoned in a tower but eventually finds, in response to prayer, the door unlocked, the ship in the harbour to take her away and to bring about a resolution. In this tale of wish-fulfilment in adulterous love Marie shows herself adept at creating what later came to seem archetypal romance effects: a wounded hero and an imprisoned heroine, decorative courtly settings, intense conversations about love and constancy, the power of love and truth to overcome obstacles. The age and tyrannical jealousy of the husband, on whom no sympathy is wasted, implicitly justify the act of adultery. In the comparable tale of *Yonec*, magic wish-fulfilment is even more to the fore, since the young wife of the old jealous husband is from the start imprisoned in a tower and it seems to be her sorrowful lonely wish for love and companionship that leads to the arrival of a hawk–knight through her window to love and impregnate her. The focus here is on the suffering of the incarcerated wife, the malice of the husband (who has iron spikes placed in the window by which the hawk is mortally wounded) and the aftermath when the pregnant wife escapes and follows the drops of blood to the palace where the dying lover gives her a ring to protect her and his sword to pass to their son. The erotic symbolism of *Guigemar* is given a religious twist in this tale; the hawk–knight has, by taking communion, proved himself not to be a demon before he becomes the lady's lover and the culminating scene is set at the site of the father's rich tomb in an abbey, where the story is told, the sword entrusted to the son (Yonec) before the mother dies and the son becomes king. In both of these lays the longing of the *mal-mariée* is answered and, in a sense, condoned by supernatural events that enable a correction of what was wrong, though in one case it is in terms of a happy ending while in the other the reassertion of right has to wait until the next generation.

In *Milun*, Marie's most melodramatic plot, some of the same motifs are rearranged. For twenty years Milun and his beloved communicate by means of a swan–messenger which bears their letters until their son is old enough to seek out his parents and (helped by the convenient death of his mother's husband) to unite them. The obstacle to their marrying had in this case been not a jealous old husband but social difference: Milun was only a poor Welsh knight, the beloved a rich nobleman's daughter, though with sufficient resources to conceal her pregnancy and to arrange for the boy to be brought up in Northumbria by her sister; she is forced to marry while Milun makes a career as a mercenary soldier. The story-material can be made to sound quite close to that of a realistic novel and there are naturalistic moments, notably the scene where the father's fighting the son in a tournament in Brittany is halted by the young man's unhorsing the older and seeing the father's grey hair beneath his helmet, but the long span of time and the movement from place to place make this the least well-anchored of the tales. What registers most sharply is another instance of 'irregular' love, treated by Marie as right and capable of outlasting social convention. Outwardly the woman fulfils her role as noble daughter and wife while Milun follows a path determined by his birth, but in reality she is mistress and mother, Milun is husband and father in waiting, and the swan's flight between them expresses this creation of life across the boundaries.

Marie's women are not always right. The adulterous wife of the seneschal in the 'cautionary tale' *Equitan* ends up hoist with her own petard as she and her lover, King Equitan, are scalded to death in the bath she had prepared for her husband; the mother who had rid herself of an unwanted twin daughter in *Le Fresne* is brought to repent her action and to make amends for it; the beautiful lady in *Chaitivel* who accepts the love of four valiant knights but makes them compete for her is implicitly blamed for the death of three and the frustrated misery of the fourth—again the title of the lay becomes the expression of the poem's emotional core when the lady's 'The Four Sorrows' is resisted by the surviving knight who calls it 'The Unhappy One'. However, the moral themes are most complexly treated in *Bisclavret* and *Eliduc*. The wife in the former is punished for her betrayal of her husband, but the fact that his absence for three days a week is caused by his being a werewolf disturbs any clear sense of what right behaviour might be: does a wife's duty to respect her husband's confidence and not take advantage of intimate knowledge obtained from him by emotional blackmail outweigh the 'natural' objection to Bisclavret's transformation? Or does the noble behaviour of the wolf (the unrecognized Bisclavret) at the king's court expose the actual bestiality of the self-serving wife and her new husband, and so reassert a sense of justice? The eventual punishment of the wife and the restoration of Bisclavret to human form and to his worldly position would seem to say so. The longest of the lays, *Eliduc*, goes furthest in its stretching of moral categories by telling a story of adulterous love from which both wife and mistress emerge with moral credit, and the lay's alternative name is a pairing of the two women. Even more striking than the generosity of Eliduc's wife, when she discovers the affair, heals the apparently dying mistress, and yields her husband to her, is Marie's resolution of the situation in the wife's establishing an independent life as abbess in charge of her own order and its rules. The emphasis in the tale is on good conduct, generosity, and the keeping of faith.

The interest of Marie's lays is not only that of recognizing the formation of a distinctive kind of short romance fiction, with qualities of delicacy and vividness in the treatment of love relationships and courtly manners, but the cumulative fascination of the collection as a whole. The lays form a body of work, provided with a kind of frame by Marie's prologue and by the settings in Brittany, Normandy, Cornwall, Wales, and northern England, within which the range in the scale of treatment and in the complexity of plot material serve to test the possibilities of the form. The non-heroic themes turn the attention of the developing romance genre towards psychological exploration. Marie is particularly drawn to stories of substitution or pairing, as with the twin sisters in *Le Fresne*, the shape-shifting figures of Bisclavret the werewolf and the hawk–prince in *Yonec*, the occupation of the role of sovereign lady for which Guenevere proposes herself in *Lanval* by the ideally beautiful fairy and the exchange of places of wife and mistress in *Eliduc*. The doubling gives depth to the themes of frustration, imprisonment, and desire by extending wish-fulfilment into an alternative reality. Marie's treatment of ethics in sexual relationships and the range of her women characters may be traced in later romance writing in both French and English.

An even greater sense of the literary interest in romance in the late twelfth century is to be gained from the leading individual writer of the period, Chrétien de Troyes (*c*.1135–*c*.1183) who is known to have written for the court of Marie, countess of Champagne, daughter of Eleanor of Aquitaine, and for Marie's cousin, Philip of Alsace, who became count of Flanders in 1168 and who is the dedicatee of Chrétien's Grail romance. His artfully shaped prologues were discussed in the first chapter and the five Arthurian romances which are Chrétien's main achievement are too well known to need summarizing here.[53] If Wace made the transfer of Geoffrey of Monmouth's chronicle material into the courtly French form of a narrative in couplets, it was Chrétien who saw the possibilities of the single tale, created by following the adventures of one knight or focussing on one type of adventure as in his Grail narrative. Chrétien invented Arthurian romance[54] and turned the material away from celebration of conquest and knightly triumphs on the battlefield towards chivalric conduct, the courtly play of tournaments and the relationship between knight and lady. Though his most extreme story is in *Lancelot (The Knight of the Cart)*, often read as the classic courtly love romance where Lancelot is forced to obey every whim of Guenevere, the imperious queen and sovereign lady in the love relationship, even deliberately fighting badly at her behest, it is even more significant that his other love romances are about either married love (in *Erec* and *Yvain*) and the tensions in the chivalric world between the knight's public, bachelor role in winning reputation and the demands of love and loyalty between husband and wife, or (in *Cligés*) about remaining virtuous when love and married duty conflict. *Cligés* (*c.*1176) may have been composed in reaction to the story of Tristram and Yseult and therefore intended to exalt pure love as against adulterous passion. Each of Chrétien's romances has a central quest, though the later romances *Yvain* and *Perceval* show more complex interweavings of plot elements. Monologue, dialogue, and description are all features of Chrétien's narration; sensibility, wit, and irony the hallmarks of his style. His influence on later writers in French is substantial and he is the source of Arthurian romance in other

---

[53] Chrétien de Troyes, *Arthurian Romances*, trans. with Introduction and Notes by William W. Kibler with Carleton W. Carroll (Harmondsworth, Penguin Books, 1991).

[54] Although it is possible to argue, as Simon Gaunt does, that Chrétien 'did not so much invent romance as guide it firmly in a direction it had already taken', in, for example, the romances of antiquity. Simon Gaunt, 'Romances and other genres', in *The Cambridge Companion to Medieval Romance*, ed. Roberta L. Krueger (Cambridge U.P., 2000), pp.45–59 (quotation from p.52).

European languages, most immediately of the German adaptations in Hartmann von Aue's *Erec* (1180s) and *Iwein* (*c*.1200), in Wolfram von Eschenbach's *Parzival* (*c*.1210), and much later of the Middle English *Ywain and Gawain* and *Sir Percevall de Gallys*.

The period in which Marie and Chrétien were writing was the major formative one for romance and within the space of about seventy years (1150–1220) the transition from style to style and from language to language seems to have been extraordinarily rapid. Courtier–clerics such as Walter Map and Gerald de Barri, both educated at the University of Paris and both, at slightly different times, members of the court of Henry II and travelling on quite a number of occasions between France and England, even as far as Rome, included romance material in their Latin writings. So, for example, both Walter in his *De Nugis Curialium* ('Of the Follies of the Court') which he began writing in the 1180s, and Gerald in his *Gemma Ecclesiastica* ('The Jewel of the Church'), written about 1197, include a story of a potential adultery that does not happen, part of the theme of the later story which Chaucer uses for *The Franklin's Tale*. In Walter's version Resus, a handsome young nobleman, is at first repulsed by the wife of Rollo, a chivalrous hero, but he is so successful in making himself worthy of a woman's love by feats of arms that Rollo knights him, praising him so highly that his wife has second thoughts and makes a secret assignation with Resus; however, when the young man discovers from the wife that it is because of her husband's praise that she has yielded, he restrains his ardour, recognizing that 'it would be discourteous to stain that couch . . .'[55] In Gerald's telling the names are different but the point is the same, though Gerald is more sexually explicit; it is at the very moment when the intending lovers are in bed and 'enjoying each others' desired embraces before intercourse' that Reginald (as he is called here) learns of the praise of the man he is about to betray, and amends his conduct:

Then I too will change my mind . . . I will never illicitly love my beloved to the extent of injuring her husband who spoke those praises, and for his sake I will abstain forever from these embraces I have so greatly desired.[56]

---

[55] Walter Map, *De Nugis Curialium (Courtiers' Trifles)*, ed. and trans. M.R. James, revd C.N.L. Brooke and R.A.B. Mynors (Oxford, Clarendon Press, 1983), Distinctio III.

[56] Gerald of Wales, *Gemma Ecclesiastica*, trans. John J. Hagen *as The Jewel of the Church* (Leiden, E.J. Brill, 1979), ch. 12.

Gerald tells the story as an *exemplum,* a 'laudable example of contin-
ence', but both writers are obviously interested in the story as demonstrating a point of honour and courtesy in love such as would
seem at home in the poems of Marie de France and Chrétien de
Troyes. They both tell a number of other stories turning on fine
judgement of points of conduct, such as Walter's most substantial
narrative of *Sadius and Galo* which balances the strength of friend-
ship between men against the wiles of a powerful but malicious
woman.

The movement of entertainment for court audiences of the late
twelfth and early thirteenth centuries may be observed also in the
different surviving versions of the story of Tristram and Yseult. On
the basis of a guessed-at Celtic tale (with some signs of earlier influence from or origins in the myth of Theseus and curious resem-
blances to several oriental tales), the story of the love of Tristram and
Yseult, his uncle's wife, is the subject of the 'pre-courtly' romances of
the Norman poet Béroul (*c.*1190) and the German Eilhart von Oberge
(*c.*1180), the 'courtly', chivalric narrative of the Anglo-Norman
Thomas of Britain (1160s) from which Gottfried von Strassburg took
the subject for his *Tristan* (*c.*1200), and the long *Prose Tristan* (1230–50)
where the story has become entangled in the suffocating coils of the
Arthurian cycle. The texts of Béroul and of Thomas are both
incomplete, so that one can only have a partial sense of the differences between them; nevertheless these are striking. Béroul's *The
Romance of Tristan* consists of vivid, dramatic episodes which focus
on the central conflict between the lovers and King Mark, the
attempts to expose them, and their skill and courage in evading
detection and punishment. These tense scenes of dangerous play-
acting are told in a forceful style, full of exclamations, outbursts,
violent acts, creating a vigorous impression of suspense and danger
which spills over from time to time into the grotesque and humorous.
The poet is in complete support of the lovers despite their obvious
breaches of decency and honour. Much of the story consists of elaborate construction of lies by the lovers, but they are portrayed as
noble and their deception of Mark as a triumph. This moral dilemma
is, of course, at the heart of all treatments of the story; Béroul tells the
version in which the effect of the love-potion is limited to three years
(Eilhart makes it four) which allows the notion that the lovers cannot
help their actions being, as it were, corrected. It is the unconventional,

'uncivilized' behaviour of the characters that has led to its being thought of as primitive or pre-courtly, but the episodic quality of the narrative has suggested a text in which the transition from *chanson de geste* to romance may be identified. Béroul writes in the typical romance form of rhyming couplets not in *laisses* but the sense of treating each episode as a separate unit is more in the spirit of epic than lyric narrative.[57] The *Tristran* of Thomas survives only in a number of separate fragments but a sense of what the whole work was like can be reconstructed from Gottfried's poem and from the Norse translation, *Tristramssaga*, made by the Norwegian Friar Robert in 1226.[58] The Thomas narrative is concerned to trace the course of love, using long monologues to reveal the lovers' states of mind, and to emphasize moral truth, and the problems of contradictory psychological impulses. He is much more interested than Béroul in conduct and the inner life of his characters, and less in action. The potion is no excuse for lack of control in love but rather a symbol expressing the tragic dilemma of the lovers; much of the writing is in the form of inner debate about the tension between passion and abstention or between pleasure and pain. Gottfried followed the lead given by Thomas, bringing the resources of rhetorical training and courtly knowledge to create an aristocratic, learned version of the story, which takes the hero even further from Béroul's athletic violent figure towards an image of the romance hero as cultured and skilled, expert in the craft of hunting as in music, languages, and chess. It is Gottfried who conveys the greatest intensity in the love relationship, to which he attributes a mystical, almost liturgical, fervour, using language reminiscent of medieval interpretation of the Song of Songs; in the idyllic scene in the cave the lovers require no food but feed on each other's gaze, rapt in a beatific vision.

If the original epic motives and situations have become intellectualized by stages in Thomas and Gottfried, they become generalized and blurred into a pattern of knight-errantry in the *Prose*

---

[57] See Béroul, *The Romance of Tristan*, trans. Alan S. Fedrick (Harmondsworth, Penguin Books, 1970).

[58] The *Tristran* of Thomas is translated by A.T. Hatto in the same volume as his translation of Gottfried von Strassburg, *Tristan* (Harmondsworth, Penguin Books, 1960). Friar Robert, *The Saga of Tristram and Isond*, trans. Paul Schach (Lincoln, Nebr., University of Nebraska Press, 1973).

Tristan,[59] which, in contrast to the single manuscript of Béroul and the scattered fragments of Thomas, survives in over eighty manuscripts. Other adventures are woven into the story so that the singularity of the love theme is lost; incidents from the Tristram poems are used as focal points in the early part but the narrative takes on the cast of a biographical romance which includes episodes outside the love story, as with the malice of Tristan's stepmother and his involvement with women other than Iseut. In the later part, influenced by other Arthurian prose texts such as the *Prose Lancelot*, it becomes a Round Table romance with Tristan as a leading knight among others, although there are included lays, sung to the harp by a minstrel or one of the leading characters, which maintain a poetic aspect to the tale. These various narratives of Tristram demonstrate the range of distinct guises that can be assumed by a single plot, though they are all identifiable as romances with the basic theme of love in conflict with duty, and noble characters caught in the crosscurrents of public and private feelings. The tragic outcome of the tale, as with the story of Arthur, puts it into the category of historical romance, with some similarities to the French and Anglo-Norman 'romances of antiquity'.

From mid twelfth century onwards there survive a number of these from the *Roman de Thèbes* (c.1150), the *Roman d'Eneas* (c.1155), and the *Roman de Troie* of Benoît de Sainte-Maure (c.1160) to late-twelfth-century examples such as the Anglo-Norman *Roman de Toute Chevalerie* (also called the Anglo-Norman *Alexander*) of Thomas of Kent. These poems which mingle dynastic history with courtly love and exotic adventure seem mainly to have been the work of clerkly court poets writing for aristocratic patrons interested in ideas of empire and power, entertainingly flavoured with fashionable analysis of love in the courtly Ovidian style. The ancient stories take elements from both the narrative manner of the *chansons de geste* and of *romans courtois* such as those of Chrétien. The heroic past provided a language in which to think of the political ambitions of the present, and the interaction of love and politics extended the historical material. Christopher Baswell describes them as 'the *romans d'antiquité* which consciously occupy a meeting place of history and

---

[59] The Old French *Prose Tristan*, trans. Renée L. Curtis as *The Romance of Tristan*, World's Classics (Oxford U.P., 1994).

the imagination'.[60] A similar eclecticism may be seen in other Anglo-Norman romances from the period 1150–1230, which saw the relative stability of the early part of Henry II's reign disrupted by the rivalries of Henry's sons and the baronial unrest of the reigns of John and Henry III. Romances written for an audience of French-speaking nobles living in England reflected the continuing concern with establishing dynastic stability in the new realm, and with issues of law and government, as Rosalind Field points out.[61] An interest in tales of exile and return is shown is several Anglo-Norman romances, *Waldef*, *Boeve de Hamtune*, and the *Romance of Horn*; respect for law and social duty is expressed in romances reacting, like Chrétien's *Cligés*, to the disruptive Tristram story (the only Anglo-Norman example of courtly romance, *Amadas et Ydoine*, and the *Romance of Horn*).

The earliest surviving romances in English are a miscellaneous group from the thirteenth century, registering interest in homespun heroes who win kingdoms and brides against usurping regents (*Havelok the Dane*) and Vikings disguised as Saracens (*King Horn*), and in young love triumphant over circumstance (*Floriz and Blauncheflour*). Some of the earlier romances, as with *Havelok* and *King Horn*, but also (from the end of the century or early in the fourteenth) *King Alisaunder*, *Sir Tristrem*, *Amis and Amiloun*, and *Guy of Warwick*, are Middle English versions of stories already treated in Anglo-Norman. But it is difficult with the large body of Middle English romances, many of which survive in manuscripts from long after the date of composition, to distinguish a clear line of historical development. There are English romances on most of the well-known medieval themes—Alexander stories, Charlemagne stories, Arthurian stories, and so on (i.e., the three great 'matters', of Rome, France, and Britain), as well as more distinctly English historical subjects (the so-called 'Matter of England').[62] In terms of poetic form there are

---

[60] Christopher Baswell, 'Marvels of translation and crises of transition in the romances of Antiquity' in *The Cambridge Companion to Medieval Romance*, ed. Roberta L. Krueger (Cambridge U.P., 2000), pp.29–44 (quotation from p.36).

[61] Rosalind Field, 'Romance in England, 1066–1400', in *The Cambridge History of Medieval English Literature*, ed. David Wallace (Cambridge U.P., 1999), pp.155–62.

[62] This is the traditional method of grouping followed in bibliographies such as J. Burke Severs (ed.), *A Manual of the Writings in Middle English, 1050–1500*, vol. I, *Romances* (New Haven, Connecticut Academy of Arts and Sciences, 1967). It is also used, with a historical introduction, by W.R.J. Barron, *English Medieval Romance* (Harlow, Longman, 1987).

romances in octosyllabic couplets in the French manner, but also in alliterative metres and in tail-rhyme stanzas, each of which suggest possible 'schools' of composition.[63] In terms of length there are short poems readable at a sitting and vast sagas such as *Guy of Warwick* which might take several weeks.[64] In terms of plot motifs there are romances of child heroes going through rites of passage towards winning a kingdom and a bride, of families disrupted and reunited, of heroines threatened and ill-treated but returned to safety, of exiled heroes returning to reclaim their rights, and so on. All these reveal interesting things about a large body of narrative, almost all in verse until the late fifteenth century when prose romances gradually become more frequent, catering for a wide variety of audiences from the educated and sophisticated to the ignorant and undiscriminating. However, to get a sense of historical development, probably the best one can do is to sample romance at selected points to see what a snapshot reveals.

An impression of romance in England in the early fourteenth century may be obtained from the contents of the Auchinleck manuscript, a miscellany from London, compiled about 1330–40 probably from pre-copied booklets or fascicles made up to order into a composite collection of romances, works of popular piety, and historical and humorous texts to provide entertainment and edification for an English household.[65] This is a professionally prepared miscellany, showing signs of editorial supervision of content and of the form in which the texts were presented and arranged. The contents are almost entirely in English, which is another sign that this is a manuscript for lay readers; contemporary clerical and learned miscellanies mix together texts in Latin, French, and English. Nearly three-quarters of the large manuscript (244 leaves out of a total of 332) is given to romances, seventeen of them, if one counts the two parts of *Guy of Warwick* as a single text. Of the seventeen romances ten concern

---

[63] Couplet and tail-rhyme romances are discussed by Derek Pearsall, 'The development of Middle English romance', *Mediaeval Studies* 27 (1965), 91–116, reprinted in *Studies in Medieval English Romances*, ed. Derek Brewer (Cambridge, D.S. Brewer, 1988), pp.11–35.

[64] Grouping of romances in terms of length is used by Mehl, *Middle English Romances*.

[65] *The Auchinleck Manuscript*, Nat. Lib. of Scotland Advocates' MS 19. 2. 1, facsimile, with Introduction by D. Pearsall and I. C. Cunningham (London, Scolar Press, 1979).

English heroes, as Turville-Petre points out, from Arthur to Richard the Lion-Heart, Guy and Bevis, and many are either given English settings (as in *Lai le Freine* and *Sir Orfeo*) or are angled to reflect the history of 'our elders' (as in *Horn Childe*).[66] He also draws attention to the focus on either English knighthood, with Guy of Warwick's role as a model highlighted by the division of the romance into two and the addition of the sequel about Guy's son, *Reinbrun*, or Christian knighthood in the several romances set against the background of the Crusades, as in the Charlemagne romances, *Roland and Vernagu* and *Otuel*, and in the conversion story, *The King of Tars*. There are several different narrative patterns. The three heroic, historical romances *King Alisaunder*, *Richard Coeur-de-Lion* and *Arthour and Merlin* are evidence of the establishment of lengthy English narratives (all over 5000 lines in rhyming couplets) which mix epic and chivalric-romance modes in a popular style. *Richard Coeur-de-Lion* and *Arthour and Merlin* both have explicit statements about the English language in their introductory sections, as in:

> Of Freynsch no Latin nil y tel more
> Ac on Inglisch ichil tel therfore;
> Right is that Inglische understond,
> That was born in Inglond;
> Freynsche use this gentilman
> Ac euerich Inglische Inglische can;
> Mani noble ich haue yseighe
> That no Freynsche couthe seye.
>
> (*Arthour and Merlin*, 19–26)

In both of these romances the narrative is a loose stringing together of battles, but *King Alisaunder* is a tauter composition largely because its source, the Anglo-Norman *Roman de Toute Chevalerie* mentioned above, is a competent mixture of entertainment and information. This is probably the best example of an English adaptor's ability to assimilate the rhetorical features of the French epic into the formation of an English 'minstrel' style, which can handle not only the bustle of battle but the world of courtly values and romantic love. The editor of the poem sees in the poet's use of such devices as the

---

[66] Thorlac Turville-Petre, *England the Nation: Language, Literature and National Identity, 1190–1340* (Oxford, Clarendon Press, 1996), pp.108–41.

seasonal headpieces, figures of speech, and irony signs of the kind of sophistication in narrative that marks the poem as a forerunner of Chaucer and Gower.[67]

Another significant presence in the manuscript is that of the Breton lay: *Lai le Freine* is a direct adaptation of Marie de France's poem with what perhaps became a standard prologue, shared with *Sir Orfeo*[68] and the basis of Chaucer's definition of the genre in *The Franklin's Tale*; in addition *Sir Degare*, set in Brittany, looks like a compilation of familiar motifs of the type. These poems indicate an awareness of the lay as a distinct romance kind, though the prologue may be intended to introduce the genre to readers unfamiliar with Marie's and other French examples.[69] The tail-rhyme romance is even more strongly in evidence, here associated with pious themes in *The King of Tars, Amis and Amiloun,* and *Roland and Vernagu,* but also the vehicle for chivalric adventure in the Guy of Warwick group and in *Horn Childe.* Alliterative romances would not have been a likely choice for this London collection but they seem to have developed later, with *William of Palerne* in the 1350s the earliest. Also strikingly absent are adventures of knights of the Round Table, though *Arthour and Merlin* moves on from the biographies of Merlin and Arthur to accounts of campaigns and conquest for others, with Gawain as the leading knight. The version of the Tristram story, *Sir Tristrem,* a condensation of the narrative in an elaborate eleven-line stanza, caters less for an interest in intensities of feeling than in a hero's complete life story (Tristrem too is identified as an English knight when caught up in Irish politics), with many changes of scene, dramatic incidents and sudden transitions. Despite the unusual verse form, the treatment makes the story more similar than likely to aspects of *Horn Childe* and *Floriz and Blauncheflour.* There is thus quite a wide range of narrative types, in terms of theme, length, and form, which one presumes current in the early fourteenth century; in this collection the favoured elements include sentiment and piety, patriotism and Christian idealism.

Fifty years later *The Canterbury Tales* provides a strikingly different

---

[67] G.V. Smithers (ed.), *Kyng Alisaunder,* EETS OS 237 (London, Oxford U.P., 1957), pp.28–40.

[68] The beginning of this poem is actually missing in the manuscript but the prologue occurs in other texts of the poem.

[69] For discussion see Archibald, 'The Breton lay'.

perspective, expressing questions of critical taste and the division between educated, literary ideas of romance and what was acceptable to a bourgeois audience. At first glance Chaucer is dismissive of romance and scornful of its popular forms; his comment in *The Nun's Priest's Tale* that the story of Lancelot is something that 'wimmen holde in ful greet reverence' recognizes Arthurian romances as a type but one not worth serious attention, and the Wife of Bath's contrast between the old days of King Arthur when fairies were dancing in the meads and the present when only friars are lurking in the bushes labels Arthurian romance as nostalgic, supernatural make-believe out of touch with the real world. It is the parody of romance in *Sir Thopas* that brings the whole genre into question, exposing the narrative clichés of tales of chivalrous heroes, and mentioning several whose stories occur in the Auchinleck collection— Bevis, Guy, Horn; a host of other Middle English romances have been suggested as Chaucer's targets, *Sir Isumbras, Torrent of Portyngale, Ipomedon*, the romances of Thomas Chester, and so on. On this evidence Chaucer despised the hack-work of contemporary romancers, but on the other hand his easy mixture of literary and everyday language shows that he had absorbed their colloquial narrative style. Several critics have shown that even high style works of Chaucer such as *The Knight's Tale* and *Troilus and Criseyde* are full of allusions to romances and qualities of expression that echo them.[70] As I suggested in an earlier chapter, *Sir Thopas* focusses on romance as a genre, helps to identify it as one of the main ingredients in the narrative medley of *The Canterbury Tales*, and suggests standards by which the reader is encouraged to judge the other romance tales which Chaucer includes. The prologue to *The Franklin's Tale* draws attention to the fact that the narrative is offered as a sample of the Breton lay and even the Wife of Bath's comments on Arthuriana invite a reading of Chaucer's version of the story of the 'loathly lady' as a demonstration of narrative mannerism, a joking version of the *roman courtois* debate about love and honour and the relationship between the sexes, deliberately adapted in this case to form an extension to the digressive, colloquial, and biassed prologue. In fact all Chaucer's romances may be seen as

---

[70] For example, B.A. Windeatt, 'Troilus and the disenchantment of romance', in *Studies in Medieval English Romances*, ed. Derek Brewer (Cambridge, D.S. Brewer, 1988), pp.129–47.

demonstration pieces, chosen to represent narrative types and they are all identified by their narrators as literary texts in which the audience's interest is invited in the way the narrative is being conducted and how it should be received.

This is most obviously so in *The Clerk's Tale*, Chaucer's assault on the romance of tested virtue, where Petrarch's version is identified in the prologue and where the epilogue encourages the reader to engage in debate about the morality of the tale and its contradiction of real experience. The lengthy prologue to *The Man of Law's Tale*, which may mark this as one of the first of the Canterbury series when Chaucer was still working out how to compile his collection, directs the reader to compare his highly rhetorical telling of the tale of Constance to the contemporary work of Gower, whose own adaptation of the story in Book II of *Confessio Amantis* was, like Chaucer's, based on Nicholas Trevet's moralistic version of this widely diffused story, which is also the subject of the romance *Emaré*. Similar audience awareness and textual manipulation is a feature of all of Chaucer's Boccaccio-based romances, *The Franklin's Tale, Troilus and Criseyde*, and *The Knight's Tale*, all three of which absorb features of French courtly *dits amoreux* into their narrative, in the form of complaint and debate in particular. Even in Chaucer's most original, though unfinished, romance, *The Squire's Tale*, the mixture of exotic settings, magic, courtly grandeur, and pathos invites recognition of the tale as a composite of textual devices, far removed from any idea of a simple demonstration of a hero's prowess and truth. Chaucer's romances are a major fourteenth-century achievement in the genre, based on but deliberately distanced from contemporary forms of popular romance; they explore the genre's interest in morality, idealism, and sensibility. Though Chaucer shows little interest in some central romance themes—recovery of a lost kingdom, a young hero's chivalrous winning of his spurs and a bride, and so on—he raises the level of English romance writing, sharing with some contemporary writers, Gower and the authors of *Sir Gawain and the Green Knight* and the Alliterative *Morte Arthure*, the ability to see in the genre the possibilities for subtlety and depth of meaning.

Nearly a hundred years after *The Canterbury Tales* Malory put together his *Morte Darthur*, a major influence on writers ever since as a classic summing-up of the Arthurian tales and a translation into the form most familiar to post-medieval readers of fiction, the long prose narrative. The publication of Malory's work by Caxton associates it with other prose romances which he translated and printed, such as *The Foure Sonnes of Aymon* (a tale harking back to the time of Charlemagne's son) or *Blanchardyn and Eglantine* (with its origin in a thirteenth-century French imitation of Chrétien), and therefore with the vogue for prose romance on old-fashioned themes at the court of Philip of Burgundy in mid-century.[71] By the end of the fifteenth century this was becoming the normal form for romance in English, although verse romances were still being copied and most of the texts of Middle English romances survive in fifteenth-century manuscripts. In addition new verse romances were still being composed. A distinctive form of late verse romance, of which *The Squire's Tale* is perhaps the earliest example, is found in a group of poems christened by Wells 'Composites of Courtly Romance',[72] *Sir Degrevant, Generydes, The Squire of Low Degree*, and a few others, none of which represents any particular branch of subject matter, but which consist of narrative elements 'derived from sophisticated courtly romances'. They could be said to provide evidence of how familiar the horizons of expectation for romance had become, though as with the *Morte Darthur* they represent the closing stages of the medieval literary tradition.

Malory's work is well known and some discussion of the Arthurian cycles is included in the later chapter concerning tale collections, but it is appropriate to ask, before leaving the subject of romance, how Malory fits into the genre. Was Malory writing romance, or reverting to chronicle? The table of contents suggests both, and that the *Morte Darthur* may be seen as a prose version of the 'composite of courtly romance', with sections devoted to the adventures of individual knights—Lancelot, Gareth, Tristram—cheek by jowl with the chronicle material of Arthur's conflict with Lucius and the final civil war, with the Grail quest tucked in for good measure. However, Malory's treatment of his mixed material raises questions. Terence McCarthy among others has pointed out how Malory shaved much of his material of what might be considered the central romance qualities in

---

[71] See Margaret Schlauch, *Antecedents of the English Novel, 1400–1600* (Warsaw: Polish Scientific Publishers; London, Oxford U.P., 1963), especially ch. iii 'The late phase of medieval romance'.

[72] J.E. Wells, *A Manual of the Writings in Middle English, 1050–1400* (New Haven, Yale U.P., 1926), p.141.

his sources, especially aspects of the tales which deal with private feeling and identity. As he says: 'In *Le Morte Darthur* we are rarely privy to the characters' thoughts and feelings; Malory keeps us at a distance, [as] he keeps his characters at a distance from one another.'[73] He focusses on public events, gives characters their public titles and dignities; so it is always 'Queen/Dame Guenevere' after her marriage and Malory never gets to the point of admitting that she was Lancelot's mistress. It has often been noted that Malory's prose style is modelled on that of chronicles,[74] and McCarthy argues that 'he may have sought to invigorate his material by stripping away the excessive concern with sentiment and by turning back to older, more sturdy modes of perception.'[75] The chronicle style, tending to a succession of statements of equal weight with limited use of subordinate clauses, has sometimes been seen as a primitive or crude way of writing, but Jeremy Smith argues that, far from using a simple-minded mode with little consciousness of style, Malory is constantly exercising stylistic choice in his adaptation of his source material, and that such syntax is not a limited kind of expression but has positive stylistic benefits: 'The paratactic style is intensely audience-centred in that, avoiding making causal relationship overt, it leaves the audience to draw its own conclusions ... Malory is claiming for himself the traditional role of the romancer: the enunciator of his audience's ethical ideology.'[76] It is in this non-subordinating presentation that Malory's availability to readers of the many generations since may be said to lie, since there is a communal acceptability to it, augmented by the use of direct speech to give dramatic immediacy to the action.

As significant as Malory's reduction of the expressed sentiments of his characters and his choice of laconic, factual narration is the structure and design of the narrative sequence. From the multiplicity of adventures and characters in the middle books, which works well to convey the cross-currents in the chivalric world, Malory moves to

---

[73] Terence McCarthy, '*Le Morte Darthur* and romance', in *Studies in Medieval English Romances*, ed. Derek Brewer (Cambridge, D.S. Brewer, 1991), pp.148–75 (quotation from p.153).

[74] As in P.J.C. Field, *Romance and Chronicle: A Study of Malory's Prose Style* (London, Barrie & Jenkins, 1971).

[75] McCarthy, '*Le Morte Darthur* and romance', p.174.

[76] Jeremy Smith, 'Language and style in Malory', in *A Companion to Malory*, eds. Elizabeth Archibald and A.S.G. Edwards (Cambridge, D.S. Brewer, 1996), pp.97–113 (quotation from p.104).

more sharply focussed narrative in his last two books. In Book VII after the episodes of the poisoned apple and the Fair Maid of Astolat's doomed love for Lancelot, both drawn from the main source material in the French *Mort Artu* and the English Stanzaic *Morte Arthur*, Malory inserts in succession the Great Tournament (his own invention), the story of Lancelot as 'the Knight of the Cart' (from the Prose *Lancelot*), and the great set piece of 'The Healing of Sir Urry' (source unknown). This is no simple chronicling of historical events but a selection of narrative material designed, on the one hand, to emphasize Lancelot's loyalty and virtue and his relationship to Guenevere and, on the other, to recapitulate the picture of the whole Round Table, the virtues of good fellowship and the principles of chivalry. Memories of the past and the mustering of knights in the last episode celebrate 'noblesse' at the same time as events around Lancelot and Guenevere are increasing in tension and the cracks in the society are beginning to show. In the last book, where these splits grow wider and the pace increases towards war, tragedy and closure, Malory responds to the subject matter by creating full-scale dramatic scenes at the Siege of Joyous Gard and Lancelot's return of Guenevere to Carlisle, in which description of settings, substantial speeches, and shorter, bitter exchanges allow enough narrative space to show in action the dilemmas of the three main characters, Gawain, Lancelot, and Arthur. At the end, Malory's invention of Ector's tribute to Lancelot equally shows him finding the rhetorical flourish that the material needs for its emotional power to work.

Malory's going back for his story to the French Vulgate Cycle of over two centuries before might be thought to indicate that the tradition of medieval romance had come to its end, and that the stories of chivalry had by the late fifteenth century become an antiquarian matter. But his influence on later writers suggests rather that he was far enough from the original creation of the stories to have a strong nostalgia for what they represented and to realize that the best way of retelling them so that they would communicate their idealistic concept of a non-existent chivalric world was to treat the whole subject as historical fact. Malory presents the most contradictory version of that medieval conflict between fiction and truth, an absolute conviction of manner with almost complete unreality of content. Though it may seem difficult to accommodate Marie de France's small-scale stories and Malory's sprawling sequence within the same genre, the celebration of the values of chivalry and love is a central theme for both. Marie conveyed her version through the imagery and allusiveness of the lay, Malory through the paratactic prose chronicling of apparently real events. Both find ways of expressing kinds of truth, whether or not they are reporting true history.

5

Comic tales

From fabliau to novella

Modern discussion of medieval comedy tends to focus on Mikhail Bakhtin's theories of the carnivalesque, expressed in several of his writings but particularly in his study of Rabelais. Bakhtin describes medieval men as existing simultaneously in two lives, the official and the carnival life: 'Two aspects of the world, the serious and laughing aspect, coexisted in their consciousness.'[1] Because he sets up a constant opposition between the carnival spirit and the world of gloom and seriousness (which naturally includes the teachings of the medieval church) Bakhtin identifies comedy as expressing itself in antithetical forms, particularly parody, and he characterizes medieval writing as the 'laughing, parodic-travestying literature of the Middle Ages'. Among classical influences on medieval forms of expression he looks to Menippean satire and the tradition of Roman Saturnalia to explain the mocking humour of turning things upside down. Parody is, in Bakhtin's terms, a meeting of two styles, or two languages, and medieval narratives are often stylistic hybrids:

Every type of stylistic hybrid is more or less dialogized. This means that the languages that are crossed in it relate to each other as do rejoinders in a dialogue; there is an argument between languages, an argument between styles . . . But it is not a dialogue in the narrative sense . . . rather a dialogue between points of view, each with its own concrete language that cannot be translated into the other.[2]

---

[1] M.M. Bakhtin, *Rabelais and His World* (1966), trans. H. Iswolsky (Bloomington, Ind., Indiana U.P., 1984), p.96.

[2] M.M. Bakhtin, 'From the prehistory of novelistic discourse' (probably written in 1940 but published in Russia in 1967), in *The Dialogic Imagination: Four Essays*, trans. Caryl Emerson and Michael Holquist (Austin, University of Texas Press, 1981).

Chaucer's placing of *The Knight's Tale* and *The Miller's Tale* side by side at the head of his narrative series in *The Canterbury Tales* seems an example of medieval narrative particularly responsive to interpretation in Bakhtin's dialogic terms of one piece of writing reacting to another and the serious and comic standing cheek by jowl, and in this case the dialogue is an argument between genres and the languages appropriate to each. But how far do the particular narrative genres used in the medieval period or the theories of comedy of which medieval writers were conscious correspond to this twentieth-century conception of the contraries within 'Gothic' style?

Umberto Eco in *The Name of the Rose* has an idea in tune with Bakhtin's when he imagines a medieval manuscript of a book of devotion which has been provided by its illuminator with a richness of marginal fantasy, where with impressive vivacity are depicted imaginary monsters and human–animal hybrids, together with bustling scenes of rustic life:

This was a psalter in whose margins was delineated a world reversed with respect to the one to which our senses have accustomed us. As if at the border of a discourse . . . of truth, there proceeded . . . a discourse of falsehood on a topsy-turvy universe.

(*The Name of the Rose*, First Day)

However, a more complex exploration of medieval comedy follows and when the main character, William of Baskerville, at last gets his hands on the book which has been the object of much curiosity and deadly stealth, the supposed second book of Aristotle's *Poetics*, he no longer really needs to read what Aristotle had to say about comedy, because he could form a hypothesis about its content from reading other books; so, in William's voice, Eco fictionalizes his own intelligent guesses about the ancient theory of comedy.

'Gradually this second book took shape in my mind as it had to be. I could tell you almost all of it, without reading the pages that were meant to poison me. Comedy is born from the *komai*—that is, from the peasant villages—as a joyous celebration after a meal or feast. Comedy does not tell of famous and powerful men, but of base and ridiculous creatures, though not wicked; and it does not end with the death of the protagonists. It achieves the effect of the ridiculous by showing the defects and vices of ordinary men. Here Aristotle sees the tendency to laughter as a force for good, which can also have an instructive value: through witty riddles and unexpected metaphors, though it tells us things differently from the way they are, as if it were lying, it actually obliges us to examine them more closely, and it makes us say: Ah, this is just how things are, and I didn't know it. Truth reached by depicting men and the world as worse than they are or than we believe them to be, worse in any case than the epics, the tragedies, lives of the saints have shown them to us.'

(*The Name of the Rose*, Seventh Day)

Eco picks up from the explanation of Dante's intentions in his *Divina Commedia* provided in the *Epistle to Can Grande* the medieval etymology of 'comedy' from *comos*, 'a village' and *oda*, 'a song', but combines it with the preferred modern alternative *komos*, 'revel' or 'merrymaking'. This notion of rustic song is related in the text to the idea that it is appropriate to use a humble style, 'lax and unpretending' (that is the vulgar tongue 'in which women and children speak', in contrast to the use of Latin and the lofty style appropriate to tragedy) for a narrative which begins with misfortune in the *Inferno* and concludes with happiness in the *Paradiso*. Eco also includes the classical idea of the corrective power of laughter, expressed by Horace among others. Dante in his turn had absorbed the terms of the medieval rhetoricians. John of Garland in his *Parisiana Poetria* offers the 'peasant song' etymology as justifying comedy's treatment of low and humorous matter and though he was thinking primarily of Roman drama he describes a typical comedy in terms which come near to medieval narratives:

A correct comedy has the following cast: a husband and a wife, an adulterer and the adulterer's accomplice (or his critic) and the adulteress's servant or the husband's servant ... A comedy is a humorous poem beginning in sadness and ending in joy ...[3]

John also identifies comedy as the kind of narrative that belongs in the Ciceronian category of *argumentum*, that is dealing with events which are fictitious but plausible, 'a realistic fiction'. John's definitions apply to many of the individual examples of comic tales that one finds in medieval collections and even to the more literary versions used by Boccaccio and Chaucer. Boccaccio's own comments on comedy provide an interesting mixture of his thoughts on Dante's definition of comedy and his own practice. He explains realistic fiction in terms similar to those of John of Garland: 'comedies recount things which never chanced to happen, although they are not so

---

[3] John of Garland, *Parisiana Poetria*, ch. 4, p.81.

diverse from the habits of men that they may not have happened'.[4] How far this covers the range of effects and types used by medieval authors will perhaps be apparent in the examination of some of them.

The comic tales which Chaucer wrote for his less refined pilgrims, Miller, Reeve, Cook, and Shipman, are usually known as fabliaux and so identified with thirteenth- and fourteenth-century French tales of adultery, tricks and deceits, slapstick revenges, outwittings for money, and the like. The tales that he devised for his Friar and Summoner, which also turn on tricks and rely on effects of broad, physical comedy, belong to the same stock of comic narratives. The French tales, of which over 150 survive, are short, humorous but callous, often indecent tales in verse, dealing with middle- and low-class characters. The fabliau is usually a fairly brief narrative and the plot is simple in nature, often little more than a joke rebounding on its perpetrator. The favourite topic is sex and the characters often consist of husband, wife and lover or father, daughter and lover; the main alternative is lavatorial joking. There is a continuing debate about the likely audience for fabliaux: Bédier (1895) thought of it as a bourgeois form but the more authoritative treatment of the subject by Nykrog (1957) shifted attention to the idea of an aristocratic audience and part of the pleasure the element of parody of romance in the fabliau treatment of love and sex; Muscatine (1986) in turn related medieval interest in compiling collections of fabliaux to the growth of urban culture and commercialism and others have seen the emphasis on ambition and profit in fabliau plots as in tune with an increase in emancipation of the peasantry and in literacy of the bourgeoisie.[5] Some of them look like professional compositions, perhaps collected by jongleurs to be used as entertainment, whether in private houses or in public places, and some of the manuscripts may represent working notebooks, compiled piecemeal rather than designed, as others were, as tale collections. The word *fablel/fabliaus*, used as a label in tales from Picardy in the thirteenth century though not generally

---

[4] In the prologue to his *Esposizioni sopra La Comedia di Dante*, trans. N.S. Thompson in his *Chaucer, Boccaccio, and the Debate of Love* (Oxford, Clarendon Press, 1996), p.180.

[5] The works referred to are Jean Bédier, *Les Fabliaux*, 2nd edn (Paris, Champion 1895); P. Nykrog, *Les Fabliaux* (Copenhagen, Ejner Munksgaard 1957); Charles Muscatine, *The Old French Fabliaux* (New Haven, Yale U. P., 1986).

until post-medieval times, is derived from *fabula/fable* and has become a useful pigeon-hole by which one can distinguish between 'contes à rire en vers', as Bédier famously called them, whose morality, if there is any, is rough and ready, and *exemplum* and fable which shape their anecdotes of everyday life to a didactic purpose.

The written versions of French fabliaux are often given a conventional moral as a way of bringing the tale to a close: so the tale of *Les Trois Boçus* ('The Three Hunchbacks')[6] is rounded off by the apparent lesson:

> Honiz soit li hons, quels qu'il soit,
> Qui trop prise mauvès deniers . . .

(Shame on any man, whoever he may be, who cares too much for sinful money.)

But, as Muscatine points out, the story itself suggests that money can buy anything.[7] The tale is typically of town life and the beautiful young wife of an ugly husband, in this case a rich hunchback who gets the lovely bride by means of his wealth but thereafter is never free of jealous anxiety, so much so that he keeps his doors locked and sits on the threshold. Only at Christmas do events take a turn, when three hunchbacks arrive to claim some hospitality and the master of the house, who is no miser, entertains them well, gives them money, but then clears them out, forbidding them ever to enter his house again on pain of a ducking in the river that runs nearby. The wife, starved of pleasure, when the husband for once goes out, has the three brought back to sing for her and to make merry, but she has hastily to find a hiding place for them on the husband's unexpected return, and crams them into the three sections of a large box bed which stands near the fire. Up to this point the story has been developing on reasonably plausible lines, given the circumstances, but fabliau thrives on confusion, exaggeration, and elements of mechanistic plot construction, often building towards farce and mayhem. When the husband leaves her, the wife finds all three hunchbacks have suffocated and she desperately offers thirty pounds to a passing, young street porter to do a job for her—that is, to throw a corpse into the river.

---

[6] A thirteenth-century fabliau attributed to one Durand: edited in R.C. Johnston and D.D.R. Owen, *Fabliaux* (Oxford, Blackwell, 1957); trans. Peter Rickard in *Medieval Comic Tales*, ed. Derek Brewer, 2nd edn (Cambridge, D.S. Brewer, 1996), pp.5–8.

[7] Muscatine, *Old French Fabliaux*, pp.91–2.

Providing the corpse and a sack to put it in and then, when the porter returns for payment, indignantly pointing out that the job remains to be done since the hunchback's corpse is still there, repeating the performance of dragging a body out from the bed in the porter's absence and this time pretending to be amazed when she sees the corpse still there, the wife manages to get rid of all three. The lively fun of the tale, which counteracts the brutality of the action, lies in the exchanges between wife and porter:

'You insolent lout!' she exclaimed, 'How dare you try to make a fool of me? The dwarf has just turned up again: you didn't throw him into the water at all . . .'
    'How in the name of all the devils in hell did he get back into the house? . . . He was dead wasn't he? He must be Antichrist himself, but, by St Remy, it won't do him any good!'[8]

The three castings into the water give the tale the symmetry of folk tale and build up the action to the ironic climax when before the porter gets to the top of the stairs in the house for a third time to claim payment, he sees the hunchback husband returning and, thinking in fury that the corpse is once more coming back to the house, he seizes a club and brains him, pops him into the sack and dumps him in the river, this time still inside the sack. At last he gets paid:

The lady did not feel disposed to haggle, and paid the young man the full amount—thirty pounds and no less. She paid him to his complete satisfaction, for she was herself highly satisfied with the bargain . . . She felt sure all her troubles were over for life . . .

This lively but casual tale, cynical and worldly, is a typical piece of fabliau black comedy, where the fun of making a farcical narrative pattern out of four hunchbacks' deaths rides over any sense of justice or of natural conduct. What is celebrated is the wife's ingenuity and the porter's gullible, indefatigable willingness to do the same actions over and over again. As Muscatine puts it: 'The fabliaux do not honor vice for its own sake, but they do celebrate the getting of money, goods and pleasure through wit.'[9] Getting rid of an ugly, rich husband is high on the list of acquisitive fabliau pleasures.
    French fabliaux are marked by an interest in material things—food

---

[8] Brewer, *Medieval Comic Tales*, pp.6–7.
[9] Muscatine, *Old French Fabliaux*, p.92.

and drink, sex, money, possessions, and so on—and the stories are full of references to physical objects, the geography and furniture of houses, manoeuvrings in and out of beds, cupboards and sacks, parts of the body, the ingredients of meals, and so on, and much of the humour develops from the need to cope with the physicality—a wife hiding a lover, or two lovers, when the husband unexpectedly returns, or having to persuade the husband that he has not seen what his eyes perceive. Muscatine's characterization of the ethos of fabliau puts a strong emphasis on 'the essential traits of concrete things' and the overall spirit of 'materialistic hedonism'.[10]

The best-known instance of fabliau writing in English before Chaucer, *Dame Sirith*,[11] is the story of a clerk whose lust for Margery, a merchant's wife, is helped to fulfilment by a wily old bawd, who, for 20 shillings and with the aid of a dose of pepper and mustard, pretends that her weeping dog is really her daughter, transformed by the clerk (who being educated may be assumed to be a wizard) for rejecting his advances: Margery is panicked into adultery. The single surviving text of this tale, in the well-known thirteenth-century MS Digby 86, is identified by the rubric at the head as 'le fablel e la cointise de dame Siriz' (the fabliau and the trickery of Dame Sirith) and, though this is the only English text identified as a *fablel*, the manuscript also contains an Anglo-Norman example of the type. The even more significant collection of texts in the early-fourteenth-century MS Harley 2253, best known as a unique anthology of Middle English secular lyrics, includes four Anglo-Norman fabliaux, together with other French humorous and satirical pieces: English comic poems such as 'The Man in the Moon' and comic invective such as the 'Satire on the Consistory Courts' help to define the robust, sharp-edged comedy which the compiler seems to have used in meaningful juxtapositions with antifeminist pieces, and in the manuscript overall in intertextual balance with courtly love lyrics and pious texts.[12] That these fabliaux are in Anglo-Norman rather than English may indicate that by the beginning of the fourteenth century fabliaux for a narrowing, French-speaking audience in England were primarily obscene

---

[10] Muscatine, *Old French Fabliaux* pp.73ff.

[11] Edited in Bennett and Smithers, *Early Middle English Prose and Verse*, pp.77–95.

[12] See Carter Revard, 'From French "fabliau manuscripts" and MS Harley 2253 to the *Decameron* and the *Canterbury Tales*', *Medium Aevum* 69 (2000), 261–78.

entertainment, rather cruder than those written for a truly French audience, as the Harley fabliaux, which include two of the fabliaux best designed to produce a courtly snigger or a lewd guffaw, 'Le Chevalier qui fist parler les cons' ('The Knight who Made Cunts Talk') and 'Les trois Dames qui troverent un vit' ('The Three Ladies who Found a Prick') suggest.[13] Both these manuscripts support the idea that Chaucer's fabliaux were not necessarily importations into English of continental texts : some at least may be instances of an educated poet taking up stories already circulating in England. The Middle English Dictionary does not recognize *fablel/fabliau* as a Middle English word, despite its use in MS Digby 86 as a label for an English text, but the word and the idea were known in England in the thirteenth and fourteenth centuries.

Chaucer does not himself use a clear genre-word for his comic tales: the nearest he came to giving a generic label to them is in the prologue to *The Miller's Tale* where, in the voice of the poet-narrator he tells us that

> . . . this Millere
> He nolde his wordes for no man forbere,
> But tolde his cherles tale in his manere.
>
> (*CT*, I, 3167–9)

The dramatization of the Miller's entry into the tale-telling has presented him as an intrusive storyteller, who insists on telling a tale out of turn, breaking the decorum that the Host is attempting to establish. So, even before the audience knows what the story is to contain and becomes aware that its frankness about sex and the body may offend, Chaucer has distanced himself from the tale and identified it as outside the category of polite writing. It is a 'cherles tale', something low-class, likely to be vulgar. He further detaches himself in the passage quoted earlier where he claims the necessity of repeating the pilgrims' tales word for word and asks 'every gentil wight' not to blame him for including distasteful material.

> The Millere is a cherl; ye knowe wel this.
> So was the Reve eek and othere mo,

---

[13] See N. van den Boogaard, 'Le Fabliau Anglo-Normand', in *Third International Beast Epic, Fable and Fabliau Colloquium, Munster 1979*, Cologne/Vienna, 1981, pp.66–77, quoted in the discussion by John Hines, *The Fabliau in English* (Harlow, Longman, 1993), pp.39–42.

And harlotrie they tolden bothe two.
Avyseth yow, and put me out of blame,
And eek men shal nat maken ernest of game.
(*CT*, I, 3182–6)

So Chaucer provides three terms from which one may assess his sense of the comic tales included in *The Canterbury Tales*: 'cherles tales', 'harlotrie', and 'game'. If, on the one hand, he may seem to be apologizing for including such stories by classing them as unfortunately unavoidable, since his pilgrims were free to narrate what they liked and he had to record their doing so, on the other he is excusing them as 'game', licensed to be vulgar because comic. It sounds as if, for Chaucer, there is no fixed idea of the comic tale and that he is simply referring to the common stock of popular narratives shared by all the main European languages. The fabliau was, it would seem, no more stable as a genre than romance, though every language had words by which such tales could be specified. Benson and Andersson list as medieval genres akin to the fabliau: 'novella, Shrovetide play, Märe, Schwank, facetia, mock epic, fable, exemplum, ballad.'[14] It is not surprising that Chaucer should have known examples of some of these: what is unexpected is that he, like Boccaccio, chose to give literary treatment to fabliau plots.

MS Digby 86 is not the only pre-Chaucerian manuscript to include comic material in English. The early-fourteenth-century anthology of English texts gathered in the Auchinleck MS contains a couple of humorous narratives: one of these is a tale known as 'A Pennyworth of Wit'.[15] This is the story of a merchant, his wife, and his mistress, on whom he lavishes gifts of silk and fur, gold and jewels; preparing to travel abroad on business he asks first the mistress what clothes and jewels she would like him to bring her; then, belatedly, he offers to get his wife any jewels for which she gives him the money, but she, having in any case no silver to spare, merely gives him one penny, saying:

---

[14] Larry D. Benson and Theodore M. Andersson, *The Literary Context of Chaucer's Fabliaux* (New York, Bobbs-Merrill, 1971), p.x.

[15] Edited in E. Kölbing, 'Kleine Publicationen aus der Auchinleck-hs', *Englische Studien* 7 (1884), 113–17. The tale is found also in two fifteenth-century manuscripts and is known in this later, slightly shorter, version as 'How a Merchant did his Wife Betray'; this text was printed in W. Carew Hazlitt, *Remains of the Early Popular Poetry of England* (4 vols., London, Russell Smith, 1864–6), i, pp.193–208.

'Haue a fair peni here,
& as ʒe be mi trewe fere,
Bi þerwiþ a peniworþ witt,
& in þine hert fast it knitt!'
('A Pennyworth of Wit', 45–8)

The merchant thinks his wife mad and puts the penny in his purse in scorn. He then sets out on his voyage and buys the best of jewels and handsome attire for his 'leman'—'As ani leuedy wald desire'—but nothing for his wife until he remembers the unspent penny and mentions it to his servant in the hearing of an old man who, on questioning the merchant and discovering the circumstances, offers to sell him a pennyworth of wisdom. He proposes subterfuge on the merchant's return: he should don poor clothing and go to his mistress, pretending to have lost everything, to have killed a man, and become a fugitive from the law—will she give him shelter? Then he should tell the same story to his wife and see what answers he gets from the two: which is better in time of need, mistress or wife? And, in any case, the old man asks, why does he need two women? It will cost too much to provide for both and one is enough to provide 'gamen vnder þe gore'. The merchant takes the point and hands over the penny. On his return he follows the old man's advice and the result is as one would expect: the mistress, peering out to see who is knocking at her door, sees him poorly clad and shuts the door on him, will speak to him only through her maid and not only will not offer help but is ready to make threats of reporting his crime in order to get rid of him; the wife, on the other hand, welcomes him, unquestioningly provides him with a change of clothes, asks how he has fared, unhesitatingly comforts him and proposes remedies, offers her own money, to plead his case before the king, and to work to recover his lost fortune. The merchant gets the message and on the next day visits the hypocritical mistress and tricks her into displaying all the gifts he had made her, which he gathers up and brings to his wife:

'Lo, dame!' he seyd, 'bi mi chaffare
Ichaue ybrouʒt þi peniworþ ware . . .'
('A Pennyworth of Wit', 387–8)

This is clearly a moral tale which could in the right context pass for an *exemplum*; recognizably a test story of a wife's fidelity, it could sit beside the more familiar medieval test case of Griselda, but in this version its turning on subterfuge and tricks, together with its social setting (the merchant class, town life, commerce, and pride in ownership) and the consequent sense of valuing life in terms of consumer goods, all identify the fabliau links. The quality of writing is throughout that of comic realism rather than of moralistic illustration. At each stage there is plenty of detail and lively speech which gives some naturalistic bite to the situations, as in the maidservant's conveying the mistress's message to the merchant:

> 'Fle, ʒif þou wilt þi liif haue,
> For þi leman nil þe nouʒt saue!
> Mi leuedi haþ her oþ ysworn
> Bi him þat was in Bedelem born,
> Þat sche nil do þe no socour.
> Noiþer in soler no in bour,
> No ben yfounde wiþ swiche tresoun,
> For to sustene þe kinges feloun!'
> ('A Pennyworth of Wit', 227–34)

The wife offering with her maid to 'swete & swinke' to make money 'Wiþ brewing, bakeing & oþer chaffare' is in neat antithesis to this reported high-flown indignation and the list of reclaimed goods, which the mistress displays to disprove what she takes to be the wife's slander (that she has given them to another lover), makes an appropriate climax to the tale:

> Sche sprad a caneuas on þe flore,
> Þat was boþe gret & store,
> & brouʒt forþ her riche þinges,
> Broches of gold & riche ringes,
> Sextene schetes milk white,
> VIII chalouns & V couerlite,
> Oþer juwels mani on t[o]ld,
> Masers riche, coupes of gold:
> 'Now miʒt tow leue & wite & see
> Dame old crate, þi wiif, oþer me!'
> ('A Pennyworth of Wit', 349–57)

The features that one recognizes as typical of fabliau include the main characters (merchant, wife, mistress), the situation (the journey and encounter, the return and test), the poetic justice of the end, together with the whole neat, plot-focussed structure. There is no preacher's voice to point any moral but simply emphasis on the outcome: the wife is glad that the husband has 'turned his þouȝt' and the poet's summing-up is a mere drawing of a line under the tale:

Þai ferd miri & so mot we.
Amen, amen, par charite!
('A Pennyworth of Wit', 399–400)

One might argue that the tale is too near to a demonstration of the rewards of virtue to sit comfortably within the fabliau genre, unlike *Dame Sirith* where the cunning stratagem, as Bennett and Smithers express it, 'is typical of the genre in awarding success to a disreputable person and discomfiture to a virtuous and innocent one'.[16] However, the use of stock characters and everyday settings creates a simple picture of the contemporary world with issues of family and social relationships, of worldly dealings with money, marriage, sex, power, and possession, which seems close to the fabliau world of other tales.

The word novella has a longer and more complex history than fabliau, and, as with the term romance, post-medieval uses blur the edges of its sense. The Italian novella, developed from Medieval Latin prose *exempla*, can be identified as a vernacular form of narrative in the thirteenth-century *Cento novelle antiche*, known as *Il Novellino*, a collection of short tales in prose, many of which are simple anecdotes and only a few of which have plots of a fabliau type, though one of the several manuscripts does contain a version of the 'pear-tree episode' which Chaucer used in *The Merchant's Tale*. In the hands of Boccaccio in the *Decameron* (first written in 1351, revised 1370–1) the novella became a richly varied form of prose storytelling and the range of material covered in the hundred tales shows that Boccaccio drew not only on contemporary Italian popular narrative but also on the French fabliau tradition of bawdy tales, on French romances, and on older literary material from Ovid and other classical poets. So, though it is possible to say that 'Boccaccio is fully medieval in his selection of stories, which are from the general international fund',[17] one has to recognize that there is some distance between such a rich exploration of the genre of novella in the *Decameron* and the basic notion of the form, as there is between fabliau and Chaucer's use of

---

[16] Bennett and Smithers, *Early Middle English Prose and Verse*, p.77.
[17] Brewer, *Medieval Comic Tales*, p.xxviii.

the form in *The Canterbury Tales*. The quality of the novella is described by Brewer as 'everyday secular realism', as with other types of medieval comic tale, interpreted with a fair degree of 'artistic and social polish'. Boccaccio himself, in the prologue to the *Decameron*, glosses the word novella, suggesting the variety within it:

intendo di raccontare cento novelle, o favole o parabole o istorie che dire le vogliamo ... (I propose to tell a hundred tales [or fables or parables or stories or what you will.])[18]

One could translate *favole* as 'fabliaux', since there are some stories, particularly the several stories concerning the tricksters Bruno and Buffalmacho who exploit the gullibility of their fellow artist Calandrino, which are, as Hines points out, 'distinctly fabliau-like'.[19] On the other hand the novella is not necessarily comic. All the tales of the fourth day (except the last by the licence given to Dioneo as narrator) are of love that ends in tears: the tales of the second and fifth days have happy endings but tell stories of misfortune overcome, and so, while illustrating the classic definition of comedy, are not humorous. The stories that are based on jokes and tricks, particularly the tales of the sixth day which turn on prompt or witty ripostes, are short, while the narratives of misfortune overcome take longer, as do the tenth day's stories of acts of generosity, which include the tale which Chaucer retold as *The Franklin's Tale* and the final story of Griselda where, like Chaucer in *The Clerk's Tale*, Boccaccio followed Petrarch. Boccaccio's *novelle* create a spectrum, expressive of his middle-brow cultural range, stretching from serious to trivial. N. S. Thompson, in his comparative study of the *Decameron* and *The Canterbury Tales*, gives a whole chapter to the subject 'The Comic Tales: Fabliaux or Novelle?', seeing the fabliau as essentially a bawdy tale using a stock plot and stock characters, whereas in the novella: 'Stock types and plots become miraculously transformed by local settings and particularized individuals who occupy worlds of surprising moral ambiguity.'[20]

Boccaccio's precision about the places in Italy where his

---

[18] Giovanni Boccaccio, *The Decameron*, trans. Guido Waldman, with Introduction and Notes by Jonathan Usher, World's Classics (Oxford U.P., 1993), p.5.

[19] The stories are *Decameron*, VIII, 3, 6, and 9; IX, 3 and 5. See Hines, *The Fabliau in English*, p.234.

[20] Thompson, *Chaucer, Boccaccio, and the Debate of Love*, p.220.

contemporary works are set is matched by Chaucer in his tales of modern life. Fabliau represented, within the literary medley of *The Canterbury Tales*, not only 'game' but the here and now and localized action. The tales of Miller, Reeve, Cook, and Summoner are set respectively in Oxford, Cambridge, London, and Yorkshire, all more directly knowable backgrounds of social activity than ancient Athens, Rome, or Brittany, which appear in the tales of Knight, Man of Law, and Franklin, let alone the fantasy world of the Wife of Bath's Arthurian adventure or the Squire's Tartary. The other tales that are placed in contemporary settings are all comic or satirical in intent: rural England (Nun's Priest, Friar), the suburbs of a town (Canon's Yeoman), or the not-too-distant France (Shipman) or Flanders (Pardoner and, jokingly, *Sir Thopas*). It is striking that, though Chaucer seems to be the first English writer to make extensive use of fabliau material, he did not have to translate specific borrowed texts. Versions of *The Reeve's Tale* and *The Shipman's Tale* occur in the *Decameron* and also as French fabliaux; for the rest there are no more than general analogues and similarities, in Flemish, Italian, and German for *The Miller's Tale*, in Latin and German for *The Friar's Tale*, in French for *The Summoner's Tale*, and in various places for the medley of *The Merchant's Tale*. Something similar may be said of some other types of tale dealing with 'modern' life: the story told in *The Pardoner's Tale* is widespread, but there is no one obvious direct source, and there is no known source for the narrative parts of *The Canon's Yeoman's Tale*. This suggests that Chaucer's tales of contemporary life were versions of anecdotes and tales in general circulation; they retain something of the oral and improvisatory, though they have been given textual sophistication.

Chaucer's fabliaux and beyond

The Shipman's Tale is the nearest of Chaucer's stories to basic fabliau ideas. The plot, known in folk-tale terms as the story of 'the lover's gift regained', is based on the classic fabliau triangle of husband, wife, and aspiring lover: the husband is a merchant and so has available cash which the hopeful lover can borrow in order to buy the wife's favours; the joke is in the ingenuity of the lover's returning the loan to the husband by means of the wife, who needs to conceal her adultery. In the version of this plot which Boccaccio includes as Tale 1 on the eighth day the setting is Milan, with Genoa as the end of trade journeys from home. The focus is on the lover, a German mercenary with a reputation for prompt payment of debts: he is the complete 'money' figure, fighting for money and getting sex by its means. There is a good deal of irony, therefore, when he courts the wife of a rich merchant and finds that she will yield to him in exchange for 200 gold florins, in the fact that he is shocked by the wife, Ambrogia's, mercenary nature: 'How sordid could she be!' The theme of the stories on the eighth day is the tricks men play on women and Ambrogia from this moment becomes Gulfardo's victim. And so the borrowing of the money from the husband is the first stage of a careful plot against her and at the end, after Gulfardo has staged the return of the money in the presence of a witness, she is 'the thwarted wife' who has to hand back to her husband 'the squalid price of her shameless conduct'. The 'canny lover' wins and the adultery is characterized as the wife's readiness to prostitute herself. Boccaccio's story is brief and makes its effect, as is usual in the *Decameron*, as part of the sequence: first the storyteller, Neifile, recalls earlier stories both of women's tricks and of the need to be honest in love, and then the story that follows repeats the plot of bargaining for sexual favours, but here the woman is the attractive wife of a peasant and the scheming lover a village priest who lusts after the jolly little Belcolore much as Absolon does after Alison in Chaucer's *Miller's Tale* and tries to impress her 'as he entoned the Kyrie or Sanctus for all the world like a donkey braying'. Boccaccio plays variations on a theme and the sympathy shifts from tale to tale: if in the first tale of men's trickery the tale favours the lover, in the second the wife does rather better.

Chaucer sets his longer tale in St Denis with Paris and Bruges providing the off-stage centres of commerce: the French setting may indicate an unknown French fabliau source. From the start Chaucer fills out the bare outline of the plot with details that illustrate a well-to-do household and a world which thinks entirely in terms of profit and loss, and of marriage in terms of how much wives cost husbands. The lover figure is a monk but a worldly one, not only in his frank sexual desire for the merchant's wife but also in being the monastery's estate manager, riding out to supervise farms and barns, buying animals and bringing, as a visitor to the house of the merchant whom he has known from childhood, generous gifts:

> . . . a jubbe of malvesye,
> And eek another ful of fyn vernage,
> And volatyl [game-fowl], as ay was his usage . . .
> (*CT*, VII, 70–2)

The monk, 'Daun John', moves about accompanied by objects that register his comfortable prosperity, the 'portehors' (breviary) which he carries and on which he swears, the 'chilyndre' (portable sundial) by which he knows it is dinner time. Chaucer also amplifies the tale with plenty of direct speech, used particularly to establish the intimacy between monk and wife and to give him the opportunity to insinuate and her the opportunity to complain and negotiate; the morality of business is also the subject of speech as the merchant lectures his wife on the need for vigilance, since 'we moote stonde in drede/Of hap and fortune in oure chapmanhede' (*CT*, VII, 237–8). Chaucer's substitution, if that's what it was, of monk for soldier as lover shifts the possibility for moral blame, but the characters are presented without clear moral colouring, so that guilt is balanced and the reader is ready to accept the wife's ingenuity in escaping from the consequences at the end.

> This wyf was nat afered nor affrayed,
> But boldely she seyde, and that anon,
> 'Marie, I deffie the false monk, daun John!
> I kepe nat of his tokenes never a deel;
> He took me certeyn gold, that woot I weel—
> What! Yvel thedam on his monkes snowte!
> For, God it woot, I wende, withouten doute,
> That he hadde yeve it me bycause of yow
> To doon therwith myn honour and my prow,
> For cosynage, and eek for beele cheere
> That he hath had ful ofte tymes heere.'
> (*CT*, VII, 400–10)

If, in some ways, the world of *The Shipman's Tale* seems completely materialistic, and the equation of money with sex and the commercial vocabulary used for marriage and adultery give an unpleasant moral hardness to the story, there is also a sense of relaxed acceptance of the ways of the world: of the money she has received, for which her husband asks, the wife simply says that she has spent it, without fearing any drastic consequences. The focus is not on adultery, which is the point of criticism in the Italian story, but money and methods of payment. It is the husband who must pay, at the end as at the beginning of the tale, and if he is to get any return it is in terms of sexual satisfaction, as his wife makes clear:

> '. . . be nat wrooth, but lat us laughe and pleye.
> Ye shal my joly body have to wedde;
> By God, I wol nat paye yow but abedde!
> Forgyve it me, myn owene spouse deere,
> Turne hiderward, and maketh bettre cheere.'
>   This merchant saugh ther was no remedie,
> And for to chide it nere but folie,
> Sith that the thyng may nat amended be.
>   (*CT*, VII, 422–9)

The life of Chaucer's tale, which in terms of plot could be seen as a routine piece of fabliau tale-telling, is in the lively speech between the characters, spiced by some punning and sexual innuendo, and the worldly believability of the feelings expressed. The tale is an extended joke about the idea of conjugal debt, as Thompson points out,[21] but, conversely, it offers a positive image of commercial ethics, with a portrait of the merchant as sober, single-minded, and in control of complex dealings.[22] His wife may experience his careful management as stinginess but the end of the story shows that she has learned from his example in developing her own language of commerce. There is no specific satirical target or edge to the tale but the textual oddities represented in the use of first-person pronouns with reference to wives in the first twenty lines of the tale have usually been read as indicating that Chaucer first wrote this tale for the Wife of Bath: if this was the case Chaucer might be seen as rescuing the tale from Boccaccio's using it as a criticism of women, though this touches on the still-debated question of whether Chaucer actually knew the *Decameron*.[23]

---

[21] Thompson, *Chaucer, Boccaccio and the Debate of Love*, pp.210–12.

[22] See Carol T. Heffernan, 'Chaucer's *Shipman's Tale* and Boccaccio's *Decameron*, VIII, 1: Retelling a story', in *Courtly Literature: Culture and Context*, eds. Keith Busby and Erik Kooper (Philadelphia, John Benjamins, 1990), pp.261–70.

[23] See Peter G. Beidler, 'Just say yes, Chaucer knew the *Decameron*: or bringing the *Shipman's Tale* out of limbo', in *The Decameron and The Canterbury Tales: New Essays on an Old Question*, eds. Leonard Michael Koff and Brenda Deen Schildgen (Madison, Associated University Presses, 2000), pp.25–46.

The related question of how much elaboration fabliau plot material can take before it turns into something else is even more intriguing in the two versions which Boccaccio and Chaucer made out of the story known as *Le Meunier et les deux clercs* (that is Boccaccio's Day IX, Tale 6 and Chaucer's *Reeve's Tale*). Boccaccio sets his tale in the countryside outside Florence and treats it as a love story: Pinuccio, a young gentleman from the city, has fallen for the daughter of the country innkeeper and deliberately arranges to get stranded one night with his friend Adriano so that the goodman has to offer them a bed and thus provide Pinuccio with the opportunity to make love to the willing Niccolosa, and less expectedly for Adriano to enjoy the host's wife. The pleasure of the story is in the farcical nippings in and out of bed in the dark bedroom punctuated by the movements of a cat and a cradle, and the ingenious sorting out of the tangle by the wife's quick-wittedness, backed up by the astute Adriano, so that the host's anger is diverted, the love affair concealed, and harmony restored. This sophisticated, neat tale works as a comedy of misunderstanding, with no satirical edge and a sympathetic treatment of young love. In contrast to this example of how the subject matter of novella, the stratagems of young lovers, can make use of the farcical slapstick elements of fabliau, Chaucer's version of the tale, set in the environs of Cambridge and so bringing in the rivalry of town and gown, is sharply angled, so that its feeling is more bitter and its action more violent. The Reeve as storyteller is characterized as a sour ageing man infuriated by the Miller's tale of an elderly carpenter ridiculed as a gullible cuckold and telling his own story as an act of revenge: hence the host in the story becomes a miller and is from the start made the target of the tale's satire. The literary treatment of fabliau can often become interesting by means of individualizing touches which turn stock figures into believable characters, and there are moments in *The Reeve's Tale* where this happens (particularly when the daughter, Malyne, suddenly comes to life with her affectionate farewell to Aleyn and her giving away her father's thieving) but the treatment of the miller, 'deynous Symkyn' is hardly in this naturalizing style: what Chaucer does here is create an exaggerated satirical caricature of provincial pretentiousness, giving plenty of space before the story begins to a ludicrous tableau of the bald, snub-nosed, quarrelsome swaggerer, bristling with weapons as he sets off for church with his 'somdel smoterlich' wife, ready to strike out if anyone remembers that she is the priest's bastard, as she now flaunts her estate in the red dress that matches her husband's hose. Chaucer's use of sarcasm in the description of these two establishes a tone distinct from that of *The Miller's Tale*, in the following lines, for example:

> A wyf he hadde, ycomen of noble kyn;
> The person of the toun hir fader was.
> With hire he yaf ful many a panne of bras,
> For that Symkyn sholde in his blood allye.
> She was yfostred in a nonnerye;
> For Symkyn wolde no wyf, as he sayde,
> But she were wel ynorissed and a mayde,
> To saven his estaat of yomanrye.
>   (*CT*, I, 3942–9)

Symkyn's pride is clearly set up to be brought down and his cheating the two students by sharp practice in his milling adds crime to misdemeanour: hence the denouement of the story becomes an act of punishment and the outcome is identified as poetic justice—'A gylour shal hymself bygyled be' (l.4321). However, Chaucer makes the contest between the cheater and his supposed victims interesting by a number of witty strategies, replacing the wife's quick wit on which Boccaccio's tale turns. Here the climax is pure slapstick with the fight in the dark turning into blind mayhem as the wife delivers the coup-de-grace with a blow to her husband's bald head gleaming in the dark and mistaken for a student's nightcap, and there is no subtle explaining it all away, but the shifts earlier in the tale offer the reader more nuance. These shifts are in terms of the balance of power in the story between cleverness and stupidity. The two young students start their adventure confident of their own cleverness and ability to catch the miller out in any attempt to cheat them in turning the college's grain into flour: and so they watch the milling process closely, adopting a naive interest in the mechanics of it all. The miller has no trouble in seeing through this; it redoubles his determination to outwit them, which is expressed through his practical ability and his scorn for the intellectualism which to him they represent.

> This millere smyled of hir nycetee,
> And thoghte, 'Al this nys doon but for a wyle.
> They wene that no man may hem bigyle,

> But by my thrift, yet shal I blere hir ye,
> For al the sleighte in hir philosophye.'
> (*CT*, I, 4046–50)

Once the miller has furtively released their horse and John and Aleyn have gone chasing it like a couple of idiots, Symkyn can get on with his thieving and his gloating superiority.

> He seyde, 'I trowe the clerkes were aferd.
> Yet kan a millere make a clerkes berd,
> For all his art; now lat hem goon hir weye!
> Lo, wher he gooth! Ye, lat the children pleye.'
> (*CT*, I, 4095–8)

When the horse has at length been caught and John and Aleyn return, wet, bedraggled, and thoroughly outmanoeuvred, having to sue for a night's lodging, the opportunity is too good for Symkyn to miss and the anti-academic scorn is at its ripest.

> 'Myn hous is streit, but ye han lerned art;
> Ye konne by argumentes make a place
> A myle brood of twenty foot of space.
> Lat se now if this place may suffise,
> Or make it rowm with speche, as is youre gise.'
> (*CT*, I, 4122–6)

The miller's sarcastic use of intellectual ideas and vocabulary is one half of a language game: the other half is Chaucer's characterizing these two Cambridge students as northern lads who talk in fourteenth-century Geordie, especially when frantic, as John is at the loss of the horse.

> 'Allas!' quod John, 'Aleyn, for Cristes peyne
> Lay doun thy swerd, and I will myn alswa.
> I is ful wight, God waat, as is a raa;
> By Goddes herte, he sal nat scape us bathe!
> Why ne had thow pit the capul in the lathe?
> Ilhay! By God, Alayn, thou is a fonne!'
> (*CT*, I, 4084–9)

It is only when thoroughly humiliated and outplayed in physical and linguistic terms that Aleyn and John begin to find a way to recover their fortunes, and it is through a mixture of youthful sexual cheek and mental reasoning, as first Aleyn argues his way to justification for going to the daughter's bed.

'Som esement has lawe shapen us,
For, John, ther is a lawe that says thus:
That gif a man in a point ben agreved,
That in another he sal be releved.
Oure corn is stoln, sothly, it is na nay,
And we han had an il fit al this day;
And syn I sal have neen amendement
Agayn my los, I will have esement.
By Goddes sale, it sal neen other bee!'
(*CT*, I, 4179–87)

The northern forms now combine with a more student-like awareness of legal terms, which stand out in this often monosyllabic plain
style, combined with ready oaths. John in his turn, left alone in bed,
argues his way towards his own sexual adventure.

'Allas!' quod he, 'this is a wikked jape;
Now may I seyn that I is but an ape.
Yet has my felawe somwhat for his harm;
He has the milleris doghter in his arm.
He auntred hym, and has his nedes sped,
And I lye as a draf-sak in my bed;
And when this jape is tald another day,
I sal be halde a daf, a cokenay!
I wil arise and auntre it, by my fayth!
"Unhardy is unseely", thus men sayth.'
(*CT*, I, 4201–10)

And so the narrative poise shifts as the reader sees the action now
through Aleyn and John (and briefly Malyne): the language is kept
quite simple and yet it is full of cross-currents which give flexibility
and interest to the unfolding of the tale. At one moment sarcastic and
rhetorical, when the priest's ambition to make his granddaughter his
heir is scornfully identified, at another supplying literary echoes,
when the lovers Aleyn and Malyne part in terms that echo the dawn
complaints of courtly sweethearts, the narrating voice is both
anonymous and full of involved intonation, which swings the balance
back against the proud miller; he has to endure a physical beating,
sexual humiliation as father and husband, and financial loss when the
students recover their meal and ride off without paying for their
board and lodging. The rights and wrongs represent Chaucer's
roughest version of fabliau justice.

It is difficult to think that there is much of the carnivalesque about *The Reeve's Tale*: its comedy seems nearer to the idea of corrective satire in that the retributive pattern of fabliau, whereby a trickster is tricked back, is used to punish a character identified at the start as proud and overbearing. The pleasure of the tale remains, as in Boccaccio's version, in the comedy of five adults and a baby in a confined space in the dark, but the outcome in fighting and injury is at odds with Boccaccio's graceful ease in leaving the characters with their dignity and with the same enjoyment still open to them.

Although there is not much dignity left, at least to the male characters, at the end of Chaucer's *Miller's Tale*, it comes nearer to that graceful ease and achieves, partly by its own qualities as narrative and partly by the context Chaucer created for it, the greater literary richness which leads Thompson to read it as novella rather than fabliau. It is in the treatment of character that he sees the closest similarity between Boccaccio and Chaucer and where he locates the distance between the two genres. As he says: 'such is the concentration on character in Chaucer's so-called fabliaux, that it forms the point of greatest similarity ... with the novella ... character absorbs the whole of the interest in narration, bar the plot.'[24] The satirical flavour of fabliau is strongly present in the passages of character description here as in *The Reeve's Tale*: in both, excess in clothing and appearance is a major theme. Absolon, the Oxford parish clerk, going through all the motions of love longing, playing his guitar yearningly under the beloved's window in the small hours, is portrayed as a precious dandy with exaggeratedly curly, fan-shaped hairdo, fashionably ornamented shoes, red hose, and light blue tunic; his gleaming white surplice is seen as part of his ensemble rather than a sign of his office, though his tripping, dancing legs and his strutting about as Herod on the mystery play's scaffold suggest that he was more often than not seen without it. Kissing Alisoun's behind is a particular humiliation for 'this joly lovere', delicate about personal hygiene, 'squaymous of fartyng' and preparing for his night-time wooing by chewing spices, combing his hair, and sucking a lozenge. This is a richer, more barbed exposure of folly than the character descriptions in the *General Prologue*. 'Deynous Symkyn' in *The Reeve's Tale* is a more dangerous

---

[24] Thompson, *Chaucer, Boccaccio and the Debate of Love*, p.217.

case, but Absolon's vanity and Symkyn's pride are the keynotes of the town life Chaucer sketches in for Oxford and Cambridge respectively, waiting to be punished by the quicker-witted student characters. Chaucer sets up a more ambiguous picture in his wonderfully vivid portrayal of Alisoun, the sexy wife of the older carpenter, John. Partly an admiring male evocation of feminine physical allure, the portrait adds greatly to the freshness and comic vigour of the tale; with the weasel's slender litheness, the breath of honey and apples, the colt's skittishness, the spring newness of pear blossom, the sweet voice of the swallow, Alisoun is a fine realization of a masculine ideal with just enough exaggeration to give the passage comic flair. Undercutting complexity is added by touches which convey Alisoun's vanity in her appearance (the plucked eyebrows, the dramatic black-and-white costume, the low collar with its large brooch to direct the eye, the lacing of the shoes high up the legs) and which suggest in the final lines her possible history:

> She was a prymerole, a piggesneye,
> For any lord to leggen in his bedde,
> Or yet for any good yeman to wedde.
> (CT, I, 3268–70)

We are not told that this is what had happened, but this town wife, looking and smelling like a country girl, but shining as brightly as a newly minted coin, has ended up married to an honest, well-meaning and well-to-do, but stupid carpenter; who knows by what means she arrived there? In the other two characters, John and Nicholas, Chaucer furnishes the tale with the fabliau stereotypes of aged husband and youthful lover in the form of landlord and lodger, 'riche gnof' and 'poure scoler', the one jealous and gullible, the other apparently angelic but in reality randy and artful. Though they are not as fully described as Alisoun and Absolon, the relationship between the two is the most developed by speech and action and acquires a ripe comic balance in the succession of pantomime scenes, as John wakes Nicholas from his assumed trance and becomes the anxious recipient of the dreadful news of the second flood, and allows himself to be persuaded, largely through his affection for Alisoun, 'his hony deere', to prepare the three barrels hanging from the beams, from which in the literal denouement of his cutting the rope he eventually comes crashing down to break his arm and be declared mad.

In the telling Chaucer makes the story work on two levels at once. The fabliau plot of trickery and adultery in which the old husband is deceived by the clever young student and the willing wife, together with the subplot of the foolish rival lover humiliated and stung into revenge, is told with a finely controlled pace and structure, building up to a supremely farcical climax: the building up is done by means of detailed naturalism and effects of plausibility, in terms of the physical details of the settings—bedroom, books, door, cat, and so on—and a sense of life going on around—bells ringing, the blacksmith at his anvil—so that a kind of literal plausibility makes the idiotic sequence of events seem almost logical. The overall liveliness of manner and language make it one of the brightest and most zestful of Chaucer's stories, with racy direct speech and and swift neat narration. Whereas in *The Knight's Tale* the stately unfolding of the story was accompanied by flourishes of narratorial activity ('But stynte I wole of Theseus a lite,/And speke of Palamon and of Arcite', and so on), here the narrator has almost disappeared: the transitions within the tale are made to seem natural, not the manipulation of the writer.

> And thus lith Alison and Nicholas
> In bisynesse of myrthe and of solas,
> Til that the belle of laudes gan to rynge,
> And freres in the chauncel gonne synge.
> This parissh clerk, this amorous Absolon . . .
> (*CT*, I, 3653–7)

And so the narrator unobtrusively moves from one place in the story to another by means of the church bells which make the shift to the parish clerk seem a natural passage of thought.

The other level at which the tale works is that provided by its context and by the stylistic indicators which give the nod to the sophisticated reader that this 'natural' tale-telling is by no means as innocent as it looks. Chaucer's placing of *The Miller's Tale* after *The Knight's Tale* at the opening of *The Canterbury Tales* is a declaration of intent: here the terms of narrative variety are laid down. If the adaptation of a grand epic story of the ancient past into an elaborate, rhetorical romance of honour, virtue, and tragedy, albeit with a courtly knowingness of tone, seems an appropriate opening for a long series of tales, what does an undignified comedy which ends in farce and slapstick say to the audience but that this is to be a game of contraries, of shifting styles and changing stances? And if the spirit of Bakhtin's carnivalesque is to be recognized in the parodic juxtaposition of romance and fabliau, contrasting most in the two heroines, Emily, a bodiless ideal of golden-haired femininity as an angel singing in a garden and womanly virtue at prayer, as opposed to the giggling, lithe-bodied Alison, skittishly flashing her buttocks, something more complex develops as the tale unfolds. Like *The Knight's Tale* this story is of two young men who are rivals for the same woman; the fourth character (Theseus, John) provides the element of age to turn the plot into a conflict of generations as well as between rivals. Whereas the pagan setting of the first tale identifies Palamon, Arcite, Emily, and Theseus with Venus, Mars, Diana, and Saturn, here the Miller's promise to 'telle a legende and a lyf/Bothe of a carpenter and of his wyf' and the characterization of Nicholas as an innocent-looking 'sweete clerk', singing *Angelus ad virginem*, invite the reader to recognize the characters as mocking parodies of Joseph, Mary, and the angel Gabriel, with attendant priest in the shape of the golden-haired Absolon swinging a censer, like the figures in some devout fresco who are suddenly brought to life and refuse to stay in place. As Steve Ellis expresses it, 'it is a tale rife with carnivalesque images . . . a tale of play, of licence, of holiday.'[25] The turning of John into an object of mockery is in tune with the carnival punishment of authority figures (the older man, the husband, the landlord) and the emphasis on physicality in the presentation of Alisoun provides an extreme instance of carnivalesque turning of things upside down, when she presents for kissing her bottom in place of her face. Accompanying this recognition by Chaucer that a fabliau plot can provide him with an extreme reversal of courtly romance and scriptural decorum is his perception of similarity and relatedness of motive and role, a narrator's recognition that all plots belong ultimately to quite a small stock of story-types, and that what characters do in stories is inevitably full of echoes.

One of the major differences between Chaucer's literary versions of fabliau material and the fabliau-type is the degree of linguistic sophistication. Here, on the one hand, in comparison to *The Knight's Tale*, Chaucer is creating a faster-moving style by using a lot of short words and including expressions that are non-courtly: not just the

[25] Steve Ellis, *Geoffrey Chaucer*, Writers and Their Work Series (Plymouth, Northcote House/British Council, 1996), pp.43–4.

references to the body (*hole, ers, queynte, pisse, fart,* etc.) but words of lower social register such as *wenche, lemman, popelote,* and colloquial backchat such as the blacksmith's address to Absolon:

> 'Why rise ye so rathe? Ey, benedicetee!
> What eyleth yow? Some gay gerl, God it woot,
> Hath broght yow thus upon the viritoot.
> By Seinte Note, ye woot wel what I mene.'
> (*CT*, I, 3768–71)

But on the other hand there is a good deal of ironic use of recurrent words (*hende* Nicholas, *joly* Absolon) and debased courtly expressions (*Of deerne love he koude and of solas*), together with comic uses of the clichés of courtly love lyrics, as with the words sung by Absolon to his guitar outside Alisoun's window:

> 'Now, deere lady, if thy wille be,
> I praye yow that ye wole rewe on me.'
> (*CT*, I, 3361–2)

Nicholas's glib talk of 'Goddes privitee' in his tricking of John equally associates language with pretence. Half the time in *The Miller's Tale* words are to be imagined in italics or in inverted commas. At any moment such cartoon figures may be given a balloon of speech from any literary source:

> This carpenter answerde: 'Allas, my wyf!
> And shal she drenche? Allas, myn Alisoun!'
> (*CT*, I, 3522–3)

Thus John, suddenly reappearing as caring husband in a moment of lyric lament. Or:

> 'What do ye, hony-comb, sweete Alisoun,
> My faire bryd, my sweete cynamome . . .
> I moorne as dooth a lamb after the tete.
> Ywis, lemman, I have swich love-longynge
> That lik a turtel trewe is my moornynge.'
> (*CT*, I, 3698–9, 3704–6)

This time it is Absolon, echoing the Song of Songs. Such allusions are part of the highly worked quality of the tale, to add to the satirical portraits full of innuendo, the stylistic games, the dovetailing of details, the interweaving of two sets of action, the careful pacing.

More expenditure of poetic craft went into this tale than most, whether or not to 'justify' the inclusion of such material is not clear; certainly this is the showpiece of the fabliau genre, an experimental narrative mixing elements from other types of writing, which create perspective for it.

Chaucer's *Miller's Tale* and *Reeve's Tale* are linked by the fabliau material of sexual pranks and manoeuvres, stories of youthful student characters as disrupters of order and old husbands as the butt of jokes and knockabout humour, but there are differences between them: the free-for-all carnival spirit of *The Miller's Tale* represents one end of a spectrum, the irresponsible carnivalesque end, whereas in *The Reeve's Tale* and its effect of paying out one recognizes the other end, that of corrective satire and the exposure of folly and vice by means of ridicule. *The Miller's Tale* does not have a moral. As Helen Cooper puts it, 'It is that rare thing, a mediaeval tale with no further meaning whatever . . . There is no sense of any order beyond the everyday world . . . a world of cheerfully amoral disorder, with no metaphysical depth whatever.'[26] In this Chaucer may be said to have pushed the fabliau as far from the *exemplum* as made sense within the context of his Canterbury series.

The subsequent history of the comic tale in English is a discontinuous mixture of imitations of Chaucer[27] and examples of the two faces of fabliau, which Hines identifies as 'the pursuit of conventional, exemplary morality, or just the reduction of the complexity of the comedy of tales to the cursory "merry jests" of the sixteenth century.'[28] Lydgate in the prologue he devised for *The Siege of Thebes* and the anonymous author of *The Tale of Beryn* (written perhaps in the 1420s) both invent more jesting and backchat for Chaucer's Canterbury pilgrims to provide comic frameworks for narrative and the latter extends the prologue into a fabliau episode of the Pardoner's frustrated lust for a barmaid called Kitt and a lively chase through the inn ending in knockabout farce. The story of Beryn which follows consists of more decorous but duller comedy: Beryn loses a fortune but turns the tables on the confidence tricksters who have cheated

---

[26] Helen Cooper, *The Structure of the Canterbury Tales* (London, Duckworth, 1983), pp.115–16.

[27] See Helen Cooper, 'Imitations of the *Canterbury Tales* 1400–1615', in *Oxford Guides to Chaucer: The Canterbury Tales* (Oxford, Clarendon Press, 1989), pp.413ff.

[28] Hines, *The Fabliau in English*, p.278.

him and wins back what he had lost. This is in the spirit of the fairly numerous scattered comic tales surviving from the fifteenth century.[29] More distinctive comic voices, though in satirical lyrics, mock-heroics, and extended lampoons, are found in the poetry of Dunbar and Skelton, both drawing on the traditional comic abuse of flyting, though the racy vignettes of a low-class alehouse and the women who frequent it in *Elinor Rumming* build up a kind of narrative comparable to Langland's scene of Gluttony and his cronies in the tavern.

More persistently narrative in form and showing the continuation of a tradition of comic tales towards sixteenth-century humanist satire is the famous German collection of 'merry pranks' associated with Till Eulenspiegel.[30] In the prologue the supposed author, N, says he is writing in 1500, collecting tales in response to his friends' requests with the avowed intention 'to create a happy feeling in hard times'. It is clearly, despite its popular style, not a communal work of folk origin but a single writer's literary compilation (attributed by some scholars to Hermann Bote [*c.*1467–1520]), giving a picaresque continuity to many separate episodes. The tradition of German Schwankbücher, jest-books on which *Till Eulenspiegel* depends, is attested as early as the thirteenth century, but kinship to Latin humanist fools' literature is also apparent—some influence of Poggio Bracciolini's *Facetiae* (1438–52) and attitudes similar to Sebastian Brant's *Das Narrenschiff* (1494—translated into English as *The Ship of Fools* through Latin a few years later) and Erasmus' *In Praise of Folly* (1509). Many of the pranks of Eulenspiegel are, like the *Facetiae*, obscene and scatological and many are short, crude scenes where shit serves as wit, but the stories acquire interest as part of a collection, in that a range of tricks is given a sense of illustrating principles. Eulenspiegel particularly punishes looseness of language (often with looseness of bowels) by understanding everything literally: the effect is of taking down a peg those who think themselves superior. When he is told by a merchant who has been infuriated by his tricks that he

---

[29] Some of which have been edited by Melissa M. Furrow in *Ten Fifteenth-Century Comic Poems* (New York, Garland, 1985).

[30] *Till Eulenspiegel: His Adventures*, trans with an Introduction by Paul Oppenheimer, World's Classics (Oxford U.P., 1995). The first edition of the German text was probably that printed in Strassburg in 1510–11, but the editions, illustrated with woodcuts, of 1515 and 1519 are the basis of modern editions. An English translation, *Howleglass*, was printed in Antwerp *c.*1510; the first English edition was that of W. Copland, 1528.

must clear out while the merchant is at church, Eulenspiegel clears out the whole house of furniture, pots, pans, candles, and all: when reproved Eulenspiegel laments: 'I do everything I'm told and still earn gratitude nowhere.' Eulenspiegel is a truth-teller exposing pedantry, superstition, and gullibility and some of the longer tales develop this into a more ambitious expression of satirical themes. Thus, for example, in Tale 27[31] Eulenspiegel appears as artist, when the Landgrave of Hesse (who thinks the trickster may be an alchemist) is impressed by some paintings Eulenspiegel has acquired in Flanders and which he pretends are his own work, and commissions the supposed artist to paint sumptuous scenes on the walls of his ceremonial chamber which will display the Landgrave with other princes and the King of Hungary with lots of pomp and flattery. Eulenspiegel gets the Landgrave to pay 100 guilders on account (of the 400 promised) and after getting out of the way the assistants appointed to help him is assumed to be hard at work for four weeks, when the patron wants to see how the masterpiece is progressing. Having explained that the paintings will be visible only to those of legitimate birth, he goes through an elaborate explanation of what is depicted on the wall:

'. . . no one can censure my work, so artistic it is and managed with such beautiful colours.'

The Landgrave can see only a white wall but expresses satisfaction and leaves; his wife and her ladies similarly pretend that they can see the fresco, but the court jester (female!) says:

'Dear master, maybe I'm to remain a whore's daughter for the rest of my life, but I don't see any painting there!'

Eulenspiegel laughs this off but sees that he will have to leave:

'This isn't good at all. If fools start telling the truth, then I, in truth, must do some travelling.'

The Landgrave realizes the trick and tells Eulenspiegel that before paying him the rest of his fee the whole court must see the work: the prankster manages to wangle another 100 guilders out of the steward and leaves before he can be exposed. The real exposure, obviously, is of the pretension of the prince and his court, and the familiar fable of

[31] Oppenheimer, *Till Eulenspiegel*, p.51.

the emperor's clothes is given an effective broadness of application by being fused into the idea of universal insecurity about the facts of one's own begetting.

These tales are a strong expression of the materialism of fabliau, in Eulenspiegel's case often a gross materialism of the body, ruled by belly and bowels, used as a weapon against authority and the imposition of order. Eulenspiegel is a traveller and so the stories accumulate into a review of the world encountered in many places, along the road, in towns and taverns. This creates out of fabliau episodes a comic panorama. Till Eulenspiegel is the apotheosis of the figure of the cheeky rascal, the tormenter of priests, innkeepers, respectable matrons, figures of authority, all those who represent the tidy rule of what is. These tales of disruption and the rude and disgraceful fit readily at the bleaker end of the idea of the carnivalesque.

6

Fantasy and dream

Voyages and otherworld journeys

The form of narrative with which medieval theorists and commentators were least comfortable was *fabula*, imaginative fiction, because it contained events that were untrue. Even the Aesopic fable was treated with suspicion and had to be justified by the moral truth enclosed within the story, the fruit concealed by the husk. Macrobius in the influential text in which he rewrote Cicero in Christian terms, *The Dream of Scipio*, justified classical fabulous narrative by explaining stories as holy truth masked by allegory, and medieval commentators put the idea into practice by reading such a tale, for example, as that of Orpheus and Eurydice as an allegory of the conflict between virtue and lust or between heavenly and earthly love. Nevertheless, medieval authors produced a large amount of what a modern reader identifies as unrealistic fiction or fantasy. I am using the word rather in the sense that Tolkien attributes to it:

in a sense, that is, which combines with its older and higher use as an equivalent of Imagination the derived notions of 'unreality' . . . of freedom from the domination of observed 'fact'.[1]

Medieval access to fantasy was by various sorts of acceptable subterfuge. Dreams, which I will discuss in more detail in the next section, were usefully ambiguous: the experience of the dreamer could be regarded as a truthful record of mental adventure even if the content of the dream was bizarre, and debating the truth of dreams could be made part of the argument of the work, as Chaucer demonstrates not only in the disagreement between Chauntecleer and Pertelote but also in the introductory sections of several of his

---

[1] J.R.R. Tolkien, 'On fairy-stories', in *The Monsters and the Critics and Other Essays*, p.139.

dream poems. Magic and miracle occur frequently in both religious narratives and romances, with wide variation in the degree of truth claimed for supernatural events: is the Green Knight's surviving decapitation more or less untrue than St Margaret's stepping unharmed from the belly of the dragon? A third area where there was a blurring of the dividing line between truth and fiction was in travel narratives.

The best known of these, Mandeville's *Travels*, was originally written in French about 1360 but had been translated into most European languages by 1400; about 250 manuscripts survive, some of them magnificently illustrated and indicating the appeal of the work to an aristocratic audience. Its author, presenting himself as an English traveller, Sir John Mandeville, may in fact have been a French-speaking Englishman from St Albans as he claims, but the authenticity which the writer asserts for his supposed eyewitness accounts of travels in the Holy Land, the Middle and Far East, is no more than a clever rhetorical ploy.[2] The assemblage of travellers' tales, wonders, strange peoples, the realms of the Great Khan and of Prester John, and so on has become a kind of universal language of far-fetched fantasy, drawn on by Shakespeare to provide Othello with a wide repertoire of tales with which to charm Desdemona, and still available to Umberto Eco for the experiences of his Baudolino; though really a romance tale of exotic wonders which belongs to the history of literature, it went on being regarded as a useful practical guide to travel for an astonishingly long time. It was based in part on some genuine travel narratives, as for instance the *Itineraries* of the friar Odoric of Pordenone and of William van Boldenseele, both early-fourteenth-century travellers, but includes material from encyclo-paedias, such as the *Speculum Historiale* and *Speculum Naturale* of Vincent of Beauvais, and episodes from exotic romances such as the stories of Alexander. The various extracts have been skilfully woven together into a continuous sequence of journeys and countries. The concentration on the Holy Land in the early part of the narrative provides a kind of religious justification for the text and Mandeville imitated the style of pilgrims' manuals to give an appropriate devo-tional tone and sense of worthy purpose. And so he learns about

---

[2] *The Travels of Sir John Mandeville*, trans. C.W.R.D. Moseley (Harmondsworth, Penguin Books, 1983).

some of the places where events related in the Old Testament occurred and gets as near as he can to the Earthly Paradise:

And yee schulle vnderstonde that no man that is mortelle ne may not approchen to that Paradys. For be londe no man may go for wylde bestes that ben in the desertes and for the high mountaynes and grete huge roches that no man may passe by for the derke places that ben there and that manye. And be the ryueres no man may go, for the water renneth so rudely and so scharply because that it cometh doun so outrageously from the high places abouen that it renneth in so grete waves that no schipp may not rowe ne seyle agenes it . . . no mortelle man, as I said, may approche to that place withouten specyalle grace of God, so that of that place I can sey you no more. And therfore I schalle holde me stille and retornen to that that I haue seen.[3]

At the same time his identification of abuses within the church and his comparison of Christianity with other forms of religion in the later parts of his supposed travelling gives a satirical edge to the treatment of religious themes. Despite the derivative nature of most of the content, Mandeville's *Travels* has to be recognized as a significant text simply in describing a wide range of peoples and faiths; compared to the narrow-mindedness of many medieval texts about religion, this is an enlightened work, handling some major topics such as the differences between the western and eastern churches and the teaching of the Koran, though, as Moseley points out, some of these ecumenical impulses were censored in later copies of the text.[4] However, it is the accumulation of exotic legends and the medley of facts and fancies, the wondrous tales of 'men whose heads do grow beneath their shoulders', the sciapods and barnacle geese, that guaranteed the work its long literary currency. This fiction which pretends to be an account of a genuine journey and incorporates factual material, written in fluent, easy prose is in a classic narrative form recognizable in many later fictions, such as *Gulliver's Travels*. The most interesting aspect of the narration is the construction of the persona of the narrator, that of a modest Englishman speaking in understatement, candid and truthful, carefully checking on the authenticity of the stories he tells (especially when he is telling the biggest lies). This is one of the most successful of medieval self-portraits, the honest inquirer with the open mind, intelligent,

[3] *Mandeville's Travels*, ed. M.C. Seymour (Oxford, Clarendon Press, 1967), pp.221–2.
[4] See *The Travels of Sir John Mandeville*, Introduction, p.27.

reasonable, and humorous, which is a good stance from which to cast a satirical glance at the situations he reports.

A much earlier medieval model of the travel narrative is to be found in another widely translated story, *The Voyage of St Brendan.*[5] The Irish saint Brendan (c.486–575) is the subject of a traditional *Vita Brendani* as well as the *Navigatio sancti Brendani abbatis*; the life is based on oral tradition and is largely fictional as is the story of the voyage. In the *Life of Brendan* the saint and the monks from the community on an island off the coast of Kerry set out in three coracles to seek the land which Brendan has been promised in a vision; they return after several years and adventures; Brendan then sets out on a second voyage with sixty companions and after two years and more adventures they reach the promised island, a place of paradisal beauty and permanent health and peace. The *Navigatio* tells of a single voyage lasting seven years in which the monks visit a number of different islands, some of which are described in detail; this is why the *Voyage* has been read as an account of actual travels and is the source of the idea that Brendan reached America by the 'stepping stone' route (the Hebrides, the Faeroes, Iceland, Greenland), the journey retraced by Tim Severin in a leather boat in 1976–7.[6] The earliest texts of the Latin prose *Navigatio* are from the tenth century; a large number of variant versions of the text and of imitations and translations of it exists, making it one of the most widely known of medieval narratives. Of particular interest are the Anglo-Norman verse version, written by one Benedeit in the early twelfth century and dedicated to Queen 'Aaliz' (Adeliza of Louvain who became the second wife of Henry I in 1121)[7] and the shortened English version which appears in the late thirteenth-century *Early South English Legendary*.

The *Navigatio* is an archetypal medieval narrative which should be read by anyone interested in the period or in tale-telling. It may be understood on several levels, first as a traveller's tale and as an example of the specific Irish tradition of sea journey known as an *immram* (literally a 'rowing around'), a tradition associated with self-testing spiritual ventures into the unknown in search of the other world, such

---

[5] *The Voyage of St Brendan: Representative Versions of the Legend in English Translation*, eds. W.R.J. Barron and Glyn S. Burgess (Exeter, University of Exeter Press, 2002).

[6] Tim Severin, *The Brendan Voyage* (London, Hutchinson, 1978).

[7] One manuscript reads 'Mahalt' which presumably refers to Henry's first wife Maud, who died in 1118.

as has been at times suggested as the subject of the Old English *Seafarer*, the story of Brendan shares features with the *Immram Maelduin*, though it is not clear which came first. The *Navigatio* consists of a series of episodes that may be read simply as a sequence of adventures but which are arranged to form a repeated annual cycle based on the monastic year, so that each year of the voyage sees the monks celebrating the calendar festivals in the same place; fasting, praying, and rowing represent allegorically the pattern of the monastic life. At the same time the variety of scenery, such as the coagulated sea and the strange column wrapped round by a huge-meshed net, and the quick succession of strange incidents present the voyage as a quest narrative with the promised land of saints as its object. The quest begins with a visitor to Brendan's community at Clonfert, St Barrind, telling of the voyage he had made to be reunited with his son who had left to live the life of a solitary, and having found the 'Delightful Island', had remained and founded a community there; from this place father and son had set out to seek the 'Promised Land of Saints', where they had remained for a year. Barrind's account of this blessed place inspires Brendan's own journey with his chosen companions; after the building of the ship the adventures of the company of monks follow as they encounter in turn the Isle of Sheep, Jasconius the giant fish, and the Isle of Birds where birds chant the canonical hours, and then continue on their spiritual mission through dangers and marvels with the protection of divine guidance. The various islands that they pass or land on represent a mixture of physical aspects of sea travel (the anxiety about provisions answered by divine gifts of food) and the sense of a journey to the otherworld. They have contrary encounters: on the one hand with demons, as on the Isle of Smiths where they dare not land, the mountain of fire where one of the three monks who had joined the voyage uninvited is snatched by devils, and thirdly in the strange encounter with Judas Iscariot marooned on a rock who tells of the torment of his punishment; on the other with images of holiness as on the island of the Three Choirs and the island inhabited by Paul the Hermit. Surprisingly Brendan's eventual achieving of his quest is dealt with briefly and the story ends soon after as he returns to his home, gives an account of his journey and dies. In this combination of the geographical realities of a voyage and the allegorical representation of the span of human life and the observances of the monastic order, joining physical with Apocalyptic imagery, *The Voyage of St Brendan* creates a powerful narrative of earthly pilgrimage and fantastic otherworld journey.[8]

Such journeys, which usually include descriptions of heaven and hell or both are a central theme of medieval imaginative fiction.[9] A major example is the story of St Patrick's Purgatory, told in the late-twelfth-century Latin prose *Tractatus de Purgatorio Sancti Patricii*, written by a Cistercian monk from Huntingdonshire; it records the journey of an Irish knight, Owein, through Purgatory to the Earthly Paradise and was widely translated. It contains elements of vision and of travel literature, like *The Voyage of St Brendan*; it prefigures Dante's *Divine Comedy* and was associated with a specific place (Station Island in Lough Derg, County Donegal) which became a place of pilgrimage. The story came into English more than once in the medieval period: it appears in *The Early South English Legendary*;[10] a slightly later version in which the knight comes from Northumberland is found as *Owayne Miles* in the Auchinleck MS, and there are at least two distinct fifteenth-century treatments.[11] The main subject matter in all the texts is Owain's eyewitness account of the punishment of sin and his experience of the pains of purgatory, but this is followed by a description of the 'eorþelich parays þat Adam was Inne ibrouȝt',[12] whence the knight is given a glimpse of the golden gates of heaven, and receives the benison of its gleaming light:

> A manere brez fram heouene adoun, þat schon wel clere and briȝte,
> Þat ouerspradde al þat lond and a cler leome þare-withoute,
> And opon euereches heued aliȝte adoun wel faire, withouten doute,
> And opon þis kniȝtes heued also, an þoruȝ him smot anon,
> And þoruȝ euerech lime and lith of him þat swete liȝt gan gon;
> Þat so much wille and ioye, him þouȝte, neuere he nadde.
>
> (*Early South English Legendary*, 35, 575–80)

The English version found in the Auchinleck MS, which Easting

[8] See Dorothy Ann Bray, 'Allegory in the *Navigatio sancti Brendani*', *Viator* 26 (1995), 1–10.

[9] Translations of most of the well-known examples are collected in *Visions of Heaven and Hell before Dante*, ed. Eileen Gardiner (New York, Italica Press, 1989).

[10] *The Early South English Legendary*, ed. Carl Horstmann, EETS OS 87 (London, Trubner & Co., 1887), 35. *Purgatorium sancti Patricii abb[at]is*, pp.199–220.

[11] In Ms Cotton Caligula A ii/Yale University Library MS 365, and as *The Vision of William of Stranton*. See *St Patrick's Purgatory*, ed. Robert Easting, EETS OS 298 (Oxford U.P., 1991).

[12] *The Early South English Legendary*, 35, l.527.

argues is not translated directly from the Latin, but is a translation
and reworking of an Anglo-Norman verse version,[13] is particularly
interesting for its elaboration of the description of the Earthly Paradise by details of precious stones and comparison of divine skill in
craftsmanship to that of earthly goldsmith or painter:

> Forþermore he gan yse
> A gate, non fairer miȝt be
> In þis world ywrouȝt;
> Tre no stel nas þeron non,
> Bot rede gold and precious ston,
> And al God made of nouȝt:
>
> Jaspers, topes and cristal,
> Margarites and coral,
> And riche safer-stones,
> Ribes and salidoines,
> Onicles and causteloines,
> And diamaunce for þe nones.
>
> In tabernacles þai wer ywrouȝt,
> Richer miȝt it be nouȝt,
> Wiþ pilers gent and smal,
> Arches ybent wiþ charbukelston,
> Knottes of rede gold þeropon,
> And pinacles of cristal.
>
> Bi as miche as our Saueour
> Is queinter þan goldsmitþe oþer paintour,
> Þat woneþ in ani lond,
> So fare þe gates of paradis
> Er richer ywrouȝt, forsoþe ywis,
> As ȝe may vnderstond.
>
> (*St Patrick's Purgatory*, Auchinleck text, Stanzas 130–3)

The relationship between such otherworld exploration and travel
literature which gives details of the wonders of the orient and so on,
as in Mandeveille's *Travels*, is obvious in such passages. The successive
descriptions of music, heavenly carolling, birdsong, and so on are all
richly wrought, with some unusual vocabulary, resulting from
detailed enumeration (of different kinds of flowers, for example)
rather than any stretching towards alliterative diction. The distinction
is made quite explicitly between 'paradis terestri/ þat is in erþe here'

---

[13] Easting, *St Patrick's Purgatory*, p.xliv.

and 'paradis, Godes riche' (Stanza 70) and the privileged movement from one to the other explained. Scenic and doctrinal detail are intertwined, so that the knight Owein is taken, as is the dreamer in a poem such as *Pearl*, to a point where he can receive, not in this case a glimpse of but a breath from heaven as one on a physical journey through mountains to the golden entrance gate. At the same time he is taught the conditions that operate in the passage through purgatory, by such means (among others) as the suggestive comparison between the swift purgation from sin of a newborn child and the laborious process needed for an old man:

> Þe child þat was yborn toniȝt,
> Er þe soule be hider ydiȝt,
> Þe pain schal ouerfle.
> Strong and heui is it þan,
> Here to com þe old man,
> Þat long in sinne haþ be.
> (*St Patrick's Purgatory* Auchinleck text, Stanza 167)

In another version of the otherworld journey, *The Vision of Tundale*, the Irishman Tundale, near death after a seizure, has an 'out-of-body' experience and testifies to his spirit's journey through the regions of Hell where he sees the punishment of sinners, to the region beyond where, though souls cleansed of sin enjoy the comforts of a typical medieval *plaisance* around the well of life, infidelity in marriage is punished (by burning from the navel down for three hours a day) in a jewelled golden house; so earthly paradise and purgatory combine. Finally Tundale is shown by the angel who guides his way the seven regions of heaven, in which, beyond a golden wall, are the jewelled thrones where the saints and martyrs enjoy sweet scent and melody, where gold-crowned souls live beneath the branches of the fruitful, sweet-smelling tree of Holy Church, and where, within a further wall of jewels, are the orders of angels, the Trinity, and God. This popular legend, composed in mid twelfth century and surviving in Latin in over fifty medieval manuscripts, was translated into English in the late fourteenth or early fifteenth century and is extant in four fifteenth-century manuscripts including the miscellanies, MS Cotton Caligula A.ii, and the Heege MS. This is perhaps the most detailed medieval imagining before Dante of the geography of Hell, Purgatory, and Heaven and the journey through Hell in particular might serve as a blueprint for the Inferno. Hell is divided according to punishments for particular sins; it has fiery pits, mountains of fire and ice, obstacles such as narrow bridges, tormenting monsters. Tundale's angel guide engages in dialogue with him as they pass through the various scenes, discussing questions of justice and mercy. Another feature echoed by Dante is that Tundale encounters people he had known in life and men of power and importance whom he recognizes. The light and the clarity of vision allowed to Tundale enables him to see 'Alle þe worlde boþe ferre & ner . . . /All at ones in þat bryȝte place' (ll.2155, 2159). This brilliance, the divine light, is a quality frequently emphasized in medieval visions of heaven. The luminosity and splendour of the empyrean picks up from scripture its imagery of gold and precious jewels and creates a home vibrant with light for the blessed souls after death. 'The bodies of the blessed will shine seven times brighter than the sun', wrote Thomas Aquinas and justifies his claim from the symbolism of light in the New Testament, the account of the Transfiguration as well as descriptions of angels.[14] The idea is pervasive, so that it appears in simple otherworld texts such as *The Vision of Tundale* at one end of the scale and in Dante's vision of Beatrice in the company of the blessed at the other. Tundale, again like the Dreamer in *Pearl*, would like to have seen more and wishes to stay in the world of which he is given privileged knowledge:

> 'I haue sen ioye & myrþe inowe!
> Dere Lorde, I pray þe of þy grace
> Lede me not fro þys ioyfull place
> For I wolde not fro þys place wende,
> But dwelle her ay wythowte ende.'
> (*The Vision of Tundale*, 2246–50)[15]

But the angel tells the unhappy traveller that he must return to his body, taking with him the memory of what he has seen and heard:

> Then grette Tundale & made yll chere
> And sayde, 'Lorde, what haue Y done
> That I shall turne agayne so sone
> To my body full of wrecchedness
> And leue all þys ioye þat her [e]s?'

[14] See Colleen McDonnell and Bernhard Lang, *Heaven: A History* (New Haven, Yale U.P., 1988), pp.80ff, quoting Aquinas, *Summa Theologica*, Supplement, 91.3.

[15] *The Vision of Tundale*, edited from MS Cotton Caligula A ii by Rodney Mearns (Heidelberg, Carl Winter, 1985).

The angell answerde on þys manere
And sayde: 'þer may non þus dwelle here
But only virgyns þat haue bene
Chaste & kepte her bodyes clene,
That for þe loue of God Allmyȝty
Haue forsake[n] þe worlde all hooly
And to God gyfen hem from all ylle
Wyth all her herte & all her wylle;
But such þowȝte was not in þe . . .'
                    (*The Vision of Tundale*, 2256–69)

And so Tundale returns to earth to bear witness and to live out his life in pious teaching both by word and example.

In most of the other medieval examples of visits to the otherworld the vehicle is a vision rather than an actual journey; this is so in the Vision of Dryhthelm, narrated by Bede, and in those of the Monk of Evesham (1156) and of the peasant Thurkell (1206), both of which appear in the *Chronicle* of Roger of Wendover.[16] However, there is a sense of being taken into another place even in vision. Dryhthelm, after apparently dying, is taken to the mouth of Hell, through the limbo of intervening fields where souls wait to the threshold of heaven, guided by an angel who rescues him from devils before returning him to life; the Monk of Evesham, on the point of death, is guided by St Nicholas through places of punishment—plains, mountains, water—and places of glory, including the Heavenly Jerusalem; Thurkell, an Essex labourer guilty of not paying his tithes, is taken by St Julian into the large church of heaven, then to the mount of joy past a purgatorial fire, a cold salt lake and a bridge with thorns and stakes, and finally to a theatre where devils watch sinners re-enacting their sins and being tormented before being returned to their seats, as if in some hideous game-show. They all have the journey-and-return structure which links them to travel narratives such as *The Voyage of St Brendan* and identifies them as rites of passage or transitions across a threshold into a mentally suspended state, in this case between waking and sleeping, comparable to the condition in a traveller's tale when the known world is left behind.[17]

---

[16] All of these visions are translated in Gardiner, *Visions of Heaven and Hell before Dante.*

[17] Kathryn L. Lynch explores the idea of liminality in these visions of the other world in *The High Medieval Dream-Vision: Poetry, Philosophy and Literary Form* (Stanford U.P., 1988), pp.46ff.

Dante's *Divine Comedy* belongs to this tradition of the otherworld journey, though the greater literary scope and complexity of the work obscures the relationship and makes it far too large a topic to be undertaken in this book; I simply note some features of the poem that relate to the narrative type. Though Dante travels not across the surface of the earth as Brendan does but down through the earth and out on the other side, the concept is similar in essence, the representation of a spiritual quest in terms of physical images of place and the idea of a troubled progress along a route full of astonishing sights and encounters. In comparision to the rather episodic structure of earlier otherworld journeys Dante's is, as George Holmes expresses it, 'the most carefully wrought and the most precisely and intricately symmetrical of great literary works'.[18] After an introductory canto, each of the *Inferno, Purgatorio,* and *Paradiso* consists of thirty-three cantos, making a total of 100, and the three-lined stanzas of *terza rima* establish the tripartite structure in even the smallest unit in which the poem may be defined, as it is in the largest, the Trinity itself. Dante uses the guide found in other vision literature, but has two figures, Virgil and then Beatrice, to explain the meaning of the different scenes through which he passes. This is a first-person narrative in the manner of the visionary describing what has been experienced in dream, though it is presented as a literal journey. The personal, autobiographical perspective is densely and repeatedly reinforced by references to contemporary people and events. While the literal level of the story is richly circumstantial the sense of the work is also allegorical and *The Divine Comedy* is probably the medieval narrative most often read in terms of layers of meaning. This was encouraged by the well-known *Letter to Can Grande,* the authorship of which is still disputed. In this explanatory commentary Dante or some member of his circle says:

It must be understood that the meaning of the work is not of one kind only; rather the work may be described as 'polysemous', that is, having several meanings; for the first meaning is that which is conveyed by the letter, and the next is that which is conveyed by what the letter signifies; the former of which is called literal, while the latter is called allegorical or mystical.[19]

---

[18] George Holmes, *Dante,* Past Masters Series (Oxford U.P., 1980), p.41.
[19] *Epistle to Can Grande della Scala,* translated extract in Minnis and Scott, *Medieval Literary Theory and Criticism,* p.459.

Dante's journey has often been seen as the progress of the human soul through stages of understanding, stages which have a personal reference to Dante's own life, and a historical one communicated particularly by the transition from the teaching of Virgil, the wise pagan philosopher, to that of Beatrice, the messenger of Christian revelation.

If the sublimity of Dante's imaginative enlargement of the other-world journey represents the summation of the genre, its status as a genre is ironically confirmed at the ridiculous end of the spectrum. The text known as *The Land of Cokaygne*, probably composed in Ireland in the thirteenth century, though with analogues in French and Dutch, describes an Earthly Paradise flowing with milk, honey, oil, and wine, with an abbey whose walls are of pasties and cakes and which is full of all delights to eye, tongue, and ear; all is gleaming light and much time is spent in play, the young monks having to be called back from hawking by the sight of a young maiden's bare bottom, flourished by the abbot. This jolly vision of freedom from restraint leads up to the lively Goliardic romp of young nuns, playing naked in the river on summer days and being chased and caught by the young monks who:

> ... techiþ þe nunnes an oreisun
> Wiþ iambleué [dancing] vp and doun.[20]

More a parody of the literary idea than any kind of satire on monastic life, the poem sets the seal on the association between fantasy and the otherworld.

Visions and courtly dreams

Dream was a rich narrative resource for medieval writers. Because of the strong emphasis on the idea of historical truth in medieval narrative theory and the consequent preference in high style poetry for retelling great historical events, writers looked to dream to provide opportunities for greater freedom. This might be freedom to be more

---

[20] *The Land of Cokaygne*, 165–6, in Bennett and Smithers, *Early Middle English Verse and Prose*, p.144.

investigative, philosophical, and abstract in the truth that they examined and more imaginative in the means that they could use to do it, but it might also mean freedom to be satirical and even irreverent in commenting on the contemporary world. Hence the interest in writing poems that follow a journey into some other state of knowledge, which could be exploited in a variety of ways. The journey could be inward: dreams of the inner life, of spiritual exploration and progress, perhaps an overcoming of mental stress, as in the Boethian dialogue, or the process of learning from a divine source or other higher being or, more mundanely, from a book. At the other end of the scale the journey could be outward and beyond; the mental world could grow and encompass transformed images of society. So *Le Roman de la Rose* began with a process of animation in which courtship was expressed through abstractions and the allegorical garden created as an image of the world of polite society and youthful ardour, but, when Jean de Meun took over, turned into academic debate and bookish philosophy about man's role in nature, love, sexual relationship, and social conduct. The existing tradition of dreams based on classical and biblical examples provided an authoritative point of reference. Most writers on medieval dream poetry stress the great variety of subjects possible, from apocalyptic visions to erotic adventures, fanciful bird debates, political satires, and tableaux of moral abstractions, and the ways in which dream allows mixtures of traditions and styles.[21]

Paradoxically dream poems, which in their subject matter may differ widely from one another, have the best-defined form of all medieval narratives. They are framed narratives which offer the reader two related but separate states of understanding, the waking consciousness of a first-person narrator figure, often given an apparently autobiographical identity, and the reporting of a dreamer figure, who sometimes adopts the stance of a camera eye simply recording what is seen in the dream, but sometimes is an active participant in dramatic scenes of debate and questioning. This extradiegetic/ intradiegetic combination is, as I suggested earlier when discussing prologues and narrators, particularly associated with the dream-poem

---

[21] For example Helen Phillips in the General Introduction to Phillips and Havely, *Chaucer's Dream Poetry*; Peter Brown, 'On the borders of Middle English dream visions' in *Reading Dreams*, ed. Peter Brown (Oxford U.P., 1999), pp.22–50.

tradition that takes the Boethian dialogue as its model. Boethius' *Consolation of Philosophy* is not presented as a vision, but the encounter between a troubled, first-person narrator and an authoritative teaching figure is one of the basic dream patterns described by Macrobius, whose definition of dreams in his commentary on Cicero's *Dream of Scipio* was frequently cited by medieval poets, as, for example, Guillaume de Lorris in the opening lines of *Le Roman de la Rose*. Macrobius distinguished five types of dream, two insignificant ones, the *insomnium* (a nightmare resulting from physical causes) and the *visum* or *phantasma* (an apparition or confusion of impressions), and three which might be thought to communicate some significant truth or foretell future events: the *somnium* (an enigmatic dream needing interpretation), the *visio* (a prophetic vision), and the *oraculum* (in which an authoritative figure appeared to give advice).[22] These could overlap and Macrobius explains that Scipio's dream is simultaneously enigmatic, prophetic, and oracular. Although this classification dismisses some types of dream as meaningless, they are all potentially interesting to a writer. The argument in *The Nun's Priest's Tale* between Chauntecleer and Pertelote is a debate about the interpretation of dreams; the proud cockerel claims that his dream of a marauding orange-coloured beast is a forewarning, a prophetic vision, but his wife pooh-poohs the idea by arguing that it is merely a sign of imbalance in his digestive system (i.e., that the dream was an *insomnium*) and that a laxative will deal with it; Chauntecleer brings forward a stream of examples of dreams that have come true to support his point. In this joking instance Chaucer is capitalizing on the uncertainties of dream and the irony of the mock-heroic tale is that the opinionated, pretentious cock is proved right, when common sense might be thought to be on Pertelote's side; the world is indeed turned upside down if divine foreknowledge has to be brought into operation for cocks to look out for foxes.

In his earlier dream poem *The Parliament of Fowls* Chaucer had used the uncertainty as an introductory strategy. The poem begins with the troubled narrator educating himself by reading *The Dream*

---

[22] See *Chaucer: Sources and Backgrounds* ed. Robert P. Miller (New York, Oxford U.P., 1977), pp.49–52, for a translation of this passage of Macrobius, and A.C. Spearing, *Medieval Dream Poetry* (Cambridge U.P., 1976), pp.8ff. for discussion of the influence of Macrobius, and the book in general for a survey of the whole tradition.

of Scipio which was the best-known model of *oraculum*, in which Scipio's grandfather, Africanus, appears in a dream to take his grandson on a tour of the heavens, to show him the littleness of earth in relation to the universe and to teach him the vanity of human wishes. After a summary of the content of the Cicero/Macrobius work the narrator puts down the book and passes into sleep, offering as he does so contradictory explanations of the dream that is to follow. It might be understood as simply stimulated by physical or psychological causes:

> Can I not seyn if that the cause were
> For I hadde red of Affrican byforn
> That made me to mete that he stod there,
> But . . .
> (*The Parliament of Fowls*, 106–9)

This is the explanation of dreams as continuations of waking activity, preoccupation dreams in which 'The juge dremeth how his plees ben sped' (l.101) or wish-fulfilment dreams in which 'The lovere met he hath his lady wonne' (l.105). On the other hand the dream might be a supernatural message as the narrator suggests in invoking Venus (under another of her names, Cytherea):

> Cytherea, thow blysful lady swete,
> That with thy fyrbrond dauntest whom the lest
> And madest me this sweven for to mete,
> Be thow myn helpe in this . . .
> (*The Parliament of Fowls*, 113–16)

So, are dreams divine communications sent from beyond into the mind of the dreamer, revelations of the future such as the dreams of Pharaoh interpreted by Joseph, messages from one's ancestors such as Scipio's dream, awful warnings such as Nebuchadnezzar's dream of the great statue interpreted by Daniel, or are they all one's own fault, the product of mental stress or indigestion? Chaucer seems more interested in opening up the reader's mind to the possibilities than in answering the question. Other literary uses of the meaningless kinds of dream would include Gower's vision in Book I of his Latin poem *Vox Clamantis* of the Peasants' Revolt as a rabble of animals turning on their masters, which has the quality Macrobius attributes to the *phantasma* of hosts of spectres aimlessly rushing about. As with Chaucer's references to the question of the truth or falsehood of dreams, the effect is of setting up a satirical position more than an ethical debate.

Dream literature is at its most serious in the visions of the other-world already mentioned and in dreams which are presented as revelations of religious truth or meditations on moral themes, as in *The Dream of the Rood*, night visions of the Virgin Mary, debates between moral abstractions as in *Winner and Waster, The Parliament of the Three Ages*, and the fifteenth-century *Disputation between the Body and the Worms*,[23] the dialogue on death and salvation in *Pearl*, and, though this is a more mixed and complicated case, *Piers Plowman*. In the first of these the double first-person voice is imaginatively employed in a clever fusion of poetic ideas. The basic concept is of the dream as divine revelation as in Bede's well-known story of the reluctant monk–poet Caedmon, who, when urged to sing by a divine messenger in dream, is miraculously supplied with words celebrating the Creation which he remembers when he wakes; he is then ever after able to compose holy words to sing to the harp. In *The Dream of the Rood* the visionary dream is combined with the speaking object, as in Anglo-Saxon riddles or the personification implied in inscriptions such as that on the Alfred Jewel: 'Aelfred mec heht gewyrcan' ('Alfred ordered me to be made'). The two voices in the poem are, first, that of the dreaming witness, who describes the cross on which Christ was crucified as it has become, transformed by jewels and gold into a sign, a beacon shining across the world but with blood gushing from its side, and then the voice of the cross itself telling its own life story from tree to gallows to honoured instrument of healing. A return to the narrator completes the design. The combination of vivid imagery in the narrator's description and the dramatic direct-witness account of the Crucifixion builds a powerful effect but a deliberately oblique one—the voice of Christ is unheard, except as transmuted through the words of the cross. The pattern of dream poem proves in this case a very effective slant on a sublime theme. The much later night visions of Mary do not include a major narrative element but do use the voice of Mary herself, enclosed in dream-poem manner within the observations of a narrating voice. In the best known example it is only the refrain that implies dreamer and dream:

---

[23] All three of these debates may be found in *Middle English Debate Poetry: A Critical Anthology*, ed. John W. Conlee (East Lansing, Mich., Colleagues Press, 1991).

> Sodenly afraide,
> Half wakyng, half slepyng,
> And gretly dismayde,
> A woman sate wepyng.[24]

At the end, 'And with that word she vanysht away', the dream frame for the *pietà* scene of the Virgin's complaint is completed; the narrative content is in the narrator's description and the sense of personal witnessing of the dramatic scene and participation in the dialogue that follows. Similar dream or dreamlike introductions occur in a number of other Marian lullabies and laments, as in:

> In a tabernacle of a toure,
> As I stode musyng on the mone,
> A crouned quene, most of honoure,
> Apered in gostly syght ful sone.[25]

The narrative content of the allegorical debates is more developed, but dream is used only as an enabling framework so that the poet can create a tableau of figures, more or less picturesque in the various instances, who then express their allegorical nature. In the case of *Winner and Waster*, which has often been thought an analogue or even a source for the Lady Meed episode in *Piers Plowman*, the topic is the proper use of worldly wealth and the presence as judge between the two contending figures of a king who appears to be Edward III gives a specific historical base to the debate. In *The Parliament of the Three Ages* the picturesque is strongly in evidence both in the elaborate poaching scene used as the waking frame and in the descriptions of the moral disputants, Youth, Middle, and Old Age; the introduction of a tableau of the Nine Worthies further turns the poem towards allegorical medley.[26] In the Body and Worms debate the setting is macabre rather than colourful, a tomb with the body of a fine woman who has died of the plague, 'In þe ceson of huge mortalitie' as the opening line says, but this is simply a body-and-soul debate dressed up as a dream. In fact all of these debates make a convenience of dream as a supposed explanation for the unreality of the scene and the abstract identity of

---

[24] In *Religious Lyrics of the XVth Century*, ed. Carleton Browne (Oxford, Clarendon Press, 1939) pp.17–18. See Rosemary Woolf, *English Religious Lyrics in the Middle Ages* (Oxford, Clarendon Press, 1968), pp.265–6.

[25] In *Religious Lyrics of the XIVth Century*, ed. Carleton Browne, 2nd edn revd G.V. Smithers (Oxford, Clarendon Press, 1957), p.234.

[26] See below in Chapter 8 for further discussion of the poem.

the speakers, with no sense of transition into another state of seeing.

The sense of 'gostly syght' is, however, strongly present in *Pearl*, since one of the threads in its dense texture is that of the otherworld journey which allows a privileged glimpse of heaven. The dreamer is given sight towards the end of the poem of the heavenly Jerusalem and from the other side of the stream which separates him from the other world sees the shining city on the hill in jewelled splendour borrowed from the Book of Revelations. The poem thus uses the idea of the direct witnessing of scriptural scenes which was mentioned earlier as a feature of Mandeville's *Travels*; this, however, is the time-traveller's experience of being present at the actual Apocalyptic moment when the wounded Christ may be seen processing through the streets of the city with 144 000 virgins in his train. In such passages as this, and in the earlier stages of the dialogue where the Pearl-Maiden narrates the parable of the workers in the vineyard and explains the nature of heavenly reward, the poem claims the status of *oraculum*. The ignorant dreamer functions as questioner and observer faced with a blessed inhabitant of the heavenly world who assumes the role of guide and teacher. The beatified girl is reminiscent of Beatrice acting as guide to Dante in Paradise and the fact that this authoritative figure is a child teaching her father reinforces the contrast between earthly and heavenly values. However, the beginning has established another of the literary threads that make up the poem, the idea of the Boethian consolation, stemming from the passionate grief of the narrator at the loss of an enigmatic precious jewel which is gradually identified as a dead child. Dream is a transition from elegy to otherworld vision, where the beauty of the dream landscape and then of the pearl-adorned ghostly Maiden are themselves consoling. With the beginning of dialogue in which his disordered emotional claims are answered by cool explanations and reproofs, the quality of the poetry shifts into the teacher–pupil mode. The intensity of emotion and poetic language in the early stages of the poem establishes a stronger identity than is usual in dream poems for both the extradiegetic narrating function of the poet and the intradiegetic experiencing function of the dreamer: the poem is as much about bereavement as about heaven. Just as Chaucer deliberately confuses the reader by offering both types of explanation for dreams, so the poet of *Pearl* destabilizes the revelatory authority of the otherworld vision by cross-hatching it with the dream of personal trouble. If the governess in *The Turn of the Screw* may be read as either the innocent witness of supernatural horrors or the hysterical origin of the trouble, then *Pearl*, cryptic about circumstances and offering the relationship between narrator and ghostly Maiden as an enigma, leaves the reader with a similar alternative. Are we reading a poem about divine revelation or about wish-fulfilment in response to the narrator's urgent emotional needs? The tension in the poem is an extreme form of the narrative doubleness of dream poetry which is always facing the reader with the question of where the narrative current is flowing strongest. Is the plot a three-part progress from a narrator who begins troubled, has an enlightening spiritual adventure, and then wakes changed? Or is the real experience in the fictional drama of the dream and the framework merely a tacked-on device concerned with recording and justification?

Many questions about the working of dream narrative arise in the course of reading *Piers Plowman*, though Langland's treatment of the waking/dreaming relationship is, for the most part, casual. His narrator walks abroad in the summer, falls asleep, and dreams; he wakes up from time to time but is usually soon asleep and dreaming again. The waking interludes separate the poem into a number of distinct dreams and so define stages of argument or changes of theme and perspective, but only rarely does Langland create continuity between the dream and the waking life, though he does so effectively at the close of Passus XVIII in the B-text, where the completion of the debate of the Daughters of God in reconciliation and celebratory song wakens the Dreamer to the sound of bells which causes him to call his wife and daughter to go to the Easter mass. The question of continuity does not usually arise in dream poems because they normally deal each with a single dream from which the dreamer may awake to resolve to write up the experience and so create the poem (as in *The Book of the Duchess*), or to make a good resolution such as to read and think more (*The Parliament of Fowls*), or to regret the loss of the vision but accept its lesson (*Pearl*), or to escape from a threatening nightmare (Skelton's *The Bowge of Court*), or simply to return to the course of normal life (*The Parliament of the Three Ages*). Langland is unusual in creating a series of dreams, eight separate ones in the B-text of *Piers Plowman*, with two inserted dream episodes in the third and fifth visions, making a total of ten. There is no close parallel to this multi-dream structure, or 'poly-narrative', as John

Burrow suggests one might think of it, in the course of examining the nearest precedent to the form of *Piers Plowman*, the pilgrimage poems of Guillaume de Deguileville.[27] This French Cistercian poet produced, between 1330 and about 1360, a trilogy of dream poems, *Le Pelerinage de Vie Humaine, Le Pelerinage de l'Ame,* and *Le Pelerinage de Jhesucrist*, which are linked as a sequence of visions though on a larger scale than Langland's curious box of narrative lantern slides. The first of these has the narrator reading *Le Roman de la Rose* before the dream begins and the subsequent progress towards salvation is a religious response and contrary allegory to the earlier poem. As Burrow points out, Langland makes use of several types of dream ending but the abrupt waking produced by a dramatic moment is the most frequent: all three of Deguileville's pilgrimages use this effect. Five out of ten of Will's dreams in the B-text end suddenly, as with the disappearance of Imaginatif at the end of Passus XII and the consequent occasion for reflection at the beginning of Passus XIII:

> . . . and right with that he vanysshed.
> (*Piers Plowman*, B-text, XII, 295)

> And I awaked therwith, witlees nerhande,
> And as a freke that fey were, forth gan I walke
> In manere of a mendynaunt many yer after,
> And of this metyng many tyme muche thought I hadde:
> First how Fortune me failed at my mooste nede,
> And how that Elde manaced me, myghte we ever mete . . .
> And how that Ymaginatif in dremels me tolde
> Of Kynde and his konnynge . . .
> And whan he hadde seid so, how sodeynliche he passed.
> I lay down longe in this thoght, and at the laste I slepte . . .
> (*Piers, Plowman*, B-text, XIII, 1–6, 14–15, 20–21)[28]

This is one of the longer interlude passages with a fuller than usual comment on the content of the preceding dream, but it is typical of Langland's handling of the relationship between the dreaming and the waking life. His dreamer is driven 'witlees' by what he witnesses and is still at odds with life and aware mainly of its penalties and

---

[27] John Burrow, *Langland's Fictions* (Oxford, Clarendon Press, 1993), ch.1, 'A Gathering of Dreams', pp.6ff., and see Appendix A, 'Langland and Deguileville: *Le Pelerinage de Jhesucrist*', pp.113–18.

[28] William Langland, *The Vision of Piers Plowman*, a complete edition of the B-text, ed. A.V.C. Schmidt, revd edn, Everyman's, Library (London, J.M.Dent, 1995).

injustices; the only good is what he has seen in his dream and he can't wait to get back to sleep.

Sleeping and dreaming become the desired state of being in *Piers Plowman* and the gaps between dreams are as remarkable for their brevity as much as for suddenness in waking. At the end of the first dream his regret at not seeing more keeps him awake for the space of five lines (Passus V, 3–8); at the end of the third dream, even though he says that a long time of unhappiness passes when he is scorned and held a fool, it takes only ten lines of raving in his folly 'Til reson hadde ruthe on me and rokked me aslepe' (Passus XV, 11). Again the sense is clearly that reason operates in the dream world, as against the injustice and folly of the waking life. Even briefer, though to the same effect, is the waking at the end of the fourth vision where it takes only three lines to record a long period spent as a wastrel, 'Til I weex wery of the world and wilned eft to slepe' (Passus XVIII, 4). The significant Easter waking mentioned earlier takes only the last six lines of Passus XVIII and the first five lines of Passus XIX before he is asleep again, though this interlude does register the use of the time to record what has been dreamt.

> Thus I awaked and wroot what I hadde ydremed.
> (*Piers Plowman*, B-text, XIX, 1)

With the two inset dreams, or dreams within dreams, (Passus XI, 4–404 and Passus XVI, 20–167) both begin in a moment of high emotion, the first in anger and tears when Will is disparaged by Scripture, the second in an ecstatic swoon at the name of Piers the Plowman, but both end in a typical sorrowful regret. The exit from dream is repeatedly a return to bitterness and confusion, even complete disorientation.

The only waking interludes that develop the extradiegetic aspects of the poet–narrator, apart from the brief mention of writing down what he had dreamt at the beginning and again in the very last line of Passus XIX, are the long passage in Passus VII/VIII after Piers' tearing of the pardon and the beginning of Passus XX where a number of years pass by. The first of these is the only substantial passage in the poem which allies *Piers Plowman* to the tradition of the literary dream poem, since here the poet poses the question of the truth of dreams and cites familiar Old Testament examples associated with Daniel and Joseph, before expressing his uncertainties about the meaning of the pardon rejected by Piers and, with a flourish of academic debating language, identifies himself as a cleric and begins to focus on the idea of Do-wel. The passage marks the major shift in the narrative from the social, satirical allegory of the early passus, based on the Field full of Folk, to the mental, moral allegory and shifting scenes of the central sections of the poem. In the late long waking section at the beginning of Passus XX Will is accosted by Need who urges him to live a temperate life, eating only what he needs; the idea relates to the recurrent theme of poverty and attacks on religious involvement in wealth. Thus even the longer interludes in the B-text are used more as thematic connectives than as the place to show how dream-learning is brought to bear on the narrator's waking life.

A sort of characterization of the narrator, in the guise of the fictional self-representation Long Will, is built up in the course of the poem in these interlude passages, but there is nothing like the emotional intensity of the *Pearl* narrator, nor the joking intimacy of Chaucer's self-portraits in his dream poems. Will is a wanderer and seeker who 'Wente wide in this world wondres to here'; once asleep he is identified in the dreamer's necessary roles of observer and questioner, stimulated by what he sees and hears to seek Truth, to pursue Do-wel, Do-bet, and Do-best and to find Piers the Plowman. Thus his role within the dreams is active and developing but outside the dreams he hardly exists except as a malcontent, a wastrel, rough-clad and obsessive, intent only on escaping from the real world into the other state of knowledge in dream.

This is one area where the C-text of the poem creates a somewhat different impression, largely by the introduction of a substantial characterization of Will the Dreamer, in a passage which has often, if controversially, been called 'autobiographical'.[29] This occurs at the beginning of the second dream, before the confessions of the Seven Deadly Sins, and the implication is that by the time Langland wrote this 'final' revision of the poem he wanted to give a stronger self-representation to his narrator, identifying him as living in London with his wife, earning his bread as a clerk in minor orders and prepared to defend himself against criticism (represented by the figure of Reason who reviews possible ways of living usefully) by giving a short

[29] See George Kane, *The Autobiographical Fallacy in Chaucer and Langland Studies*, Chambers Memorial Lecture (University College London, 1965).

outline of his education and a justification of his way of life. The work of an itinerant bedesman with prayers for the souls of the living and the dead as the tools of his trade, is, he argues, appropriate to a tonsured cleric. Confessing, in response to his conscience's accusation, that he has not always kept up the high standards of active piety that he describes, but has been reduced to begging and so has 'ytynt tyme and tyme myspened', he resolves to 'bigynne a tyme/That alle tymes of my tyme to profit schal turne' (C-text, Passus V, 100–01[30]). The passage may be read as providing a typical role for Will the Dreamer and giving a personal perspective to the theme of confession and contrition which is the subject of the section of the poem which is to follow, but there is the possibility that the characterization is to be read literally: as a dreamer about sin it is appropriate that he should recognize his own failures, but it is perhaps as a poet of moral ideas that he has the need to defend his own life.

Langland was little interested in the dream poem as an art form. At the beginning he shows awareness of the conventional May morning opening as found in *Le Roman de la Rose*, but his use of it is perfunctory and he shifts quickly into the dream world. Of the eight visions that follow in the B-text only the sixth (Passus XVIII) achieves concentrated impact as a dream poem. The particular kind of dream found here is an aspect of the otherworld journey, in this case a series of scriptural witnessings, beginning with Jesus' entry into Jerusalem on Palm Sunday, the prospect of the joust against Satan which the knight Christ in the arms of Piers is to undertake, and then the Crucifixion itself; next comes a shift of scene into a supernatural realm where the Debate of the Daughters of God encloses a dramatic report of the Harrowing of Hell before reaching reconciliation between Justice and Mercy and the Dreamer's Easter waking. The powerful material of this self-contained section of the poem has drawn from the poet sharp focussing on scene and speech and consistent holding of the perspective of Dreamer as witness to great moments of religious history; this is the nearest any Middle English poet gets to the imaginative use of dream seen in *The Dream of the Rood*. Elsewhere the dreams are more of a medley of effects and types of scene and action. At the beginning the Prologue turns the review

---

[30] William Langland, *Piers Plowman*, an edition of the C-text, ed. Derek Pearsall (Berkeley, University of California Press, 1978).

of the world (in the style of estates satire) into the symbolic panorama of the Field full of Folk, inserts some other kinds of allegory,
particularly the fable of the rats, mice and cat, and then shifts into
teacher–pupil dialogue in Passus I. The exchanges with Holichurche
push the Dreamer into the required role of simple-minded learner
addressed as 'Thow doted daffe!' and the like, which easily passes into
the observer of allegorical debate in the Lady Meed scenes. The second vision surveys the field of human sin through confessional dramatic monologues and the panoramic abstraction of society at work
in the ploughing of the half-acre; from this dramatic allegory emerge
the figure of Piers the Plowman and the concerted action of the
pilgrimage to Truth. The most striking image in these initial dreams,
and in the poem as a whole, is the Field full of Folk set between the
Tower of Truth and the Dungeon of Falsehood; against this background pictures of the world in action are filled with type figures,
with only Will the poet/dreamer and Piers the Plowman the exemplar
and moral guide providing continuity. The overall character of the
dreams appears to be social/moral satire, akin to *Winner and Waster*
and to a number of French social poems, not all of them dreams,
some of which may have influenced Langland.[31]

Between these opening dreams and Passus XVIII Langland shifts
into the allegorical mode closer to *Le Roman de la Rose* and to contemporary French works of a more religious type, as well as to the
older tradition of the *psychomachia*, the conflict between good and
evil within the human soul represented as a battle between personi-
fied virtues and vices. The use of such a conflict, where the vices are
led by Antichrist, is one of the motifs in *Li Tornoiemenz Antecrist*
(1234–5) of Huon de Meri, a contemporary of Guillaume de Lorris,
which has led to its being identified as a possible source for Langland;
this is not a dream poem but has some familiar touches such as the
springtime opening, and themes such as the allegory of the human
body as a castle and the central topic of the allegorical tournament.
The narrative in *Piers Plowman*, from Passus VIII onwards, turns
into a number of encounters between Will and authoritative teaching

---

[31] See Stephen A. Barney, 'Allegorical visions', in *A Companion to Piers Plowman*, ed.
John A. Alford (Berkeley, University of California Press, 1988), pp.117–33, who refers not
only to Deguileville but to several other allegorical pilgrimage dreams, such as *La Voie
de Paradis* of Rutebeuf (late thirteenth century) and *La Voie d'Enfer et de Paradis* of
Jean de la Mote (1340).

figures, in which the dreamer's role is often reduced to that of listener to lengthy discourses, though monologue is interspersed with teacher–pupil dialogue and with passages involving more than two speakers in a 'parliament' mode. In these sections Langland only fitfully exploits the imaginative possibilities of the dream form, but the representations of mental processes by means of personifying the different active forces in the mind, Thought, Study, Imagination, the Soul, and so on, and the development of Will's understanding from the idea of Do-wel to the concepts of Patience and Charity clearly belong to the realm of fiction. Narrative is being used to explore concepts metaphorically, rather than in terms of literal experience or historical evidence. Langland's use of dream poetry transforms his social and moral themes into pictures and dramatic confrontations. One has only to compare *Piers Plowman* to some of the medieval poems which treat similar material in more literal ways, such as *The Simonie*, a 'bitter review of the secular and spiritual ill-health of the earlier fourteenth century',[32] with a range of material similar to that of Langland's Prologue and Passus I–IV, to understand the transfiguring power added by casting social satire into dream images.

Compared to Langland Chaucer is more sophisticated and subtle in his use of dreams, though less serious. He was seldom content simply to follow fashion and to write completely within genre boundaries and this is as true of his dream poems as the various types of narrative included in *The Canterbury Tales*. His dream poems are recognizably alike in that he prefaces them with speculation about the nature and truth of dreams and with literary examples from the past but the likeness does not go far beyond the initial stages. In *The Book of the Duchess* the dream is introspective, exploring images of melancholy and anxiety; in *The House of Fame* the dream is a spectacularly extrovert venture into medieval science fiction, and the dream in *The Parliament of Fowls* is a literary pot-pourri of images of love—temple, garden, and debating birds. I pointed out in the earlier discussion of *The Book of the Duchess* the two different first-person narrators and the adaptation of dream to the purpose of tribute to the dead duchess of Lancaster, but another striking feature of the poem is Chaucer's

---

[32] Elizabeth Salter, '*Piers Plowman* and "The Simonie" ', *Archiv* 203 (1967), 241–54 (quotation from p.248). One of the surviving texts of *The Simonie* is found in the Auchinleck manuscript, suggesting London circulation.

absorption of material from several contemporary French poems of the type known as *dits amoreux*. There are similarities in the Black Knight's complaint and story to Guillaume de Machaut's *Jugement dou Roy de Behaigne*, in some of the description of the lady to Machaut's *Remède de Fortune*, in the story of Ceyx and Alcyone to Machaut's *Dit de la Fonteinne amoreuse* and in the use of dream as a frame to Jean Froissart's *Le Paradys d'Amours*, as well as several other poems by the same two poets.[33] Chaucer's poem is very derivative, saturated with the sentiments and expressions of contemporary French courtly poetry, a distillation of the spirit of love complaint and melancholy yearning, but the very number of borrowings requires a refocussing of the material to characterize his mourning knight who is observed from the outside by the detached poet/narrator. The effect is akin to Picasso's showing a human figure from several angles at once.

The House of Fame is much more explicitly a work of the imagination, using the central motif of dream as a spiritual journey through the universe and applying it to the idea of the poet's seeking for material. It is the nearest Chaucer comes to writing a grand serious dream poem. It is provided with an elaborate machinery of three books with epic invocations and many classical allusions. The architectural settings are imposing, with reminiscences of the descriptions of the dwellings of Fame and of Fortune in Ovid's *Metamorphoses*, in Nicole de Margival's *Panthère d'Amours*, and Froissart's *Temple d'Honneur*. The tableau of the nine companies seeking fame in the weighty allegorical set piece in Book III has some resemblance to Dante's ranging through the evils and follies of mankind in the *Inferno*. Interesting themes are opened up, the instability of fame, the role of poets in substantiating the reputations of the great, and so on. It is also the most obviously influential of Chaucer's dream poems, despite its being unfinished: Lydgate's *Temple of Glass*, Douglas's *Palice of Honour*, Skelton's *Garland of Laurel* all use Chaucer's work as a starting point and the whole idea of centring an allegory in the building devoted to a divine power or a moral abstraction has Chaucer's poem as one of its main sources in later English poetry, in *The Faerie Queene*, for example. And yet *The House of Fame* is

[33] See B.A. Windeatt, *Chaucer's Dream Poetry: Sources and Analogues* (Cambridge, D.S. Brewer, 1982).

obviously not meant to be taken seriously. It begins with a good deal of scepticism as Chaucer muses on dreams:

> For hyt is wonder, be the Roode,
> To my wytte, what causeth swevenes
> Eyther on morwes or on evenes,
> And why th'effecte folweth of some
> And of some hit shal never come;
> Why that is an avision
> And why this a revelacion,
> Why this a dreme, why that a swevene,
> And noght to every man lyche evene—
> Why this a fantome, why these oracles,
> I not—but who so of these meracles
> The causes knoweth bet then I
> Devyne he . . .
> (*The House of Fame*, 2–14)

This reminiscence of the dream classifications of Macrobius makes the foundations of the vision look shaky even before it starts and though Chaucer the dreamer is later quite clearly participating in an 'oracle' as he is instructed in the principles of physics and the transmission of sound by his all-knowing guide, the fact that his tutor is a garrulous eagle and that the hapless Geoffrey is having to receive instruction while speechlessly flying through the air in the eagle's claws casts the whole process in a comic light which encourages questions. Is *The House of Fame* a parody of dream poetry? By introducing his own name and envisaging the celestial journey as an attempt to get the poet out and about and provide him with tidings of love to give him something to write about, Chaucer turns the dream experience into an enjoyable game, full of busy activity and inventive images, especially in the phantasmal House of Rumour.

In contrast to the three books of *The House of Fame*, consisting of 2158 lines in loose octosyllabic couplets but still unfinished, the 694 lines of *The Parliament of Fowls* in neat rhyme-royal stanzas (plus final roundel) looks a model of taut expression and poetic form. Though the exact dating of the two poems is not sure, it is very tempting to think that the shorter poem represents a more intellectually controlled idea of what the dream poem could do, which in Chaucer's hands was to invent new angles on fashionable court topics. In the restricted space of this poem he flashes from one end of the spectrum to the other, beginning with the theme of love and the classic authoritative text of *The Dream of Scipio* with its inherent promise that any dream which follows will be serious, philosophical, about the world and man's place in it, and about judgement of good and bad lives. With the teasing tone of a writer who is playing with his readers, the narrator tells us the mood in which he went to bed:

> And to my bed I gan me for to dresse,
> Fulfilled of thought and besy hevynesse;
> For bothe I had thinge which that I nolde,
> And eke I ne had thyng that I wolde.
> (*The Parliament of Fowls*, 88–91)

With the confusing alternatives about the possible source of dreams which I quoted earlier the narrator turns into a dreamer and finds himself thrust by his august guide through the challenging gates into the garden of love, the temple of Venus, and the assembling of all the birds in the world in Nature's court on St Valentine's Day and so into the debate of birds which occupies the second half of the poem. This rapid transit through different scenes is poetic shorthand since Chaucer is passing through snatches of the imagined worlds of *The Divine Comedy, Le Roman de la Rose*, Boccaccio's *Teseida*, and Alain de Lille's *De Planctu Naturae* ('Of the Complaint of Nature') on the way to a courtly *demande d'amour* about rivalry in love which might come from a Machaut *dit*, which gradually descends to an unseemly squabble among impatient factions of birds:

> The noyse of foules for to ben delyvered
> So loude rong: 'Have doon, and let us wende!'
> That wel wende I the woode had al toshyvered.
> 'Com of!' they cride, 'allas, ye wol us shende!
> Whan shal youre cursed pledynge have an ende?
> How shulde a juge eyther party leve,
> For ye or nay, withouten any preve?'
>
> The goos, the duk, and the cukkowe also
> So criden: 'Kek! kek!', 'Kukkowe', 'Quek, quek!' hye
> That thorgh myn eres the noyse went tho.
> (*The Parliament of Fowls*, 491–500)

The authority of Nature and the conventions of debate that allow matters to end in suspended judgement bring a satisfactory cheerful close in St Valentine's Day celebration and so Chaucer signs off with panache. What better demonstration could there be of the usefulness and freedom of the dream poem form? An apparently serious opening has managed to slip and slide by degrees through a whole repertoire of fourteenth-century notions of dream towards playful fun and in so doing has managed to create something of the inconsequence and fantasy of dream experience. Chaucer is the only medieval poet who invented dreams that are actually dreamlike, while remaining unmistakably fictional and linked to his professional interest in analysing what were the proper subjects for poetry. His use of dream in the *Prologue to the Legend of Good Women* is as a kind of defence of poetry, or at least a plea for the poet's freedom to select material from 'old books' and to interpret it as he wishes.

Chaucer started a native tradition of courtly dream poems about love and poetry, often full of ceremony and colour, in English from Clanvowe's *The Cuckoo and the Nightingale* to Lydgate and Skelton, and in Scots from *The Kingis Quair* to the poems of Henryson, Dunbar, and Douglas. Though the attraction of the dream poem to fourteenth-century poets must have been the exploration of states of 'altered consciousness'[34] and the opportunity to claim that their visions had greater truth than observations of real life, fifteenth-century imitations and developments of Chaucer and of French courtly poets expose the weaknesses as much as the imaginative possibilities of the form. Dreams may be an excuse, rather than a means for probing analysis of self and society; in Lydgate's *Temple of Glass*, for instance, the dream is little more than a frame for an anthology of complaints. Of these later poets only Skelton did much more than to create variations on what Chaucer had done with the dream as a narrative form.

[34] As argued by Peter Brown in the essay in *Reading Dreams*, which echoes Lynch, *The High Medieval Dream-Vision*, in stressing the anthropological concept of liminality, or crossing thresholds.

7

Two versions of tragedy: *Troilus and Criseyde* and the Alliterative *Morte Arthure*

Tragedy

Peter Brooks argues that narrative always makes the implicit claim 'to be in a state of repetition'—'a *sjuzet* repeating the *fabula*'.[1] This idea that narrative is a going over again of ground already covered has a particular application to medieval narrative, which is nearly always based on 'borrowed' plot material. Medieval rhetorical teaching of the art of composition always assumed that subject matter would be well known and that the artist's task was not that of invention but of expression and interpretation. Hence the space that arts of poetry give to the question of judging the appropriate scale for a narrative and to the basic choice between developing a subject at greater length (*amplificatio[n]*) and reducing a diffuse subject to its essence (*abbreviatio[n]*); with that goes the decision about where to begin— whether to follow the Aristotelian maxim of constructing a narrative

---

[1] Brooks, *Reading for the Plot*, p.97.

with a beginning, middle, and end or the Virgilian example of plunging into the current of action. Medieval poets seem comfortable with the idea that their purpose in writing was not to devise new plots (though the authors of dream poems and allegories took more liberties with narrative content) but to exercise their imaginations in the realization of existing ones. The two poems I have chosen to discuss, Chaucer's *Troilus and Criseyde* and the Alliterative *Morte Arthure*, both tell known stories. The alliterative poem is a retelling in 4346 alliterative long lines of the version of the story of King Arthur that omits his birth and achievement of the throne and most of the chivalrous, romance stories of the knights of the Round Table, in order to focus on his wars, first against Lucius, emperor of Rome, and then against his treacherous nephew, Mordred, which leads to Arthur's death. The material comes from the chronicle-cum-epic tradition of Geoffrey of Monmouth, Wace, and Laȝamon discussed in an earlier chapter, though the poet seems not to be translating or adapting a single identifiable text of any one of them but building up his own narrative effectiveness from an amalgam of these and other chronicle sources, while adding several episodes from texts outside the Arthurian tradition. Thus, while the poet is selecting from the Arthurian material and omitting or rejecting aspects of the narrative which had been explored in other works (particularly the story of Lancelot and Guenevere, the quest for the Holy Grail, the wisdom of Merlin) and so producing an abbreviated version of the whole cycle, he is at the same time adding to the story and reshaping the course of the narrative. The stance he adopts towards his discourse is that of a sober moral chronicler, aiming to write worthily, 'That nothyre voyde be ne vayne', and to narrate the noble deeds of the past.

> And I salle telle ȝow a tale, that trewe es and nobylle,
> Off the ryealle renkys of the Rownnde Table
> That chefe ware of cheualrye . . .
> (AMA, 16–18)

Chaucer, on the other hand, in creating his ambitious narrative from an episode in the story of the fall of Troy, might be seen as even closer to Brooks's idea: the claim of narrative to be regarded as an act of repetition is expressed in the epic poet's initial statement of intent—'I sing of . . .' or 'I tell of . . .'—and this is Chaucer's model in his opening lines, where he declares:

> The double sorwe of Troilus to tellen,
> That was the kyng Priamus sone of Troye,
> In lovynge, how his aventures fellen
> Fro wo to wele, and after oute of joie,
> My purpos is, er that I parte fro ye.
>
> (*TC*, I, 1–5)

He later presents himself as a translator whose personal feelings are not involved in the subject but who is simply doing his best to render a foreign text into English.

> . . . of no sentement I this endite,
> But out of Latyn in my tonge it write.
>
> (*TC*, II, 13–14)

Further he is not responsible for the work's inadequacies, especially in expressing love, since he is merely following his source.

> Disblameth me if any word be lame
> For as myn auctour seyde, so sey I.
>
> (*TC*, II, 17–18)

What he says is true to the extent that he does have one main source, the Italian poem *Il Filostrato* ('The Love-Stricken One') by Boccaccio, which Chaucer amplifies into a poem of 8239 lines in seven-line, rhyme-royal stanzas (replacing the eight-line—*ottava rima*—stanzas of the Italian), divided into five books. But he never identifies 'myn auctour' beyond disguising his source under the name Lollius, and he by no means produces a verse-by-verse rendering of the Italian. The story of the Trojan prince, Troilus, and his doomed love for Criseyde, a widow left in Troy when her father, the soothsayer Calkas, crosses over to the Greeks, is set against the background of the besieged city and the uncertainty of warfare; this material from classical epic is, to some extent, augmented by Chaucer, though still subordinated to the love story whose brief time of happiness is succeeded by separation, unfaithfulness, and the hero's death. Like the alliterative poet, Chaucer mixes into his main story elements taken from other sources as well as his own invented scenes, details, and comments.

Both poems, in very different ways, present the reader with intriguing paradoxes. The Alliterative *Morte Arthure* has often been praised for its realism, particularly in the stark expression of the brutalities of war. It is full of physicality about fighting and mutilation and has been compared to the contemporary chronicles of

Froissart and seen as a reflection of particular battles of Edward III in the Hundred Years War; yet it is completely fictional and the campaign against Lucius, which Malory turns into Book II of his *Morte Darthur* using this poem as his source, is (in terms of historical credibility) the least persuasive part of the Arthurian story. The poet's concentration on Arthur as leader leaves no room for themes of love or spiritual quest. *Troilus and Criseyde* has puzzled readers too: are we reading epic or romance? When is it all supposed to be happening—in the pagan past or the Christian present? Chaucer's amplification of passages expressing the thoughts and feelings of the three main characters moves them on from Boccaccio's stereotypes of autobiographical young hero, fickle mistress, and neutral confidant/go-between: should one read it in terms of plot and character, as if it were a novel, or in terms of its lyrics and soliloquies as if it were a courtly *dit*? Both poems have been called 'tragedy' and that idea provides a useful perspective from which to examine them.

I referred earlier, in the discussion of genres, to Chaucer's definitions of tragedy in his translation of Boethius and in the prologue to *The Monk's Tale*, where he explains tragedy as a story 'Of hym that stood in great prosperitee/And is yfallen out of heigh degree/Into myserie and endeth wrecchedly.' This is the idea of tragedy associated with the turning of Fortune's wheel and the fall of princes, the *de casibus* tragedy of Boccaccio's series of stories in Latin prose concerned with the falls of famous men. Boccaccio does not actually call these stories tragedies, and there is a broader medieval sense of the word, closer to Aristotle and the ideas of classical drama, which sees tragedy simply as a serious story concerned with noble characters and written in high style, 'beginning in joy and ending in grief', as John of Garland expresses it. Though in writing *The Monk's Tale* Chaucer shows that he is taking Boccaccio's stories in the limited sense of worldly position brought to a sudden end, his use of the word in the closing stages of *Troilus and Criseyde* is perhaps less circumscribed. It is particularly striking that, as Chaucer says farewell to his work, he not only provides a generic label for it but contrasts it in rhyme with its opposite:

> Go, litel boke, go, litel myn tragedye,
> Ther god thi makere ʒet, er that he dye,
> So sende myght to make in some comedye . . .
>
> (*TC*, V, 1786–8)

As Windeatt points out, Chaucer is using terms that are not an accustomed part of the contemporary English literary vocabulary: his self-deprecating phrase 'litel myn tragedye' might seem anxious not to claim too much and yet he is declaring that his poem aspires to equality with the great classical poets.[2] That liking for explicit identification of genre which was noted earlier in *The Canterbury Tales* is in operation here. The occurrence of the word focusses the reader's attention and forces one to ask the question of how far and in what respect *Troilus and Criseyde* fulfils an idea of tragedy.

The author of the Alliterative *Morte Arthure* does not give one a handle so ready to be grasped but the fall of a prince is unavoidably the central theme. *Morte Arthure* may be read, in terms of narrative content rather than structural divisions or episodes of equal length, as made up of seven elements:

1. The challenge to Arthur from the Emperor Lucius (1–624);
2. The mustering of armies (625–839);
3. The giant of Mont St Michel (840–1221);
4. Three battles against the Romans (1222–1616; 1617–1960; 1961–2370);
5. The conquest of Lorraine (2371–3217);
6. Arthur's second and major dream (3218–3455);
7. Civil war and the death of Arthur (3456–4346).

The poem begins as an epic account of King Arthur's just wars against a tyrant. The tone is serious and heroic, concerned with justice and nobility, set against a background of ceremony and vigorous speech and action. The episode of the giant is closer to the spirit of romance, a piece of supernatural adventure testing Arthur's individual courage rather than his kingship but also presented as a fight against a tyrant and so fitting into the pseudo-chronicle material of the war; Arthur releases the people from bondage and evil and the episode may be taken as symbolic, displaying Arthur's heroic nature before the actual battles. The battle scenes weave together two main elements, heroic speeches and energetic accounts of hand-to-hand fighting between individuals. The three battles and the defeat of Lucius complete Arthur's original mission: from 2371 onwards the

---

[2] B.A. Windeatt, *Oxford Guides to Chaucer:* Troilus and Criseyde (Oxford, Clarendon Press, 1992), p.154.

poem changes direction as Arthur is motivated by the desire to conquer further realms; these campaigns appear to be fought for the sake
of dominion, rather than in the just defence of right. At the same
time the poet changes course in another sense, in that he introduces
new material into the narrative, which is mainly based on the epic/
chronicle material descending from Geoffrey of Monmouth, Wace,
and Laʒamon, but which now incorporates episodes which associate
Arthur with the exploits of Alexander and Charlemagne. Then follows the elaborate dream of Arthur and the wheel of Fortune, which
brings allegory and symbolism into the narrative in preparation for
the climax of the poem in Arthur's war against Mordred.

From the start the treatment is expansive and high-flown, particularly in its heroic tone and in the importance attributed to formal,
boasting speeches, some of them lengthy; the figures who speak in
the council scene, where the possible responses to the challenge from
Lucius are debated, are important as attitudes rather than as characters. The early scenes convey concern with states and nations: the
summoning by Lucius of kings and nobles from all corners of the
Roman Empire to fight against Arthur, together with giants, witches,
and warlocks, accumulates through exotic place names a sense of
epic sweep and a richly populated political arena. Arthur's mustering of his own forces, his entrusting the kingdom to Mordred in a
farewell speech, the traditional epic motif of the sea crossing and
Arthur's first dream, of the dragon fighting against the bear, all
sustain the bold heroic style of the opening. Though the encounter
with the giant of Mont St Michel is a self-contained episode typical
of romance meetings with monsters and marvels, and accompanied
by characteristic romance embellishments—the birds singing in the
grove, the mourning widow, the grotesque description—epic motifs
continue to appear, as in Arthur's arming, the leaving behind his
accompanying knights, his speech of challenge, the jesting between
Arthur and Bedivere. Whereas the hero's role in Arthurian romances
has so often passed to Lancelot, Gawain, or some other knight, here
it is Arthur who is displayed as hero. In the three battle scenes the
speeches and narration of attack and bloodshed are akin to the
movements of a dance, ritualized displays of defiance and courage;
some individualization is added by emphasis on particular British
knights, by touches of the exotic in references to giants, ele-
phants, and so on, by the dying speech and death of Kay, and by the

culmination of the battles in the death of Lucius and the ironic delivery of the belated tribute to Rome together with Lucius' embalmed body. The poet could have left Arthur's European ventures there and moved on to the recall of Arthur to deal with rebellion at home, but instead he enlarges his theme. Arthur now sets out to conquer Lorraine and with a boasting speech lays siege to Metz; a foraging party which includes Gawain gets involved in a series of adventures which culminates in a battle against the duke of Lorraine, a stirring victory for Gawain and the other knights, and then a full assault on Metz. This episode has been seen by most critics as the turning point in the action of the poem, in that Arthur is no longer engaging in a just war, but is embarking on war of conquest and self-aggrandizement. However, even if one does not read moral judgement into the treatment of this period of conquest, the subsequent dream makes it clear that fortune will change for Arthur—he has gone far enough. The foraging party and its adventures is imported from the French Alexander episode known as *Li Fuerres de Gadres*, and the encounter with Priamus from the *chanson de geste* stories of Charlemagne, specifically from the episode concerning Fierabras. The touches of narrative elaboration, such as the description of the foraging party in the meadows listening to the song of the birds, and the concern with fighting for personal 'nobelay' in the encounter between Gawain and Priamus highlight the turning aside from the high road of the narrative. The furthest reach of diversion from the main current of action comes with Arthur's conquests in Lombardy and Tuscany and the message from the Pope that Arthur will be crowned sovereign in Rome. As Arthur glories in conquest and plans to hold the Round Table in Rome, the voice of one riding for a fall is clearly heard:

> Than this roy royalle rehersys theis wordes:
> 'Now may we reuelle and riste, fore Rome is oure awene! . . .
> We salle be ouerlynge of alle that one the erthe lengez!'
>
> (AMA, 3206–7, 3211)

This hubris is soon answered in the fearful dream that follows. Although the pattern of dream and philosopher's explanation resembles the earlier dream of the dragon and the bear, that was a simple prophetic dream using symbols; this second dream is a much more portentous affair, an enclosed vision poem using allegory.

Arthur, in recounting it, acts as the dream narrator who observes and is taught and who then awakes and ponders on the meaning; the philosopher takes up the poet–teacher's role. Again the poet introduces subject matter from outside his main source material in the form of the pageant of the Nine Worthies, taken from *Les Voeux du Paon*, a story attached to French versions of the conquests of Alexander. I will examine the content of the dream in more detail later, but for the moment note that the conjunction of Arthur's pride in his conquests and the dream of the Wheel of Fortune signals unambiguously the poet's sense of his subject as an instance of *de casibus* tragedy. In the climactic phase of the action that remains the signs are that he saw the completion of his task in terms of raising the level of discourse to the high style appropriate to epic. Dramatic narrative and scene-painting with a number of the topoi associated with epic—a messenger's speech for Cradok, a sea battle enlivened by some of the tackle and trade vocabulary that alliterative poets particularly like—prepare the way for the first part of the climax that leads to the death of Gawain; Gawain's rashness, his concern for his men and his exhortation to them to face death well, his battle frenzy, the slow-motion effect of the fight between Gawain and Mordred are all identifiable as epic gestures and they culminate in the finest passage in the poem, Mordred's noble tribute to the courage of the enemy he has just killed.

> 'He was makles one molde, mane, be my trowthe;
> This was syr Gawayne the gude, the gladdeste of othire,
> And the graciouseste gome that vndir God lyffede,
> Mane hardyeste of hande, happyeste in armes,
> And the hendeste in hawle vndire heuene riche . . .'
> (AMA, 3875–9)

In the last part of the poem dealing with Arthur's final battle the outstanding features are Arthur's lament for Gawain, the formal ceremonial of the drawing up of battle lines and the speeches that are preliminary to battle, and the dignity and soberness of the ending: there is no magic or mystery but simply a laconic, bleak completion of the tale. The poet leaves all the emotional force to Arthur's short speeches, remaining himself in the unobtrusive role of chronicler of events, which do not include any strange ladies in barges, or any mention of Avalon, but which end in a suitable ceremony of burial.

With alle wirchipe and welthe that any wy scholde.
Throly belles thay rynge, and *Requiem* syngys,
Dosse messes and matyns with mournande notes . . .
Whas neuer so sorowfulle a syghte seene in theire tyme!

(A*MA*, 4331–3, 4341)

In contrast, Chaucer uses his narrator's voice much more manipu-
latively in *Troilus and Criseyde*. Not only does he at the end provide
the reader with the word 'tragedy' as a measuring-glass through
which to look back at the poem but from the start he draws attention
to the idea of the rise and fall of the fortune of the hero: 'how his
aventures fellen/Fro wo to wele, and after out of joie'. Discarding the
twenty-two-year-old Boccaccio's prologue in which the poet claims
that Troilo's story has been chosen as a vehicle for his own sorrow,
Chaucer, in his mid-forties when he wrote the poem, takes up the
detached stance of the writer trying to render a difficult text and a
distressing theme. His interest in not concentrated on the discarded
lover's sorrow and so the proportions of the narrative shift; more
time is made for the preliminary episodes, falling in love, overcoming
of despair, processes of courtship, the uncertainties of both hero and
heroine. Chaucer's first three books present an expanded version of
Boccaccio's Cantos 1–3, with particularly substantial additions in the
long scene between Criseyde and Pandarus at the beginning of Book
II and the longer scene at Pandarus' house in Book III which leads to
the consummation of the love affair. Chaucer's Book IV (dealing with
the plan for Criseyde to be exchanged for Antenor and so to leave
Troy) follows Boccaccio more closely, though complaint and speech
are added for Criseyde and the predestination soliloquy for Troilus.
The material in Boccaccio's Cantos 5–8 is condensed into three scenes
in Chaucer's Book V dealing with Diomede's wooing of Criseyde and
Troilus' despair as he hopes for her return, followed by his eventual
recognition that the love affair is over, and the events leading to his
death; Boccaccio's short last canto in which he bids farewell to his
work and reiterates its moral, the fickleness of women, is replaced by
Chaucer's complex mixture of strategies of closure which includes
Troilus' looking down at the earth after his death, adapted from
Arcita in Boccaccio's *Teseida*.

The imagery of rising and falling is a recurrent thread in the poem,
from Troilus' falling in love in Book I (seen as a bringing down of his
former pride and a climbing on to Fortune's stair) to his dreaming in

Book V 'as though he sholde falle depe/From heighe o-lofte' (V, 258–9).
The sense of the rise and fall of Fortune's wheel is marked out by the
structure which Chaucer has imposed on the material of Boccaccio's
Il Filostrato: for the prose prologue and the nine cantos of the Italian
source Chaucer has substituted the pattern of five books (modelled
on Boethius' *Consolation of Philosophy*) and marks out each book as a
significant stage of the action by means of prologues to the first four
books and an epilogue to the last. The workings of the machinery are
thus highly visible and these passages of structural support are characterized by conspicuous elements of high style poetry, particularly in
the form of invocations of divine aid and of the poet's own comments on his artistic endeavour, and by the poet's addresses to and his
engagement in debate with his audience. So, as he approaches the
highest point of Troilus' fortunes in love in the central book of the
five, Chaucer calls both for the help of Venus, as the power of love,
and of Calliope, the muse of epic poetry, to 'telle anon right the
gladnesse/Of Troilus', but by the beginning of Book IV he is already
pointing out to us that 'al to litel, weylawey the whyle,/ Lasteth swich
ioie' and recording the change of fortune's favours.

> From Troilus she gan hire brighte face
> Awey to writhe and tok of hym non heede,
> But caste hym clene out of his lady grace,
> And on hire whiel she sette vp Diomede.
> (*TC*, IV, 8–11)

These authorial comments function almost as marginal indicators for
the reader, so that the story develops within a frame of ironic awareness: one knows where the story is going and one knows further that
its author has accepted it from elsewhere and has no choice about its
outcome.

This question of choice becomes one of the issues in the poem,
since Chaucer not only expresses a sense of the constraint which the
story exercises upon him but develops discussion within the fiction of
the extent to which the characters have any choice. Fortune is quite
frequently referred to in the work, but there is no sense that the
modern reader has to accept that the action is controlled by some
pagan deity spinning a wheel: the image is there as a representation of
the changes of situation which affect the characters, but the question
of their freedom is made more open than the image might suggest. In

Book I as Pandarus tries to persuade Troilus that his falling in love with Criseyde is not a cause for despair but for hope, Chaucer, in one of the passages he has added to Boccaccio, develops a debate between the two in which Troilus' role is that of the pessimist who can see little opportunity for determining his own fate:

> 'Ful hard were it to helpen in this cas,
> For wel fynde I that fortune is my fo;
> Ne al the men that riden konne or go
> May of hire cruel whiel the harm withstonde;
> For as hire list she pleyeth with free and bonde.'
>
> (*TC*, I, 836–40)

However, Chaucer uses the pragmatic voice of Pandarus to resist this:

> Quod Pandarus, 'than blamestow fortune
> For thow art wroth, ȝe, now at erst I see;
> Wost thow nat wel that fortune is comune
> To eueri manere wight in som degre?'
>
> (*TC*, I, 841–4)

Fortune is no more than the normal uncertain condition of life—the wheel has to keep turning and is just as likely to produce an up as a down:

> 'What woostow if hire mutabilite
> Right as thy seluen list wol don by the,
> Or that she be naught fer fro thyn helpynge?
> Paraunter thow hast cause for to synge.'
>
> (*TC*, I, 851–4)

This debate lies behind the longer treatment of the question of free will which Chaucer expresses in Book IV by giving to Troilus the soliloquy adapted from Boethius concerning predestination, in which he characterizes his hero's despair as a philosophical determinism:

> 'For al that comth, comth by necessitee,
> Thus to ben lorn, it is my destinee.'
>
> (*TC*, IV, 958–9)

This is characteristic of the intriguing cross-currents in the poem. Chaucer gives to the story the veneer of Virgilian (or Statian) epic and the plot is one of the fall of a prince, showing him in bliss and moments of success but ending with his defeat and death, though his role as military hero is pushed aside and happens, like his death, off-stage; the fall of Troy, which we all know is imminent, remains only a threat. If the work is to be seen as a tragedy, it is nevertheless not, as the *Morte Arthure* is, the sort that reaches its climax on the battlefield.

To some readers Chaucer's addition to the plot-material of the epilogue in which Troilus looks down after death at 'this litel spot of erthe',

> . . . and fully gan despise
> This wrecched world, and hold al vanite
> To respect of the pleyn felicite
> That is in hevene above . . .
>
> (*TC*, V, 1816–9)

takes the story beyond tragedy into Christian 'comedy' and consolation, while to others this realization of 'worldly vanity' is the most tragic part of the ending. The sudden reversal of the hero's fortune has occurred at the beginning of Book IV and the rest of the poem consists of a slow working through its effects and consequences. Book IV is the most melodramatic part of the poem: 70 per cent of it is in direct speech in alternating passages of soliloquy and dialogue. Complaints for hero and heroine in turn are countered by argument often from Pandarus, and this dramatic structuring is highlighted by an extreme style of rhetoric and action, which includes fury and rage, wringing of hands and tearing of hair. The story is treated here on a plane of high tragedy and culminates in Criseyde's death-like swoon with Troilus lamenting over her body and contemplating his own suicide (*TC*, IV, 1182–6). From the tragic brink the characters and the poet draw back, but it is significant that Chaucer does not mute Boccaccio's moment of high theatre, which indicates one literary version of what might befall noble characters in an epic tale. What does in fact happen in Book V is more complex, an interweaving of two sets of action (Criseyde and Diomede in the Greek camp, Troilus and Pandarus in Troy) and two levels of discourse, one dealing with the seduction of Criseyde and Pandarus's attempts to divert Troilus which at times verges on the style of a comedy of manners, and the other, in a sequence of lyric passages and letters, mainly expressing the growing desperation of the hero. The tragedy lies in Troilus' having to suffer the slow recognition of lack of steadfastness and in the failure of love, for both Criseyde and Troilus, to overcome the force of circumstances.

The Use of Dreams

Both poems make significant use of dreams to create a sense of the mental dimensions within which the characters move. The prophetic dream is a feature in Arthurian chronicles and romances from Geoffrey of Monmouth onwards. In the *Historia Regum Britanniae* Arthur falls asleep in the ship which is bearing him from Southampton to take up arms against the Emperor Lucius, and the reader shares his dream of a flying bear meeting a terrifying dragon from the west and engaging in aerial combat; the dragon attacks the bear again and again and finally hurls its burning body to the ground. On waking he tells the dream to those near at hand who offer him the favourable interpretation that the dragon is himself and that he will win a contest with a fierce giant: Arthur considers it may have a different meaning related to his challenge to Lucius (and to the golden dragon on his own personal standard). However, he does soon encounter a hideous and predatory giant whom he defeats in single combat, so that the dream both forecasts an episode in the narrative and creates a more far-reaching sense of menace. Other heroic battle narratives have absorbed the ancient tradition of divine dreams such as those which punctuate the *Chanson de Roland*, where the crusading battles against the pagan enemy have angelic warnings as part of their machinery of ironic foreknowledge: so Charlemagne is told in a vision that Roland will be defeated at Roncesvalles and after Roland's death he is forewarned of the impending battle against the returning Saracen horde. Interestingly Geoffrey leaves the ambiguity, as if hesitating between the clear-cut divine warning, with the structural irony it adds to the narrative, and the dream as a device of suspense. Wace keeps this double sense of the dream but Laȝamon, while making more of the actual scene, leaves the dream's meaning a mystery: he does not take the reader into Arthur's dreaming consciousness but conveys the terror of a hideous dream from which Arthur wakes groaning aloud and sorely troubled, praying that Christ bring his dream to a good outcome. In response to the pleas of his companions Arthur narrates the dream—the terrible bear, the fiery dragon, the ferocity of their contest, the departure of the victorious dragon. The bishops and learned men, we are told, speak with wisdom in interpreting this but are too afraid to read anything ominous in it and so the dream represents an unspecified foreboding.

Laȝamon is interested in portents and visions nevertheless and at a later stage in the story gives Arthur a second dream (not present in either Geoffrey or Wace). This occurs at the point when the news of Mordred's treachery is about to be broken to the king by a young knight who can not bring himself to utter the bad news on the evening when he arrives. Again it is only when Arthur wakes next morning that the reader, along with his companions, learns of troublesome dream knowledge. The king describes a scene in which, as he sits astride a hall with Gawain placed before him, Mordred approaches with a great host and attacks the pillars supporting the hall with a battle-axe, joined by Guenevere who is pulling down the roof. Arthur falls, breaking his arm, and when Mordred gives the hall a final blow, it collapses, breaking both Gawain's arms. Arthur beheads Mordred, hacks Guenevere to pieces and thrusts her into a pit, and is then left alone, wandering over the moors among hideous griffins and threatening birds, but taken by a golden lion into the sea from which a fish brings him to land, weary and sick with sorrow. Arthur knows that this dream foretells the end of all his happiness and, though the knight to whom he has told the dream (whom we now realise is the knight who has still to break the news of Mordred's betrayal) attempts to avert the omens by confidence that, even if Mordred had betrayed his trust, Arthur would be mighty enough to gain vengeance, Arthur's own declaration of faith in Mordred and Guenevere has to face the belated communication of the news that the betrayal has already occurred. Laȝamon's use here of the hall, that powerful symbol in Old English poetry of authority and power, is given a bizarre dream vividness by the picture of Arthur and Gawain riding it like a horse only to be brought tumbling to the ground.

In the Alliterative *Morte Arthure* the two dreams of Arthur appear again but here dream is no longer being used just as a narrative device to add depth or colour or irony but has been enlarged to become a substantial element in the story. The poet combines the bear and dragon dream, inherited from Geoffrey of Monmouth through Laȝamon, with a much elaborated dream of the wheel of Fortune, a version of which appears in the contemporary Stanzaic *Morte Arthur*, a poem in eight-line stanzas based on the French *La Mort le Roi Artu*; in the alliterative poem elements from the French poem are combined with the theme of the Nine Worthies from *Les Voeux du Paon*, possibly augmented by knowledge of *The Parliament of the Three Ages*. These two dreams are placed far apart in the poem, the first (760–805) on board the ship taking Arthur's army across the channel to undertake the campaign against Lucius, as in the *Historia Regum Britanniae*, and the second, longer dream (3223–393) brought forward from the position established by Laȝamon so that it no longer falls in the trough created by Mordred's treachery but is placed, with much greater narrative panache, at the moment of Arthur's triumph in the conquest of Lorraine and his further campaign in Tuscany. An embassy from the Pope offers him the glory of being crowned at Christmas in Rome and it is at this point that Arthur utters his boasting speech:

> 'Now may we reuelle and riste, for Rome is oure awene! . . .
> We salle be ouerlynge of alle that one the erthe lengez!
> We wille by the Crosse dayes encroche theis londez,
> And at the Crystynmasse daye be crowned theraftyre;
> Ryngne in my ryalties, and holde my Rownde Table,
> Withe the rentes of Rome, as me beste lykes;
> Syne graythe ouer the grette see with gudmene of armes,
> To reuenge the renke that one the rode deyde!'
>
> (*AMA*, 3207, 3211–17)

Despite Arthur's final promise to lead a crusade, this moment of hubris marks the highest rung of the king's progress up the ladder of achievement, and the 'dredefulle dreme' that follows marks with a clap of thunder a check to further ambition. The placing of the dream, and the enlarged content, make clear the poet's interpretation of Arthur's history as an example of *de casibus* tragedy in the tradition of Boethius and Boccaccio.[3] The two dreams thus mark the beginning and end of the campaign of conquest which is the main subject matter of this English *chanson de geste* version of the Arthurian story: the models of Alexander and Charlemagne colour not only the characterization of Arthur but also the poem's rhetoric and form.

The poet is not concerned with psychological realism nor with creating an emotional atmosphere of apprehension: in the first dream

---

[3] See Anke Janssen, 'The Dream of the Wheel of Fortune', in *The Alliterative Morte Arthure: A Reassessment*, ed. Karl Heinz Göller (Cambridge, D.S. Brewer, 1981), pp.140–52.

he takes the reader into Arthur's sleeping consciousness to show the dream as it happened. What he does do, in comparison to the other versions of this bear/dragon dream, is greatly to enhance the visual detail: the dragon appears first, and the reversal of the usual order increases the dragon's importance; it is described in mainly positive terms, as a magnificent creature, glittering in azure and silver scales, mailed in sharp irridescence with sable feet and breathing flame. This resplendent image is succeeded by the black bear, massive and ugly, with frothing mouth, rampaging and roaring: negative aspects are dominant here.[4] The technicolour effects provided by the rich flourishings of alliterative vocabulary have much more of the quality found in separate dream poems than is usual in included dreams; the scene is not subordinated to the narrative moment but asserts itself as an alternative reality. The vigorous fight between the beasts leaves the king 'wery fore-trauaillede' and in need of two philosophers to tell him what it means, which they do favourably and in surprising detail, interpreting the dragon's coloured wings as Arthur's many kingdoms and the tail as the army now embarked with him to face tyrants, or it may be that Arthur will face some giant in single combat, but whatever, victory is assured. No doubts are expressed; Arthur does not demur and so the dream stands as a picturesque banner of expectation, flashing colour and ferocity without any depth of meaning, unless we choose, as Göller does, to read later events into the ambiguous symbolism, both dragon and bear suggesting dangerous and destructive aspects later exposed in Arthur's nature. If such suggestions are present they are latent, since the dream is placed at the threshold of the action.

The elaborate second dream carries more weight and the poet chooses the more dramatic way of presenting the dream: only when the king wakes and his philosophers have been sent for is the content revealed, in a staged narration and explanation scene. Again the poet augments the colour and descriptive detail. First Arthur finds himself alone in a wood among wild beasts which are licking the blood of his knights from their teeth; he flees to a meadow among mountains, the space enclosed by silver vines with golden grapes, other trees, and fruits. An elegant lady appears, richly adorned with jewels and

---

[4] See Karl Heinz Göller, 'The Dream of the Dragon and the Bear', in Göller, *The Alliterative* Morte Arthure, pp.130–9.

bearing a turning wheel in her hands to which crowned kings are clinging, though six have fallen and lament their fate. Each one speaks of his time of glory and his sudden fall; only two are still attempting to climb to the silver, jewel-encrusted chair at the wheel's apex. Arthur is greeted by the lady and placed in the seat, given kingly sceptre, diadem and a jewelled globe—'In syngne that I sothely was souerayne in erthe' (3357). Finally he is taken back to the wood where the branches of the trees offer fruits to his hand and the lady fetches him wine from the spring. But by midday all changes and the gracious lady turns harsh:

> 'Kyng, thow karpes for noghte, be Criste that me made!
> For thou shall lose this layke, and thi lyf aftyre,
> Thow has lyffede in delytte and lordchippes inewe!'
> Abowte scho whirles the whele, and whirles me vndire,
> Tille alle my qwarters that whille whare qwaste al to peces!
>   (AMA, 3385–9)

As far as Arthur is concerned the message is clear, as the philosopher emphasizes in his first words: 'Freke,' sais the philosophre, 'thy fortune es passede!' (3394). But the poet hammers home the point by religious instruction that Arthur should prepare for his end, make amends for his sins, and found abbeys for those he has killed in France. What does need interpretation is the allegorical scene the poet has added to the dream, the kings on the wheel, their identities and fates. The pageant of the Nine Worthies unfolds as the six fallen kings are named as Alexander, Hector, Julius Caesar, Judas Maccabeus, Joshua, and David, and the two clinging aspirants to greatness as Charlemagne and Godfrey of Bouillon (identified as lord of Lorraine) who will gain Christ's crown and the lance that pierced him and the true cross. Arthur himself will be celebrated in chronicle and romance for his doughty deeds, but now must prepare both to repent his sins and to face the enemies who are mustering to attack him. The explanation has both to provide moral judgement and to make the transition from the earlier accounts of triumph to the reversed fortune now to be faced: hardly has Arthur dressed himself in fine ceremonial robes than the messenger who is to break the news of Mordred's treachery arrives and the inevitable movement of the narrative begins towards the last battles, the death of Gawain, finally the deaths of Mordred and Arthur himself, and the passing of an age.

Dream in this instance has ceased to be a punctuation of the story or part of the orchestration and evaluation which takes the reader through a narrative with many episodes; it has assumed the character of foreground meaning. In terms of genre one recognizes it as an included dream poem which could stand by itself, given that the story of Arthur was at the time of writing already well known. By linking the *topos* of Fortune's wheel (usually described and pictured with anonymous figures, such as four representative kings at different stages of rise and fall) with the *topos* of the Nine Worthies (usually offered as examples of great achievement, rather than of the vanity of human power) the poet has both created a significant shift of perspective between the episodes of Arthur's triumphs and his doomed civil war, and added moral substance to the work. Arthur acts as the vision narrator who is taught, the philosopher having the role of poet (and reader) who weighs the evidence. The scene-painting in the dream narration creates the sense of an abstract mental space in which the allegorical tableaux can be staged: the sequence of narration and interpretation turns these images into demonstrative tools through which the action of the poem can be fitted into a larger moral scheme.

Chaucer, using different tools, creates an effect in *Troilus and Criseyde* which has something of the same character. In this poem too there are two significant dreams, one early and one late. The first is given to Criseyde as the culmination of the long scene at the beginning of Book II in which Pandarus, by a mixture of intimate avuncular cajolery and emotional blackmail, has persuaded Criseyde to entertain the idea of taking Troilus as her lover; after seeing from her window Troilus in his guise as handsome warrior and prince riding through the streets of Troy and experiencing a moment of intoxication—'Who yaf me drynke?'—she is lulled to sleep by the romantic song of the nightingale:

> And as she slep, anon right tho hire mette
> How that an egle fethered whit as bone
> Under hire brest his longe clawes sette,
> And out hire herte he rente, and that anone,
> And dide his herte into hire brest to gone—
> Of which she nought agroos ne nothyng smerte—
> And forth he fleigh with herte left for herte.
>
> (*TC*, II, 925–31)

Criseyde had already greeted Pandarus as a fulfilment of her previous night's dreams at the beginning of the scene. This later one, it is implied, is as likely to forecast the future; Chaucer's addition increases the sense that Criseyde's surrender to persuasion is partly unconscious and outside her control; the violent image in the dream suggests the element of victim in her role.[5] There is a sense of predatory sexuality in the action of the eagle but at the same time the image is a royal, heraldic one and the exchange of hearts can be understood as a symbolic act akin to devices on a shield. Criseyde feels in the dream no fear or pain and so appears as the passive, helpless, even perhaps willing victim of the violation.

Troilus' dream in Book V is an enlargement of the same procedure. First the subject of the likelihood of dreams coming true is introduced in general. Troilus dreams of dreadful things, that he is alone in a fearful place or surrounded by enemies (V, 246–59). From such dreams he wakes with a start in trembling and sorrow, but, when he tells Pandarus of his experience (V, 316–22), his fears and foreboding are dismissed, and Pandarus is used as the spokesman for the rational reaction to the idea that dreams are supernatural warnings:

> 'Thi sweuenes ek and al swich fantasie
> Drif out and lat hem faren to mischaunce,
> For they procede al of thi malencolie,
> That doth the fele in slepe al this penaunce.
> A straw for alle sweuenes significaunce!
> God helpe me so, I counte hem nought a bene;
> Ther woot noman aright what dremes mene.'
>
> (*TC*, V, 358–64)

Before Troilus' significant dream, dream experience is thus questioned and Pandarus does a thorough demolition job while he is at it, condemning the arbitrariness of priests' interpretations of 'celestial' dreams that supposedly come from divine sources, of doctors' equally contradictory notions of dreams produced by bodily conditions ('animal' dreams that come from physical causes) and of the insecurity of explanations of the third kind (the 'natural' dream produced by psychological factors, such as preoccupation). Complete scepticism about the likelihood of truth being revealed during sleep is, therefore,

---

[5] See Windeatt, *Oxford Guides to Chaucer. Troilus and Criseyde*, p.222.

in the reader's mind and Pandarus could hardly go further in utter scorn:

'Wel worthe of dremes ay thise olde wiues,
And treweliche ek augurye of thise fowles,
For fere of which men wenen lese here lyues,
As rauenes qualm, or scrichyng of thise owles:
To trowen on it bothe fals and foul is.
Allas, allas, so noble a creature
As is a man shal dreden swich ordure!'

(*TC*, V, 379–85)

All of this creates the pattern for the exchange which occurs when Troilus has a dream of direct relevance to his situation.

So on a day he leyde hym doun to slepe,
And so byfel that yn his slepe hym thoughte
That in a forest faste he welk to wepe
For love of here that hym these peynes wroughte;
And vp and doun as he the forest soughte,
He mette he saugh a bor with tuskes grete,
That slepte aʒeyn the bryghte sonnes hete.

And by this bor, faste in his armes folde,
Lay kyssyng ay his lady bryght, Criseyde—
For sorwe of which, whan he it gan byholde,
And for despit, out of his slep he breyde,
And loude he cride on Pandarus & seyde,
'O Pandarus, now know I crop and roote—
I nam but ded; ther nys non other bote.

My lady bryght, Cryseyde, hath me bytrayed . . .'

(*TC*, V, 1233–47)

Chaucer is translating Boccaccio here but he has changed the content of the dream from a fierce boar charging through the forest and tearing out Criseida's heart, to her apparent pleasure (clearly the origin of Chaucer's earlier dream of the eagle), and he then omits the stanzas in which Troiolo himself interprets the boar as Diomede. By envisaging a boar sleeping in the sun embraced by Criseyde, Chaucer has increased the erotic charge of the image as well as giving it a grotesque vividness, akin to Shakespeare's picture of Titania and Bottom, much more offensive to the startled Troilus, whose dislocated frenzy is expressed in the stanzas that follow. Pandarus dismisses his fears and interprets the dream away as caused simply by

Troilus' 'owene drede' or, if it has to have a meaning, then perhaps he has seen Criseyde with her old dying father. With this he turns Troilus' thoughts for the time to the writing of a letter to Criseyde but the dream goes on festering in his mind as a divine message that has revealed 'in figure' Criseyde's lack of faith. His desire to have his suspicions quashed leads to his arranging a meeting with Cassandra, identified merely as a sister of Troiolo in *Il Filostrato* but here appearing in her role as Sybil, prophetess of doom. (Chaucer has ceased translating Boccaccio at this point and invents the scene that follows.) Troilus' seeking an interpretation of the dream is thus built up into a significant moment in the story and when Cassandra has heard the dream narrated, her first reaction is to offer her own narration in return. She tells the story of Meleager and the boar from Ovid's *Metamorphoses* and the subsequent Theban war, the subject of Statius' *Thebaid*; in most manuscripts of *Troilus and Criseyde* a twelve-line Latin summary of the content of the twelve books of the *Thebaid* is included in the text at V, 1498. At length Cassandra returns to the question of the dream and to Diomede, descended from Meleager and now identified with the boar in the dream:

> 'And thy lady, wher-so she be, ywis,
> This Diomede hire herte hath and she his—
> Wepe if thow wolt or lef, for out of doute,
> This Diomede is inne and thow art oute.'
> (*TC*, V, 1516–19)

Now that the identification has been made Troilus furiously rejects it and is angry enough to leave his bed and resume the life of a royal soldier but Chaucer's side glance in the next stanza at Fortune, about to 'pull away the fetheres brighte of Troie', indicates what good that will do.

Chaucer's handling of Troilus' dream is intriguing in its complexity. Though Pandarus' dismissive attitude undermines it, the postponement of the identification of Diomede turns it into an instrument of suspense, but then the revelation assumes the curious form of a textual raising of the stakes: Diomede is not merely identified as Troilus' rival but as the inheritor of Meleager's power to start a war. Troilus' fierce rejection of the meaning of the dream is psychologically right, even though he has already recognized that Criseyde has deserted him, but what is the reader to make of the debate between the idea that dreams are not to be trusted and the apparent evidence that in this instance a dream has not only shown what is true but has tuned in to a historical line of inevitable meaning? Is it simply the copyists of the text or Chaucer who have wanted to attribute the authority of classical epic to Cassandra's explanation, or is this a sign of the medieval poet's sense of being uncomfortably controlled by the ancient story? Elsewhere Chaucer seems to be expressing the idea that he is struggling with his material and that the ethics of this pre-Christian story are outside his and his audience's range: here is an example of 'the forme of olde clerkis speche/In poetrie' and of the 'payens corsed olde rites' of which he speaks at the end of the poem (V, 1849–55). Troilus' dream, in Chaucer's handling of it, is not merely a way of creating dramatic irony, nor of indicating the inevitability of the movement of the plot towards Troilus' ultimate sorrow and death, but a textual indicator of the unmanoeuvrability of historical tragedy.

Intertextuality

Chaucer's introduction of material from Statius into the scene of Cassandra's exposition of Troilus' dream is one example of a feature of *Troilus and Criseyde* which may be understood as a form of intertextuality. This concept is particularly associated with the critic Julia Kristeva who, in her interpretation and development of the ideas of Bakhtin, argued that no text is completely free of other texts; writers provide the reader with a frame of reference from other works to which the text in one way or another alludes. She explains Bakhtin's idea of the 'literary word' as an intersection of textual surfaces or a dialogue among several writings and offers this definition:

The term *intertextuality* denotes th[e] transposition of one (or several) sign-system(s) into another; but since this term has often been understood in the banal sense of 'study of sources', we prefer the term *transposition* because it specifies that the passage from one signifying system to another demands a new articulation . . .[6]

---

[6] Julia Kristeva, *The Revolution in Poetic Language*, trans. Margaret Waller (New York, Columbia U.P., 1984), p.60; the passage is printed in *The Theory of Criticism from Plato to the Present: A Reader*, ed. Raman Selden (Harlow, Longman, 1988), p.417–18.

Kristeva makes it clear that she is not thinking of the sort of use that Chaucer makes of Boccaccio's *Il Filostrato* as an example of intertextuality, although the kind of adaptation that he and other medieval writers made of their source material is too complicated to be thought of as translation, but of the presence in texts of assumptions, sometimes hidden, transferred from elsewhere. The way in which Kristeva's idea has been applied in the analysis of texts may be stated more simply as the recognition that a text 'does not function as a closed system' but is 'shot through with references, quotations and influences of every kind'.[7] It is a striking aspect of *Troilus and Criseyde* that Chaucer includes within his adaptation of Boccaccio a mosaic of passages from elsewhere as well as allusions to a number of classical and medieval writers: the 'Canticus Troili' in Book I is a translation of a Petrarch sonnet; the song of love uttered by Antigone in Book II is a courtly lay in the style of de Machaut; Troilus' hymn to love in Book III is from Boethius as is the predestination soliloquy in Book IV; the descriptions of Diomede, Criseyde, and Troilus in Book V are from Joseph of Exeter; the final stanza of the poem includes lines from Dante's *Paradiso*. Perhaps Kristeva would class all these as 'study of sources' but the occurrence of these scattered passages within a long narrative text seems to me somewhat different. The alliterative poet of the *Morte Arthure* does not intersect quite so many 'textual surfaces' but there too intertextuality plays a part in the creation of the sense of the whole.

The episode in which Gawain encounters the Saracen knight Priamus is taken from the story of Fierabras (the subject of the Middle English romance *Sir Ferumbras*); it occurs when Gawain leaves the foraging party to seek adventure. When he meets an armed knight, a fierce fight with spear and sword follows; subsequently the two exchange names and formal courtesies. This is the most obviously chivalrous section of the poem and its purpose might be seen as that of building up the importance of the figure of Gawain, whose death is to be as significant a part of the climax as that of Arthur himself. However, its romance style—an arbitrary challenge between knights for no more substantial reason than a demonstration of chivalric honour—is at odds with the seriousness of the text's treatment

---

[7] Michael Worton and Judith Still, *Intertextuality: Theories and Practices* (Manchester U.P., 1990), p.1.

of battle. Göller suggests that the introduction of this material creates 'structural irony' and that the poet's intention is 'to highlight the frivolity and triviality of knightly combat in order to use it as a foil for the brutality of war . . . By inserting this romantic *aventure*, the poet relativises the whole concept of romance, setting it in a world of reality.'[8] In this case the chivalric jousting from a Charlemagne romance may be thought, according to Göller's view that it appears no more than 'a ridiculous game', to strengthen the seriousness of the main parts of the narrative by an intertextual comparison; the episode also acts as an indicator in this Arthur-centred war story of all the other adventures of the knights of the Round Table which are mostly not being narrated here.

The text's other allusions also work to substantiate and aggrandize the presentation of Arthur and the campaigns which he leads. The poet draws on the histories of the conquests of Alexander in both the episode of the foraging party and in the dream sequence of the Nine Worthies. The effect is to augment the idea of empire in Arthur's career, as William Matthews argues, and to draw Arthur towards the typological pattern of *de casibus* tragedy.[9] Arthur is raised higher by being seen in the company of Alexander and the other great heroes of history and so he has further to fall. Whether or not this increases the tragic effect is a matter of debate; one might see Arthur's appearance in the company of the other worthies as a categorization which reduces his fate to that of a moral example rather than a cathartic end. Intertextuality is not perhaps a major aspect of the narrative strategy of the *Morte Arthure*, which is dominated by virtuoso displays of alliterative technique and by the large amount of description and speech with which the basic plot-material is embellished. There are lots of pictures of fleets setting sail, of knights in battle, of light sparkling on armour, flames flashing from swords, running blood, cloven shields; some of the set pieces, such as the feast given to Lucius' ambassadors or the grotesque description of the giant, accumulate detail into colourful focal points. The language is flamboyant in places; the poet's liking for successions of lines alliterating

[8] Karl Heinz Göller (with R. Gleissner and M. Mennicken), 'Reality versus romance: a reassessment of the Alliterative *Morte Arthure*', in Göller, *The Alliterative* Morte Arthure, p.23.

[9] William Matthews, *The Tragedy of Arthur* (Berkeley, University of California Press, 1960).

on the same letter requires a large vocabulary, even if many phrases are traditional collocations. Despite the many local flourishes, however, it is impossible by the late fourteenth century for any narrative of Arthur to be read in isolation; even within the Middle English versions there are sharp contrasts, as is obvious from the Stanzaic *Morte Arthur* in which all of the story of adultery and guilt finds expression, together with the melancholy, elegiac regret for the passing of an age which is robustly excluded from the stoic alliterative text. Consciousness of the other possibilities of the story material provides in itself an intertextual perspective for the tale.

In the case of *Troilus and Criseyde* the 'transposition of sign-systems' is much clearer, particularly in the case of Statius' *Thebaid* which provides Chaucer not only with the substance of Cassandra's interpretation of the dream in Book V, but also with the book of 'romance' to which Criseyde is listening when Pandarus visits her at the beginning of Book II, and possibly with much of the epic machinery in the form of invocations with which he adorns his prologues. As Windeatt points out,[10] Chaucer could have derived from the story of Thebes the sense of the inevitability of the downfall of the city and of the vanity of the pagan gods: Chaucer, unusual among medieval writers in expressing a sense of historical relativity, uses the story of Thebes to provide a sense of the past for his Trojan characters. This idea of the pressure of history, which invites comparison of Troilus with Oedipus and other past victims of fatal passion, has been explored by several commentators on the poem, as for example Lee Patterson who finds *Troilus and Criseyde* 'massively saturated with Thebanness',[11] which he sees Chaucer using to characterize Troilus' lack of self-knowledge. Statius' epic is thus identifiable as what Michael Riffaterre calls an 'intertext', defined as a text 'which the reader must know in order to understand a work of literature in terms of its overall significance'. Sometimes a writer's allusions tell the reader all that is necessary for understanding, but a passage such as Cassandra's interpretation of Troilus' dream is cryptic and the inclusion of the Latin summary of the *Thebaid* by most of the scribes of the Troilus manuscripts indicates that one needs to know more. As Riffaterre expresses it:

[10] Windeatt, *Oxford Guides to Chaucer:* Troilus and Criseyde, in the chapter on sources, pp.121–5.

[11] Lee Patterson, *Chaucer and the Subject of History* (London, Routledge, 1991), p.132.

The urge to understand compels readers to look to the intertext to fill out the text's gaps, spell out its implications . . .[12]

The Theban material provided Chaucer's text with an important strand in its historical texture, contributing particularly to the sense of pre-Christian fatalism through which Chaucer interpreted his hero.

If epic is one direction in which Chaucer allowed his story to be pulled, a contrary force draws it towards the intimacy of conversation and lyric. The expression of feeling and the use of direct speech are major elements in Boccaccio's text but Chaucer invents and imports more of both, by developing longer dramatic scenes and increasing the number of occasions for lyrical monologue for the hero, with the help of Petrarch, de Machaut, and Boethius. The idea of an 'intersection of textual surfaces', in this case of narrative and lyric, is particularly evident in Book V where the plot material is simple and conveyed in relatively few lines and where the function of narration is often to link together the passages of sorrowful complaint and the direct expressions of feeling in formal lyrics, in letters between Troilus and Criseyde and in conversation; much of the book may be read as a lyric sequence such as Dante wrote in *La Vita Nuova* or as a hybrid courtly narrative akin to Guillaume de Machaut's *Voir Dit*. Into this current of plangent expressiveness Chaucer makes a startling intertextual intrusion in the form of the three descriptions of Diomede, Criseyde, and Troilus (*TC*, V, 799–840); the passage, based on the descriptions in Joseph of Exeter's 'Latin Iliad', appear with something of the same effect of a marginal gloss as the summary of the *Thebaid* in Book IV. Here in three set portraits, almost at the end of the story, the narrator's voice takes over to describe the new lover, the 'hardy, testif' Diomede, 'of tonge large' and the old lover, Troilus, 'ʒong, fressh, strong' and 'trewe as stiel'; between them is Criseyde, 'tendre-herted, slydynge of corage', not very tall perhaps but with Paradise 'formed in her eyen'. These frozen pictures, offered before the narration has been finished, nevertheless tell the reader that the story is over and that the characters are fixed in time. It is a vivid instance of the way that one text can comment on another.

Chaucer repeats the device in his epilogue. Having completed the

[12] Michael Riffaterre, 'Compulsory reader response: the intertextual drive', in Worton and Still, *Intertextuality*, pp.56–78 (quotations from pp.56 and 57).

narrative, said his farewells, and labelled the work as 'litel myn trag-edye', Chaucer decides to look back through the intertextual glass of Boccaccio's *Teseida,* enhanced by the *Dream of Scipio* of Cicero/ Macrobius. And so he treats the actual death of Troilus as an anti-climax but extends his existence by transposing the flight of the soul of Arcita (omitted from *The Knight's Tale*) into Troilus' ascent to the eighth sphere, whence he takes a detached view of his own folly, the transitoriness of earthly love, and the pointlessness of human grief. By means of this intertextual glossing of pagan history from specifically Christian texts the poet too can detach himself from the narrative, and does so with another flurry of strategies of closure: a rhetorical summing up of Troilus' fate, an address to the potential lovers in his audience, a dismissal of the pagan gods, a dedication of the poem to his contemporaries and colleagues, and the final prayer. Among the questions left is the reader's curiosity as to why Chaucer was willing to give himself the trouble of writing over 8000 lines of poetry cele-brating 'blynde lust, the which that may not laste', if it is to be seen as pointless. Whatever else it is, *Troilus and Criseyde* is an act of textual commitment on Chaucer's part. He uses the narrator's voice to indicate that it is no easy matter:

> Owt of thise blake wawes for to saylle,
> O wynd, o wynd, the weder gynneth clere;
> For in this see the boot hath swych travaylle,
> Of my connyng, that unneth I it steere.
> This see clepe I the tempestuous matere
> Of disespeir that Troilus was inne . . .
>
> (*TC*, II, 1–6)

Chaucer thus dramatizes the writing of the work, so that his achievement of the goal of completing it runs alongside his rehearsal of the known story. And by the end he registers a sense of this achievement as he bids his poem be humble in the presence of the great classical poets but prays for his work to be accurately communicated and read.

> And for ther is so gret diversite
> In Englissh and in writyng of oure tonge,
> So prey I God that non myswrite the,
> Ne the mysmetre for defaute of tonge;
> And red wherso thow be, or elles songe,
> That thow be understonde, God I beseche!
>
> (*TC*, V, 1793–8)

Troilus may have committed himself to the pursuit of vanity but there is no suggestion that the poet has done so. As text, with all its transpositions and interfaces, it is a success, ending on a note of triumph.

8

Putting narratives together

Tale collections

How far does it change one's perceptions of a narrative to read it as part of a collection, as one of a series or as a unit within a miscellany? The question is not one which it is necessary to ask about most modern novels, though it applies to the separate parts of a trilogy such as *The Lord of the Rings* or a tetralogy such as Ford Madox Ford's *Parade's End* or the even longer sequence of Proust's *À la Recherche du Temps Perdu*; in a different way one could ask it of one of such a series as Trollope's Barsetshire novels or novels in which the same characters appear as in Henry James's *Roderick Hudson* and *The Princess Casamassima*. However, one would be more likely to treat as a tale collection those types of narrative which, because of their length or their subject matter or both, were published together, as with short stories, whether by a single author or in a multi-authored anthology. Tale collections are a common medieval form of narrative writing and they come in just as wide a range of kinds as with modern fiction. Models range from Aesop's fables and Ovid's *Metamorphoses* to the Bible and oriental teaching collections such as the text known as *Disciplina Clericalis*.[1] In the simplest sort of tale collection the framework that encloses the stories is no more than the manuscript or 'book' in which the tales have been collected, and the

---

[1] For a survey see ch.1, 'The genre of the story-collection', in Cooper, *The Structure of* The Canterbury Tales, pp.8–55. See also R. Clements and J. Gibaldi, *Anatomy of the Novella: The European Tale Collection from Boccaccio and Chaucer to Cervantes* (New York U.P., 1977).

characteristics of the tale type may be little more than brevity, as with the modern collection of short stories. One might take the Auchinleck manuscript once again as an example, where alongside the several romances of medium length such as *Floriz and Blauncheflour* and *Sir Orfeo*, the lengthy romance *Guy of Warwick* has been tailored into three consecutive narratives of manageable length, *Guy of Warwick I*, *Guy of Warwick II* and a 'son-of-Guy' romance *Reinbrun*, neatly adapted from Anglo-Norman; the set is accompanied by a text of religious instruction, the *Speculum Guy of Warwick*, to develop the moral perspective of the story. This would seem to represent part of the user-friendly aspect of this composite London manuscript, intended perhaps to provide entertainment and instruction for a bourgeois household. The two manuscripts associated with the name of Robert Thornton, a fifteenth-century Yorkshire gentleman who seems to have been compiling the manuscripts for his own or his family's interest and entertainment, also contain a substantial number of romances. John J. Thompson has pointed out that in the larger and more varied of the two, the Lincoln Thornton MS (Lincoln Cathedral MS 91), the arrangement of the secular and religious material is not random: apart from grouping romances together, it looks as if Thornton began a new gathering (i.e., the section in the manuscript that would make up a separate booklet) with the Alliterative *Morte Arthure* and then removed some pages of the preceding section in order to bring this Arthurian epic narrative closer to the prose *Life of Alexander* with which the compilation opens.[2] To put Alexander and Arthur in conjunction suggests that the theme of the Nine Worthies was in Thornton's mind (and the other Thornton MS [British Library MS Additional 31042, known as the London Thornton MS] contains *The Parliament of the Three Ages* which describes the Worthies); the *Morte Arthure* is then followed by the texts of *Octavian*, *Sir Ysumbras*, and *The Erl of Tolous*, so that the Alliterative *Morte Arthure* appears as a kind of head-piece for the following romance group; later on the sequence of religious and devotional texts also begins a new gathering with a substantial main piece, a prose text called the *Privity of the Passion*. While both the

---

[2] See John J. Thompson, 'The compiler in action: Robert Thornton and the "Thornton Romances" in Lincoln Cathedral MS 91', in *Manuscripts and Readers in Fifteenth-Century England*, ed. Derek Pearsall (Cambridge, D.S. Brewer, 1983), pp.113–24.

Auchinleck MS and the Lincoln Thornton MS are miscellaneous compilations, they thus show signs of editing, grouping, and placing of texts so that they contribute to an overall sense of formal or thematic relationship.

Another common type of collection is the assembling of narratives of like kind as in a collection of *exempla* such as the *Alphabet of Tales*, a preacher's handbook organized alphabetically to illustrate abstinence, anger, avarice, and so on, or in a series of saints' lives, of which the best-known example is probably the Latin *Legenda Aurea* or *Golden Legend*, compiled by an Italian Dominican friar Jacob de Voragine (*d.*1298) about 1266 and widely copied and translated; it consisted of a prologue and 177 chapters organized chronologically according to the saint's feast day, so that a kind of frame is provided by the liturgical calendar.[3] Collections of narratives related by their subject matter or didactic purpose tend to have uniformity imposed upon them, as one may see in such a compilation as the *Gesta Romanorum*, where the *exempla* fall into a pattern consisting not only of story plus allegorical interpretation but also a similar ordering within the narratives, most of which begin with a chronological placing in the reign of a particular Roman emperor or a king or prince. Similar patterning is visible in the *Legenda Aurea* where most of the lives follow the same format consisting of the etymology of the saint's name, the narrative of the 'life', and a series of miracles. The etymologies now seem a strange element in this pattern, particularly since most of them are linguistic nonsense, but it is interesting that even when a saint's life is removed from the context of the series the pattern survives, as it does in Chaucer's *Second Nun's Tale*, the life of St Cecilia, which is based in part on the version of Jacob de Voragine, and which completes the prologue with five stanzas of fanciful discourse on the meaning of 'Cecilia'. The *Legenda Aurea* was known in England from the late thirteenth century on and was already being used as a source of English versions of saints' lives in the latter part of the *South English Legendary*; later it formed the basis of the *Festial* of John Mirk and Osbern Bokenham's *Legendys of Hooly Wymmen*; it was translated into English as the *Gilte Legende* in the 1430s and translated and printed as *The Golden Legende* by Caxton in 1483. It

---

[3] Jacobus de Voragine, *The Golden Legend*, trans. Christopher Stace, with Introduction and Notes by Richard Hamer (Harmondsworth, Penguin Books, 1998).

was therefore a recurrent presence as a model for the single-authored one-genre tale collection. Others of these, such as the collection of fables by Marie de France, were given an overall coherence not only by repetition of narrative formulae and recurrence of situations and themes, but by a defining prologue which explained the purpose of the collection and estabished the narrator's voice. This is the pattern that Chaucer used in writing *The Legend of Good Women*.

Chaucer calls this work, when he refers to it in *The Man of Law's Prologue*, 'the Seintes Legende of Cupide', indicating its hybrid nature; he is embarking on a legendary of martyrs, but martyrs to love rather than religious faith, and stories from the ancient, pagan past rather than the Christian heroism of a later age. This is not an 'innocent' tale collection but an artificial exercise: it is not that the stories were there waiting for a compiler to give them collective form but that Chaucer, knowing the form of the series of saints' lives, sets himself to produce an imitation, a kind of spoof of the genuine narrative kind. And so the elaborate prologue creates a framework for the tales which relates to Chaucer's own self-consciousness as a poet and his dramatizing his audience's supposed reaction to his works. Because he has allegedly maligned women in translating *Le Roman de la Rose* and in writing of Criseyde's faithlessness, now he is arraigned in the court of the God of Love and given the penance of writing of 'good' women, the martyrs to love's cause who were betrayed by men. The poem is incomplete in the texts that are known, consisting of the prologue (which survives in two different forms) and nine tales, the last one of which breaks off before the end; however the work is referred to in the 'Retractions' at the end of *The Canterbury Tales* as the Book of the xxv Ladies (though some manuscripts say xv and some xix) and some scholars have been ready to accept that Chaucer may have composed more tales which have been lost.[4] There is a good deal of confusion about Chaucer's own sense of his work since he refers in both versions of the Prologue to nineteen women and in *The Man of Law's Prologue* to sixteen, including Chaucer's defender, Alceste. Whether or not Chaucer actually wrote more than the nine tales that survive, the various references suggest that he was, over a period of time, considering the idea of a substantial series

---

[4] See A.J. Minnis, *Oxford Guides to Chaucer: The Shorter Poems* (Oxford, Clarendon Press, 1995), pp.326–7.

of short classical narratives. This work is presumably Chaucer's first experiment in compiling a collection of tales and all readers would agree that, in comparison to *The Canterbury Tales*, this version exposes the weakness of the idea of making up a series from stories of the same kind. When Chaucer did this again in *The Monk's Tale*, he presents it as a narrative failure deliberately interrupted as monotonous and depressing. What the prologue to the series sets up as a frame is the idea that the tales that follow are created to order as a test of the poet's mettle and his powers of empathy with abused women; what Chaucer produced has left readers uncertain how seriously he meant to be taken.[5] There are comic and parodic elements in some of the stories, particularly in the gleeful attack on Jason, but Chaucer's treatment of the classical tales, many based on the letters of complaint in Ovid's *Heroides*, may be read in the spirit in which one reads Lamb's *Tales from Shakespeare*, as condensations of stories with a few narrative highlights. But apart from the special questions that stem from Chaucer's subject matter in this poem, there are the broader issues of the tale collection: how does the author create continuous interest for the reader in a series of tales? If the stories are all similar to one another, how can each one be anything but a repetition of effects already experienced? There is variety of treatment in *The Legend of Good Women*: sometimes Chaucer focusses on scenic effects as with the battle of Actium, sometimes on the lamenting heroine as with Ariadne, sometimes on the wickedness of the man in the story as with Jason (comically) and Tarquin (seriously), sometimes on vivid moments in the story as with Pyramus and Thisbe. But the requirement that every story should illustrate the same idea, that virtuous women are the victims of deceiving men, is a constraint on the narratives that even Chaucer's ingenuity in playing gender games is insufficient to outmanoeuvre.

There is stronger integration between tale and framework in the type of collection where a narrator's voice continues through the series and introduces the stories as illustrations of varying and developing themes. This is the pattern of the collection of *exempla* in the *Manual des Pechiez* and Robert Mannyng's English adaptation in his *Handlyng Synne*, and in the later French instruction book, translated

---

[5] See Phillips and Havely, *Chaucer's Dream Poetry*, pp.291–3 for a discussion of the degree of seriousness in the poem.

into English in the fifteenth century as *The Book of the Knight of la Tour Landry* and printed by Caxton as *The Book of the Knight of the Tower*, in which the author compiles a 'boke of ensaumples' for the education of his daughters. Slightly more complex in its working is the alliterative poem *Cleanness*, which appears alongside *Pearl*, *Patience*, and *Sir Gawain and the Green Knight* in the Cotton Nero A x manuscript. The poet defines the theme, God's hatred of impurity, uses the New Testament parable of the man without a wedding garment as an introductory instance and then retells the Old Testament stories of the Flood, the destruction of Sodom and Gomorrah, and Belshazzar's feast as three demonstrations of God's uses of power in the destruction of earthly houses of moral corruption. The linking passages mainly function to make the transition from tale to tale but also present the poem's positive images of cleanness, the discoloured pearl restored to gleaming whiteness by being cleansed in wine and the pure house of Mary' womb. The narrator's voice is anonymous and instructive, although there are some ironic cross-currents in the relationship among the tales. More sophisticated, literary dramatizations of the tale-telling process are produced when the storytellers are fictional characters rather than the preaching author. So the stories in *The Seven Sages of Rome* are all exemplary but the frame story creates a context in which the identity of the teller and the hearer's response to the story are as important as the moral point being made. In this widely disseminated romance, originally an ancient oriental narrative but known in the west from mid twelfth century and translated into most European languages, the fifteen tales are shared among the wicked empress/stepmother whose seven tales are designed to prejudice the emperor against his son and bring about the son's death, the seven masters who each tell a tale to win back the emperor's favour for the boy, and the prince himself, who breaks his enforced silence to tell the final tale which rescues him from death and exposes the empress's malice. Stories are thus not only moral examples but weapons in a debate and devices for delaying death as in the more famous oriental delaying narrative of Scheherazade. The shorter tales are subordinate to the frame story which carries the main narrative interest.

This is true, though in a different way, of the ingenious Spanish *Libro de Buen Amor* ('The Book of Good Love'), written by Juan Ruiz, Archpriest of Hita, who completed a revised version of his book in

1343.[6] It consists of a prose prologue, which many have read as ironic, in which the author declares his purpose as that of warning the innocent against women and the snares of worldly love, followed by a first-person account in verse of a series of love affairs which acts as a framework for about thirty fables and exemplary anecdotes and two allegories (a debate with the God of Love and a battle between Lent and Carnal Appetite), together with songs to the Virgin and various digressions. Its form, apart from the interspersed lyrics in a variety of metres, is that of the learned school of poets who used the four-line, monorhymed stanza known as the *cuaderna via*; the line has fourteen syllables with a marked caesura and is thought to have its origin in Latin. The work is rich in proverbs and axioms and is written in a lively style with plenty of dialogue. Among the influences on it that may be readily identified are Ovid's *Ars amatoria*, Goliard satire, the French *pastourelle* and other troubadour lyrics, and Arabic story collections with a frame. Beginning in prayer and praise of the Virgin, the Archpriest soon shifts into carnivalesque mode with praise of laughter and confession of his several courtships. Stories, mainly fables, are put into the mouth not only of the narrator; fictional characters use tales to persuade and to argue. The first woman to whom he sends messages fends him off with salutary fables; after his male messenger has betrayed him in a second love campaign, he attacks Love, going through all its unfavourable aspects under the heading of the deadly sins, with a fable to illustrate each, but the God of Love, ready with quotations from Ovid, answers back 'con mesura' (in moderation) and offers practical advice about selecting the right woman to fall in love with and how to choose a good go-between, 'one of those old women who frequent churches and know all the alleyways'. The God of Love too is ready with examples and fables. When the Archpriest falls for a lively young widow called Endrina (in an episode close to a twelfth-century Latin comedy called *Pamphilus*), the narrator puts the advice he has received into practice and finds himself a suitable old woman as go-between rejoicing in the name *Trota-conventos* ('Convent-trotter'). Soon she and Endrina are engaged in the elaborate Ovidian strategies of persuasion towards love; the old woman sets fables to work

---

[6] Juan Ruiz, *The Book of Good Love*, trans. Elizabeth Drayson Macdonald, Everyman's Library (London, J.M. Dent, 1999).

towards a love affair beginning with the story of 'The Bustard and the Swallow' (the fable Henryson tells as *The Preiching of the Swallow*) which she turns into a warning to the young widow that she and her house need the protection of a man. Thus included tales are woven into the liveliness of conversation and exchanges of folk wisdom. With parodies of the pastourelle to recount his frolics with mountain maidens and the conflict between Love and 'Don Carnal', Ruiz accommodates the satirical spirit of the Latin Goliard poets, and the juxtaposition of mockery and piety brings the *Libro de Buen Amor* closest of medieval narrative works to the carnivalesque of Bakhtin referred to earlier in the chapter on comedy. As a tale collection the frame story takes precedence over the medley of intercalated items, lyrics as well as narratives; the tale-telling is dramatized to include the effect of the stories on the hearer and on the argument. It makes an interesting comparison with the English 'book of good love', the *Confessio Amantis* of Gower, which is also a mixture of forms (and of languages).

The frame story here is of preparation for love rather than reminiscence of past experience, and the aspiring lover, Amans, is not simply telling the reader his thoughts and feelings but is distanced from us in a dialogue with his confessor, Genius, the priest of Venus, whose task it is to catechize the lover to find out if he is a worthy entrant to Love's court. The tales are all (except for one minor example) told by Genius as exemplary instances, organized in the early stages under the headings of the seven deadly sins, for the edification of Amans. Gower has thus combined the two ideas of the instruction manual full of *exempla* and the autobiographical lover's confession in a dream-like encounter with an allegorical teacher—*Le Roman de la Rose* plus *Handlyng Synne*, as it were. Gower elaborates his long, ambitious fiction in various ways: by a substantial political prologue which sets the theme of love in the perspective of politics and relates the harmony of the individual to the need to resolve division in the body politic; by a scholarly series of Latin epigraphs; by allowing the structural scheme of the seven deadly sins to merge, in Book VII, into the broader educational theme of the education of a prince; and by adding a sort of epilogue in the form of a series of French ballades. But, despite these techniques of enlargement, the focus remains on the lover's story and the tales he is told; it is this story which provides the surprising ending to the poem, where Venus appears to the lover, asks his name, which is supplied as 'John Gower' rather than as 'Amans', and confronts him with the unwelcome reminder that he is an old man and no longer a suitable applicant to join her court. It needs another kind of tale (an included allegorical dream in which the forces of Youth and Age confront one another) to resolve the matter and to release the lover into thoughts of prayer and preparation for death. Considered as a tale collection *Confessio Amantis* lacks the variety that comes from the use of multiple tale-tellers: the teaching voice of Genius is always the one heard in the narratives and so Gower has to keep the reader's interest in other ways. The topic being illustrated moves on all the time, through the sins and with each sin through several subdivisions. The tales vary in length, some being no more than allusions taking a few lines, others full-scale narratives of several hundred lines, with two really long narratives, the story of Constance in Book II and the tale of Apollonius of Tyre (the source of Gower's appearance as a Chorus character in the Shakespeare collaboration *Pericles*) which takes up most of Book VIII. Then again the nature of the exemplification varies a good deal from the simple moral illustration which Amans accepts as instructive, to the tale which leaves its moral theme behind and may come to seem irrelevant and which the lover protests has nothing to do with him; sometimes the lesson is obvious, sometimes ingeniously indirect so that questions arise from it. Because Amans talks a lot about his own feelings, *Confessio Amantis* is a more introspective work than most Middle English romance writing and the tales work in conjunction with this to create effects through echoing, repetition, resemblance, and contrast.

The actual sources of the exemplary tales range widely, with the result that the poem may be read as an anthology. A number of medieval manuscript miscellanies include extracts from *Confessio Amantis*, treating it as a sort of narrative supermarket where one can select from different shelves. Ovid's *Metamorphoses* was a favourite source and the tales of Actaeon and Diana, Narcissus, Acis and Galatea, Hercules and Deyanira, Pyramus and Thisbe, Phoebus and Daphne, Dido and Aeneas, Pygmalion, Daedalus and Icarus, Ceyx and Alcyone, Jason and Medea, Theseus and Ariadne are scattered through the various books, together with some less familiar ones. Mixed into this classical pot-pourri are biblical tales such as that of Nebuchadnezzar, stories from the *Gesta Romanorum* and the encyclopaedic tradition of Isidore of Seville and Vincent of Beauvais, a few tales from Germanic sources, stories also used by Boccaccio. Particularly interesting is the material Gower shares with Chaucer, as is the case with most of the tales in *The Legend of Good Women* where Gower's version provides a touchstone of comparison, and the stories of Chaucer's *Man of Law's Tale, Wife of Bath's Tale, Manciple's Tale, Physician's Tale.*

Perhaps the most interesting aspect of *Confessio Amantis* as a tale collection is Gower's interweaving of two kinds of narration which stem from the competing voices of the two narrators. Genius is the source of the rich storehouse of examples which he conveys in the voice of the teaching narrator: he is fertile and inventive and extends the world of the fiction by his many comparisons and images from the world beyond the confessional. Amans/Gower offers the reader the first-person confessional narration of inner experience and self-analysis, which appropriately leads into the dream narrative that brings the poem to its conclusion. Chaucer's disciple, Thomas Hoccleve, extends this effect of dual narrative in his *Series*, in which autobiographical sections, the *Complaint* and the *Dialogue with a Friend*, form a framework for two exemplary tales from the *Gesta Romanorum* and an *Ars Moriendi* translated from Suso, together with passages of prose moralization after each tale and groups of linking stanzas which provide a kind of continuity from the *Dialogue*. The whole work amounts to a self-referential debate about writing. The opening *Complaint*, in which Hoccleve dramatizes his own mental breakdown and his friends' reaction to it, is the most powerful piece of writing and establishes the autobiographical theme. Each of the texts that follows is in response to the friend or to a patron, so that the production of the series becomes a demonstration of the poet's shifting from a solitary, self-communing state into dialogue and social reintegration, as Roger Ellis notes.[7] The recurrence of complaint, solitariness, and death as themes maintains the debate about Hoccleve's own usefulness as a writer and translator, as the friend's voice is used to continue urging him to write and arguing with him about the subject-matter of the tales. This is, as James Simpson puts it: 'a poem whose single unifying plot is the story of its own

---

[7] *'My Compleinte' and Other Poems* by Thomas Hoccleve, ed. Roger Ellis (Exeter, University of Exeter Press, 2001), p.33. This is the most convenient text of the *Series*.

composition'.[8] Juan Ruiz, Gower, and Hoccleve all show that in the tale collection the personal frame-story may be inventive and exploratory and not merely a convenient ordering device.

Nevertheless Boccaccio and Chaucer are the only two medieval writers who triumphantly solve the problems inherent in writing a tale collection—how to create unity and coherence in the series and yet leave room for individuality and constant surprise in the tales. Boccaccio tried out several versions of the tale collection, as did Chaucer later, both in the Italian vernacular and in Latin. The *Filocolo*, written about 1336, introduces into a retelling of the story of Floris and Blauncheflour a lengthy digression set in a Neapolitan garden where noble courtiers engage in a game of love questions and debate; some of the questions arise from stories, as with the one which became Chaucer's *Franklin's Tale*. The *Ameto*, written in the early 1340s, has nymphs speaking of their own love adventures in a pastoral, springtime setting on the day of a festival of Venus, though the fiction has an unexpectedly allegorical, Christian ending. In both these, as with the *Decameron*, the frame-story provides the thematic emphasis for the included tales. There is no frame-story in Boccaccio's later Latin compilations, the *De Claris Mulieribus* ('Concerning Famous Women'), which provides a parallel to *The Legend of Good Women*, though Chaucer does not obviously draw on the earlier work except possibly in the story of Cleopatra, and the *De Casibus Virorum Illustrium* ('Concerning the Falls of Famous Men'), mainly telling of the downfall of tyrants and obviously close to Chaucer's *Monk's Tale* and the model also for Lydgate's *Fall of Princes*. Boccaccio thus provides comparisons both for Chaucer's two thematic compilations, where the unity of the series lies simply in a moral theme, and the more varied type of tale collection in which multiple narrators entertain one another with a wide range of subjects and of narrative effects.

Some of the strategies used by Boccaccio in the organization of the hundred tales of the *Decameron* have already been mentioned in the earlier discussion of comic tales, but will perhaps bear being repeated. The frame-story itself, telling how ten young people agree to leave Florence to avoid the plague and to spend time in leisurely retreat, is

---

[8] James Simpson, 'Madness and texts: Hoccleve's *Series*', in *Chaucer and Fifteenth-Century Poetry*, ed. Julia Boffey and Janet Cowen (London, King's College, 1991), pp.15–29.

full of interest in its picture of the suffering in the city and of the layering of Florentine society, the relationships among the company of seven women and three men and the several country estates where they spend the two weeks that the action requires. The hundred tales are rendered comprehensible as a totality by the division into ten sets of ten and the setting of themes day by day (and this is made flexible enough to allow the subjects for two of the days to be left to individual choice); Boccaccio thus builds into his scheme differences of theme and variation of mood from the comic effects of tales of witty rejoinders to the more moving and dramatic moments involved in the stories of difficulties overcome and the debating material for the mixed company in the stories of men and women outwitting one another. Within each day there is the twist brought by Boccaccio's giving to Dioneo the privilege of telling his tale last and ignoring the day's theme when he wants to. Even when the day's theme does not determine the subject matter many tales pick up some reference from the preceding tale as a starting point. The dynamics of relationships in the group shift from day to day as each one in turn takes on the role of queen or king of the storytelling. As a result of these devices and of his range of story material Boccaccio brings off the conjuring trick that the tale collection requires, the trick of making the stories work both as units and as part of the cumulative effectiveness of the whole.

Chaucer was nothing like so thorough, but then his work is incomplete. If the scheme proposed by the Host (that each of the pilgrims should tell two tales on the way from Southwark to Canterbury and two on the way back) is taken as a serious statement of Chaucer's intent, then *The Canterbury Tales* was meant to contain 120 or so tales and so to be even longer than the *Decameron*, but then one would guess that he would have had to work in tales of a much shorter type to stop it becoming unwieldy. As it is, only about a fifth of that number was written and some of the tales that exist are unfinished. The major effect that Chaucer decided to exploit which distinguishes his collection from Boccaccio's is the idea of a wide variety of genres to go with his variety of narrating voices: this is, even in its incomplete state, a virtuoso collection of most of the kinds of narrative known at the time, and the result is that deliberate contrasts create Chaucer's version of the unexpectedness that tale collections need. That this is his intention is made plain at the outset with the shift in subject matter and style between *The Knight's Tale* and

The Miller's Tale, and later on in the series (in the few cases where the tales survive as a sequence) it seems that Chaucer did not want to settle into writing groups of stories of the same kind but wanted to surprise—hence the mixture of Fragment VII, where the tales of Shipman and Prioress themselves contrast in style and kind but are further trumped by the tales of Chaucer, Monk, and Nun's Priest, all of which are in different ways surprising, even bizarre. Boccaccio's exchanges among narrators have plenty of lively disagreement, but the rivalries are mainly those of gender: the irreverence and cheeky boldness about sex of some of the male narrators interplay with the more decorous stories of the young women. Chaucer has a more mixed social group and exploits the possibilities of quarrelling and mutual criticism; the Host's proposal that the storytelling they engage in along the road shall be a competition introduces the idea that the very act of telling a story is part of the game and has an element of rivalry in it, so that the question of storyteller's skill becomes an issue. Chaucer thus turns his pilgrims into critics as well as narrators and it is through the dynamics of the process of narrating and record-ing audience response that Chaucer creates his complex layers of narrative illusion.

Narrators and commentators in *The Canterbury Tales*

In much medieval narrative poetry the poet simply asks his audience to listen while a story is passed on:

> If ȝe wyl lysten þis laye bot a littel quile,
> I schal telle hit astit, as I in toun herde.
> (*Sir Gawain*, 30–1)

The implication might appear to be that the hearer's role is receptive but passive. But because oral delivery offered the opportunity for the poet to act out his narrative and because much of the poetry which achieved written form was probably composed for a sophisticated audience, more often the poet assumes a critical awareness in his hearers and is prepared to give directions or ask for feedback:

> ... if ӡe fynde fables or foly þeramonge,
> Or any fantasie yffeyned, þat no frute is in,
> Lete youre conceill corette it and clerkis togedyr,
> And amende þat ys amysse and make it more better.
> (*Mum and the Sothsegger*, 57–60)

The underlying intention may, as much as with a modern blurb, be indirectly to persuade the reader that the book is worth reading, but the direct speaking voice seems to offer a real opportunity to respond: the poem promises not to be perfected and closed off but still in progress and open to disagreement. More than any other medieval English writer Chaucer became adept at exploiting this apparent openness, even to the extent of treating literary works as if they were unfinished conversations between presenter and recipient. In many poems he speaks not with an anonymous narrative voice, but with a distinctive set of attitudes and mannerisms; by exaggeration and self-deprecation he exploits the comic possibilities of the relationship between poet and audience and by direct rhetorical exhortation he skilfully moves his audience from distance to intimacy. By the time he came to write *The Canterbury Tales* he had worked his way through several versions of the deferential, bookish, and inexperienced character which he created for himself out of medieval traditions of modesty and the function of the learning figure in dream poems. He had also begun to indicate aspects of the role of the audience—what reactions he expects and the degree of sympathy and intelligence he requires in such commands as 'Now herkneth with a good entencioun' (*Troilus and Criseyde*, I, 52) where he reminds the audience of the relevance of their own experiences of love to their judgement of Troilus' behaviour.

On the basis of earlier explorations of the roles of teller and listener Chaucer invented the fascinating narrative complexity of *The Canterbury Tales* and its variety of invented voices. The character called Chaucer, who becomes a member of the group of pilgrims at the Tabard Inn and reports on his fellow-travellers, has apparently the most reticent of the voices, even though it is the one that repeats the words of all the rest. The Host's voice is, in contrast, loud and clear enough to fulfil the roles of master of ceremonies and proposer of the game of tale-telling. The voices of the pilgrims are used both to tell the stories and to express the audience's reception of them: all are simultaneously tellers and listeners, narrators and commentators. By putting the receivers of the narratives into the fiction, instead of merely identifying those out there listening as 'ye loveres' or 'every lady bright of hewe', Chaucer immensely enlarges his self-conscious exploitation of the narrative process. Even in its unfinished state *The Canterbury Tales* has always appeared the earliest English work with an ambitious and imaginative narrative plan—not merely a great assembling of stories but a continuous and shifting fiction which fills the imagination with inter-threaded strands of themes, characters, literary kinds, levels of style, and layers of illusion. The roles that Chaucer developed for himself, for the Host, and for the pilgrims as creators, instigators, and tellers of tales and as commentators upon them are an important part of the work's effects of richness and flexibility.

The figure of the poet is the one who is most surprising to the reader unfamiliar with Chaucer's earlier works. One might expect him to control the content, to represent the authority of the creator, and to act as the voice of common sense, but Chaucer has chosen to conceal his performance of these functions. So in the *General Prologue* he appears a man whose 'wit is short', who accepts the pilgrims' evaluation of themselves and who combines description of character and appearance with a deliberately ingenuous pleasure which augments the satirical and moral effect in an implicit, subtle way. He presents himself as a mere reporter and recorder, whose task it is 'To telle yow hir wordes and hir cheere', and who apologizes for the fact that some of the material may be offensive; he can not leave it out because then it would not be true.

> But first I pray yow, of youre curteisye,
> That ye n'arette it nat my vileynye,
> Thogh that I pleynly speke in this mateere,
> To telle yow hir wordes and hir cheere,
> Ne thogh I speke hir wordes proprely.
> For this ye knowen al so wel as I,
> Whoso shal telle a tale after a man,
> He moot reherce as ny as evere he kan
> Everich a word, if it be in his charge,
> Al speke he never so rudeliche and large,
> Or ellis he moot telle his tale untrewe,
> Or feyne thyng, or fynde wordes newe.
>
> (*CT*, I, 725–36)

Here Chaucer claims to be avoiding the very thing that is the foundation of his and every poet's art, the invention of incidents and the original composition and arrangement of words. The insistence on the exact truth of the record, the closeness to supposed reality, shows Chaucer more concerned to encourage belief in his fictional world than to take credit for its invention, but because the reader knows that the insistence on exact copying of reality is not true, the passage functions to increase our awareness of the complexity of reality and the poet's relationship to it.

In the Prologue to *The Miller's Tale* he plays the same game, claiming that he must record the words of churls or else be guilty of falsifying the matter, even if to record 'harlotrie' may risk offending those who are 'gentil'. His way out of the problem is to insist on the freedom of the audience not to listen to nor to read what they do not like:

> . . . every gentil wight I preye,
> For Goddes love, demeth nat that I seye
> Of yvel entente, but for I moot reherce
> Hir tales alle, be they bettre or werse,
> Or elles falsen som of my matere.
> And therfore, whoso list it nat yhere,
> Turne over the leef and chese another tale;
> For he shal fynde ynowe, grete and smale,
> Of storial thyng that toucheth gentillesse,
> And eek moralitee and hoolynesse.
> Blameth nat me if that ye chese amys.
> The Millere is a cherl; ye knowe wel this.
> So was the Reve eek and othere mo,
> And harlotrie they tolden bothe two.
> Avyseth yow, and put me out of blame;
> And eek men shal nat maken ernest of game.
>
> (*CT*, I, 3171–86)

The primary intention of this is to win acceptance for and to enhance the writer's creation; the pretence is that the fictional world is the reality and that it is too masterful to be denied. The writer must not 'falsen' his material and if one looks beyond the immediate occasion of the statement (which is to justify the inclusion in *The Canterbury Tales* of scurrilous fabliaux), one can see the start of a debate about the relationship between fiction and reality which surfaces on several occasions. The point made here is that the poet must truthfully record men's words and the implication is that the writer's function is to give an accurate record of experience. There have been plenty of readers willing to take Chaucer at his word and to read *The Canterbury Tales* as an eyewitness account of the medieval world, but the list of types of tale that follows reminds us that it is only the act of telling the tale that Chaucer is claiming to report exactly; the actual 'mateere' of the tales varies widely in its relationship to literal experience and what the passage really says is that in fiction one can *choose* the degree of closeness to literal truth; for those readers made uncomfortable by imitation of men's actual behaviour there are plenty of alternatives. In this apparently defensive passage Chaucer is really claiming the right to compose as he chooses. At the same time as claiming that the fictional world is real experience outside himself Chaucer is also establishing the idea of variety in the type of tale: the work is to be a medley in which some things are serious, some merely 'game'; major and minor works stand side by side and all are equally available if not equally important, history, romance, exemplary tales, and pious legends as well as comic anecdotes. The most interesting effect of the passage is ostensibly to transfer responsibility for discrimination among these various narrative pleasures from writer to reader; Chaucer rejects responsibility for deciding that one kind of fiction is preferable to another, but he is really staking a claim to try out all kinds; all is grist to the writer's mill, even trivial stuff of doubtful taste.

When he comes to tell his own tale he shows another facet of his idea of the role of the poet. Partly he is just having fun and making a joke at his own expense, as he does also in *The Man of Law's Prologue* where he has his pilgrim imply that Chaucer the poet has written far too much and is not very good at metre, rhyme, and the whole business of writing English. The spirit of game is clear enough in the 'merry words of the Host to Chaucer' where the Host teases the poet for always looking down at the ground and for the sly deceit suggested by the combination of a substantial manly shape with an 'elvysh' countenance, and the tale of Sir Thopas is a good joke: fair enough in a tale-telling competition to characterize the one poet among the company by doggerel, cliché, a naive mishmash of fairy bride, giant, armour, and high-sounding bravado. But when the tale is halted in mid-flow by the Host, the debating point lying beneath the joke is apparent. The poet protests:

'Why so?' quod I, 'why wiltow lette me
More of my tale than another man,
Syn that it is the beste rym I kan?'
(*CT*, VII, 926–8)

The consequence of supposedly giving freedom to all tellers is that you have to put up with bad art. In response to the Host's criticism of his incompetence, the great writer tartly offers an alternative, which 'oghte liken yow, as I suppose . . ., It is a moral tale vertuous'; the Host has earlier shown his approval of a meaty piece of *sentence* and his reaction to the story of Melibee is duly appreciative of its improving morality, but other readers have not been quite so certain of their reaction to Chaucer's 'lytel thyng in prose'.

This section of *The Canterbury Tales* marks an important stage in Chaucer's exploration of the extent and nature of authorial responsibility. In earlier works he had presented himself as a bookish observer rather than an active participant in experience; in *Troilus and Criseyde* he proclaims himself inadequate to find words to express intensity of feeling, unable fully to control his material, and unwilling to express the moral judgements which his fable seems to require. The suggestion is that Life, Love, Art are all bigger than he is. Though one recognizes the poet's modesty as a way of enhancing the significance of his matter, the accumulated instances identify a poet apparently unwilling to categorize, to judge, or to claim the special insight or the moral privilege of containing fiction within a theoretical frame. In *The Canterbury Tales* he even denies responsibility for tale-telling itself. First he can not control the tellers. Now he presents himself as professionally incompetent; he can not write decent verse and can tell a moral tale only in a pedestrian way, the worthy intention having to compensate for the lack of art. The ability to tell and to judge belongs to others. The only roles Chaucer will accept openly are those of innocent recorder of what he hears and sees and the purveyor of other writers' virtuous examples.

Chaucer's double act in *Sir Thopas* and *Melibee* remains a challenge to the reader. It looks as if Chaucer thought that the author figure was a suitable mouthpiece for two extreme types of narrative but quite how he would have defined those extremes is not clear. It is not possible to read the lengthy *Melibee* as a second jest, a parody of the moral tale, as some have suggested, although there is an element of joking in the poet's failure in verse being paid for by some unambitious didactic prose. The terms of the tale-telling contest in *The Canterbury Tales* provide the more convincing antithesis of the Host's call for 'tales of best sentence and moost solas': in *Sir Thopas* Chaucer shows by exaggeration where writing only for 'solas' can lead; escapism without sense is a logical extreme of the avoidance of serious purpose in narrative. *Melibee* can be seen as the other extreme, 'sentence' without much 'solas'. There is some textual support for this view within the tale itself: before Dame Prudence takes over, Melibeus is advised by his friends and 'oon of thise olde wise' argues against war, but his words are not received well:

And when this olde man wende [thought] to enforcen his tale by resons, wel ny alle atones bigonne they to rise for to breken his tale and beden hym ful often his wordes to abregge. For soothly, he that precheth to hem that listen nat heeren his wordes his sermon hem anoieth.

(*CT*, VII, 1043–4)

In the light of what follows this is clearly a reproof to the impatient hearers, rather than a criticism of the speaker and the tenor of the rest of the tale is to lay stress on the worth of judicious counsel, with little regard for what is pleasing to the hearer. If pursuit of the pleasing risks empty folly, insistence on moral importance may cost the audience's delight.

If one looks beyond the context in *The Canterbury Tales* then other aspects of the writer's position in the fourteenth century may be seen reflected in the antithesis of the two tales. The material of *Sir Thopas* is a comic comment on what can happen when a poet ranges freely and uses his imagination and his inventive capacity. Instead of liberation of the poet's creative powers one gets lack of control; to create a new fable the poet links stale romance motifs, loosened and blurred into mere archetype. At the other extreme the writer is tied to his source: Chaucer accepts the text of (the French version of) the *Liber Consolationis ad Consilii* of Albertanus of Brescia as a task for translation and renders it word for word in places. The two tales thus comment on one another: if the sober accuracy of *Melibee* is an object lesson for the author of *Sir Thopas*, the irresponsible verbal comedy and skipping metre of the poem cock a snook at the plodding sentences of the prose.

R. F. Green suggests another dimension to the contrast: the two tales reflect contrary aspects of the role of the court author. *Melibee* can be placed with Book VII of Gower's *Confessio Amantis* as political and moral instruction for the young Richard II and thus identified with the idea of poet as adviser to princes and with court respect for the practical value of literature; the handbook for rulers is one of the best-attested literary traditions of the medieval period. *Sir Thopas* belongs with the older tradition of the kind of entertainment expected of the court minstrel, identified by the time of Richard II either with the old-fashioned days when the court's social life was centred in the hall or with the crude entertainments of those outside the sophisticated circle of the King's Chamber.[9] *Sentence*, translation of worthy material and virtuous example characterize a possible way for the serious writer and it is a way which Chaucer seems to approve in his other problematic statement about his own work in *The Canterbury Tales*, the so-called 'Retractions'. His final repudiation of his 'enditynges of worldly vanitees' and those tales in the Canterbury series 'that sownen into synne' in favour of his translation of *Boece* and 'legendes of saintes and omelies and moralitee and devocioun' has never been acceptable as a straightforward literary judgement— indeed it runs counter to what all readers of the tales have found most enjoyable and worthwhile in Chaucer's writings. In terms of Chaucer's handling of the idea of the responsibility of the writer, it seems the culmination of the process that starts with his disclaiming responsibility for the contents of his work, continues with his rejecting originality in relationship to it and a display of professional incompetence as a poet; only a modest demonstration of serious moral intent is within his powers. It is, in its way, logical that such a narrator should wash his hands of virtually the whole realm of fiction and of tale-telling. Fortunately Chaucer did not allow that logic to inhibit his exploration of the full range of medieval narrative kinds with verve and independence. What he is saying in the 'Retractions' amounts to a recognition that secularity, or at least the suspension of explicit belief, is necessary to the author of fiction. Chaucer's response to Boethius as much as to the pagan philosophy and history involved in *The Knight's Tale* and *Troilus and Criseyde* shows how willing he was to examine that territory. But the role of the poet which he chose to adopt did not allow admission of the fact. Deference and a show of modesty had become a habit, a useful defence,

[9] R. F. Green, *Poets and Princepleasers: Literature and the English Court in the Late Middle Ages* (Toronto, University of Toronto Press, 1980), p.143.

and perhaps a genuine bedrock of substance and security in the shifting areas of literature and imagination, of the instability of medieval courts and of Chaucer's personal assessment of his own life. It might seem an unnecessary self-restraint for an exuberant poet, were it not that he had devised for himself several alternative outlets in his work.

Some of the responsibities that Chaucer refuses to bear in his own person he gives to the major figure in the interlude sections of *The Canterbury Tales*, the Host, who is at the start of the journey designated 'oure governour/And of our tales juge and reportour'. As this indicates, Harry Bailly's main function is the control and organization of the tale-telling and of the good behaviour of the company. He is to be judge of the storytelling competition to decide which pilgrim tells the tale of 'best sentence and moost solas' and to award the prize, a free supper at the Tabard Inn.[10] Since this prize is within his gift, the Host thus functions as a homely version of the literary patron. It is also the Host's task to supervise the order of the tale-telling, from the drawing of lots which gives to the Knight the task of beginning the game to the subsequent calling on others to take their turn, in the course of which the reader gets a running commentary on aspects of literary decorum. Sometimes the Host asks with politeness and tact (Prioress); sometimes the next teller has to put up with teasing (Clerk, Monk); sometimes the Host is rough and impatient (Franklin, Cook). At times the pilgrims will not do what they are told (Miller) or quarrel among themselves (Friar and Summoner). Harry occasionally loses his temper (Pardoner) or, on the other hand, has to remain calm and to smooth over a temporary break in good fellowship (Cook and Manciple). By the accumulation of these passages Chaucer establishes not only a lively characterization of a loud, cheerful, short-tempered innkeeper, with a taste for fun, sound moral lessons on behaviour, pathos, and the whole-hearted enjoyment of physical pleasure, but also a perspective of everyday experience which becomes a point of reference for the tale-tellers and the tales they narrate. Through the Host Chaucer dramatizes and externalizes the

[10] See Alan T. Gaylord, 'Sentence and solaas in Fragment VII of *The Canterbury Tales*: Harry Bailly as horseback editor', *PMLA* 82 (1967), 226–35 and L.M. Leitch, 'Sentence and solaas: the function of the Host in *The Canterbury Tales*', *Chaucer Review* 17 (1982–3), 5–20.

choices that he was making in the composition of the work and the idea of a natural mixture of narratives.

Harry Bailly does not only tell the pilgrims which of them is to speak next, but also has quite a lot to say about the tales themselves. Sometimes he indicates at the beginning what he would like; at other times he says what he thinks when the tale is over. He functions as commentator both in the specific sense of expressing approval or disapproval of particular tales and in the general sense of voicing literary preferences. So he is moved by *The Physician's Tale*, the sad story of Virginia whose 'beautee was hir deeth'; that the gifts of Fortune and Nature should be the cause of death adds a bitter comment to the poignancy of her particular tragic fate and the Host needs the help of 'corny ale' or 'a myrie tale' as a restorative—otherwise 'Myn herte is lost for pitee of this mayde.' Through the Host Chaucer displays the unselfconscious emotional response to this melodramatic tale and establishes the principle of tales balancing one another, since one kind is seen as some kind of answer to another. He is used again to define the effect of a tale on the audience in the discussion with the Knight after the latter has interrupted *The Monk's Tale* and criticized it for being depressing and boring: the Host speaks up for optimism and liveliness. At other moments he expresses the naive but common way of judging a tale purely with reference to his own experience. So with comic exaggeration Harry reveals himself as a henpecked husband whose ill-named wife Goodelief could learn a lesson from the tale of Melibee. All the reactions of this type which Chaucer put into *The Canterbury Tales* contribute to the sense of the life of the tale spilling over. This is not to say that the work is a continuous dramatic performance and the 'Human Comedy' school of reading which insists on viewing tales as dramatic monologues undervalues Chaucer's interest in literary judgement and comparison. The stories exist as separate fictional worlds and examples of narrative kinds and as part of an ebb and flow of argument and mood, as one tale pleases and another annoys, or as one confirms the hearer's beliefs and another causes controversy.

If one looks for a central principle in Chaucer's presentation of the Host, the expression in his words of the spirit of game in *The Canterbury Tales* seems the most significant. He proposes the competition which brings the idea of contest into the tale-telling. He discourages the pilgrims from becoming too serious and so upholds the sense of narrative as play. His reproof of the Reeve for his melancholy words on old age identifies holy writ and preaching with miserable thoughts and he later expresses a similar attitude of mind by discouraging the Clerk from being too learned and didactic:

> 'For Goddes sake, as beth of bettre chere!
> It is no tyme for to studien heere!
> Telle us som myrie tale by youre fey!
> For what man that is entred in a play
> He nedes moot unto the pley assente.
> But precheth nat, as freres doon in Lente,
> To make us for oure olde synnes wepe,
> Ne that thy tale make us nat to slepe.'
>   (*CT*, IV, 7–14)

This is consistent with a view of the Host as a worldly, superficial judge of things, who just wants life to be cheerful—and there are some good passages which establish this idea, particularly *The Manciple's Prologue* where the Host's character as *bon viveur* and as innkeeper who praises wine and laughter as peacemakers is displayed:

> 'I se wel it is necesarie,
> Where that we goon, good drynke we with us carie;
> For that wol turne rancour and disese
> T'acord and love, and many a wrong apese.
> O thou Bacus, yblessed be thy name,
> That so kanst turnen ernest into game!'
>   (*CT*, IX, 95–100)

But that is not all there is to it. Chaucer has given his Host a good strain of common sense, as well as his liking for a joke. The terms of *The Clerk's Prologue* (apart from their relevance to Chaucer's literary purpose in the tale that follows and the subtlety of the contrast between the Host's commands and the Clerk's fulfilment of them[11]) identify the ground rules of all the tale-telling: this is the arena of 'play', which requires a suspension of the habits and outlook of scholar and priest and of the larger existence within which those offices are carried out. The division of literature from life is as clear here as in the 'Retractions'.

---

[11] See Anne Middleton, 'The Clerk and his Tale: some literary contexts', *Studies in the Age of Chaucer* 2 (1980), 121–50.

The most pointed literary criticism attributed to the Host is found in the two passages where he condemns a tale. His impatient dismissal of *Sir Thopas* as badly told and worthless, in which Chaucer 'doost noght elles but despendest tyme', leads to a request for something else in which there is 'som murthe or sum doctryne'; this restatement of the literary principle of 'lust and lore' allies the Host with standard medieval literary tastes and identifies his role as that of the middle-of-the-road, reasonably knowledgeable layman. He may have little appreciation of the finer points of rhetoric or of philosophy, but he has absorbed the classical justification of literary composition as involving profit and pleasure, even if he is prepared to accept them separately. Equally indicative of Chaucer's use of the Host to express the commonsense view based on ordinary experience is his comment on *The Monk's Tale*. In an echo of the passage quoted above from *Melibee*, he says:

> 'Whereas a man may have noon audience,
> Noght helpeth it to tellen his sentence.'
> (*CT*, VII, 2801–2)

But whereas in *Melibee* the context makes it clear that an audience should be prepared to listen to sensible practical advice, here the foregoing instance of the Monk's series of the tragic falls of great men directs the reader to agreement with the Host; worthy lessons fail if they are exemplified so often that the audience is too bored to pay attention.

The relationship between serious and comic, or 'ernest' and 'game' as the Host expresses it, thus becomes a point of debate in the interludes and it is most significantly the point of disagreement between Host and Parson in the prologue to *The Parson's Tale*. Here the Host's request for the tale which is, according to this version of things, to be the last, since 'every man, save thou, hath toold his tale', reminds the Parson of the spirit of the game: 'ne breke thou nat oure pley'. But the Host's command 'Telle us a fable anon' meets with a refusal which is a rejection of the whole business of the tale-telling and of the rules of the game:

> 'Thou getest fable noon ytold for me,
> For Paul, that writeth unto Thymothee,
> Repreveth hem that weyven soothfastnesse
> And tellen fables and swich wrecchednesse.

> Why sholde I sowen draf out of my fest,
> When I may sowen whete, if that me lest?'
> (*CT*, X, 31–6)

What the Parson offers is 'Moralitee and vertuous matere' which will make an appropriate end to the pilgrimage, since he, with Jesus' aid, may be given the grace to show how this pilgrimage is an earthly image of the perfect glorious pilgrimage to the heavenly Jerusalem. The pilgrims accept this as suitable, but the Host does not let the Parson begin without a reminder that they *are* still in this world and that there is a limit to the length of time any sermon should last:

> 'Say what yow list, and we wol gladly heere.'
> And with that word he seyde in this manere:
> 'Telleth,' quod he, 'youre meditacioun.
> But hasteth yow, the sonne wole adoun.
> Beth fructuous, and that in litel space.
> And to do wel God sende yow his grace!'
> (*CT*, X, 69–74[12])

There is much of interest in this exchange.

First there is the word 'fable'. The Host may be thought to use it in an appropriate sense, to mean a fictitious narrative (especially one based on legend) or a short narrative designed to convey a moral. But the Parson takes it in the sense of an idle tale, a falsity, as Chaucer uses it in *The Legend of Good Women* (l.702): 'This is storial truth, it is no fable', and in *Lak of Stedfastnesse*: 'Trouthe is put doun, resoun is holden fable.' Through the ambiguity of the word Chaucer shows the ambiguity of the tale-telling itself; 'solas' may include lies; 'game' may mean vanity, triviality, immorality. *The Parson's Tale* is not a fable in either sense, nor a story of any kind, not in fact a 'tale' at all, unless that word is reduced to meaning merely 'discourse'; it is a didactic tract on penitence and the deadly sins, a rejection of fiction and the 'solas' of narrative, and, of course, a rejection of the Host's game, and the whole idea that one can suspend moral imperatives for the sake of art; the tale promises no pleasure and gives none.

Secondly, there is the question of the breadth of implication of

---

[12] Lines in the order of the manuscripts, though *The Riverside Chaucer*, gen. ed. Larry D. Benson, 3rd edn (Oxford U.P., 1988) prints lines 69–70 after line 74, following John M. Manly's edition of *The Canterbury Tales* (1928).

the passage. Some commentators have seen the exchange between Host and Parson as controlling the meaning of the end of *The Canterbury Tales* and hence of the work as a whole. The Host has been seen by some critics as yielding his role of ruler and governor to a higher authority. However, Chaucer makes it clear that the Host would prefer not to have to listen to a sermon and so the characterization remains consistent: the Host continues to be representative of the audience, allowed to require brevity and cogency.

So in the figure of Harry Bailly Chaucer accepts one kind of responsibility, that of controlling narrative, and explores some of the perspectives from which it asks to be regarded; he bears witness to the power of narrative to create feeling, to communicate, to amuse, and to teach, but also to its capacity to weary the attention. By detaching these responsibilities and perspectives from himself Chaucer leaves room to distance his authorial sympathies from the world of fiction when it seems fitting to put tale-telling back into its place.

Chaucer also leaves his authorial figure free of implication in the practical, physical and temporal aspects of the Canterbury series. The unfinished state of the work and the evidence of the manuscripts that others had to some extent to organize Chaucer's writings after his death make it difficult to see the effect of this absolutely clearly, but the various fragments were obviously being fitted into a not yet fully worked out time scheme and into the stages of the physical journey and it is the voice of the Host that becomes particularly associated with reminders of time and place. The description of him as 'oure aller cok' in the *General Prologue* and the conjunction of time and space in his closing exhortation to the Parson invite the reader to identify the Host from beginning to end as the type of the earthbound, secular man, living only in the immediate present[13] and at the conclusion of the work in dramatic opposition to the Parson with his spiritual and eternal perspective. To Harry Bailly the insult of *Sir Thopas* is that it wastes time, and elsewhere Chaucer develops the thought as one of the Host's themes:

> 'Lordynges, the tyme wasteth nyght and day,
> And steleth from us, what pryvely slepynge,
> And what thurgh necligence in oure werkynge,

---

[13] See Barbara Page, 'Concerning the Host', *Chaucer Review* 4 (1969–70), 1–13.

> As dooth the streem that turneth nevere agayn,
> Descendynge fro the montaigne into playn.
> Wel kan Senec and many a philosophre
> Biwaillen tyme more than gold in cofre;
> For "Los of catel may recovered be,
> But los of tyme shendeth us," quod he.'
>
> (*CT*, II, 20–8)

This is only one aspect of references to time in *The Canterbury Tales*; the consciousness of time of day and month attributed to the Host, and echoed by others among the pilgrims within and without their tales has to be related to the seasonal time of the opening of the *General Prologue* and to the references to 'this present lyf' and 'the day of doom' in the closing words of the 'Retractions' to form another of Chaucer's multiple effects. As Pandarus' practicality is used in *Troilus and Criseyde* to put Troilus' behaviour within a worldly perspective while leaving the hero free of the trivialities of circumstance, so Chaucer uses the Host to express some of his purpose and concern and to characterize part of the nature of tale-telling, but to leave it in tension with other aspects expressed through the poet's deferential withdrawals from authority and through the rest of the invented voices in the work, those of the pilgrims.

Through his adopted narrating voices Chaucer shows the ambiguities involved in being a tale-teller. To ask someone to tell a tale is to ask them, in the context of the Canterbury series, to be judged. The tale is presented as a public performance, and even if Chaucer did not pursue very far into each tale the dramatic character of the individual teller (except in the cases of the Wife of Bath and the Pardoner and, to a lesser extent, the Canon's Yeoman), still he is assuming a role. Chaucer's invention of the pilgrims as his storytellers enables him to engage in a virtuoso tour de force of medieval narrative kinds and styles. In this respect it is irrelevant that it is the Squire who tells an exotic eastern tale of magic or that it is the Reeve who presents a comic tale of provincial snobbery and cheating; what is significant is that two such tales should be brought together in the same work and so create range and variety. But, at the same time, the use of invented characters to tell the stories allows Chaucer to display them, when he wishes, as the product of class, education, personality, taste, and skill (or the lack of it). Tale-telling becomes a metaphor for life itself. The convention of authorial modesty can be given a dramatic point in prologues which express different degrees and kinds of self-consciousness, or, on the other hand, of self-confidence.

Some of the pilgrims are characterized as irresponsible narrators. The Miller flouts the ruling of the Host by insisting on telling his tale out of turn and threatens decorum by telling a tale which may offend; the Reeve is offended, though not by the words and actions, and some variation of reaction among the others is suggested. The Friar finds even the Wife of Bath far too serious-minded and too inclined to preach, but the result of his speaking only of 'game' is also to offend and cause a bitter reaction from the Summoner. The two pairs of fabliaux use personal resentment as a motive in tale-telling; the stories of Reeve, Friar, and Summoner are used as weapons like the stories in *The Seven Sages of Rome*. More subtly one tale may be used to present a version of reality which challenges that of another tale, as the Miller's fabliau may be said to do in relation to the Knight's romance. These examples of one tale 'quitting' another also help to build up an intermittent discussion of the rules for and the standards of narration. This debating theme provides a way for Chaucer to use incompleteness (a characteristic of only too many of Chaucer's works) as a literary device. So Chaucer the poet is also irresponsible in his first effort at tale-telling and the Monk is characterized as a failed narrator, at least in the eyes of Knight and Host, through monotony and a negative outlook. The Squire is an ambiguous case but some readers have taken the incompleteness of his tale to contribute to the same effect. Chaucer's intentions are quite clear, though, when he includes an explicit reproof in the linking material or within the prologues: the grumbling Friar's complaint that 'this is a long preamble of a tale' confirms the reader's suspicion that, however lively a performance Chaucer devised for her, *The Wife of Bath's Prologue*, twice as long as her tale, is a piece of literary cheek, and it makes it more likely that her use of her tale as a vehicle for her own obsessions and prejudices is being drawn to our attention. With the Pardoner the fault of separating narrative effect from narrative intent is identified unambiguously. Chaucer characterizes him as a professional tale-teller who boasts of his persuasive arts and describes his own manner of speech, his abiding theme and the tricks of his trade. Finally the division between act and motive is declared:

'Thus kan I preche agayn that same vice
Which that I use, and that is avarice.
But though myself be gilty in that synne,
Yet kan I maken oother folk to twynne
From avarice, and soore to repente.
But that is nat my principal entente;
I preche nothyng but for coveitise . . .'
(*CT*, VI, 427–33)

The cynical artifice to which the attention is directed here is Chaucer's extreme instance of creating pleasure for the reader from irresponsible narration; by identifying the idea of story being manipulated for a purpose, Chaucer directs our critical attention to enjoyment of rhetorical bravura and skilful composition. The vivid power of *The Pardoner's Tale* becomes oddly ironical as a result and Chaucer needs to use the Host at his most brusque and crude to reassert some sense of the right judgement of the narrator's persuasive arts.

Chaucer explores narrative from another angle by characterizing some storytellers as making the audience conscious of the questionable truth of what they are saying. So in the Prologue to *The Clerk's Tale* the Host, as I mentioned earlier, virtually forbids the Clerk to be didactic or penitential in his storytelling and enjoins on him the rules of 'play': in response the Clerk accepts the Host's temporary authority and says he will try to please, with just a slight touch of qualification:

'Ye have of us as now the governance,
And therfore wol I do yow obeisance,
As fer as resoun axeth, hardily!'
(*CT*, IV, 23–5)

How far reason is controlling the narrative becomes a point at issue in the story of Griselda and is presented as a debating theme in the Envoy which Chaucer added to the Petrarch/Boccaccio tale. First his narrator makes it plain that the events of the tale are not likely to be confirmed by experience:

But o word, lordynges, herkneth er I go.
It were ful hard to fynde now-a-dayes
In al a toun Grisildis thre or two . . .
(*CT*, IV, 1163–5)

And then, calling on the response of the fictional audience of pilgrims by making a deferential gesture 'for the Wyves love of Bath', the narrator signs off with a brilliant satirical lyric advising men not to test their wives:

> No wedded man so hardy be t'assaille
> His wyves pacience in trust to fynde
> Grisildis, for in certein he shal faille.
>
> (*CT*, IV, 1180–2)

After this one stanza addressed to men the song's other five verses gleefully offer advice to wives, advice which completely contradicts the moral of the tale: Griselda should not be taken as a model, but wives should take command and use their 'crabbed eloquence' to quell their husbands' tyranny:

> Be ay of chiere as light as leef on lynde,
> And let hym care, and wepe, and wrynge, and waille!
>
> (*CT*, IV, 1211–12)

Whatever one makes of the tale itself, the Prologue and Envoy show Chaucer using the tale-telling framework to mediate between the audience and the story, and using the commentator's voice to complicate our sense of the relationship between fiction and reality. Less explicit but somewhat similar is *The Nun's Priest's Tale*, another highly literary composition. Here the narrator, who brings with him no suggestions of 'character' but who is an anonymous stand-in for Chaucer, is again used to offer to the audience alternative ways of understanding the tale: the freedom which the reader is apparently offered at the end to decide what part of the story is wheat and what chaff has the effect of creating greater uncertainty in our minds about the relationship between the pleasure of fiction, the nature of reality and the good of morality. Similarly the literary values of the audience are brought into question by the shifts of level in *The Merchant's Tale* and by Chaucer's characterizing others (such as the Man of Law and Franklin) as self-conscious literary performers.

Part of the sense of richness of *The Canterbury Tales* as a narrative work results from Chaucer's inclusion of the various questionings and discussions of tale-telling. By changes of style, by criticism, objections, and answered accusations, by parody and burlesque, by discussion of the responsibility of the narrator, and by putting his tales into the mouths of speakers who move from a tale-telling role to a commenting role, Chaucer makes narrative into a complex process not just a temporarily assumed activity. The journey is a succession of stories, not a succession of places and the sense of progression is marked by ends of tales, links, and new beginnings. Storytelling acts as a metaphor for living in the world and the road to Canterbury of the path of life. Narrative is the game of the road, to be put aside when the journey comes to an end, but meanwhile the state in which the pilgrims exist. The participants in the game are both narrators and commentators, both actors and observers: telling stories to an audience is a vivid equivalent for the sense of life as a continously interrupted performance of one's self. So versions of living are modified by corrective alternatives, as when the view of deceived old age in *The Miller's Tale* is exposed as superficial and callous by the Reeve's meditation on the miseries of age. Chaucer has pretended that his narrators are independent of him. By this means he demonstrates the varied possibilities of tale-telling and its arbitrariness, but the most convincing reason for his adopting this stance is his unwillingness to be pinned down. Narrative for Chaucer is never just exemplification of moral principle; it is also a public performance for others, and so an exploration of the possibilities of 'telling one's tale', which include giving an account of oneself and possibly telling lies, as well as keeping the audience happy.

At the end of *The Canterbury Tales* Chaucer withdraws from narrative and from its metaphorical implications; the journey and the life of the road come to an end and storytelling is overtaken by 'vertuous sentence'. The poet's voice fuses with that of his Parson to identify the goal of pilgrimage with rejection of its processes and stages. The game of the road and the current of life are put behind in a mood of repentance. But Chaucer left a number of ironies and questions in the mind of the reader when he determined on this closure. His original conception was that all should return to the Tabard Inn where the supper awaits and the Host would remain in command. By then each pilgrim should have presented a set of four tales to be assessed for their combination of *sentence* and *solas*. However fitting an arrival at Canterbury *The Parson's Tale* makes (and that is open to question), it is quite certain that the Parson would not have been awarded a free meal back in Southwark. The greatest irony of the tale-telling itself is that the most effective short story is given to the pilgrim who expresses the greatest cynicism about the truth of fiction; the Pardoner stands for absolute manipulation of fiction with no moral conviction behind it. In contrast

Chaucer the poet, of all the pilgrims presumably the one most committed to tale-telling by his career, presents the 'best rym that I kan' and a sorry thing it is.

Cycles and composites

The collections of tales which I have mentioned so far have been, with some variations, assemblings in the same place or within a constructed framework, of stories which in their origins had a separate existence. Tales are drawn into groups by a collector, a compiler, a pigeon-holer who is either stacking like things together for convenience or filling up a storehouse which has a narrative label like Boccaccio's hundred tales or Chaucer's 'Canterbury' tales. Tale collections are centripetal, in the sense that separate items are being drawn towards the centre. The opposite medieval way of putting stories together is the centrifugal variety where it is the narrative centre from which the energy derives. This is the case with the *Ysengrimus* and the various versions of the *Roman de Renart* referred to in the chapter about fables. Once the character of Reynard the Fox together with a group of other stock figures, the wolf, the lion, and so on, are seen as the nucleus of comic narrative, a whole series is generated which continues to grow as long as writers think of new adventures and new twists to the original situation; the impulse to use animals for exemplary lessons has been overtaken by inventive interest in the multiplicity of ways in which known characteristics can be shown in action. Similarly the figure of Till Eulenspiegel, once invented, can become the hero of dozens of tales that are essentially repetitions of the first with variations. The series of adventures for the same characters is the basis also for the cycles of *chansons de geste* and, most prolifically of all, for the vast number of medieval narratives concerning Arthur and the knights of the Round Table. In this latter case the beginning and ending were, in a sense, fixed, but the centre was infinitely expandable, since within Arthur's story the adventures of every other knight could become the subject of a series, of sequels and prequels, of reinterpretations, expansions, and continuations.

The process by which lengthy cycles developed from a narrative core has been described in various ways. Historically it may be seen as

part of the early-thirteenth-century movement in France from individual verse romances to longer prose narratives. Several stages are
involved. One statement of the sequence is as follows: 'the segmenta-
tion of the narrative into episodes, the use of analogy to build intra-
and intertextual patterns, the interlacing of narrative segments.'[14]
A significant text which provided a stimulus to proliferation was the
unfinished *Perceval* of Chrétien, of which several continuations were
produced by other writers in the late twelfth and early thirteenth
centuries; these in turn may be seen as stages towards the development
of the vast Grail romance in prose, *Perlesvaus*, produced soon after
1200 and already displaying the complex interweaving of episodes
which is characteristic of the medieval Arthurian cycles and which,
following Vinaver, is usually referred to as 'interlace'.[15] The invention
of episodes for the hero Lancelot and the linking of the consequent
Lancelot cycle with the Grail stories and the death of Arthur led to
the formation in the first quarter of the thirteenth century of what
used to be known as the 'Vulgate Cycle' (now often referred to simply
as the Lancelot–Grail cycle).[16] Stories of Merlin and of Gawain and
his brothers provide other growth points and the Arthurian saga even
expands centripetally by absorbing the originally quite separate narrative material concerning Tristan, Yseult, and King Mark. The Prose
Lancelot and the Prose *Tristan* are perhaps the high points of this
phase of medieval French romance; the nearest in English to the vast
scope of these narrative forests is the selective version which Malory
created in the late fifteenth century out of a mixture of French and
English sources in his *Morte Darthur*. The overall impression made
by the French cycles is of complexity of incident and excess of narrative
lines. As Vinaver expresses it:

Arthurian romance in its most advanced cyclic form becomes a work so
complex as to defeat at first every attempt to discover any semblance of
rational principle behind it. The knights-errant who indefatigably make their

[14] Matilda Tomaryn Bruckner, 'The shape of romance in medieval France', in *The
Cambridge Companion to Medieval Romance*, ed. Roberta L. Krueger (Cambridge U.P.,
2000), p.23.

[15] Vinaver himself credits an earlier French historian, Ferdinand Lot, with identification of the device. See Vinaver, *The Rise of Romance*, p. 71, referring to Lot's study of the
prose *Lancelot* (*Étude sur le Lancelot en prose*, 1918) where he discusses 'le principe de
l'entrelacement.'

[16] For an outline of the growth of the Arthurian cycles see Derek Pearsall, *Arthurian
Romance: A Short Introduction* (Oxford, Blackwell, 2003), ch. 3, pp.40–59.

way through a forest—that ancient symbol of uncertain fate—are apt to abandon at any time one quest for the sake of another, only to be sidetracked again a moment later . . .[17]

Vinaver argues that those modern critics who have condemned the medieval cycles for want of coherence, clarity, unity, the lack of a central theme, and so on have failed to recognize that the Aristotelian model of literary unity is not the only narrative structure that works. What Tasso called 'natural multiplicity' and C. S. Lewis 'polyphonic' or interwoven narrative is Vinaver's 'poetry of interlace'. His metaphor suggests a parallel between cyclic narration and woven materials, such as tapestries, and more specifically the curving interwoven patterns of Romanesque design in architectural sculpture and in manuscript illumination. Romanesque 'ribbon' ornament, 'which has no beginning, no end, and above all no centre'[18] is nevertheless coherent; it combines *acentricity* and *cohesion*, as do the romance cycles which Vinaver praises for their 'satisfying sense of a vast design, of a continuous and constantly unfolding panorama'.[19] Vinaver's view is essentially an argument for the aesthetic appeal of the richness of the composite, many-branched narrative, full of digression and return, repetition and parallel, change and shift, the uncertainty of adventure even when it repeats a pattern encountered before.

This aesthetic informed Vinaver's editing and criticism of Malory, after the Winchester manuscript of Malory's work came to light in 1934 and made it clear that Caxton's *Le Morte Darthur*, which is all that had been known hitherto, was by no means a simple transfer into print of a uniquely authoritative work. Caxton had made changes (particularly to the alliterative text of the Arthur and Lucius episode) and had imposed his own narrative structure of books and chapters. However, what emerged in Vinaver's first edition of the Winchester text (1947) proved to be just as controversial. In comparison to the French cycles Malory's narrative appeared simpler and Vinaver characterized him as a writer who was cutting through some of the interwoven threads. This makes sense in so far as it explains what Malory did in separating the episode of Arthur and Lucius

---

[17] Vinaver, *The Rise of Romance*, ch. v, 'The poetry of interlace' (quotation from p.69).

[18] Vinaver, *The Rise of Romance*, p.77.

[19] Vinaver, *The Rise of Romance*, p.91.

from the death of Arthur and in organizing what became Books III
and IV in Vinaver's version around the adventures respectively of
Lancelot and Gareth; but the corollary was that Vinaver viewed
Malory's writing as consisting of eight tales and, discarding Caxton's
title which had become sanctioned by nearly 500 years' usage, published his edition as the *Works* of Malory, arguing that the eight parts
should be read as separate narratives.[20] Debate inevitably followed
between Vinaver's view and objectors who argued that, even if the
chronology is not exact, the tales create a logical sequence. P.J.C.
Field who revised Vinaver's edition[21] sticks to the idea of 'the hoole
book of kyng Arthur' and argues that Malory's creation of the parts
of the story: 'in their present order made a story with completeness
and coherence . . . [with] a satisfying symmetry in the plot: the rise,
supremacy, and fall of Arthur's world'.[22] Vinaver explained away
Malory's inconsistencies (such as finding a character alive who had
been killed forty pages earlier) because his tales are separate entities,
and characterizes his treatment of sources as carving from the
French cycles a novel-like narrative with beginning, middle, and end.
Others reasonably pointed out that inconsistencies occur not only
between but within tales, and that Malory structured his narrative in
polyphonic style in Book I and Book V, which is nominally devoted
to Tristram but includes many other episodes, including the murder
of Lamorak and the birth of Galahad. The instabilities and
inconsistencies in the text have to be accepted and most readers are
prepared to read on two levels at once, following the coherent central
narrative of the Arthurian court at the same time as the mass of
loosely linked subsidiary episodes which reflect on the major characters and incidents. The narrative and the history of its composition
unfold together.

The cross-referenced multiplicity of interlaced narrative is well
illustrated in Malory's Book V which is based on a hybrid version of
the French Prose *Tristan*, where the process of Arthurianizing the

---

[20] *The Works of Sir Thomas Malory*, ed. Eugene Vinaver (3 vols., Oxford, Clarendon
Press, 1947).

[21] *The Works of Sir Thomas Malory*, ed. Eugene Vinaver, 3rd edn., revd P.J.C. Field
(Oxford, Clarendon Press, 1990).

[22] P.J.C. Field, 'Sir Thomas Malory's *Le Morte Darthur*', in *The Arthur of the English*,
ed. W.R.J. Barron (Cardiff, University of Wales Press, 2001), pp.225–46 (quotation from
p.241).

story had already changed its force. Tristram's joining the Round Table and demonstrating the virtues of fellowship and chivalry become more significant than the love-potion and the tragic outcome of passion. The Tristram–Yseult–Mark triangle is turned into a mirror for the relationship of Lancelot–Guenevere–Arthur, the simplification of Mark into a type of corrupt kingship sharpening the contrast between them. So it is that, though Book V has struck many readers as a narrative muddle and a digression from the main lines of the Arthurian story, it is possible to make out a strong case for its functioning as the heart of Malory's work, where the main narrative tide reaches its height and begins to turn.[23] The coming to court of Tristram (with a flashback account of his birth and youth) marks a new beginning, a renewal of the chivalrous narrative and a confirmation of the values of brotherhood. Later in the book the included, self-contained stories of 'La Cote Male Tayle' and 'Alexander the Orphan' may at first register as digressions but have features which reflect the stories of Gareth and Tristram. The madness of Lancelot echoes the earlier madness of Tristram, while the plotting of Gawain and his brothers against Lamorak, a major indicator of the turn towards dissension and division of the brotherhood, demonstrates a different version of the results of adultery and the quest for vengeance. By such means polyphonic narrative achieves some depth in the treatment of character and situation.

I suggested earlier that the unfinished state of Chrétien's Grail romance was a stepping stone towards the longer cycles; the opportunity to complete something half-written was taken by several writers. But, apart from this particular stimulus, Chrétien's romances in general established the Arthurian court as the setting for adventure, the primal scene from which knights ventured out and to which they returned, and the Grail quest had the potential to involve all the knights of the Round Table and so to function as a framework for a series of individual episodes; diversity of adventure could be combined with singularity of theme. This remains true in Malory's Book VI, even though the Grail material had passed through many hands between the 1180s and the 1470s, and it gives superficially a greater sense of unity to Malory's Grail book than is visible in the Book of

---

[23] Such a view is presented, for example, by Dhira B. Mahoney, 'Malory's "Tale of Sir Tristram": sources and setting reconsidered', in *Tristan and Isolde: A Casebook*, ed. Joan Tasker Grimbert (London, Routledge, 2002), pp.223–53.

Tristram. However, the nature of what is narrated is a good deal more mixed so that one sees how heterogeneous interlaced narrative can be. The Grail cycle had absorbed religious commentary and interpretation to add to the touches of the exotic already present in the visualization of the Fisher King's court, of chapels, symbolic dishes, chalices, lances, and so on; Malory's narrative includes dreams, visions and mysterious sea voyages, the voices of commentating hermits and wise men who offer allegorical meanings, in addition to the basic subject matter of questing knights moving through the landscape of forest, lake, chapel, and castle. The combination of secular and spiritual adventure is already present in Chrétien's *Perceval*. Because the poem is unfinished the relationship is not fully defined but Perceval's single-minded pursuit of an ideal of purity and his gradual education in the life of service seems to represent an antithesis to the series of adventures into which Gawain stumbles. Such a contrast presents a more concentrated form of interlaced narrative. What Malory does with the theme is to draw up a kind of balance sheet of spiritual achievement in the quest with Galahad, Percival, and Bors at one end, Gawain at the other, and Lancelot, the most fully explored character, winning a tortured half-grace in the middle.

It is perhaps in the history of polyphonic, cyclic narrative that the explanation of some shorter medieval composite structures lies. Cycles consist of many repetitions with variation and present multiple stories of heroes embarking on parallel adventures. A similar concept is at work on a smaller scale in narratives with two heroes such as the fifteenth-century romance *Valentine and Orson*, the story of twin brothers, and the father-and-son romance *Generides*. There are more problematic pairings which put together narratives of different types, creating conjunctions of naturalism and allegory or of courtly and supernatural, which suggest a medieval tolerance of shifts of narrative illusion which modern readers have sometimes found difficult to accept. Is this the problem, for example, with the fifteenth-century alliterative romance *The Awntyrs of Arthur*? This is a poem in two episodes. In the first Arthur and his knights ride out hunting, leaving Guenevere and Gawain in a leafy bower in the forest, where they are confronted by a hideous ghost who proves to be the Queen's dead mother, appearing in order to warn Guenevere and the court against pride, adultery, and failure to observe Christian virtues. In the second episode Gawain undergoes a trial by combat with a stranger called Galeron, who claims that his lands have been wrongfully given to Gawain. The Queen halts the contest, Galeron's lands are returned, Gawain is compensated, and finally Guenevere arranges to have masses said for her mother's soul. Critical discussion has focussed on the question of coherence. What have the two episodes to do with one another? Is this really two poems which by some accident of transmission have been yoked together? Late-twentieth-century critics tended to reconcile the elements in a view of the poem as a double *exemplum*. Rosamund Allen argues that it should be read 'as an intertextual work', constructing meaning from a cluster of cultural motifs—the ghostly request for redemptive masses, the loathly lady, the wildwood, the intruder in the hall, the halted duel.[24] Such a conjunction of supernatural/homiletic with an aristocratic legal argument about territorial rights in elaborate thirteen-line alliterative stanzas might be thought the literary equivalent of those medieval table decorations known as 'subtleties' which consisted of holy scenes made of pastry or sugar.

In an earlier alliterative poem, *The Parliament of the Three Ages*, a change from one mode to another does correspond to the passage from waking to dreaming: a richly described hunting scene serves as prologue to the allegorical dream-debate of Youth, Middle Age, and Old Age. The naturalistic evocation of the sights and sounds of early morning and the meticulous account of the narrator's well-trained cutting up of the deer he has poached work well enough as images of unlawful worldly pleasure and the lesson of mortality that follows makes effective contrast between the green-clad courtly lover Youth, with hawk on fist, the grey-clad property-dealer Middle Age, pre-occupied with gold and goods, and the black-clad, bent figure of Old Age, blindly telling his beads. Physical imagery eases the transition from literal to allegorical and the debate contrasts the attitudes of the three ages with corresponding sense, until Old Age attenuates his lesson with a review of the Nine Worthies, requiring the reader to accept more stilted allegorical representation, which Turville-Petre has described as 'long-winded and strangely incompetent'.[25] On the

---

[24] Rosamund Allen, 'The Awntyrs off Arthure', in Barron, *The Arthur of the English*, pp.150–5.

[25] *Alliterative Poetry of the Later Middle Ages: An Anthology*, ed. Thorlac Tuville-Petre (London, Routledge, 1989), p.68; the text of the poem is edited pp.70–100.

other hand J.A.W. Bennett describes the pageant of the Worthies, accompanied by an elegiac roll-call of the valiant and the wise, as 'the true *raison d'être* of the poem'.[26] The debate and tableau are neatly framed with a return to Old Age's message:

'Dethe dynges one my dore, I dare no lengare byde.'
(*The Parliament of the Three Ages*, 650)

and the poacher's waking and returning to town. Perhaps the composite elements here are simply not handled tactfully enough—as Bennett puts it, 'the central part of the poem forgets its beginning'— but one might also read the poem as evidence of a medieval acceptance of narrative medley.

Chaucer's *Squire's Tale* is another composite or shifting narrative, though, since it is unfinished, it is not clear what the whole tale might have looked like. As it survives it consists of two episodes. First comes a scene at the magnificent court of Cambuskan, the Tartar king, to which an impressive messenger from the king 'of Arabe and of Inde' comes bearing four magic gifts, horse, mirror, sword, and ring, each of which is described and its magic properties explained and wondered at. Chaucer appears to be embarking on a sophisticated romantic narrative, exotic in setting, courtly and highly polished in style, inventive and original, and with the promise of multiple adventures to follow. But the second part, though it puts one of the magic gifts to use, seems to change gear into the style of the French courtly *dit* as Cambuskan's daughter, Canace, uses the magic ring, which enables her to understand the lament of a distressed falcon, deserted by her lover; by turning to a bird–heroine and the language of dream poem Chaucer seems to step back from the world of chivalrous knightly combat, though the final lines promise other challenges for the king and for his two sons. Readers have disagreed about the significance of the tale and its unfinished state. Chaucer creates a structure for interlaced adventures for four characters and four magic instruments, but all we have is the frame and a curious lyric episode. Some have taken it as parody or a demonstration of the Squire's incompetence as a narrator, while others have regretted Chaucer's not going further with what might have been his most ambitious attempt at romance. As it stands it is a hybrid work and another indicator of the influence

---

[26] Bennett, *Middle English Literature*, p.52.

on the composition of narrative poems of the culture of medley or miscellany which was fostered by the making up of manuscripts piecemeal, from heterogeneous material and from pre-packaged sections.

However, in contrast to these examples of unresolved compositeness, one may reflect that something similar is to be detected in *Sir Gawain and the Green Knight*. The richness of narrative illusion and interest in this artfully constructed romance stems from the poet's ambitious linking of three separate stories, the Green Knight's challenge, the tempting of Gawain by the Lady of Hautdesert, and the game of exchanged winnings. None of these is part of the inherited Arthurian material. As I suggested earlier, when considering the poem in terms of *fabula, sjuzet*, and narration, it is the plot of Morgan la Fay against Camelot and Guenevere that is recognizable as the primary *fabula* and this includes the figures of Arthur and Gawain and the contrary elements in the knowledge that poet and audience share of them. That is the screen across which the incidents of this particular plot are to cast shadows. The three narrative motifs have separate origins in Irish and French tales but have been given a continuous identity by having the same hero slotted into their centre. The Arthurian cycles encouraged the accretion of adventures around individual heroes and the construction of strings of events, but the *Gawain*-poet has gone a step further in making several narratives depend upon one another and so become one. In so doing he has provided a justification for compositeness: Gawain is tested in terms of his sexual morality, his honest dealing, and his honour and courage by the different phases of his experience and emerges, in comparison with his romance colleagues, a more bruised but a more completely explored and more believable hero as a result. The world of the poem is imagined in sharply etched detail and yokes together opposites with a completely natural effect: indoor and outdoor scenes, the intimacy of private conversation and the bravado of public performance, vigorous physical action and sophisticated courtly talk. *Sir Gawain* is a rarity, a highly enjoyable but morally reflective tale which involves and satisfies readers at many levels. Beneath its impressive surface are structural devices not essentially distinct in kind from those found in other late medieval composite narratives; the difference is that they are so much better concealed.

Postscript

9

The variety of medieval storytelling makes one realize the more limited range of styles and effects in modern written narrative which has almost entirely, in European and American languages at any rate, restricted itself to the novel and the short story in prose. One has to look to radio and film to supply the extensions which verse-form made available in the past. Modern imitations of medieval narrative have seldom copied medieval language or poetic form unless they are actually modern versions of particular texts such as Ezra Pound's *The Seafarer*. Auden was one of the few to attempt to create an original work in a language imitating medieval syntax, vocabulary, and rhythm in his 'charade' *Paid on Both Sides* (1928), a drama in mixed prose and verse based on Icelandic sagas and Old English poetry. The story is of a feud between northern families and the situations echo such stories as that of Cynewulf and Cyneheard in the Anglo-Saxon Chronicle:

> Shot answered shot, Bullets screamed,
> Guns shook, Hot in the hand,
> Fighters lay, Groaning on ground
> Gave up life. Edward fell,
> Shot through the chest, First of our lot,
> By no means refused fight, Stephen was good,
> His first encounter, Showed no fear,
> Wounded many.[1]

Tolkien was as interested in creating a modern version of Old English poetic style as in the heroic material when he wrote a continuation of *The Battle of Maldon* in the form of a dialogue between two men who, after the battle, come in search of the body of the leader Beorhtnoth (Byrhtnoth). Here is the moment when they find him:

---

[1] W.H. Auden, *Collected Longer Poems* (London, Faber & Faber, 1968), p.18.

TORHTHELM   I've found it Tida!
Here's his sword lying! I could swear to it
by the golden hilts.
TIDWALD   I'm glad to hear it.
How it was missed is a marvel. He is marred cruelly.
Few tokens else shall we find on him;
they've left us little of the Lord we knew.
TORHTHELM   Ah, woe and worse! The wolvish heathens
have hewn off his head, and the hulk left us
mangled with axes. What a murder it is,
this bloody fighting!
TIDWALD   Aye, that's battle for you,
and no worse today than wars you sing of,
when Froda fell, and Finn was slain.
The world wept then, as it weeps today:
you can hear the tears through the harp's twanging.
Come, bend your back! We must bear away
The cold leavings . . .[2]

Other modern writers have been more likely to imitate medieval
language in the form of comic pastiche or in the rare imaginative use
of historical styles, as in the 'Oxen in the Sun' episode in *Ulysses*,
where Joyce works his way by quotation and imitation from Old
English verse to Mandeville, Malory, and beyond. More frequently
medievalist narrative is modern in its language and either of the kind
used by Peter Ackroyd, who, in *The Clerkenwell Tales*, takes Chaucer's
characters as the framework for his own evocation of medieval
London, or the Arthurian trilogy lengthily luxuriating in Celtic
atmosphere, or the work of historian–novelists who supply their
whodunits with local colour in the form of information about drains
(or the lack of them), disease, legal systems, monastic organization,
costume, or whatever is the writer's special area of interest and knowledge; they put in all the things that medieval authors are apt to leave
out. To encounter anything like the complexity of register of actual
medieval writing in modern medievalism one has to look not to
academic popularizers but to intellectual fantasists such as Tolkien
and Eco, as I suggested at the beginning. Tolkien supplies it through
his interest in invented languages and in balladry and lyric and Eco by

---

[2] J.R.R. Tolkien, 'The Homecoming of Beorhtnoth, Beorhthelm's Son', in *Essays and Studies*, n.s.6 (1953), 1–18 (quotation from pp.6–7); reprinted with *Tree and Leaf* and *Smith of Wootton Major* (London, Allen & Unwin, 1975).

spicing his modern Italian with a liberal scattering of Latin and inventing characters like Baudolino who express themselves in a potpourri of book-language and mixed vernaculars.

Complexity in medieval texts was at all stages a possible product of the expectation that the story-material for narrative would be inherited or borrowed but that the treatment would be invented or selected from a range of available forms and styles; the position of the medieval poet had some similarities to that of the modern opera director who may produce a reverent, traditional production of a well-loved classic but who more often feels obliged to invent a new take on material which might otherwise be thought stale. Hence Chaucer's recasting into the grand romance form of *The Knight's Tale* of the story of Boccaccio's *Teseida*, which was already a reinvention in a modern romance-epic form of classical episodes and ideas of noble conduct. To the classical/Italian subject matter Chaucer adds a mixture of poetic flavours by adopting an alliterative style for the martial passages concerning the Temple of War and the tournament, by developing the voices of his heroes with French-style complaint and love-debate and by scattering passages of *occupatio* through the poem so that the reader is constantly reminded of the manipulating presence of the narrator who slips seriousness on and off as the story demands. The tale was given a further variation of voice when Chaucer imported it into the frame of *The Canterbury Tales* and attributed its telling to an invented character. It was the tale collection which provided the best opportunities for intricacy in narration and Boccaccio and Chaucer in particular realized the usefulness of assuming another's voice. It was not only the bawdy incidents of the stories of 'harlotrie' that could be included for variety's sake though distanced from the author, but such a narrative as Chaucer's *Prioress's Tale*. This is made readable in the assumed voice of the sentimental nun whereas taken straight it would be relegated, because of its antiSemitism, Mariolatry, and mawkishness, to a special category of 'historical' works, to be understood as merely a cultural phenomenon. The framing of narratives in dream poems similarly makes available as images of mental exploration material which otherwise might appear simply to be spoken in a dead language.

One of the things which modern literary theory has encouraged is interest in the way narratives work as much as in what they are about. Study of the literature of the past is no longer limited to a few great works but includes a variety of discourses which provide evidence of the culture of the time. However, there are inevitable limitations, particularly those caused by the conditions of survival of medieval texts: of the small number that achieved written form only a portion still exist in manuscript. Among the material least likely to have been written down must have been a huge amount of family and social storytelling. Because most of the evidence for such forms as the ballad is post-medieval, they remain marginal to the study of medieval narrative and are not included in this book; before I close one or two other omissions and uncertainties should be identified. I have not found it convenient to include biography among the 'forms of history', though there are many medieval narratives of the lives of kings and of saints. The tradition is mainly a Latin one, stretching in England from such early examples as Bede's life of St Cuthbert (written c.700) and Asser's life of Alfred (written c.893) to the post-Conquest lives of Thomas Becket, together with biographical accounts and assessments of rulers in the chronicles of such writers as William of Malmesbury. The earliest contemporary royal biographies in English may have been of Henry V, though only Latin ones survive. Saints' lives, however, were written in English, alongside Latin ones, as early as Aelfric; over fifty manuscripts survive of the late-thirteenth-century collection of vernacular lives in the *Early South English Legendary*.[3] The normal pattern of the saint's life is an account of birth, upbringing, conversion, evidence of piety, trials, suffering, death, and miracles, and the influence of the pattern is visible in romances about a hero's whole life, such as *Guy of Warwick*. The idealized biography in the vernacular is evident in the late fourteenth century in the different forms of Chandos Herald's French life of the Black Prince and the 'romance–biography' of Robert the Bruce in John Barbour's lengthy poem *The Bruce*. Impulses towards autobiography can be identified as an aspect of the writings of the mystics, particularly those who give an account of their own spiritual progress, as with Richard Rolle and Julian of Norwich, or their own adventures in religion as with Margery Kempe.[4]

---

[3] See Thomas J. Heffernan, *Sacred Biography: Saints and Their Biographers in the Middle Ages* (Oxford U.P., 1988).

[4] See Julia Boffey, 'Middle English lives', in *The Cambridge History of Medieval English Literature*, ed. David Wallace (Cambridge U.P., 1999), pp.610–34.

Another problem of which I have been conscious is the fact that the word 'medieval' has to cover far too large a period, something like 700 years in terms of literary texts from Anglo-Saxon times to the introduction of printing. Even if one thinks only of post-Conquest literature the period 1100–1500 is as long as from Shakespeare's late works to the present: to discuss *Hamlet* and *Waiting for Godot* together as 'modern' plays might have some point but equally might be thought a touch misleading. One of the few scholars to take notice of this tendency to 'homogenize' the medieval period, John Simons, puts it as follows: 'All too often medieval texts are not debated within historical limitations and insufficient distinctions are drawn between texts which are years apart.'[5]

In discussing medieval narrative I have been guilty of ignoring historical limitations and it would smack too much of a desire to homogenize to attempt to draw conclusions. I have tried to register the interest of the main varieties of storytelling but in each and every category of narrative one is aware of contradictions, whether in changing cultural conditions over a long period of time or in the wide range of textual consciousness among writers or of possible audience response. Not even monastic chronicles were simple dis-interested records: the monks protected the interests of their own religious house and reflected regional concerns. Some chroniclers were in the employ of powerful rulers. In the case of historical epic, political polemic was enhanced by traditional poetic rhetoric, some-times with the intention of raising nationalistic enthusiasm for war or crusade; the Arthurian story was taken up by kings who saw them-selves as rulers of the New Troy as in the case of Edward III. Patriot-ism remains a central motif in historical romance but the idealism of tales of the heroic and virtuous could also be annexed by homiletic writers for whom narrative meant the opportunity for religious didacticism. Romance is the narrative form most concerned with social themes, including family relationships and the role of the indi-vidual in society, but it was the form most apt to stereotyping of character and conduct. The nearest to striking out an independent kind of narrative is found in stories about social-climbing heroes like Havelok and Gamelyn or of heroines who move up the ladder by marrying above their station like Griselda.

---

[5] John Simons (ed.), *From Medieval to Medievalism*, (Basingstoke, Macmillan, 1992), Introduction, p.3.

Medieval narratives often seem particularly conscious of the polarities between which they operate. Langland's image is of the world of his dream narrative set between the Tower of Truth and the Dungeon of Falsehood. Gower's fiction is pitched in the 'middel weie', not only between *lust* and *lore* but creating a bridge between the world 'in olde daies passed' and the 'world which neweth every dai'. For Chaucer in *The Canterbury Tales* they are expressed in several different ways: in terms of the desirable qualities for good narrative, *sentence* and *solas*, the worth of the moral meaning and the pleasure of the story, what one learns and what one likes; in terms of *ernest* and *game*, the one implying seriousness of narrative intention but also moving towards the potential tedium of being preached at, the other implying acceptance of the rules of the Canterbury bargain with the Host but liable to spill over into folly and dispute; in terms of the recurrent medieval anxiety about fable and truth. In the Retractions with which he presumably ended his series, even though he had not completed the middle parts, Chaucer's distinction was between the tales that tended towards sin and those that were religious and didactic and might contribute to the good of his soul. These definitions of boundaries suggest a theoretical notion of narrative as mediating between extremes, as a process of exploration and negotiation. Such a concept may account for some of the features of medieval narrative genres, the tolerance of medley and digression, for instance, and the interest in debates, which do not necessarily reach conclusions. In the actual handling of narrative, issues often became interestingly blurred by the writer's perception of the contradictions within the subjects and within the genre. Perhaps it is a feature peculiar to late-fourteenth-century English narratives, but there are suggestive similarities in the four best-known works of the Ricardian period. Langland's sequence of dream searches ends not with discovery or completion but with Conscience setting out on another quest. Gower's long preparation for entry into the court of Venus is cut short by the revelation that he has spent so long in the attempt that he is now too old. Gawain returns to Camelot safe and sound, congratulated by the court for his success, but chastened and regretful. Chaucer's planned pilgrimage from Southwark to Canterbury and back to a cheerful supper at the Tabard Inn somewhere lost the will for the return journey and ends instead with the Parson condemning all storytelling as mere fable and Chaucer expressing pious apologies for having written the wrong narratives. Closure in the celebration of achievement is avoided or deflected in all four. Nevertheless they all made their journeys and the journey was the story; to end in triumph might suggest that it was the goal that was the point, but readers of narrative know that that is not so. Closure is necessary but more often a matter for regret than rejoicing.

Bibliography

Works of reference

Middle English Dictionary, ed. Hans Kurath, Sherman M. Kuhn and John Reidy (Ann Arbor, Mich., University of Michigan Press, 1954).

Prince, Gerald, *A Dictionary of Narratology* (Aldershot, Scolar Press, 1987).

Severs, J. Burke (ed.), *A Manual of the Writings in Middle English, 1050–1500*, vol. I, *Romances* (New Haven, Connecticut Academy of Arts and Sciences, 1967).

Wales, Katie, *A Dictionary of Stylistics* (Harlow, Longman, 1989).

Wells J.E., *A Manual of the Writings in Middle English, 1050–1400* (New Haven, Yale U.P., 1926).

Texts and translations of Old and Middle English works

Alliterative *Morte Arthure*, ed. E. Brock, EETS OS 8 (London, Oxford U.P., 1865); edited with the Stanzaic *Morte Arthur* as *King Arthur's Death* by Larry D. Benson (Indianapolis, Bobbs–Merrill, 1974); both in *King Arthur's Death*, trans. Brian Stone (Harmondsworth, Penguin Books, 1988).

Alliterative Poetry of the Later Middle Ages: An Anthology, ed. Thorlac Turville-Petre (London, Routledge, 1989).

The Anglo-Saxon Chronicles, trans. and ed. Michael Swanton (London, Phoenix Press, 2000).

Anglo-Saxon Poetry, trans. and ed. S.A.J. Bradley, Everyman's Library (London, J.M. Dent, 1982).

Anonymous Short English Metrical Chronicle, ed. E. Zettl, EETS OS 196 (London, Oxford U.P., 1935).

The Auchinleck Manuscript, National Library of Scotland Advocates' MS 19.2.1, facsimile, with introduction by D.A. Pearsall and I.C. Cunningham (London, Scolar Press, 1979).

The Battle of Maldon, ed. E.V. Gordon (London, Methuen, 1937).

Beowulf and the Fight at Finnsburg, ed. F. Klaeber, 3rd edn (Boston, D.C. Heath & Co., 1950).

Beowulf, a glossed text ed. Michael Alexander, revd edn (Harmondsworth, Penguin Books, 2000).

Beowulf: A New Translation, Seamus Heaney (London, Faber and Faber, 1999).

Caxton, William, *The Book of the Knight of the Tower*, ed. M.Y. Offord, EETS SS 2 (London, Oxford U.P., 1971).

Chaucer, *The Riverside Chaucer*, gen. ed. Larry D. Benson, 3rd edn (Oxford U.P., 1988).

Chaucer, *Troilus and Criseyde*, ed. B.A. Windeatt (Harlow, Longman, 1984).

Chaucer's Dream Poetry, eds. Helen Phillips and Nick Havely (Harlow, Longman, 1997).

Cleanness, in *The Poems of the Pearl Manuscript*; see *Pearl*.

The Dream of the Rood, ed. Michael Swanton, revd edn (Exeter, University of Exeter Press, 1987).

Early Middle English Prose and Verse, eds. J.A.W. Bennett and G.V. Smithers (Oxford, Clarendon Press, 1968).

The Early South English Legendary, ed. Carl Horstmann, EETS OS 87 (London, Trubner & Co., 1887).

Gesta Romanorum, ed. Sidney J.H. Herrtage, EETS ES 33 (London, Oxford U.P., 1879).

Gower, John, *The English Works*, ed. G.C. Macaulay (2 vols., Oxford, Clarendon Press, 1900–01).

Gower, John, *Confessio Amantis*, ed. and abridged R.A. Peck (Toronto, University of Toronto Press, 1980).

Henryson, Robert, The Poems of, ed. Denton Fox (Oxford, Clarendon Press, 1981).

Henryson, Robert, The Moral Fables of, ed. George D. Gopen (Notre Dame, Ind., University of Notre Dame Press, 1987).

Hoccleve, Thomas, *'My Compleinte' and Other Poems*, ed. Roger Ellis (Exeter, University of Exeter Press, 2001).

Kyng Alisaunder, ed. G.V. Smithers, EETS OS 237 (London, Oxford U.P., 1957).

Laȝamon's Arthur, the Arthurian Sections of Laȝamon's Brut, ed. and trans. W.R.J. Barron and S.C. Weinberg (Harlow, Longman, 1989).

Langland, William, *The Vision of Piers Plowman*, a complete edition of the B-text, ed. A.V.C. Schmidt, revd edn, Everyman's Library (London, J.M. Dent, 1995).

Langland, William, *Piers Plowman*, an edition of the C-text, ed. Derek Pearsall (Berkeley, University of California Press, 1978).

Lydgate, John, *The Minor Poems of*, Part II, ed. H.N. MacCracken, EETS ES 107 (London, Oxford U.P., 1934).

Malory, The Works of Sir Thomas, ed. Eugene Vinaver (3 vols., Oxford, Clarendon Press, 1947).

Malory, The Works of Sir Thomas, 3rd edn, revd P.J.C. Field (Oxford, Clarendon Press, 1990).

Mandeville's Travels, ed. M.C. Seymour (Oxford, Clarendon Press, 1967).

Mandeville, The Travels of Sir John, trans. C.W.R.D. Moseley (Harmondsworth, Penguin Books, 1983).

Mannyng, Robert, *Handlyng Synne*, ed. Idelle Sullens (Binghamton, NY, Binghampton U.P., 1983).

Medieval Comic Tales, ed. Derek Brewer, 2nd edn (Cambridge, D.S. Brewer, 1996).

Middle English Debate Poetry: A Critical Anthology, ed. John W. Conlee (East Lansing, Mich., Colleagues Press, 1991).

Middle English Romances, ed. Stephen H.A. Shepherd (New York, Norton, 1995).

The Parliament of the Three Ages, ed. M.Y. Offord, EETS OS 246 (Oxford U.P., 1959).

St Patrick's Purgatory, ed. Robert Easting, EETS OS 298 (Oxford U.P., 1991).

Pearl, ed. E.V. Gordon (Oxford, Clarendon Press, 1953). Also in *The Poems of the Pearl Manuscript*, eds. M. Andrew R. Waldron, 2nd revd edn (Exeter, University of Exeter Press, 1996).

'A Penniworth of Wit', ed. E. Kölbing, 'Kleine publicationen aus der Auchinleck-hs', *Englische Studien* 7 (1884), 113–17.

Religious Lyrics of the XVth Century, ed. Carleton Browne (Oxford, Clarendon Press, 1939).

Religious Lyrics of the XIVth Century, ed. Carleton Browne, 2nd edn, revd G.V. Smithers (Oxford, Clarendon Press, 1957).

Remains of the Early Popular Poetry of England, ed. W. Carew Hazlitt (4 vols., London, Russell Smith, 1864–6).

The Seven Sages of Rome, ed. K.Brunner, EETS OS 191 (London, Oxford U.P., 1933).

Sir Gawain and the Green Knight, eds. J.R.R. Tolkien and E.V. Gordon, 2nd edn, revd Norman Davis (Oxford, Clarendon Press, 1967). Also in *The Poems of the Pearl Manuscript*: see *Pearl*.

Ten Fifteenth-Century Comic Poems, ed. Melissa M. Furrow (New York, Garland, 1985).

The Vision of Tundale, ed. Rodney Mearns (Heidelberg, Carl Winter, 1985).

Wace and Lawmen, *The Life of King Arthur*, trans. Judith Weiss and Rosamund Allen, Everyman's Library (London, J.M. Dent, 1997).

Ywain and Gawain, ed. Maldwyn Mills, Everyman's Library (London, J.M. Dent, 1992).

Translations of non-English medieval works

Aesop, *The Complete Fables*, trans. Olivia and Robert Temple (Harmondsworth, Penguin Books, 1998).

Babrius and Phaedrus, ed. and trans. B.E. Perry, Loeb Classical Library (Cambridge, Mass., Harvard U.P., 1965).

Béroul, *The Romance of Tristan*, trans. Alan S. Fedrick (Harmondsworth, Penguin Books, 1970).

Boccaccio, Giovanni, *The Decameron*, trans. Guido Waldman, with Introduction and Notes by Jonathan Usher, World's Classics (Oxford U.P., 1993).

Boethius, *The Consolation of Philosophy*, trans. V.E. Watts (Harmondsworth, Penguin Books, 1969).

The Voyage of St Brendan: Representative Versions of the Legend in English Translation, eds. W.R.J. Barron and Glyn S. Burgess (Exeter, University of Exeter Press, 2002).

Chrétien de Troyes, *Arthurian Romances*, trans. with Introduction and Notes by William W. Kibler with Carleton W.Carroll (Harmondsworth, Penguin Books, 1991).

The Poem of the Cid, a bilingual text, trans. Rita Hamilton and Janet Perry, with Introduction and Notes by Ian Michael, first published Manchester 1975 (Harmondsworth, Penguin Books, 1984).

Dante, *The Divine Comedy*, trans. Charles S. Singleton (6 vols., Princeton: Princeton U.P., 1970–75).

Eilhart von Oberge, *Tristrant*, trans. J.W. Thomas (Lincoln, Nebr., University of Nebraska Press, 1978).

Till Eulenspiegel: His Adventures, transl. with Introduction by Paul Oppenheimer, World's Classics (Oxford U.P., 1995).

Fabliaux, eds. R.C. Johnston and D.D.R. Owen (Oxford, Blackwell, 1957).

Froissart, *Chronicles*, trans. Geoffrey Brereton (Harmondsworth, Penguin Books, 1968).

Geoffrey of Monmouth, *Historia Regum Britanniae*, trans. Lewis Thorpe as *The History of the Kings of Britain* (Harmondsworth, Penguin Books, 1966).

Gerald of Wales, *Gemma Ecclesiastica*, trans. John J. Hagen as *The Jewel of the Church* (Leiden, E.J. Brill, 1979).

The Epic of Gilgamesh, trans. N.K. Sandars (Harmondsworth, Penguin Books, 1960).

Gottfried von Strassburg, *Tristan*, trans. A.T. Hatto (Harmondsworth, Penguin Books, 1960).

Henry of Huntingdon, *The History of the English People 1000–1154*, trans. Diana Greenway, World's Classics (Oxford U.P., 2002).

Jacobus de Voragine, *The Golden Legend*, trans. Christopher Stace with Introduction and Notes by Richard Hamer (Harmondsworth, Penguin Books, 1998).

Marie de France, *Fables*, ed. and trans. Harriet Spiegel (Toronto, University of Toronto Press, 1994).

The Lais of Marie de France, trans. with Introduction by Glyn S. Burgess and Keith Busby (Harmondsworth, Penguin Books, 1986).

The Nibelungenlied, trans. A.T. Hatto (Harmondsworth, Penguin Books, 1965).

The Fables of Odo of Cheriton, trans. John C. Jacobs (New York, Syracuse U.P., 1985).

Friar Robert, *The Saga of Tristram and Isond*, trans. Paul Schach (Lincoln, Nebr., University of Nebraska Press, 1973).

The Romance of Reynard the Fox, trans. D.D.R. Owen (Oxford U.P., 1994).

The Romance of the Rose, by Guillaume de Lorris and Jean de Meun, trans. Frances Horgan, World's Classics (Oxford U.P., 1994).

The Song of Roland, trans. with Introduction and Notes by Glyn Burgess (Harmondsworth, Penguin Books, 1990).

Ruiz, Juan, *The Book of Good Love*, trans. Elizabeth Drayson Macdonald, Everyman's Library (London, J.M. Dent, 1999).

Thomas (of Britain), *Tristran*, trans. by A.T. Hatto in the same volume as his translation of Gottfried von Strassburg, *Tristan* (Harmondsworth, Penguin Books, 1960).

Prose Tristan, trans. Renée L. Curtis as *The Romance of Tristan*, World's Classics (Oxford U.P., 1994).

Wace, *Roman de Brut, A History of the British*, ed. and trans. Judith Weiss (Exeter, University of Exeter Press, 1999).

Walter Map, *De Nugis Curialium (Courtiers' Trifles)*, ed. and trans. M.R. James, revd C.N.L. Brooke and R.A.B. Mynors (Oxford, Clarendon Press, 1983).

William of Malmesbury, *Chronicle of the Kings of England*, trans. J. Sharpe, revd J.A. Giles (London, Bell, 1911).

William of Malmesbury, *Gesta Regum Anglorum*, ed. and trans. R.A.B. Mynors, R.M. Thomson, and M. Winterbottom (2 vols., Oxford, Clarendon Press, 1998).

William of Newburgh, *The History of English Affairs*, Book I, trans. P.G. Walsh and M.J. Kennedy (Warminster, Aris & Phillips, 1988).

Classical and medieval rhetoric

Aristotle, *On the Art of Poetry*, in *Classical Literary Criticism*, trans. with an Introduction by T.S. Dorsch (Harmondsworth, Penguin Books, 1965).

Baldwin, C.S., *Medieval Rhetoric and Poetic* (Gloucester, Mass., Smith, 1959).

Cicero, M. Tullius, *De inventione*, ed. and trans. H.M. Hubbell, Loeb Classical Library (Cambridge, Mass., Harvard U.P., 1949).

Cicero, M. Tullius (attrib.), *Rhetorica ad Herennium*, ed. and trans. Harry Caplan, Loeb Classical Library (Cambridge, Mass., Harvard U.P., 1954).

Curtius, E.R., *European Literature and the Latin Middle Ages* (original German text 1948), trans. W.R. Trask, (Princeton U.P., 1953; with corrections, 1967).

Gallo, Ernest, *The 'Poetria Nova' and its Sources in Early Rhetorical Doctrine* (The Hague, Mouton, 1971).

Gallo, Ernest, 'The *Poetria Nova* of Geoffrey de Vinsauf', in *Medieval Eloquence*, ed. J.J. Murphy (Berkeley, University of California Press, 1978).

Geoffrey de Vinsauf, *Documentum de Modo et Arte Dictandi et Versificandi*, trans. R.P. Parr (Milwaukee, Wis., Marquette U.P., 1968).

John of Garland, *Parisiana Poetria*, ed. and trans. Traugott Lawler, Yale Studies in English 182 (New Haven, Yale U.P., 1974).

Minnis, A.J., *Chaucer and Pagan Antiquity* (Cambridge, D.S. Brewer, 1982).

Minnis, A.J., *Medieval Theory of Authorship: Scholastic Literary Attitudes in the Later Middle Ages*, 2nd edn (Aldershot, Scolar Press, 1988).

Minnis, A.J. and A.B. Scott, with D. Wallace (eds.), *Medieval Literary Theory and Criticism c. 1100–1375: The Commentary Tradition*, revd edn (Oxford, Clarendon Press, 1991).

Murphy, J.J., *Rhetoric in the Middle Ages: A History of Rhetorical Theory from St Augustine to the Renaissance* (Berkeley, University of California Press, 1974).

Murphy, J.J. (ed.), *Medieval Eloquence: Studies in the Theory and Practice of Medieval Rhetoric* (Berkeley, University of California Press, 1978).

Payne, Robert O., *The Key of Remembrance: A Study of Chaucer's Poetics* (New Haven, Yale U.P., 1963).

Payne, Robert O., 'Chaucer and the art of rhetoric', in Beryl Rowland (ed.), *Companion to Chaucer Studies*, revd edn (Oxford U.P., 1979).

Salmon, P.B., 'The "Three Voices" of poetry in medieval literary theory', *Medium Aevum* 30 (1961), 1–18.

Wogan-Browne, Jocelyn with Nicholas Watson, Andrew Taylor, and Ruth Evans (eds.), *The Idea of the Vernacular: An Anthology of Middle English Literary Theory 1280–1520* (Exeter, University of Exeter Press, 1999).

Other secondary sources

Alford, John A. (ed.), *A Companion to Piers Plowman* (Berkeley, University of California Press, 1988).

Allen, Rosamund, '*The Awntyrs off Arthure*', in *The Arthur of the English*, ed. W.R.J. Barron (Cardiff, University of Wales Press, 2001), pp. 150–5.

Archibald, Elizabeth, 'The Breton lay in Middle English: genre, transmission and the Franklin's Tale', in *Medieval Insular Romance: Translation and Innovation*, eds. Judith Weiss, Jennifer Fellows, and Morgan Dickson (Cambridge, D.S. Brewer, 2000), pp.55–70.

Archibald, Elizabeth and A.S.G. Edwards (eds.), *A Companion to Malory* (Cambridge, D.S. Brewer, 1996).

Auerbach, E., *Mimesis: the Representation of Reality in Western Literature* (1946), trans. Willard R. Trask (Princeton U.P., 1957).

Bakhtin, M.M., *Problems of Dostoevsky's Poetics* (originally published in Russian, 1929) (Ann Arbor, Mich., Ardis, 1973).

Bakhtin, M.M., *Rabelais and His World* (originally published in Russian, 1966), trans. H. Iswolsky (Bloomington, Ind., Indiana U.P., 1984).

Bakhtin, M.M., 'From the prehistory of novelistic discourse' (probably written in 1940 but published in Russia in 1967), in *The Dialogic Imagination: Four Essays*, trans. Caryl Emerson and Michael Holquist (Austin, University of Texas Press, 1981).

Barron, W.R.J., *English Medieval Romance* (Harlow, Longman, 1987).

Barron, W.R.J. (ed.), *The Arthur of the English* (Cardiff, University of Wales Press, 2001).

Bédier, Jean, *Les Fabliaux*, 2nd edn (Paris, Champion, 1895).

Bekker-Nielsen, H. *et al.* (eds.), *Medieval Narrative: A Symposium* (Odense U.P., 1979).

Bennett, J.A.W., *Middle English Literature* (Oxford, Clarendon Press, 1986).

Benson, Larry D. and Theodore M. Andersson *The Literary Context of Chaucer's Fabliaux* (Indianapolis, Bobbs–Merrill, 1971).

Blackham, H.J., *The Fable as Literature* (London, Athlone Press, 1985).

Boitani, Piero, *English Medieval Narrative in the 13th and 14th Centuries*, trans. Joan Krakover Hall (Cambridge U.P., 1982).

Boitani, Piero (ed.), *Chaucer and the Italian Trecento* (Cambridge U.P., 1983).

Boitani, Piero and Jill Mann (eds.), *The Cambridge Chaucer Companion* (Cambridge U.P., 1986).

Boitani, Piero and Anna Torti (eds.), *Poetics: Theory and Practice in Medieval English Literature* (Cambridge, D.S. Brewer, 1991).

Boogaard, N. van den, 'Le Fabliau Anglo-Normand', in *Third International Beast Epic, Fable and Fabliau Colloquium, Munster 1979*, Cologne/Vienna, 1981, pp.66–77.

Booth, Wayne C., *The Rhetoric of Fiction* (Chicago, U. of Chicago Press, 1961).

Bray, Dorothy Ann, 'Allegory in the *Navigatio sancti Brendani*', *Viator* 26 (1995), 1–10.

Brewer, Derek, *Symbolic Stories: Traditional Narrative and the Family Drama in English Literature* (Woodbridge, D.S. Brewer, 1980).

Brewer, D.S., *Chaucer: the Poet as Storyteller* (London, Macmillan, 1984).

Brewer, Derek (ed.), *Studies in Medieval English Romances* (Cambridge, D.S. Brewer, 1988).

Brooks, Peter, *Reading for the Plot: Design and Intention in Narrative* (Cambridge, Mass., Harvard U.P., 1984).

Brown, Peter (ed.), *Reading Dreams* (Oxford U.P., 1999).

Burrow, John, 'The alterity of medieval literature', *New Literary History* 10 (1978–9), 385–90.

Burrow, John, *Langland's Fictions* (Oxford, Clarendon Press, 1993).

Butterfield, Ardis, 'Medieval genres and modern genre theory', *Paragraph* 13 (1990), 184–201.

Chaytor, H.C., *From Script to Print* (Cambridge, U.P., 1945).

Clements, R. and J. Gibaldi, *Anatomy of the Novella: The European Tale Collection from Boccaccio and Chaucer to Cervantes* (New York U.P., 1977).

Clifford, Paula, *Marie de France*, Lais, Critical Guides to French Texts (London, Grant & Cutler, 1982).

Cobley, Paul, *Narrative* (London, Routledge, 2001).

Cooper, Helen, *The Structure of* The Canterbury Tales (London, Duckworth, 1983).

Cooper, Helen, 'Langland's and Chaucer's Prologues', *The Yearbook of Langland Studies* 1 (1987), 71–81.

Cooper, Helen, *Oxford Guides to Chaucer:* The Canterbury Tales, (Oxford, Clarendon Press, 1989).

Davenport, W.A., *Chaucer: Complaint and Narrative* (Cambridge, D.S. Brewer, 1988).

Davenport, W.A., *Chaucer and His English Contemporaries: Prologue and Tale in The Canterbury Tales* (London, Macmillan, 1998).

Duff, David (ed.), *Modern Genre Theory* (Harlow, Longman, 2000).

Eckhardt, Caroline D., 'Genre', in *A Companion to Chaucer*, ed. Peter Brown (Oxford, Blackwell, 2000), pp.180–94.

Eco, Umberto, *Il Nome della Rosa* (1980), trans. William Weaver as *The Name of the Rose* (London, Secker & Warburg, 1983).

Eco, Umberto, *Postscript to The Name of the Rose*, trans. William Weaver (New York, Harcourt Brace Jovanovitch, 1983).

Eco, Umberto, *Art and Beauty in the Middle Ages*, trans. Hugh Bredin (New Haven, Yale U.P., 1986).

Eco, Umberto, *Baudolino* (2000), trans. William Weaver (London, Secker & Warburg, 2002).

Eliot, T.S., *The Three Voices of Poetry* (Cambridge U.P., 1953).

Ellis, Roger, *Patterns of Religious Narrative in The Canterbury Tales* (London, Croom Helm, 1986).

Ellis, Steve, *Geoffrey Chaucer*, Writers and Their Work Series (Plymouth, Northcote House/British Council, 1996).

Everett, Dorothy, 'A characterization of the English Medieval romances', *Essays and Studies* 15 (1929), 98–121, reprinted in *Essays on Middle English Literature*, ed. P.M. Kean (Oxford, Clarendon Press, 1955), pp.1–22.

Everson, Jane E., *The Italian Romance Epic in the Age of Humanism* (Oxford U.P., 2001).

Fellows, J., R. Field, G. Rogers, and J. Weiss (eds.), *Romance Reading on the Book: Essays on Medieval Narrative presented to Maldwyn Mills* (Cardiff, University of Wales Press, 1996).

Fewster, Carol, *Traditionality and Genre in Middle English Romance* (Cambridge, D.S. Brewer, 1987).

Field, P.J.C., *Romance and Chronicle: A Study of Malory's Prose Style* (London, Barrie & Jenkins, 1971).

Field, P.J.C., 'Sir Thomas Malory's *Le Morte Darthur*', in *The Arthur of the English*, ed. W.R.J. Barron (Cardiff, University of Wales Press, 2001), pp.225–46.

Field, Rosalind, 'Romance in England, 1066–1400', in *The Cambridge History of Medieval English Literature*, ed. David Wallace (Cambridge U.P., 1999), pp.155–62.

Friend, Albert C., 'Master Odo of Cheriton', *Speculum* 23 (1948), 641–58.

Frye, Northrop, *The Secular Scripture: A Study of the Structure of Romance* (Cambridge, Mass., Harvard U.P., 1976).

Galloway, Andrew, 'Writing History in England', in *The Cambridge History of Medieval English Literature*, ed. David Wallace (Cambridge U.P., 1999), pp.255–83.

Gardiner, Eileen (ed.), *Visions of Heaven and Hell before Dante* (New York, Italica Press, 1989).

Gaunt, Simon, 'Romances and other genres', in *The Cambridge Companion to Medieval Romance*, ed. Roberta L. Krueger (Cambridge U.P., 2000), pp.45–59.

Gaylord, Alan T., 'Sentence and solaas in Fragment VII of *The Canterbury Tales*: Harry Bailly as horseback editor', *PMLA* 82 (1967), 226–35.

Genette, Gérard, *Narrative Discourse* (1972), trans. Jane E. Lewin (Ithaca, NY, Cornell U.P., 1980; Oxford: Basil Blackwell, 1982).

Genette, Gérard, *Figures of Literary Discourse*, trans. Alan Sheridan (New York, Columbia U.P., 1982).

Godden, Malcolm and Michael Lapidge (eds.), *The Cambridge Companion to Old English Literature* (Cambridge U.P., 1991).

Göller, Karl Heinz (ed.), *The Alliterative* Morte Arthure: *A Reassessment* (Cambridge, D.S. Brewer, 1981).

Gransden, Antonia, *Historical Writing in England c.550 to c.1307* (Ithaca, NY, Cornell U.P., 1973; London, Routledge & Kegan Paul, 1974).

Gransden, Antonia, *Historical Writing in England c.1307 to the Early Sixteenth Century* (Ithaca, NY, Cornell U.P., 1982).

Gransden, Antonia, 'The Chronicles of Medieval England and Scotland', *Journal of Medieval History* 16 (1990), 129–50 and 17 (1991), 217–43, reprinted in *Legends, Traditions and History in Medieval England* (London, Hambledon Press, 1992).

Gray, Douglas, *Robert Henryson* (Leiden, E.J. Brill, 1979).

Green, D.H., *Irony in the Medieval Romance* (Cambridge U.P., 1979).

Green, R.F., *Poets and Princepleasers: Literature and the English Court in the Late Middle Ages* (Toronto, University of Toronto Press, 1980).

Griffin, Nathaniel E., 'The definition of romance', *PMLA* 38 (1923), 50–70.

Grimbert, Joan Tasker (ed.), *Tristan and Isolde: A Casebook* (London, Routledge, 2002).

Heffernan, Carol T., 'Chaucer's *Shipman's Tale* and Boccaccio's *Decameron*, VIII, 1: Retelling a Story', in *Courtly Literature: Culture and Context*, eds. Keith Busby and Erik Kooper (Philadelphia, John Benjamins, 1990).

Heffernan, Thomas J., *Sacred Biography: Saints and Their Biographers in the Middle Ages* (Oxford U.P., 1988).

Henderson, Arnold Clayton, 'Medieval beasts and modern cages: the making of meaning in fables and bestiaries', *PMLA* 97 (1982), 40–49.

Hervieux, Léopold, *Les Fabulistes Latins* (5 vols., Paris, 1893–9; reprinted Hildesheim, Georg Olms, 1970).

Hines, John, *The Fabliau in English* (Harlow, Longman, 1993).

Holmes, George, *Dante*, Past Masters Series (Oxford U.P., 1980).

Hunt, Tony, 'Tradition and originality in the Prologues of Chrestien de Troyes', *Forum for Modern Language Studies* 8 (1972), 320–44.

Jauss, Hans Robert, 'Theory of genres and medieval literature', first published in French in *Poétique* (1970), 79–101, and incorporated into *Towards an Aesthetic of Reception*, trans. Timothy Bahti (Brighton, Harvester, 1982), pp.20ff.

Jauss, Hans Robert, 'The alterity and modernity of Medieval literature', *New Literary History* 10 (1978–9), 181–228.

Kane, George, *The Autobiographical Fallacy in Chaucer and Langland Studies*, Chambers Memorial Lecture (University College London, 1965).

Kay, Sarah, *The Romance of the Rose* (London, Grant & Cutler, 1995).

Kelly, H. Ansgar, 'Interpretation of and by genres in the Middle Ages', in Piero Boitani and Anna Torti (eds.), *Interpretation: Medieval and Modern*, 8th Series of J.A.W. Bennett Memorial Lectures (Cambridge, D.S. Brewer, 1993), pp.107–22.

Ker, W.P., *Epic and Romance* (London, Macmillan, 1908).

Kermode, Frank, 'Novel and narrative', in *The Theory of the Novel: New Essays*, ed. John Halperin (London, Oxford U.P., 1974), pp.155–74.

Koff, Leonard Michael and Brenda Deen Schildgen (eds.), *The Decameron and The Canterbury Tales: New Essays on an Old Question* (Madison, Wis., Associated University Presses, 2000).

Kristeva, Julia, *The Revolution in Poetic Language*, trans. Margaret Waller (New York, Columbia U.P., 1984).

Krueger, Roberta (ed.), *The Cambridge Companion to Medieval Romance* (Cambridge U.P., 2000).

Lawton, David, *Chaucer's Narrators* (Cambridge, D.S. Brewer, 1985).

Leitch, L.M., 'Sentence and solaas: the function of the Host in *The Canterbury Tales*', *Chaucer Review* 17 (1982–3), 5–20.

Lewis, C.S., *A Preface to Paradise Lost* (London, Oxford U.P., 1942).

Loomis, Laura Hibbard, 'Chaucer and the Breton lays of the Auchinleck Manuscript', *Studies in Philology* 38 (1941), 14–33.

Lynch, Kathryn L., *The High Medieval Dream-Vision: Poetry, Philosophy and Literary Form* (Stanford U.P., 1988).

MacQueen, John, *Robert Henryson: A Study of the Major Narrative Poems* (Oxford, Clarendon Press, 1967).

Matthews, William, *The Tragedy of Arthur* (Berkeley, University of California Press, 1960).

McCarthy, Terence, 'Le Morte Darthur and romance', in *Studies in Medieval English Romances*, ed. Derek Brewer (Cambridge, D.S. Brewer, 1991), pp.148–75.

McDonnell, Colleen, and Bernhard Lang, *Heaven: A History* (New Haven, Yale U.P., 1988).

McQuillan, Martin (ed.), *The Narrative Reader* (London, Routledge, 2000).

Meale, Carol M. (ed.), *Readings in Medieval Romance* (Cambridge, D.S. Brewer, 1994).

Mehl, Dieter, *The Middle English Romances of the Thirteenth and Fourteenth Centuries* (London, Routledge & Kegan Paul, 1967).

Mehl, Dieter, *Geoffrey Chaucer: an Introduction to his Narrative Poetry* (Cambridge U.P., 1986).

Middleton, Anne, 'The Clerk and his Tale: some literary contexts', *Studies in the Age of Chaucer* 2 (1980), 121–50.

Miller, Robert P. (ed), *Chaucer: Sources and Backgrounds* (New York, Oxford U.P., 1977).

Mills, Maldwyn, 'Generic titles in MS Douce 261 and MS Egerton 3132A', in *The Matter of Identity in Medieval Romance*, ed. Phillipa Hardman (Cambridge, D.S. Brewer, 2002), pp.125–38.

Minnis, A.J. (ed.), *Oxford Guides to Chaucer: The Shorter Poems* (Oxford, Clarendon Press, 1995).

Moseley, Charles, *J.R.R. Tolkien*, Writers and Their World Series (London, Northcote House in association with the British Council, 1997).

Mosher, J.A., *The Exemplum in the Early Religious and Didactic Literature of England* (New York, Columbia U.P., 1911).

Muscatine, Charles, *The Old French Fabliaux* (New Haven, Yale U.P., 1986).

Nykrog, Per, *Les Fabliaux: Étude d'histoire littéraire et de stylistique médiévale* (Copenhagen, Ejner Munksgaard, 1957).

Oinas, Felix J. (ed.), *Heroic Epic and Saga: An Introduction to the World's Great Folk Epics* (Bloomington, Ind., Indiana U.P., 1978).

Onega, Susana and José Angel García Landa (eds.), *Narratology: An Introduction* (Harlow, Longman, 1996).

Ong, Walter J., *Orality and Literacy: The Technologizing of the Word* (London, Routledge, 1982).

Owst, G.R., *Literature and Pulpit in Medieval England*, revd edn (Oxford, Basil Blackwell, 1961).

Page, Barbara, 'Concerning the Host', *Chaucer Review* 4 (1969–70), 1–13.

Patterson, Lee, *Negotiating the Past: the Historical Understanding of Medieval Literature* (Madison, University of Wisconsin Press, 1987).

Patterson, Lee, 'On the margin: postmodernism, ironic history, and medieval studies', *Speculum* 65 (1990), 87–108.

Patterson, Lee, *Chaucer and the Subject of History* (London, Routledge, 1991).

Pearsall, Derek, *John Lydgate* (London, Routledge & Kegan Paul, 1970).

Pearsall, Derek, *Old English and Middle English Poetry* (London, Routledge & Kegan Paul, 1977).

Pearsall, Derek, *The Canterbury Tales* (London, Routledge, 1985).

Pearsall, Derek, 'The development of Middle English romance', *Medieval Studies* 27 (1965), 91–116, reprinted in *Studies in Medieval English Romances*, ed. Derek Brewer (Cambridge, D.S. Brewer, 1988).

Pearsall, Derek, *Arthurian Romance: A Short Introduction* (Oxford, Blackwell, 2003).

Propp, Vladimir, *Morphology of the Folktale* (first published in Russian in 1928, first translated into English 1958), trans. Laurence Scott, 2nd edn (Austin, University of Texas Press, 1968).

Putter, Ad, 'A historical introduction', in *The Spirit of Medieval English Popular Romance*, eds. Ad Putter and Jane Gilbert (Harlow, Longman, 2000), pp. 1–15.

Raby, F.J.E., *The Oxford Book of Medieval Latin Verse* (Oxford, Clarendon Press, 1959).

Revard, Carter, 'From French "Fabliau Manuscripts" and MS Harley 2253 to the *Decameron* and the *Canterbury Tales*', *Medium Aevum* 69 (2000), 261–78.

Riffaterre, Michael, 'Compulsory reader response: the intertextual drive', in *Intertextuality*, ed. Worton and Still, pp.56–78.

Rigg, A.G., *A History of Anglo-Latin Literature 1066–1422* (Cambridge U.P., 1992).

Rimmon-Kenan, Shlomith, *Narrative Fiction*, 2nd edn (London, Routledge, 2002).

Rychner, Jean (ed.), *Les Lais de Marie de France* (Paris, Champion, 1966, 2nd edn, 1981).

Ryding, W.W., *Structure in Medieval Narrative* (The Hague, Mouton, 1971).

Salter, Elizabeth, '*Piers Plowman* and "The Simonie"', *Archiv* 203 (1967), 241–54.

Scanlon, Larry, *Narrative, Authority and Power: The Medieval Exemplum and the Chaucerian Tradition* (Cambridge U.P., 1994).

Schlauch, Margaret, *Antecedents of the English Novel, 1400–1600* (Warsaw, Polish Scientific Publishers; London, Oxford U.P., 1963).

Selden, Raman (ed.), *The Theory of Criticism from Plato to the Present: A Reader* (Harlow, Longman, 1988).

Severin, Tim, *The Brendan Voyage* (London, Hutchinson, 1978).

Shepherd, Geoffrey, 'The emancipation of story in the twelfth century', in *Medieval Narrative: A Symposium*, eds. H.Bekker-Nielsen *et al.* (Odense U.P., 1979), pp.44–57; reprinted in *Poets and Prophets: Essays on Medieval Studies*, eds. T. Shippey and John Pickles (Cambridge, D.S. Brewer, 1990), pp.84–97.

Shippey, Tom, 'Texts, relics and clever forgeries', review of *Baudolino* by Umberto Eco, trans. William Weaver, *The Times Literary Supplement*, 11 October 2002, 21–2.

Simons, John (ed.), *From Medieval to Medievalism* (Basingstoke, Macmillan, 1992).

Simpson, James, 'Madness and texts: Hoccleve's *Series*', in *Chaucer and Fifteenth-Century Poetry*, eds. Julia Boffey and Janet Cowen (London, King's College, 1991), pp.15–29.

Smith, Colin, *The making of the* Poema de mio Cid (Cambridge U.P., 1983).

Smith, Jeremy, 'Language and style in Malory', in *A Companion to Malory*, eds. Elizabeth Archibald and A.S.G. Edwards (Cambridge, D.S. Brewer), 1996, pp.97–113.

Spearing, A.C., *Medieval Dream Poetry* (Cambridge U.P., 1976).

Spiegel, Gabrielle M., *Romancing the Past: The Rise of Vernacular Prose Historiography in Thirteenth-Century France* (Berkeley, University of California Press, 1993).

Strohm, Paul, 'Middle English narrative genres', *Genre* 13 (1980), 379–88.

Strohm, Paul, *Hochon's Arrow: the Social Imagination of Fourteenth-Century Texts* (Princeton U.P., 1992).

Swanton, Michael, *English Literature before Chaucer* (Harlow, Longman, 1987).

Tatlock, J.S.P., *The Legendary History of Britain: Geoffrey of Monmouth's* Historia Regum Britanniae *and its Early Vernacular Versions* (Berkeley, University of California Press, 1950).

Taylor, John, *English Historical Literature in the Fourteenth Century* (Oxford, Clarendon Press, 1987).

Thomas, Neil, *Reading the Nibelungenlied* (University of Durham, 1995).

Thompson, John J., 'The compiler in action: Robert Thornton and the "Thornton Romances" in Lincoln Cathedral MS 91', in *Manuscripts and Readers in Fifteenth-Century England*, ed. Derek Pearsall (Cambridge, D.S. Brewer, 1983), pp.113–24.

Thompson, N.S., *Chaucer, Boccaccio and the Debate of Love: a Comparative Study of the Decameron and the Canterbury Tales* (Oxford, Clarendon Press, 1996).

Thompson, Stith, *The Folktale* (1946) (Berkeley, University of California Press, 1977).

Tolkien, J.R.R., *Tree and Leaf, Smith of Wootton Major, The Homecoming of Beorhtnoth* (London, Allen & Unwin, 1975).

Tolkien, J.R.R., *The Monsters and the Critics and Other Essays*, ed. Christopher Tolkien (London, Allen & Unwin, 1983).

Topsfield, Leslie, 'The *Roman de la Rose* of Guillaume de Lorris and the Love Lyric of the early troubadours', *Reading Medieval Studies* 1 (1975), 30–54.

Tremayne, Peter, 'Death of an icon', in Mike Ashley (ed.), *The Mammoth Book of Historical Whodunnits* (London, Robinson, 2001).

Turville-Petre, Thorlac, *England the Nation: Language, Literature and National Identity, 1190–1340* (Oxford, Clarendon Press, 1996).

Utley, Francis Lee, 'Five genres in the *Clerk's Tale*', *Chaucer Review* 6 (1971–2), 198–228.

Vance, Eugene, *From Topic to Tale: Logic and Narrativity in the Middle Ages* (Minneapolis, University of Minnesota Press, 1987).

Varty, Kenneth, *Reynard the Fox: Social Engagement and Cultural Metamorphoses in the Beast Epic from the Middle Ages to the Present* (Oxford, Berghahn Books, 2000).

Vinaver, Eugene, *The Rise of Romance* (Oxford, Clarendon Press, 1971; reprinted Cambridge, D.S. Brewer, 1984).

Vitz, E.B., *Medieval Narrative and Modern Narratology* (New York U.P., 1989).

Wallace, David (ed.), *The Cambridge History of Medieval English Literature* (Cambridge U.P., 1999).

Wheatley, Edward, *Mastering Aesop: Medieval Education, Chaucer and His Followers* (Gainsville, University Press of Florida, 2000).

Wilson, Anne, *Traditional Romance and Tale: How Stories Mean* (Cambridge, D.S. Brewer, 1976).

Windeatt, B.A., *Chaucer's Dream Poetry: Sources and Analogues* (Cambridge, D.S. Brewer, 1982).

Windeatt, B.A., 'Literary Structures in Chaucer', in *The Cambridge Chaucer Companion*, eds. Piero Boitani and Jill Mann (Cambridge U.P., 1986), pp.195–212.

Windeatt, B.A., 'Troilus and the disenchantment of romance', in *Studies in Medieval English Romances*, ed. Derek Brewer (Cambridge, D.S. Brewer, 1988), pp.129–47.

Windeatt, B.A., *Oxford Guides to Chaucer: Troilus and Criseyde* (Oxford, Clarendon Press, 1992).

Wittig, Susan, *Stylistic and Narrative Structures in the Middle English Romances* (Austin, University of Texas Press, 1978).

Woolf, Rosemary, *English Religious Lyrics in the Middle Ages* (Oxford, Clarendon Press, 1968).

Worton, Michael and Judith Still, *Intertextuality: Theories and Practices* (Manchester U.P., 1990).

Index